"In case you ever wondered how we got to the point where we could no longer house our population, look no farther. In this compact volume, Jim Burling examines the various threads of government policy that have led us to this predicament. Here, you will see how reactions to race, class, nationality, faith and fear all combined through various local, state and national policies—effectuated through planning and zoning laws—to make housing unaffordable for some and generally unavailable for others. It is a sobering read and points the finger directly at the government agencies responsible. As Walt Kelly's Pogo put it when I was growing up, 'we have met the enemy and he is us.'"

—Michael Berger, senior counsel
Manatt, Phelps & Phillips, LLP

"Jim Burling is one of America's leading property rights litigators. In this book, he offers an outstanding overview of the law and history behind the policies underlying the nation's housing crisis. Essential reading for anyone interested in the most important property rights and land use issue facing the United States today."

—Ilya Somin, professor of Law
George Mason University

"A thorough exposition of the fundamental importance of property rights coupled with a biting and well-documented indictment of superfluous governmental regulation which not only stifles such rights but also leads to a critical shortage of affordable housing."

—David L. Callies, FAICP
emeritus professor of Law
University of Hawaii

"James Burling has been one of America's most effective defenders of property rights for more than four decades, and in *Nowhere to Live*, he offers a clear and compelling account of the roots of America's housing crisis in misguided—and sometimes ill-intentioned—departures from basic principles of property law. The book is comprehensive and nuanced, without ever losing steam or focus, and I learned a lot from reading it. *Nowhere to Live* is essential reading not only for legal experts but for interested citizens seeking to understand the dynamics of America's housing crunch and the role of private property in a flourishing society."

—James Y. Stern, professor of Law and director,
William & Mary Property Rights Project

NOWHERE TO LIVE

NOWHERE TO LIVE

THE HIDDEN STORY OF AMERICA'S HOUSING CRISIS

JAMES S. BURLING

Skyhorse Publishing

Skyhorse Publishing books may be purchased in bulk at special discounts for sales promotion, corporate gifts, fund-raising, or educational purposes. Special editions can also be created to specifications. For details, contact the Special Sales Department, Skyhorse Publishing, 307 West 36th Street, 11th Floor, New York, NY 10018 or info@skyhorsepublishing.com.

Skyhorse® and Skyhorse Publishing® are registered trademarks of Skyhorse Publishing, Inc.®, a Delaware corporation.

Visit our website at www.skyhorsepublishing.com.

Please follow our publisher Tony Lyons on Instagram @tonylyonsisuncertain

10 9 8 7 6 5 4 3 2 1

Library of Congress Cataloging-in-Publication Data is available on file.

Cover design by Faceout Studio, Amanda Hudson
Jacket imagery from Stocksy and Shutterstock

Print ISBN: 978-1-5107-8153-5
Ebook ISBN: 978-1-5107-8193-1

Printed in the United States of America

Contents

Foreword by US Senator Mike Lee   *xi*

Introduction: The Crisis—Our Dystopian Reality   *xv*

**Part I: Zoning: The Racist History of Residential Zoning—
America's Obsession with Quiet Places Where Yards Are Wide
and People (of Color) Are Few**   1

Chapter 1: A Plague of Explicit Racial Zoning Is Born in Baltimore
and Dies in Louisville   3

Chapter 2: The Rise of the Tenement Slums and Urban Reform   23

Chapter 3: New York City Creates Economic Zoning   33

Chapter 4: Zoning Arrives in Euclid, Ohio, and Travels to
the Supreme Court   43

Chapter 5: Judicial Impotence, Complicity, and Zoning Challenges 62

Chapter 6: New Jersey Courts Take on Exclusionary Zoning   85

Chapter 7: An End to Single-Family Zoning as We Know It?   94

Chapter 8: The Economic Impact of Zoning and Land-Use
Regulations Has Been Devastating   100

**Part II: Eminent Domain and the Destruction of
Working-Class Housing**   111

Chapter 9: The Modern Rise of Eminent Domain and the
Destruction of Existing Housing   113

Chapter 10: The Transformation of "Public Use" into
"Politically Useful"   126

Chapter 11: The Public Use in Removing the Poor from Cities   135

Chapter 12: Tax Increment Financing and the Perversion
of Incentives   139

Chapter 13: The Unjust Compensation Gambit   143

Chapter 14: Reform of Eminent Domain at the State Level
and What Must Be Done   149

**Part III: Using the Environment to Destroy Property Rights
and Housing Opportunities**   **153**

Chapter 15: The Endangered Species Act—Humans Need Not Apply   157

Chapter 16: The Clean Water Act and Wetlands   164

Chapter 17: The Special Case of California Environmental
Land-Use Permitting   174

Part IV: Rent Control Isn't the Answer   **183**

Chapter 18: The Early History of Rent Control in the United States   185

Chapter 19: Rent Control Makes Housing Worse and More
Expensive   200

**Part V: Affordable Housing Mandates—Unworkable,
Unaffordable, Unproductive, and Unconstitutional**   **211**

Chapter 20: Extorting Developers and Home Buyers to Pay for
Subsidized Housing   213

**Part VI: The Great Emptying of the Mentally Ill onto
Our Streets**   **239**

Chapter 21: Unhousing the Mentally Ill   241

Chapter 22: From the Courtroom and Hospitals to the Streets   245

Part VII: Property Rights—A Way Out of the Housing Crisis   **251**

Chapter 23: A Short History of the Rise, Fall, and Rise of Private
   Property   253

Chapter 24: Regulatory Takings—A Way to Protect Property   272

Part VIII: The Future—Speculations and Solutions   **283**

Chapter 25: The Future of Housing in a Post-COVID AI World   285

Chapter 26: Respecting Property Rights—The Way Out of
   Our Housing Crisis   289

Final Word   *301*
Acknowledgments   *303*
Endnotes   *305*
Index   *355*
Suggested Reading   *365*

Foreword

by US Senator Mike Lee

B uying a home provides more than shelter and a place to build memories—it's also a critical tool for building wealth. For most Americans, their home is their most valuable asset and most reliable avenue toward long-term wealth accumulation.

Homeownership is the foundation of stable and secure communities. Localities with higher homeownership rates often enjoy stronger social cohesion, a more resilient tax base, better schools, and other ancillary benefits that help the community thrive, grow, and prosper. For these reasons, we recognize homeownership as a principal pillar of the American dream.

Yet, for many Americans today, this dream is growing further out of reach due to the lack of affordable housing. Housing costs are already the single largest expense in most American families' budgets, and in recent years, spiking home prices have led to unprecedented challenges in affordability and availability of homes, with the median US home price increasing by 30 percent since the COVID-19 pandemic began in 2020.[1] Higher interest rates, which make mortgages more expensive, have only compounded the challenge for lower- and middle-income Americans seeking to enter the housing market.

The central problem is one of supply and demand. By one leading estimate, the United States faces a shortage of over five million homes. The housing stock shortage is dramatically increasing prices and locking many buyers out of the market. With the pronounced inflation of recent years, the spiraling cost of raising kids, education, and health care, Americans are finding financial freedom more difficult to attain. Add to that the stark reality of stagnant wage growth, and the conclusion is undeniable: many Americans are losing their confidence.

They're certainly losing confidence in the housing market. A May 2023 Gallup poll found only 21 percent of Americans believe now is a good time to buy a house.[2] Twenty years ago, that number was 81 percent. We've witnessed a catastrophic loss of faith in the housing market—and with it, a loss of faith in the American Dream.

It's not just affected potential buyers with lower income. Increasingly, working and middle-class families, who, within recent memory, typically experienced little difficulty securing good homes, are finding themselves locked out of the market. First-time buyers are hit particularly hard. Young Americans struggling with housing costs may delay starting a family and will likely find their ability to build wealth over the long term stymied.

One of the most culpable factors is government policy constraining the housing supply. Land-use regulations, prohibitive building restrictions, exclusionary zoning laws, rent-control schemes, and a patchwork quilt of rules and restrictions (primarily at the state and local level, though federal laws and regulations have also contributed) have dampened our ability to build the homes needed to house a growing population.

Finding ways to address high costs and making housing available to more Americans would go a long way toward improving the well-being of American families and strengthening our communities.

Fortunately, Jim Burling's new book, *Nowhere to Live: The Hidden Story of America's Housing Crisis*, presents us with an insightful starting point. This book provides a crucial understanding to navigate and address the underlying issues of our nation's housing challenges. It's essential reading for those of us dedicated to fostering solutions for every American.

Nowhere to Live is perhaps best thought of as three books in one:

1. It offers a brisk and compelling historical survey of how housing policy decisions over the last century have brought us to our current situation.
2. It presents a painstaking analysis of the adverse effects, unintended consequences, and even outright failures of various government policy interventions in the housing market.
3. It provides a carefully considered set of proposals as a roadmap for getting the housing market back on track.

Burling's book does not deal in glibly rendered "heroes" and "villains." Instead, he makes it clear that many of the problems we experience in housing today are complex and systemic, stemming directly from regulations and restrictions that have constrained the proper functioning of the housing market. While these regulations and restrictions may have been rooted in good intentions, many are well past their expiration date and desperately need rethinking. We know what we're doing isn't working—we see the evidence of that failure.

The challenge is not restricted to large cities and metropolitan areas where real estate is at a premium. Take my home state of Utah, where two-thirds of our land is owned or controlled by the federal government. Unfortunately, finding available land for housing is a challenge, especially in the West.

Importantly, Burling doesn't offer a single "magic bullet" solution to address the housing crisis. Instead, he supplies a variety of suggestions based on free market principles that, taken together, would alleviate the problem. Policymakers and housing experts would do well to study Burling's ideas—and then get to work putting them into action. Because these challenges won't be overcome overnight; they result from decades of unwise decisions, and it will take time to set a new course.

We must get started right away!

While many "experts" simply repeat tired refrains, pitching the same policies that got us into this situation, we're fortunate to have thinkers like Jim Burling, who can cut through the noise and present the case for an alternative market-based approach with clarity and precision.

Burling offers a clear plan.

Homeownership is vital to promote flourishing American families and communities. Jim Burling's book is a valuable addition to the conversation, showing how we got here—but more importantly, providing a road map for where we need to go next by presenting a pro-growth, pro-family, pro-community housing reform policy that will go a long way toward restoring optimism and faith in the American dream.

The Crisis—Our Dystopian Reality

Figure 1. The New Colossus.

Not like the brazen giant of Greek fame,

With conquering limbs astride from land to land;

Here at our sea-washed, sunset gates shall stand

A mighty woman with a torch, whose flame

Is the imprisoned lightning, and her name

Mother of exiles. From her beacon-hand

Glows world-wide welcome; her mild eyes command

The air-bridged harbor that twin cities frame.

"Keep, ancient lands, your storied pomp!" cries she

With silent lips. "Give me your tired, your poor,

Your huddled masses yearning to breathe free,

The wretched refuse of your teeming shore.

Send these, the homeless, tempest-tost to me,

I lift my lamp beside the golden door!"

—"The New Colossus" by Emma Lazarus, inscribed at the base

of the Statute of Liberty (1883)[1]

America still attracts immigrants from all over the world. We still provide a degree of economic freedom and opportunity that is sorely lacking in too many nations across the globe. And we still provide a tranquility that does not exist in nations beset by war, abject poverty, ethnic cleansings, religious persecution, and unchecked violence.

However, our welcome mat is becoming frayed. The disparity between the opportunities and conditions in foreign lands and those at home is no longer as stark as it was when the Statute of Liberty first stood as a beacon for the world's poor and huddled masses yearning to breathe free. While we had poverty in the nineteenth century when Lazarus wrote the words to "The New Colossus," we also had hope. Today we have our own wretched refuse of our urban decay and our tent cities scattered across our teeming shores. Our lamp is dim, the golden door tarnished, and the hope elusive.

While it may be elusive, the hope promised in "The New Colossus" is not yet completely extinguished. We got ourselves into this mess, and we can get ourselves out of it by reembracing the inspiration for the poem and the statue: *Liberty!* As will be shown, we have simply failed to allow ourselves to build enough housing for Americans to live in. Some of this failure has been the result of a deliberate desire to exclude the newest and poorest Americans from our neighborhoods. Some has been the result of well-intentioned but shortsighted policies to elevate other values over human needs. By limiting the rights of people to build new homes, we have constrained liberty—both of the people who desire better homes to live in and of the people wishing to build those homes.

It's not for want of trying. For over a half-century, lawyers working with my organization, Pacific Legal Foundation, have fought a multitude of environmental and land-use restrictions that stand in the way of economic freedom and home building. As one roadblock is removed, government and "Not-in-My-Backyard" (NIMBY)-inspired groups impose others. The decline in property rights, especially in some of the coastal states, is proportionate to the decline in housing availability and affordability.

Unless and until we free up the pent-up desires of Americans to build new homes, America's housing crisis will grow worse, especially in large urban areas. By various measures of affordability, it is becoming increasingly difficult for poor and middle-class families to find decent housing at an affordable level. Those on the very bottom of the economic and social ladder are now often without any stable housing. Instead, we have tent cities—which suffer in comparison to many third-world shanty towns.

But the "homeless" aren't just some abstraction that we describe with numbers. These are real people. The *New York Times* recently interviewed thirty people who have, or are, experiencing homelessness across the nation.[2] Every story is different; every story is the same. A loss of a job here, an illness there, the inexorable lure of drugs and alcohol somewhere else. These are the people who have been cast out of the American dream by internal and/or external forces.

As I write this, I reflect on the young woman I saw a while ago on the sidewalk below my second-story office window. She was cursing loudly and in obvious distress. She had covered herself with a blanket, under which I saw the repeated flash of a lighter. My first fear was that she was trying to set herself on fire. But then she threw off the blanket in frustration and finally managed to light the pipe clenched between her teeth. Soon, the effect of whatever it was she smoked eased her pains, she stopped cursing, and fell into a doze.

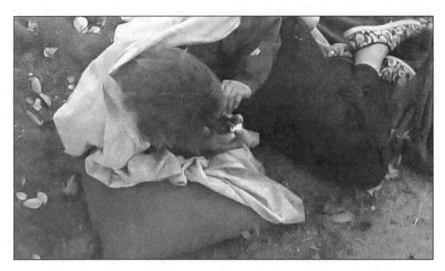

Figure 2. Unknown woman below the author's office window.

Riding our light rail a few years ago, I was assaulted by a deranged homeless man, who, after kicking my tablet out of my hands, could only scream at me, telling me to "stop f**king with me, you motherf**ker." He continued shouting and cursing at me until the train came to the next stop and he got off. It took me a long time to calm my emotions.

When approaching the door of my office, I have seen the feces that were left behind by some unfortunate soul the night before. Usually, the city cleans up the mess in a day or so. When I remarked on the mess to our receptionist, she told me how upset she was to see a young woman wrapped in blankets and bawling on the side of the freeway. And this is in Sacramento, a medium-sized city that is in the throes of something that none of us has seen on this scale before in our lifetimes. These are just a few of the stories that all of us encounter with increasing frequency day after day. How did we get here? And who are these people?

Americans fall into two categories: those with homes and those without. Neither is doing well.

Those without Homes

On end-of-the-month January weeknights in 2023, volunteers across America counted 653,104 homeless people—the highest number ever counted.[3] That's roughly equivalent to every man, woman, and child living today in a city like Oklahoma City. Those are the people on the streets, in shelters, couch-surfing, living in their cars, and otherwise without any sort of permanent home. But there may be more. Those were only the ones *counted*—not those hunkered down in some remote unreachable corner of the city hidden from the eyes of the volunteers roaming the established camps and shelters.

African Americans, who make up 12 percent of the nation's population, accounted for 37 percent of the homeless population. That stands to reason, as over a century of housing policies, by design and by inadvertence, have shunted minority populations into urban ghettos, where supply is limited, prices are high for what is available, and services are few.

Of the homeless that were counted, 256,610 were unsheltered.[4] Those are people without a roof over their head, other than the roof of their cars, their nylon tents, or the stars. That's as if every person living in Laredo, Texas, was thrown into a refugee camp, but one without regular food and care provided by the Red Cross.

And it's only getting worse.[5] Between 2020 and 2023, the number of homeless people jumped 12.5 percent nationally, 5.8 percent in California, the state with the most unsheltered homeless at 111,206 individuals. From 2007 to 2023, the homeless population in California surged 30.5 percent. Other states like New York had managed to experience a decrease over the early part of this period, with a decline of 18.7 percent from 2007 to 2022, although that success has been overwhelmed by the rising tide of immigrants coming to New York City. In the past year there has been a jump of 42.3 percent in the homeless population.[6] There, over 100,000 people are living in shelters.[7]

In December 2019, after reporters from the *New York Times* "embedded" themselves in a homeless camp in Oakland, they did a video pictorial that compared a squatters' camp in Oakland to one in Mexico City.[8] While the camp in Mexico was three times larger, the shanties there at least had some basic utilities and sanitation. But the filth and squalor of the myriad homeless camps in the United States, one of the world's richest nations, is beyond appalling. Things are so bad in some parts of Los Angeles that there has been a reappearance of the ancient scourges of tuberculosis, hepatitis A, typhoid fever, shigellosis, and trench fever.[9] Some predict that the bubonic plague will be next.[10]

In addition, those experiencing homelessness were considered to be more vulnerable to catching and spreading COVID-19.[11] Not all observers, however, blame the spread of these diseases on the homeless, noting that rats and other vermin—which have always been part of LA's ecosystem—are often to blame.[12] These progressives suggest that the focus on the resurgence of old diseases is scapegoating the poor in a thinly veiled right-wing attack on the liberal politics of the cities.[13] Nevertheless, the rat problem and homeless camps are inextricably intertwined. Sanitation departments do not usually make regular pick-ups at the homeless camps. Toilets are often unavailable, and cities resist the regularizing of the camps with such facilities, even arguing as Sacramento did in 2020, that there is no constitutional right to porta-potties in homeless camps.[14] But as sure as sanitation-free homeless camps are filthy, and as sure as rats and disease follow filth, we cannot be sanguine that every third-world disease that starts in a homeless camp won't spread into the general population.

Many people who at one time in our recent history would have been housed in cheap lodgings, boarding homes, or institutions can now be found living in squalor, outside, and without the basics of modern life. From the post-Civil War era to the Great Depression, many so-called "hoboes" lived outside in the sometimes romanticized "hobo jungles." But those communities had some measure of self-order and discipline—even with codes of ethics.[15] They were not hopeless. Today's homeless camps are characterized more by squalor, trash, addiction, disease, and desperation.

"Car-camping" no longer means family fun in the mountains; it means finding a safe parking space for the night. Some of the luckier homeless get to spend the night in a shelter. Others prefer no such accommodation because of limits on drug and alcohol use or because of their discomfort with the shelter's other clientele who do use or who are physically or mentally ill.

Especially troubling, at least 25 percent of the homeless are mentally ill, with some estimates running as high as 78 percent.[16] It's tough to get help and medicine when living on the streets. And the stress of not having a home can only exacerbate preexisting problems. When a mentally ill person goes without treatment, the illness will become worse: the depression more debilitating and the demons more compelling. If an ill person self-medicates with illicit drugs or alcohol, the illness will be compounded by the pathologies of addiction.[17]

And California, where half the nation's homeless live, witnesses more homeless deaths than anywhere.[18] In 2022, at least 4,800 homeless people died in California, nearly half from overdoses.[19] Is California a harbinger of where the rest of the nation is heading, or will we learn the hard lessons from the Golden State and reverse course before all of America is covered with shantytowns and tent cities?

Those with Homes

Even those who can afford a place to live are often forced to spend a disproportionate share of their income on housing. The old "spend only 30 percent on housing" rule of thumb is an anachronism in many cities.[20] With such a shortage of housing, working-class neighborhoods become gentrified, pushing the working poor further and further out. Blue and pink-collar workers must endure either nightmare commutes or barely habitable dwellings, often shared with other renters in equally precarious circumstances.

Over one-half of California renters pay more than 30 percent of their income in rent. One study reported that "nearly half of California's households cannot afford the cost of housing in their local market."[21] That's 9.5 million "cost-burdened" households in the state. That's not surprising considering that the median value of a home has increased 160 percent since 2013, from $307,00 to $783,666 as of March 1, 2024.[22] For a while, things seemed to be getting better . After a 20 percent increase from 2021 to 2022, prices dropped by 3.4 percent by late 2023.[23]

But alas, that was only temporary. Prices shot back up to their 2022 high by the spring of 2024.[24] Among the state's poorest populations, "nearly 100 percent are unable to afford the local cost of housing."[25] At the same time, the nationwide median price of an existing home reached $416,000 in the second quarter of 2023, nearly an all-time high.[26] Between early 2020 and 2023, home prices rose an astonishing 37 percent, and rents rose by 24 percent.[27]

Nationally, over 23 percent of Americans are cost-burdened, 23 percent of homeowners and 49 percent of renters.[28] Worse still, over 25 percent of Americas renting homes and apartments are *severely* cost-burdened, meaning they pay over one-half their incomes for housing.[29]

These statistics are at best rough measures of housing affordability. Fifty percent of a large income could be less of a stretch than 30 percent of a lower income household. Nevertheless, the overall point is that as the percentage of our incomes that we spend on housing rises, the less there is for other goods and services, and the less of a cushion we have should our incomes be curtailed, say by illness, an employer closing a business, or a pandemic. As a recent study from the Joint Center for Housing Studies of Harvard University put it, "since lower-income households are also more likely to have housing cost burdens and limited savings to cover those income losses, they are also more likely to have fallen behind on rent."[30] For the lowest income households, those earning less than $30,000 per year, 73 percent were cost-burdened in 2023. After housing costs, those households had only "$490 per month left to spend on all other needs—a full 18 percent drop in real terms from 2001."[31]

How Did We Get Here?

The problems of housing affordability and homelessness didn't crop up overnight. We didn't have vibrant urban spaces and bucolic suburbs one day and an affordability and homelessness crisis the next. It's been a long time coming. It's been coming because we haven't been able to meet the demand for housing. We have allowed zoning and excessive land-use controls to stand between the homes we need and the homes we have. Simply put, we're simply not creating enough new housing. And at the core of our inability to create enough housing, we have government policy after government policy that prevents needed housing from being built.

Nationally, just to replace aging or destroyed housing stock, one million homes must be built each year. Another million must be built to keep up with population growth. Yet, we are building only half that number.[32] Another estimate is that the national annual shortfall is 430,000 housing units per year with a total national shortfall of 6.8 million units.[33] One estimate is that California alone needs to build 3.5 million homes and apartments by 2025.[34] And where housing is being built, it isn't necessarily where people need it to be. The Bay Area and Silicon Valley have created far more jobs than homes. Developers respond by building homes in distant Central Valley locations, forcing people to make hours-long commutes every day. California doesn't build enough homes, so those states where building is easier see an influx of Californians who are uprooted to distant states to find affordable housing. And once an area begins to build enough homes to meet demand, there is often a movement to stop or slow the growth. People want affordable homes, but once they have one, they don't want any more to be built.

Despite increasing need, we are building significantly fewer homes today than we did in the previous decades.[35] For example, in the early 1970s we built from 1.4 to 2.1 million units per year. But in the post-recession years from 2015 to the present, we've averaged fewer than 1.2 million homes per year.[36] All the while, our population has increased 61 percent from 205 million Americans to 331 million.[37] As a study commissioned by the National Association of Realtors notes, "The shortfall in residential housing production extended across all regions of the country. Comparing the last two decades of annual housing production with the prior historical period (1968–2000), every major region of the country heavily underbuilt housing."[38] Moreover, the study's statistics support its conclusion that "the underbuilding gap extends across almost every major city in the country."[39] This has, the study concludes, led to higher home prices, less equity for minority families, and delay in household formation—meaning younger adults delay or put off marriage and raising families.

While there are vast open spaces in the country, and while some rural areas are losing population, the places where people want to live—the cities where the jobs and opportunities are—are most severely impacted. Nowhere is this effect more pronounced than in our coastal cities, and California is among the worst of the worst of the places that are too susceptible to no-growth anti-development NIMBYism.

According to the California Legislative Analyst's Office, just to meet that state's growing population, builders must create 210,000 new homes a year; in a good year they build just about half that number.[40] A recent study found that the state is short, *at a minimum,* a staggering two-million housing units when compared per capita to other states like New Jersey or New York.[41] Over a forty-year period, this report notes that California "added only 325 homes for every 1,000 additional people. During the same period, New York and New Jersey added 1,007 and 681 homes for every 1,000 additional people."[42] In more recent times, from 2005 to 2014, California has added only 308 units to New York's 549 per 1,000 population added.[43] In other words, California is among the worst, but even the best lags behind population gains.

Even California's attempt to create publicly funded housing has been mired in failure. In 2021, San Francisco financed a tent city at a cost of $60,000 per tent per year.[44] For only ten times that amount, in February 2022, Los Angeles could build a single permanent housing unit for the homeless.[45] But that was then. Now the price in Northern California has jumped to $1 million for each "affordable" unit.[46] In 2016, Los Angeles voters approved a $1.2 billion bond measure to build 10,000 new housing units, as if that would have made a serious dent in Los Angeles's population of 30,393 people living on the streets that year.[47] But ten thousand units is possible only in a political math class, because $1.2 billion divided by the bargain price of only $600,000 yields only 2,000 units in real math. And if the price is now a million dollars a pop, that yields only 1,200 apartments—for a homeless population in Los Angeles County that has now reached nearly 70,000 individuals in 2022.[48] Clearly, the bond measure is a failure. The government might as well buy used homes and be done with it—since the median price of a home in Los Angeles is $1 million.[49] Officials have blamed everything from union labor requirements to parking requirements to supply chain woes to a multiplicity of funding sources to local permit requirements.[50] All true, perhaps, but it's been a long time since government has been able to build anything at a reasonable cost.

Figure 3. Million-dollar union-built affordable beachfront apartments in San Francisco.

While some nations have tried to repeal the law of supply and demand, none have succeeded. Not the Soviet Union. Not North Korea. Not Venezuela. And not even California. So, unless and until we build more homes, we're not going to meet demand. And unless we meet the demand, prices will rise and rise and rise.

If the law of supply and demand requires that we build more housing, why aren't we building enough homes? And who is responsible for building them?

A 2018 survey conducted by the *Los Angeles Times* of 1,180 eligible California voters found that 28 percent of the respondents blamed the problem on "lack of rent control." A close 24 percent thought the problem was due to a "lack of funding for low-income housing." A respectable 17 percent considered the problem to be environmental regulation. But only 13 percent laid the blame on "too little housing" and 9 percent on "restrictive zoning rules."[51]

But if we are to respect the immutable law of supply and demand, then the *only* explanation for the persistent high cost of housing is a lack of supply, which means that there is too little homebuilding. Some of the other answers to the survey may explain *why* there is too little homebuilding—such as environmental regulations or restrictive zoning rules. Other responses, such as rent control or more public subsidies are distorters of the free market and are more likely to be a *cause* of the lack of new building, rather than a solution to high costs. And other responses to the poll, such as foreign or Wall Street buyers, may identify a source of some temporary aberrations in the housing market, but they are, at most, temporary factors that will invariably be averaged out—if we begin to build a lot more homes. Moreover, corporate and foreign buyers do not explain why the housing affordability problem has been with us for decades. And, indeed, it has. According to a 1991 Presidential Commission:

> In the past [twenty-four] years, no fewer than [ten] federally sponsored commissions, studies or task forces have examined the problem. . . .
>
> The regulatory environment has if anything become a greater deterrent to affordable housing, regulatory barriers have become clearly more complex, and apparently more prevalent. . . .
>
> Millions of Americans are being priced out of buying or renting the kind of housing they otherwise could afford were it not for a web of government regulations.[52]

That was written well over three decades ago. Presidents Obama, Trump, and Biden have said pretty much the same thing. The Obama White House put it this way:

> Local policies acting as barriers to housing supply include land use restrictions that make developable land much more costly than it is inherently, zoning restrictions, off-street parking requirements, arbitrary or antiquated preservation regulations, residential conversion restrictions, and unnecessarily slow permitting processes.[53]

And President Trump issued an Executive Order stating that: "Increasing the supply of housing by removing overly burdensome regulatory barriers will reduce housing costs, boost economic growth, and provide more Americans with opportunities for economic mobility."[54]

President Biden agrees:

> Today's rising housing costs are years in the making. Fewer new homes were built in the decade following the Great Recession than in any decade since the 1960s—constraining housing supply and failing to keep pace with demand and household formation. . . .
>
> Exclusionary land use and zoning policies constrain land use, artificially inflate prices, perpetuate historical patterns of segregation, keep workers in lower productivity regions, and limit economic growth. Reducing regulatory barriers to housing production has been a bipartisan cause in a number of states throughout the country.[55]

Thus, we've recognized this bipartisan problem for over a half-century, and we are no closer to solving it now than we were in 1991 or twenty-four years before that. In fact, things have gotten worse.

During the Great Depression, there were over a million homeless people, many of whom created squatter villages known as "Hoovervilles" located in public parks and on open land. Many of the dwellings were made of scrap construction materials and many of the camps had their internal governance and rules, such as "no begging."[56] Homelessness today has a different and more debilitating character than in the past with more women and children and "more medical, mental health and substance use disorders than previous generations of persons experiencing homelessness."[57]

Even in more recent history, some recall a time when we had no significant homelessness. Nan Roman, president of the National Alliance to End Homelessness, commented, "In the 1970s, there was an adequate supply of affordable units for every low-income household that needed one—and we really didn't have homelessness."[58]

In contrast to the homeless of the nineteenth century and through the Great Depression, today's homeless tent encampments spill over into downtown business districts where the homeless are beset by mental disabilities, drugs, and despair. The Great Depression has been blamed on many things from tariffs and a trade war, bad monetary policy, and government inaction in the face of the crisis. As will be shown, today's homeless crisis is largely the result of generations of bad government actions.

This book will focus on those government forces that have caused and exacerbated the housing crisis. More importantly, it will show that the solution to this mess is not more government, but less interference by the government with the free market of housing. The focus will be on zoning, both exclusionary and inclusionary, environmental regulation, land-use permitting, rent control, eminent domain, and public housing. The bottom line is that we need less interference with the free market in housing, not more. Only by freeing up builders to build what the public wants to buy and live in can we begin to tackle our problems. Giving the government more power to interfere in the market is most certainly not the answer.

Put another way, hoping that the government will solve the housing crisis with more government is like hoping that a hurricane will wash away the effects of a flood.

PART I

Zoning: The Racist History of Residential Zoning—America's Obsession with Quiet Places Where Yards Are Wide and People (of Color) Are Few

The shortage of affordable housing, especially for working class and minority populations, is no accident. It is the result of nearly a century of deliberate government policies designed to maintain economic and racial segregation. While the overt mandates forcing racial segregation lie in our past, their legacy lives on today. To understand how this began, we must first travel to Baltimore in 1910 when a lawyer decided to buy a home for his family.

Chapter 1

A Plague of Explicit Racial Zoning Is Born in Baltimore and Dies in Louisville

The collapse of housing affordability began over a century ago with the rise of zoning. On its face, zoning seems like a fair enough policy, designed to keep neighborhoods safe, clean, and healthy. However, its roots are much more sinister than that. Indeed, the history of zoning has been a history of confining poor and not-so-poor Black people to the ghettos. It started out with explicit attempts to zone out Blacks. When that was declared unconstitutional, it transformed into a more scientific and rational way of preserving "good" neighborhoods, so that the front door next door wouldn't be darkened by those who were different.

Zoning for the purpose of economic and racial segregation had its start in 1910, when Jim Crow moved to Baltimore, Maryland.[1]

As the nineteenth century turned into the twentieth, the Eutaw Place neighborhood was a very fashionable, affluent, tree-lined, all-white neighborhood in the heart of Baltimore. Only a few blocks to the west, there were Black neighborhoods—which had been expanding into the White areas as the City's Black population had been growing since the end of the Civil War. And as Black citizens became better established, they naturally sought to leave the slums and move to some of the nicer parts of the city.

In the summer of 1910, a successful, Yale-educated attorney named George W. F. McMechen and his schoolteacher wife moved to a three-story red brick row home at 1834 McCulloh Street, in the heart of Eutaw Place. While his new neighbors were all White, Mr. McMechen and his family were all Black. When the move became known, all hell broke loose.

George McMechen was born in West Virginia and attended Morgan State University in Baltimore when that school first opened in 1891. He next enrolled in Yale Law School in 1895 and, after practicing law a few years in Illinois, moved back to Baltimore and joined the Bar there in 1905. At heart, McMechen was an activist who didn't like the informal color barriers thrown up to thwart the needs of Blacks who had left the South in search of economic improvement and freedom from the more oppressive discrimination endemic in the former confederacy. He especially didn't like the difficulties Blacks faced in moving to more upscale neighborhoods like Eutaw Place.

White citizens saw the McMechens' move as the first step in the destruction of another White neighborhood. They had seen this before as the Black population expanded and entered into formerly White neighborhoods. Previously, there had been isolated instances of vandalism by Whites when Blacks moved into their neighborhoods. As Garett Power notes, "Windows were broken and black tar was smeared on white marble steps. And when a black family moved into a house on Stricker Street they were attacked and the house was stoned. But white terrorism was no match for the combined purchasing power of housing-hungry blacks. Money talked."[2]

When word got out about George McMechen's move to Eutaw Place, White Baltimoreans held a protest meeting to agitate for a halt to the perceived further destruction of their all-White neighborhoods.[3] White teens harassed the McMechens.[4] Within days, every window and skylight in the McMechens' new home was broken. Citizens presented a petition to the mayor and city council asking them to "take some measures to restrain the colored people from locating in a white community, and proscribe a limit beyond which it shall be unlawful for them to go."[5]

House 1,834 McCulloh Street in Which a Negro Lawyer Named McMechen
Moved in June, 1910, and Which Promptly Had Its Windows
Broken, as Shown in the Cut.

Figure 4. From the *New York Times*, Dec. 25, 1910.

Milton Dashiell, a lawyer with an undistinguished reputation, took it upon himself to draft an ordinance to stop Blacks from moving into White neighborhoods, like his own.[6]

There were strong objections from the Black community to a proposal to create segregation by zoning. The Baltimore *Afro-American* newspaper spearheaded the opposition, not because, it said, Black people necessarily wanted to move into White neighborhoods, but because segregation was "anti-American" and "mischievous."[7]

Despite the opposition, the city obliged its White constituency.

By a party-line vote, and over objections from the Republicans, Black leadership, and some members of the real estate business, the city council complied. In December 1910, the city adopted the nation's first racial apartheid law.[8]

The ordinance was straightforward and decreed: "That no negro can move into a block in which more than half of the residents were white." And in a cynical hat-tip to equality, it continued: "That no white person can move into a block in which more than half of the residents are colored."[9] The law had teeth. It threatened: "That a violator of the law is punishable by a fine of not more than $100 or imprisonment from [thirty] days to [one] year, or both."[10]

That's the equivalent of more than three thousand dollars in 2024 dollars.

The city solicitor, Edgar Allan Poe—a grand nephew of the American poet—opined that the law was constitutional, because "close association on a footing of absolute equality is utterly impossible between [whites and negroes and] . . . wherever negroes exist in large numbers in a white community [there is] invariably . . . irritation, friction, disorder and strife."[11] This sentiment was widely shared: the notion that Black populations were irredeemable and had to be quarantined to avoid infecting the White population with their blight. The city's progressive and reform-minded mayor signed the legislation in December 1910.[12]

It made national news. A two-page Christmas Day story in the *New York Times* noted the new law's significance:

> Nothing like it can be found in any statute book or ordinance on record in the country. It seeks to cut off from men of a certain class—black in one set of circumstances, white in another—the right to purchase and enjoy property anywhere within the limits of Baltimore, under a certain limitation saying: "Thus far shalt thou come no further." It deprives such a man of the right to enjoy property that he may own.[13]

The *Times* article had a few illustrations of the "problem," one showing a block of well-built homes and captioned, "Where the Negro Invasion Has Depreciated Values."

Baltimore Mayor J. Barry Mahool defended the ordinance, telling the *New York Times* that "one of the first desires of a negro, after he acquires money and property, is to leave his less fortunate brethren and nose into the neighborhood of the white people." Moreover, "Many

Lanv .'. bt   ·   Where the Negro Invasion Has Depreciated Values.

Figure 5. *New York Times* Dec. 25, 1910.

blocks of homes formerly occupied exclusively by whites have now a mixture of colored—and the white and colored races cannot live in the same block in peace and with due regard to property security." Later on, he claims that the ordinance "was not passed in a spirit of race antagonism; most of us concerned in its passage are the best friends the colored people have."[14]

The mayor next described the vandalism caused by the McMechens' move and that of the few Blacks that followed that year: "Window-glasses of the negroes' houses were broken with stones; skylights were caved in by bricks, descending bomb-like from the sky: there were mutterings of plots to blow up the houses; in short, we were on the verge of riot."[15]

The *Times* sought other opinions. It quoted further from Solicitor Poe who suggested that the ordinance was not derived from "mere prejudice but because experience and time have conclusively proved that the commingling of the white and colored race is an absolute impossibility and that any attempt to bring about such a result invariably leads to grave public disaster."[16]

The newspaper continued with this quote from an unnamed "lady high in Baltimore's most sacred circles" that, "It is a most deplorable thing that even the best of the well-to-do colored people should invade our residential districts. I am sure the colored race has no better friend than I. . . . From my earliest recollection my feeling for the race has been one associated with affection; my old negro 'mammy,' my little nurse-girl playmate, all are among my happiest recollections. But the idea of their assuming to live next door to me is abhorrent."[17]

After noting the rampant vandalism of the Black-inhabited homes in the neighborhood, George McMechen told the *Times*:

> "We did not move up there because we wished to force our way among the whites; association with them in a social way would be just as distasteful to us as it would be to them. We merely desired to live in more commodious and comfortable quarters. . . .
>
> "In my opinion as a lawyer [the ordinance] is clearly unconstitutional, unjust, and discriminating against the negro. . . .
>
> "So far from having any disposition to live among the whites, I vastly prefer living in the midst of my own kind. But I cannot get the comfort there that my purse permits me—and which I think I am entitled to, under the law, if I pay for it. . . .
>
> "We certainly have the right, as American citizens, to the pursuit of happiness and comfort."[18]

Figure 6. George McMechen Yearbook Photo, Yale Law School.[19]

The law was immediately challenged by both Black and White citizens of Baltimore. White real estate interests were especially unhappy and wrote the mayor that they would lose "thousands of dollars" if White landowners could not rent to Blacks in already mixed neighborhoods where Blacks were in the minority.[20] Others complained that they would suffer hardship if they couldn't rent to Whites where they were in the minority.[21]

Within a month, twenty-six criminal enforcement cases were in court, with the defendants, White and Black, challenging the constitutionality of the law.[22] They initially had some success. The county court struck the ordinance down on a technical drafting error. But the city fathers were undeterred and adopted a new version in 1911.[23] Several challenges and versions later, the law remained, with its fourth iteration ultimately surviving challenges in the state courts.

The effects of the ordinance and other subsequent segregating laws were devastating to the Black community. As its population increased, the supply of new housing was stalled. Black Baltimoreans could buy homes only in Black majority districts where there was no space for new homes. More people chased the static supply of homes and apartments. With demand rising, the incentive to maintain the existing housing stock declined. Prices rose and quality declined. Crowding increased and disease became more prevalent.[24]

The ordinance proved to be wildly popular throughout the southern and border states. In only a few short years, a dozen or so cities adopted ordinances based on the Baltimore model.[25] One such city was Louisville, Kentucky.

W. D. Binford, an employee of the mechanical department of two of the local Louisville newspapers, started the segregation ball rolling.[26] He made his first presentation to a group of White real estate men, calling for adoption of the Baltimore plan. Otherwise, he told them, they would awaken one morning "to find a Negro family had purchased and was snugly ensconced in a three-story residence in one of the best and most exclusive white squares in the city." Their purpose was "purely mercenary" and "to exact a prohibitive bonus from white residents to leave the neighborhood."[27] His first audience pretty much ignored him. However, as the *Boston Guardian* reported, a small element of Louisville's poverty-stricken Whites, spurred on by the *Louisville Times*, soon enough succeeded in getting the Baltimore copycat ordinance adopted.[28] While there was organized opposition from Blacks and White businessmen, arguments from working-class Whites that Blacks could destroy property values won the day.[29] The ordinance was adopted on May 11, 1914.[30]

William Warley was the first president of the Louisville branch of the National Association for the Advancement of Colored People (NAACP) and founder and editor of the *Louisville News*. In 1914, when Louisville passed its own Baltimore-style apartheid ordinance, the NAACP had been in existence for five years. And it was looking to take on racial zoning in the Supreme Court. The NAACP leadership knew it would not be easy.

Only eighteen years before, the Supreme Court had upheld segregation by Louisiana of Pullman railroad cars in *Plessy v. Ferguson*,[31] a case that created the notorious "separate but equal" doctrine. That case began on June 7, 1892, when Homer Plessy, a "mixed-race" thirty-year-old shoemaker bought a first-class train ticket. Two years earlier, however, in 1890, Louisiana passed a law it called the "Separate Car Act," wherein railroads had to maintain "equal, but separate" cars for Whites and non-Whites. Riding in the wrong car could subject the passenger to a fine of twenty-five dollars and twenty days in jail. Failure by a train conductor to enforce the law could make him subject to similar penalties.

The railroads were unhappy with the new law. They neither wanted to buy the extra train cars it would require nor the liability to enforce a law they didn't need. Therefore, the railroad developed a secret plan where it would arrange for Homer Plessy to board a train and be arrested for violating the law. Moreover, the railroad paid for Plessy's attorneys so that they could bring forth a constitutional challenge. To highlight the folly of the law, Plessy was chosen as the torchbearer of the case, in part because his mixed-race background was not readily obvious from his appearance.

* * *

Plessy admitted to a train conductor—who was part of the plan—that he was an eighth Black. Plessy was arrested and convicted for trying to ride in the Whites-only first-class car. There were, unsurprisingly, no identical first-class cars for non-Whites. Plessy's lawyers argued that the law violated the Constitution's Equal Protection Clause, which the nation had adopted after the Civil War. The so-called "reconstruction" of the Constitution through the Thirteenth, Fourteenth, and Fifteenth Amendments and the Civil Rights Act of 1866 were meant to forever end not only the enslavement of Black Americans, but the unequal treatment of Blacks. Henceforth, everybody would be entitled to all the rights of full citizenship.

But like a lot of post–Civil War federal lawmaking, the Equal Protection Clause was ignored in the southern states. In time, the North and the federal government began to give up on enforcing the reconstruction amendments and laws. Nowhere was this truer than with the seven-to-one ruling against Homer Plessy. The Court blithely held that "equal protection" could be the same thing as "separate but equal." While it was clear that things were *not equal*, the Court's majority upheld Louisiana's railroad Jim Crow law.

There was one stirring dissent by Justice John Marshall, who wrote:

> There is no caste here. Our constitution is color-blind, and neither knows nor tolerates classes among citizens. In respect of civil rights, all citizens are equal before the law. The humblest is the peer of the most powerful. The law regards man as man, and takes no account of his surroundings or of his color when his civil rights as guaranteed by the supreme law of the land are involved.[32]

Alas, that sentiment would not become the law of the land until over a half-century later when segregation began to tumble down in *Brown v. Board of Education*.[33]

Even more disheartening was the story of Berea College. After Kentucky adopted a law requiring that all schools in the state be segregated, the college protested and sued. After all, its Christian mission was to educate "all races of men, without distinction."[34] But in 1908 the Supreme Court upheld Kentucky's law. In order to survive, the college was forced to expel all of its Black students.[35]

With these cases in mind, the NAACP knew it had a big challenge ahead. At a meeting in a local Black church, J. Chapin Brinsmade, NAACP's new lawyer from Washington, DC, told the crowd that the "results in Louisville will be of the utmost importance in determining whether or not the Negro is to be segregated. It will not be easy to void the ordinance in the courts . . . Louisville has drawn its ordinance very carefully."[36]

Despite the promise of the Thirteenth, Fourteenth, and Fifteenth Amendments that all persons were entitled to the same liberties as every other person no matter what their color may be, as Jim Crow took hold in the South, many of the rights guaranteed by the Civil War amendments became more illusory than real for black citizens.

The title of Louisville's new law said it all:

> An ordinance to prevent conflict and ill-feeling between the white and colored races in the city of Louisville, and to preserve the public peace and promote the general welfare, by making reasonable provisions requiring, as far as practicable, the use of separate blocks, for residences, places of abode, and places of assembly by white and colored people respectively.[37]

It had the supposedly separate but equal provisions: Just as no Black person could buy property and move into a predominantly white neighborhood, so too could no white person buy property and move into a mostly Black neighborhood. However, the equality was a sham and served to keep Black Louisvillians stuck in poorer and more run-down neighborhoods rather than keeping Whites out of the better Black neighborhoods.

Just three months after the ordinance was adopted in 1914, the city prosecuted its first case. In August, Arthur Harris moved into a house in a White block. He was summoned to appear before a police court and found guilty of violating the new law. In December, the court upheld the conviction, stating that the ordinance "was extremely mild in its operation," that it had a "scrupulous regard for property," and that while the ownership of property was important, it could be regulated by the government—as settled by the Supreme Court in the *Plessy* "separate but equal" railroad car case.[38] This would be the first criminal conviction based on the law. But it was Mr. Warley's subsequent civil suit that would put it to the most serious test.

William Warley wanted to challenge the new law. So did Charles Buchanan, a White businessman who bought and sold real estate. Together, they concocted a plan. They found a block in the city that had ten households—eight of which were occupied by White families and two were occupied by Black families. Mr. Warley contracted to buy from Mr. Buchanan an undeveloped lot on the block so that Mr. Warley could build his family a home. The contract, however, had a rather unusual provision:

> It is understood that I am purchasing the above property for the purpose of having erected thereon a house which I propose to make my residence, and it is a distinct part of for said property unless I have the right under the laws of the State of Kentucky and the City of Louisville to occupy said property as a residence.[39]

In short, the contract allowed Warley to get out of the deal if he wasn't allowed to live on the property he bought. Both he and Buchanan knew full well that Warley wouldn't be allowed to move into Warley's new property, but they moved ahead in order to set up a test case to challenge the law.

After signing the contract, Warley immediately tried to back out of the deal, citing the Louisville ordinance as the reason why he could not go through with the purchase. Buchanan sued Warley, seeking to enforce the contract and make Warley buy the property. While Warley claimed that the ordinance prevented him from buying the property, Buchanan asserted that the law was unconstitutional. Thus, there was the odd circumstance of a White businessman arguing in court that the segregation ordinance was unconstitutional, while Warley, the local Black NAACP president, was relying on the ordinance to avoid a contractual obligation. It may have been a set-up, but it was brilliant. And it needed to be brilliant considering the obstacles the opponents of residential segregation faced.

With Jim Crow becoming more and more firmly entrenched in the South, and with no indication from the Court that things were about to change, the NAACP looked for a new strategy. It found it with a case decided only nine years earlier—*Lochner v. New York*.[40] The *Lochner* Court had found a regulation of working conditions in bakeries interfered with the freedom of contract between employers and employees and in doing so violated the "substantive due process" rights guaranteed by the Constitution. Substantive due process was then, as now, a controversial doctrine.

But it was a doctrine for which the NAACP had found some use. Knowing that an argument under the Equal Protection Clause of the Fourteenth Amendment would not be well-received in light of the *Plessy* and the *Berea College* cases, the NAACP had no choice but to avoid heavy reliance on the fundamental principle that segregation is an evil proscribed by the Constitution's guarantee of equal protection. Instead, it relied on *Lochner* and the Court's embrace of economic rights. If the Court couldn't understand the conflict between the Equal Protection Clause and the separate but equal doctrine, perhaps it could understand the importance of the right of a White landowner to sell his property to whomever he wanted—even if the buyer were Black.

Lochner involved New York's regulation of working conditions in bakeries. For generations, the *Lochner* decision has been derided by progressive scholars as a case that elevated property and economic rights over the ability of government to protect working people. More recent scholarship has called that narrative into doubt.

As catalogued in detail by Professor David Bernstein, the regulation at issue in *Lochner* was little more than a protectionist ordinance pushed by well-established bakeries to shut down competition from smaller and newer bakeries opened and run by immigrants.[41] Bernstein describes the conventional progressive demonization of *Lochner* this way:

> Lochner is said to have involved overworked, exploited bakery workers who had managed to win a meager but hard-fought legislative victory limiting their hours of labor to sixty per week. The Supreme Court refused to acquiesce to this minor victory for progress and social justice, and instead protected the interests of large corporations by invalidating the hours legislation under the Fourteenth Amendment's Due Process Clause as a purported violation of "liberty of contract."[42]

But, Bernstein writes, this is a myth:

> The bakers' union conceived of and promoted the hours legislation not simply to address health concerns, but also to drive small bakeshops that employed recent immigrants out of the industry. . . . Large corporate bakeries, meanwhile, *supported* and also benefited from the maximum-hours legislation invalidated in *Lochner*. The constitutional challenge to the legislation came from small family-owned bakers that were usually owned by former bakery workers.[43]

This was a classic case of what economists today call "rent-seeking." Rent-seeking behavior refers to the efforts of interest group lobbyists to gain an advantage over competitors through legislation. For example, a manufacturer might seek a law that favors the sale of products that only it makes. A union might ask for legislation that requires all construction workers on government projects to be unionized. In one famous case, a consortium of avocado farmers in California convinced that state to ban avocados with less than 8 percent oil content. Only avocados grown in California could meet this standard, thus making avocados grown in Florida illegal in California.[44]

In other words, like most cases where there is a symbiotic rent-seeking relationship between legislators, the regulators, and the regulated community, the large bakeries could more easily meet the new labor guidelines.[45] But the smaller, largely immigrant-owned bakeries, that relied more on long hours put in by family and friends, could not. The law was designed to drive them out of business. The worker-protection rationale was a pretext.

Moreover, like a lot of protectionist legislation, there was an element of anti-immigrant bias. As Bernstein relates, a state inspector reported, "It is almost impossible to secure or keep in proper cleanly [*sic*] condition the Jewish and Italian bakeshops. Cleanliness and tidiness are entirely foreign to these people."[46]

In April 1902, a factory inspector filed a criminal complaint against Joseph Lochner, a small bakery owner. The complaint alleged that Lochner had employed Aman Schmitter for more than sixty hours a week. Schmitter claimed that he agreed to work extra hours so he could learn cake-baking.[47] Interestingly, Schmitter had known Lochner for years, and continued to work for him for years after the case. David Bernstein speculates that Schmitter, Lochner, and the Utica Master Bakers Association had cooperated to set the case up as a constitutional challenge.[48]

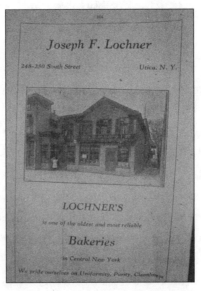

Figure 7. The Lochner Bakery.[49]

Lochner lost in New York's Court of Appeals, its highest court. The court concluded that, "the purpose of [the law] . . . is to benefit the public; that it has a just and reasonable relation to the public welfare, and hence is within the police power possessed by the Legislature."[50] By the "police power" the court was not referring to law enforcement; rather this is the term given for a local or state government's general power to pass laws and regulate in the public interest. With its focus on the beneficial nature of the law, the state court paid little attention to whether Lochner's rights had been trampled. But the United States Supreme Court did.

In what proved to be one of the most controversial decisions of its era, the Supreme Court concluded:

> That the real object and purpose were simply to regulate the hours of labor between the master and his employees . . . in a private business, not dangerous in any degree to morals, or in any real and substantial degree to the health of the employees. Under such circumstances the freedom of master and employee to contract with each other in relation to their employment, and in defining the same, cannot be prohibited or interfered with, without violating the Federal Constitution.[51]

There was a strong dissent from Justice Holmes, who famously quipped that the Court should not impose its own model of economic wisdom on the nation. Referring to the laissez-faire economist Herbert Spencer, Holmes wrote:

> The liberty of the citizen to do as he likes so long as he does not interfere with the liberty of others to do the same, which has been a shibboleth for some well-known writers, is interfered with by school laws, by the Postoffice, by every state or municipal institution which takes his money for purposes thought desirable, whether he likes it or not. The 14th[-Fourteenth] Amendment does not enact Mr. Herbert Spencer's Social Statics.[52]

While progressives have long lamented it, the *Lochner* opinion came strongly down on the side of economic rights against state interference. And it was this respect for economic and property rights that gave the NAACP a powerful tool to fight racial segregation in Louisville. The NAACP used *Lochner* to argue for the free right of contract between buyers and sellers of real estate, whatever the color of their skin.

Effective advocates in any court understand that even the best legal arguments can often lose if a party is unsavory or the idea of giving a win for the litigant makes the judges uncomfortable. While some courts can overcome their distaste for an individual and rule in that person's favor if the law is compelling enough, this is usually not so if the law is uncertain. That is why lawyers try to paint their clients in the best light possible and try to make the court understand all the good that can come out of the correct decision. The NAACP attorneys understood this well.

The NAACP's brief opposing the law was carefully tailored for its intended audience—a Court that was comfortable with the philosophy of "separate but equal." Recognizing that the prejudices of the justices ran deep, the NAACP's principal brief begins by setting up its own cringe-worthy dichotomy between good Blacks who were trying to better themselves and a "degraded and worthless class of negroes":

> That if the ordinance in question is enforced it will result in preventing the better and more prosperous element of the colored inhabitants from obtaining residences in a better locality, will have a tendency to confine those members of the colored race who are anxious to improve their condition to undesirable quarters of the city, where they and their offspring will be constantly thrown in close touch with and contaminated by the degraded and worthless class of negroes, which element predominates in those sections to which the colored race are now almost exclusively confined, and will thereby have a tendency to lower the standard of citizenship in the State among the colored citizens rather than raise it.[53]

And then, to further reassure the Court, the brief continues that the plaintiffs are seeking only a return to the status quo ante, rather than the more radical and pernicious course inherent in the ordinance:

> The purpose of the enactment . . . is to establish a Ghetto for the colored people of Louisville. . . . After white and colored people have lived side by side all over the country for nearly fifty years since the Civil War, there has come an outbreak of race prejudice, and legislation like the ordinance under consideration has been attempted in various cities. It is a disease which is spreading as new political nostrums constantly spread from State to State.[54]

And next, after making the Court comfortable with the thought of ruling for the plaintiff, the NAACP next provides a palatable legal reason for doing so that is based in the economic rights of property owners. Such rights, the NAACP argues, the ordinance "destroys without compensation rights which had become vested long before it took effect."[55] The brief admits that governments have the "police power" to regulate economic activity. However, tying the economic argument to the antidiscrimination theme, the NAACP continues that such regulations must be applied uniformly:

> We rest our case upon the fundamental principle that, while a State may make police regulations which forbid many acts which would otherwise be lawful and may add restrictions respecting the use of property to those existing at common law, such restrictions must affect all citizens without discrimination.[56]

The brief is careful to make no attempt to call for a reversal of the "separate but equal" cases of *Plessy* or *Berea College*, or to even suggest that those cases would be incompatible with a favorable outcome in Louisville. Instead, whereas *Plessy* and *Berea College* advanced some [ersatz] notion of "equality," the whole point of the Louisville ordinance was only to advance *inequality*: "Such an ordinance cannot fail to keep the negro in that condition of inferiority as respects his opportunities for advancement and self-improvement which it was the prime object of the Fourteenth Amendment to put an end to."[57]

And again, "No one . . . would imagine for an instant that the predominant purpose of this ordinance was not to prevent the negro citizens of Louisville, however industrious, thrifty, and well-educated they might be, from approaching that condition vaguely described as 'social equality.'"[58]

Working through the double-negative in that passage, the NAACP was making it clear that a victory for them would not be a threat to "separate but equal." That would have to wait for a later generation. But to win in 1917, the NAACP was compelled to agree that the "Counsel for the defendant are right in saying that the Fourteenth Amendment does not compel social equality."[59]

While the City and its supporting friends of the Court—which included the City of Baltimore—argued mightily that *Plessy* and *Berea College* protected the segregation ordinance against challenge, the NAACP would have none of it. And, more importantly, neither would the Supreme Court.

On November 5, 1917, the Court issued its opinion. The Court was far more interested in protecting rights in property than allowing segregation. First, the court emphasized the importance of property rights in American law:

> The Fourteenth Amendment protects life, liberty, and property from invasion by the states without due process of law. Property is more than the mere thing which a person owns. It is elementary that it includes the right to acquire, use, and dispose of it. The Constitution protects these essential attributes of property. . . . Property consists of the free use, enjoyment, and disposal of a person's acquisitions without control or diminutions save by the law of the land.[60]

Property rights were the key to defeating the law, because they were the one area where discrimination could not be tolerated: "Colored persons are citizens of the United States and have the right to purchase property and enjoy and use the same without laws discriminating against them solely on the account of race."[61]

As for *Plessy*, the Court paid it little mind, simply saying that *Plessy* dealt with the "classification of accommodations [which] was permitted upon the basis of equality for both races."[62]

Also, by 1917, a few other lower courts around the country had been able to get around *Plessy* when ruling that Baltimore-style copycat laws violated the federal constitution. In *Buchanan*, the Supreme Court found particularly persuasive the way the Georgia Supreme Court dealt with *Plessy* in a case from Atlanta and proceeded to quote from the Georgia opinion:

> The most that was done [in *Plessy*] was to require him as a member of a class to conform to reasonable rules in regard to the separation of the races. In none of them was he denied the right to use, control, or dispose of his property, as in this case. Property of a person, whether as a member of a class or as an individual, cannot be taken without due process of law.[63]

And because a White man could not sell his property to a Black man, just as the Black man could not buy the property of a White man, the Court found not only a lack of equality but a violation of property rights.

> We think this attempt to prevent the alienation of the property in question to a person of color was not a legitimate exercise of the police power of the state, and is in direct violation of the fundamental law enacted in the Fourteenth Amendment of the Constitution preventing state interference with property rights except by due process of law.[64]

That was pretty much the end of explicit racial zoning. Overt apartheid was dead. While a few other cities tried from time to time to pass similar laws in the hope that the courts would overlook them or reverse *Buchanan*, those attempts were promptly struck down by the courts.

But in the end, it didn't much matter. Cities soon found a more sophisticated way to protect White neighborhoods not only from Blacks but also from the "degraded and worthless class" of all races. The era of economic and exclusionary zoning was about to begin.

Chapter 2

The Rise of the Tenement Slums
and Urban Reform

Today, thanks to *Buchanan v. Warley*, we no longer have explicit racial zoning. Instead, we have "comprehensive" zoning. This is also called "Euclidean" zoning for reasons that will be explained in subsequent chapters. The essence of comprehensive zoning is that an entire city can be laid out with various uses assigned to various zoning districts. Commercial uses might be in one section and residential uses elsewhere. The problem with such zoning is that it rarely sets aside enough land for inexpensive housing—the kind that working class and minority populations can afford.

The explicit racial zoning of Baltimore, Louisville, and other cities was particularly ugly because it so overtly demeaned and debased an entire race. But despite its cosmetic surgery, modern-day zoning can be just as unattractive. But the harm isn't the same ugliness that came out of the mouths of working-class whites giving voice to their worst fears and prejudices. Rather, post-Baltimore style comprehensive zoning has a patina of professionalism imparted to it from the elite progressives concerned about the betterment of society, land planning professionals worrying about streets and traffic, and environmentalists focused on open space and nature. Most important are all those suburbanites who want to keep their neighborhoods just the way they are. In short, modern-day zoning has managed to sanitize intentional and unintentional segregation by hiding it behind the sophisticated mantle of comprehensive planning and a popular longing for large green lawns and cul-de-sacs.

Yet the origins of what came to be known as comprehensive zoning were imbued with some of the same reprehensible motivations that animated the segregation zoning in cities like Baltimore and Louisville. While the purveyors of the early comprehensive zoning laws did not overtly speak of minority exclusion, their focus on maintaining the "integrity" of residential neighborhoods paid little mind to those who had been excluded from those neighborhoods in the first place—whether that exclusion was the result of race or economics.

While the first comprehensive zoning ordinance came out of New York City in 1916, the first great legal test for the new zoning arose in the unlikely town of Euclid, Ohio. But to understand what happened in Euclid, it is essential to know the history of housing in New York City,[1] because the conditions in that city's tenement housing are almost incomprehensible to the modern twenty-first-century city apartment dweller. It is a history that made the impetus to plan and to regulate housing inevitable.

New York City's Tenement Housing and Calls for Reform

Imagine living at the top of a six-story tenement building in an apartment with no running water, no central heat, and no air. And that doesn't mean no air *conditioning*, it means no *air* because there were no windows in many apartments—only a door leading to a dim hallway and six flights of stairs. For sanitation, you would take your pail of human waste down those six flights to a central courtyard where you could dump your waste into a central privy vault. And then, hopefully with another pail, you could find a nearby pump for water that you could haul back up six flights of stairs. Under these conditions it is no wonder that cholera epidemics would rage, killing thousands.[2]

Figure 8. A room in a tenement flat circa 1910.

Figure 9. New York City tenement, circa 1900.

As Professor Richard Plunz describes it, by 1859, one New Yorker out of twenty-seven, or 3.7 percent, died on an annual basis largely of disease: "In addition to cholera the common urban killers included smallpox, typhoid fever, malaria, yellow fever, and tuberculosis."[3] Previously, in 1810, before the massive tenement-style urbanization, only one in forty-six New Yorkers died. The increase in less than fifty years was attributed to "the city's changing status."[4]

One of the great reform movements started with Jacob Riis, whose 1890 book, *How the Other Half Lives,* was the impetus for much reform. However, Riis's sense of charity ranged from sympathetic to odious. On the sympathetic side, he would sadly note, "The death of a child in a tenement was registered in the Bureau of Vital Statistics as 'plainly due to suffocation of foul air of an unventilated apartment.'"[5] Indeed, the illustrations in the book are especially compelling even today, showing the floor plans of numerous tenements that clearly lack windows or ventilation of any kind. In one, the interior rooms were "utterly dark, close, and unventilated. The living-rooms are but 10 by 12 feet; the bedrooms 6 ½ by 7 feet."[6]

It's not that the slum dwellers lived in these cramped and overly crowded apartments because they were cheap. They weren't. In fact, they were sometimes more expensive than better dwellings elsewhere. But they were where the poor could live cheek to jowl with other poor. As Riis put it: "And yet experts had testified that, as compared with uptown, rents were from twenty-five to thirty per cent higher in the worst slums of the lower wards."[7] As one nineteenth-century report put it, rents were high because the poor couldn't be expected to keep things in good order and the landlords didn't bother to try:

> Rents were fixed high enough to cover damage and abuse from this class, from whom nothing was expected, and the most was made of them while they lasted. Neatness, order, cleanliness, were never dreamed of in connection with the tenant-house system . . . containing, but sheltering not, the miserable hordes that crowded beneath smouldering, water-rotted roofs or burrowed among the rats of clammy cellars.[8]

Riis was not the only observer of these conditions. During the 1849 cholera outbreak, a doctor observed a dank cellar dwelling where the epidemic originated, "At my first visit, on the 16th of May, five human beings, one man and four women, lay upon the floor in different stages of cholera. There was nothing under them but mud and filth, and nothing over them but a few mats of the filthiest description."[9]

But on the odious side, Riis and his fellow reformers' sense of discomfort with the poor could be palpable. As Riis writes,

> The climax had been reached. The situation was summed up by the Society for the Improvement of the Condition of the Poor in these words: "Crazy old buildings, crowded rear tenements in filthy yards, dark, damp basements, leaking garrets, shops, outhouses, and stables converted into dwellings, though scarcely fit to shelter brutes, are habitations of thousands of our fellow-beings in this wealthy, Christian city."

Riis piles on:

> If it shall appear that the sufferings and the sins of the "other half," and the evil they breed, are but as a just punishment upon the community that gave it no other choice, it will be because that is the truth. . . . in the tenements all the influences make for evil; because they are the hot-beds of the epidemics that carry death to rich and poor alike; the nurseries of pauperism and crime that fill our jails and police courts; that throw off a scum of forty thousand human wrecks to the island asylums and workhouses year by year; that turned out in the last eight years a round half million beggars to prey upon our charities . . . That we have to own it the child of our own wrong does not excuse it, even though it gives it claim upon our utmost patience and tenderest charity.[10]
>
> "The City . . . was a general asylum for vagrants." Young vagabonds, the natural offspring of such "home" conditions, overran the streets. Juvenile crime increased fearfully year by year.[11]

Riis was appalled not just by the slums but by those who lived in
them. The progressive zeitgeist was as much about blaming the victims as it was about their exploitation.[12] During what can best be
described as a series of voyeuristic tours of various tenement blocks,
Riis is as contemptuous of the poor as he is of their housing. Block
by block, Riis catalogs the overcrowded and unsanitary housing
as he criticizes those who owned and managed the tenements. But
with each block he also lays into ethnic caricatures of the resident
Italians, Irish, Germans, Jews, Chinese, and Bohemians and with
slurs viler than we might expect today at a Klan rally. These ethnic
poor were described variously as being "content to live in a pig sty,"
ignorant, lazy, thieves, beggars, tramps, drunkards, greedy, stupid,
and so on.

He had special hatred for the Chinese because of their history
of "senseless idolatry, a mere grub-worship" that made them incapa-
ble of being Christianized.[13] Worse, Riis believed the vicious canard
that the Chinese routinely enslaved white girls to opium. A typical
Chinatown neighborhood is: "honeycombed with scores of the conventional households of the Chinese quarter: the men worshippers of Joss
[a.k.a. a Chinese temple]; the women, all white, girls hardly yet grown
to womanhood, worshipping nothing save the pipe that has enslaved
them body and soul."[14]

It is with a sense of resignation that Riis concludes: "Granted, that
the Chinese are in no sense a desirable element of the population, that
they serve no useful purpose here, whatever they may have done elsewhere in other days, yet to this it is a sufficient answer that they are
here, and that, having let them in, we must make the best of it."[15]

Riis was hardly alone in his contempt for people from south of the
English Channel. President Woodrow Wilson "denounced immigrants
'from the south of Italy and men of the meaner sort out of Hungary
and Poland' who possessed 'neither skill nor energy nor any initiative
of quick intelligence.'"[16]

Riis's attitude toward Blacks was somewhat more nuanced—being
more condescending than condemning. He noted that whites refused to

live where Blacks presently lived or had ever lived in the past—despite Blacks having done much to "improve" themselves since slavery. Or, as he put it, "Once a colored house, always a colored house."[17] But he admitted, as far as cleanliness went, "he is immensely the superior of the lowest of the whites, the Italians and the Polish Jews, below whom he has been classed in the past in the tenant scale."[18] Condescending as he may have been, Riis was also quite modern in his understanding of the impact of racism on the inability of Blacks to advance: "If, when the account is made up between the races, it shall be claimed that he [the Black] falls short of the result to be expected from twenty-five years of freedom, it may be well to turn to the other side of the ledger and see how much of the blame is borne by the prejudice and greed that have kept him from rising under a burden of responsibility to which he could hardly be equal."[19]

In contrast to Riis's somewhat more charitable attitude toward African Americans, other reformers harbored more negativity. They were resigned to the untrue "fact" that Black Americans were from a less evolved race and one that could not be substantially improved, if at all. Only such a belief could explain how, in 1906, Ota Benga, a member of the Mtubi tribe, could be brought over from Africa to be displayed first at the St. Louis World's Fair and then in the monkey cage at the Bronx Zoo.[20] Not coincidentally, the Bronx Zoo was run by Madison Grant, a noted eugenicist who wrote *The Passing of the Great Race; or, The Racial Basis of European History*, which argued that northern Europeans were the most advanced people in the world and advocated for anti-miscegenation laws, forced sterilizations, and immigration restrictions.[21]

Historian George M. Frederickson connected the myth of an inferior race with the supposed need to quarantine:

> If blacks were a degenerating race with no future, the problem ceased to
> be one of how to prepare them for citizenship or even how to make them
> more productive and useful members of the community. The new progno-
> sis pointed rather to the need to segregate or quarantine a race liable to be

a source of contamination and social danger to the white community, as it
sank even deeper into the slough of disease, vice and criminality.[22]

Other reformers were equally distressed by another newer minority—
the Italians. As reformer Allen Forman wrote, "By all odds the most
vicious, ignorant and degraded of all immigrants who come to our
shores are the Italian inhabitants of Mulberry Bend and the surrounding tenements . . . an eddy in the life of the city where the scum collects,
where the very offscouring of all humanity seem to find a lodgment."[23]

A few years after this was written, Riis's reform movement had
some effect. The city demolished the Mulberry Bend slum, replacing
it with the ironically named Columbus Park, the first of many great
urban improvement projects across the nation. With these projects, the
"ignorant and degraded" might not have been eliminated, but they
were displaced—and little has been written about where they went
because the reformers cared not a whit. Now the city had Columbus
Park, named for the great Italian explorer, and the site where Italian
immigrants were kicked out of their homes.

As Joel Schwartz described it, "Riis and his associates goaded city
officials to step up their police campaign against tenement violations.
For a time, the Board of Health forced closure of 400 rookeries [slum
tenements] a year . . . generat[ing] a class of refugees."[24] Indeed, like all
such redevelopment where the question of where the poor will go is an
afterthought, if it is considered at all, "Riis was puzzled by the surge in
flophouse bunks. 'Given the ability to choose targets for demolition,'
Riis wrote, 'we picked our lot . . . and the department drove the tenants out.'"[25] Ironically, Riis praised Columbus Park as the "lungs of the
poor," although between 10,000 and 13,300 of the poor were forced to
find their way to other tenements.[26] On the Lower East Side, public
projects removed another 50,000 residents.[27]

Likewise, Plunz says three hundred squatter shacks in Seneca
Village were demolished to make way for Central Park.[28] "Squatter
shacks" was how the neighborhood homes, most of them two story and
owner-occupied, were described at the time to justify their removal.

But, in fact, the so-called shacks were the locus of the most prosperous establishments of African American property owners in New York City. But to justify the destruction of the village to make way for the park, the "white and mulattoe" residents were described as squatters and their homes as shacks. Between 1600 and 5,000 residents were duly displaced.[29]

"The one thing," Riis wrote, "you shall vainly ask for in the chief city of America is a distinctly American community." Immigrants, apparently, were not Americans. Instead, they were a "queer conglomerate mass of heterogeneous elements, ever striving and working like whiskey and water in one glass, and with the like result: final union and a prevailing taint of whiskey."[30]

A common theme to the reform sought by Riis and his fellow-reformers was that they had to fix the problem of the tenements because of their disease-spreading potential. In one passage Riis manages to combine anti-Semitic xenophobia with germaphobia:

> Typhus fever and small-pox are bred here [in the Jewish sweatshops], and help solve the question what to do with him [the Jew.] Filth diseases both, they sprout naturally among the hordes that bring the germs with them from across the sea. . . . It has happened more than once that a child recovering from small-pox, and in the most contagious stage of the disease, has been found crawling among heaps of half-finished clothing that the next day would be offered for sale on the counter of a Broadway store; or that a typhus fever patient has been discovered in a room whence perhaps a hundred coats had been sent home that week, each one with the wearer's death-warrant, unseen and unsuspected, basted in the lining.[31]

The prevalence of disease was a constant concern of those who investigated slum conditions. As early as 1842, Charles Dickens wrote in his *American Notes*, of a visit to one of the tenements:

> What lies beyond this tottering flight of steps, that creak beneath our tread!
> A miserable room, lighted by one dim candle, and destitute of all comfort,

save that which may be hidden in a wretched bed. Beside it, sits a man: his elbows on his knees: his forehead hidden in his hands. "What ails that man?" asks the foremost officer. "Fever," he sullenly replies, without looking up. Conceive the fancies of a fevered brain, in such a place as this![32]

Nearly a half-century later, Riis observed pretty much the same: "Drop a case of scarlet fever, of measles, or of diphtheria into one of these barracks, and, unless it is caught at the very start and stamped out, the contagion of the one case will sweep block after block, and half people a graveyard [*sic*]."[33]

Clearly, in a trope that has resonated from before Riis's time to the present era and the COVID-19 pandemic, with their disease and crime, the slums and their inhabitants threatened not only the slum-dwellers but everyone else as well. Something had to be done because the slums were "hot-beds of the epidemics that carry death to rich and poor alike."[34]

It was a reform movement motivated not only by charity but also by an instinct for self-preservation. There was a need to stop the destruction of real Americans by the other half who dwelled in the tenements.

In Riis's mind the tenement-dwellers were not real Americans but interlopers on the scene who had brought their filth, crime, and depravity to our shores. Their natural tendencies were only exacerbated by their horrific disease-ridden conditions. Fixing the conditions might limit the contagion, but it would not cure it. And it is this sort of contempt that seems to have been an undercurrent for much of the housing reform of the era. Nativist, racial, ethnic, and disease fears were exploited to sell reform. Alternatively, reform was the vehicle used as window dressing for the real object of protecting white Anglo-Saxon Protestants from the hordes.

Chapter 3

New York City Creates Economic Zoning

The right to own and use property has never been absolute. Landowners have never had the right to use property in such a way that the use will harm neighboring landowners. Neighbors have always had the right to stop objectionable uses that rise to the level of being a nuisance. And that was the premise behind early land use regulations—instead of waiting for a nuisance to happen, the local government could step in and stop a presumed nuisance before it began. Thus, governments could ban rendering plants or brickyards in residential neighborhoods because of their offensive odors.[1] When local authorities could make a good health and safety rationale for a land use regulation, the courts were generally solicitous. But when the regulation seemed to be for some unrelated purpose, such as mere aesthetics, the courts were often less forgiving. Thus, the late nineteenth and early twentieth centuries were marked by numerous cases where land use regulations had been variously upheld or struck down, depending on whether a court could be convinced that their purpose and effect was to abate proto-nuisances and whether the rights of property owners were adequately respected.[2]

For example, in order keep Copley Square in Boston aesthetically pleasing, in 1898 the city adopted an ordinance restricting the height of nearby buildings to ninety feet. The Massachusetts Supreme Court upheld it in 1899 not so much because it could be justified under health and safety reasons but because there was a mechanism to compensate landowners for any losses caused by the restriction:

> Regulations in regard to the height and mode of construction of buildings in cities are often made by legislative enactments, in the exercise of the police power, for the safety, comfort, and convenience of the people, and for the benefit of property owners generally . . . But [this ordinance] differs from most statutes relative to this subject, in providing compensation to persons injured in their property by the limitations which it creates. In this respect it conforms to the constitutional requirements for the taking of property by the right of eminent domain.[3]

In other words, the Massachusetts high court first recognized the validity of the purpose behind the law—to protect a public park—and then found it did not infringe upon the rights of landowners because they would be compensated.

A decade later, in a separate challenge before the US Supreme Court, that Court refused to upset another decision by the Massachusetts high court in upholding the same law. This time no compensation had been offered, but the state court didn't focus on the compensation rationale because no money was paid for the height restriction. The court also rejected the notion that a purely aesthetic regulation could be lawful. But it did find that the regulation was justified because tall buildings were more difficult to stop from burning down.[4] The US Supreme Court refused to second-guess the state court, expressing "reluctance in interfering with the well-considered judgments of the courts of a state whose people are to be affected by the operation of the law."[5] Because it had no reason to second guess the fire safety rationale, it let the height limit stand.

Likewise, in 1908, Maryland's highest court allowed a height ordinance to survive despite claims that it was chiefly adopted to protect the aesthetics of a wealthy neighborhood. Instead, the court was persuaded that the ban on seventy-foot buildings (except churches) would protect the neighborhood from fire: Thus, the law's "purpose was to protect the handsome buildings and their contents, located in that vicinity, and also the works of art clustered there, from the ravages of fire" including "numerous handsome residences of private citizens, containing valuable works of art and of literature." [6]

But when a court thought the motivation behind a land use regulation was primarily aesthetics, the law would be dismissed out of hand. As Professor Revell explains,

> When judges failed to see the connection between a residential land-use ordinance and public health or safety, they tended to assume that the real motivation of the law was to beautify the neighborhood by keeping out commercial elements. And where they saw aesthetic motives as primary, judges could be quite contemptuous of efforts to limit the use of private property. . . . To extend the police power so far would constitute "the essence of tyranny."[7]

Unless compensation was to be paid, an aesthetic regulation would not be tolerated. As the California Supreme Court put it, "the promotion of aesthetic or artistic considerations is a proper object of governmental care will probably not be disputed. But . . . Such restriction is, if not a taking, pro tanto of the property, a damaging thereof, for which the owner is entitled to compensation."[8]

In this era the courts recognized that state and local governments had a general "police power" to protect health, safety, and welfare. But that power was limited. It didn't give the government broader powers than necessary to address immediate threats to public health, safety, and welfare. Just as an individual could sue to stop a nuisance, so too could a local government restrict dangerous and noxious uses of land. But, by the same measure, just as an individual couldn't sue a neighbor because the individual didn't like his neighbor's choice of architecture or paint color, neither could the government regulate the same. A neighbor might try to buy an easement from his neighbor to limit the neighbor's non-nuisance choices in architecture or paint color. Likewise, a local government could enact a regulation to the same effect—so long as it agreed to pay for the privilege. Otherwise, there had to be a legitimate health, safety, or welfare rationale for the regulation. And aesthetics alone were not a legitimate rationale. Their regulation might be a legitimate exercise of police power, but that exercise could not trample rights in private property.

This state of affairs did not sit well with a small group of proto-planners who sought to craft the nation's first *comprehensive* zoning law in New York City. The early years of the twentieth century swirled with intellectual currents of the progressive movement, which focused on achieving broad societal improvements even if that meant individual economic and property rights had to take a back seat. There was the "City Beautiful" movement that sought to instill better aesthetics and design into the cityscapes. And, of course, there were the reformers like Jacob Riis who wanted to end tenement living as it was practiced.

There were some early hesitant steps starting in the mid-nineteenth century, especially after the Civil War. Windows or airshafts were mandated for all apartments so crowded families wouldn't suffocate with bad air.[9] Running water and other sanitation measures followed. Such mandates easily survived challenge—including one brought by Trinity Church, which owned some tenement houses where the only supply of water was from backyard hydrants.[10]

By this time, the connection between cholera and tainted water was well known. In 1854, 616 people in London died from cholera. Famously, Dr. John Snow mapped every occurrence of the disease and found that they all clustered around a single water well. He ended that outbreak by locking the handle on the pump.[11] When New York tried to enforce a law requiring that each floor of the tenements have fresh running water from the city's upstate reservoir, Trinity Church sued, arguing the measure was one of mere convenience, not public health and safety. New York's highest court easily brushed aside the challenge:

> That the free use of water, especially during the summer months, tends
> towards the healthful condition of the body, by reason of the increased

cleanliness occasioned by such use, there can be no reasonable doubt. . . .
That dirt, filth, nastiness in general, are great promoters of disease; that
they breed pestilence and contagion, sickness and death,—cannot be successfully denied. There is scarcely a dissent from the general belief on the
part of all who have studied the disease that cholera is essentially a filth
disease.[12]

As the nineteenth century ended, no longer would residents have to carry
human waste down to pit vaults and haul shallow well water back up to
their windowless rooms. Health and safety regulations were imposed on
the tenements, and the new laws withstood challenges. There were even
architectural edicts that prohibited construction of apartments without windows and mandated minimum room sizes. While these measures may have alleviated some of the human misery caused by horrible
housing, they did not end it. The city was just growing too fast with
new waves of unabated immigration, which wasn't fully relieved by out-
ward migration to other regions or by the nascent suburbanization of
the metropolitan area. The city *was* going to grow, and people became
increasingly focused on exactly *how* it was going to grow.

But the sort of planning that could manage such growth and that
was advocated by the early planners was in large measure the regulation of aesthetics. While that might have been within the police power
of the state, aesthetic zoning could not survive if property owners had
to be paid for aesthetic-based restrictions on the use of their land. And
the early planners knew that was a problem. How else could they justify forbidding otherwise innocuous commercial buildings in residential neighborhoods without paying the freight? How could they stop
the proliferation of clearly profitable apartment houses, or tenements,
amongst low density homes? How could they make a serious case that
this would be all in the name of health and safety? An apartment house
was not, of course, a nuisance. Or was it? The answer wouldn't come
until later, in 1926. And until 1926, nobody really knew whether the
effort to zone without the payment of compensation was constitutional
or would survive in the Supreme Court.

Comprehensive Zoning Gets Its Start

To address overcrowding, a New York City "congestion commission" recommended "the redistribution of population from the inner city to the outlying areas."[13] Then, in 1914, the mayor appointed a commission to come up with a comprehensive zoning plan.[14] After much debate over the extent and justification for such a law, in 1916 New York City enacted the nation's first comprehensive zoning law.[15] A rationale to justify the zoning came from the collaboration of the academic Robert H. Whitten and New York attorney Edward M. Bassett. They were well aware of the challenge before them. As Bassett put it, "We must reckon with the fact that Americans take for granted their right to do on their own property anything they please regardless of their neighbors."[16] Bassett expanded on these concerns in his 1917 book *Constitutional Limitations on City Planning Power*.[17] While this may have overstated the legal environment quite a bit because there was no right to inflict harm upon neighbors, it did show that these early planners recognized that the legal acceptance of their vision of land use zoning was not guaranteed.

According to Professor Revell, the "zoning advocates overcame what they perceived to be a persistent, obstructive constitutional preference for property rights, apparently in contempt of public rights, by finding innovative ways to expand the police power."[18] Prior to the adoption of the New York law, there was much debate amongst the planners as to how to best overcome the perceived limitations placed upon the police power.[19] Courts were unsympathetic to aesthetic zoning, yet aesthetics seemed to play a role in the need to separate apartments from single-family homes. Some planners worried more about constitutional challenges than others, but they all eventually agreed that the status quo was unacceptable. As Professor Revell put it, "Because they believed zoning required the subordination of individual property rights to broader community goals embodied by a city-wide zoning plan, they saw themselves on a collision course with the Constitution."[20]

Whitten and Bassett understood that to succeed they had to encourage "a transition in police power decision-making from categorical legal reasoning to the modern balancing approach."[21] To do this, they envisioned the creation of *comprehensive* zoning, devised by so-called experts, and characterized by interlocking parts that stood together. This would serve as a new type of police power, health and safety-based regulation of property. While any one tree in the forest might not relate to the *public's* health and safety, the entire forest of comprehensive regulations would. As Alfred Bettman, another advocate for planning and zoning from Ohio, later wrote in the *Harvard Law Review*, "comprehensiveness puts the 'reason' into 'reasonableness.'"[22]

New York City's zoning ordinance was adopted in the right place at the right time in history for zoning to be accepted. There was popular will to stop the tenements that Riis so abhorred. Indeed, leading supporters of the zoning plan came from Fifth Avenue merchants who were upset by the spread of garment factories in their midst—factories usually occupied by immigrant Jews. As Joel Schwartz wrote, the Fifth Avenue Association of merchants claimed that "'Hebrews' swarmed from nearby lofts at lunchtime, driving away the patrons of exclusive shops."[23]

Of course, as zoning was being contemplated in other places, there were a few who made the argument that the poorer classes could benefit from zoning. In a modern take on Marie Antoinette's alleged "let them eat cake" remark, some early planners when advocating for single-family zoning in Seattle suggested it would actually help the poor because "'a zoning bill is a poor man's bill' in that it provided lower-income owners with protection from nuisances that wealthier individuals could prevent through expensive lawsuits."[24]

The same sort of arguments were made in other cities such as Portland, Oregon, and Boston. In Boston, while some argued that zoning would "legislate a majority of citizens—those who cannot afford to occupy a detached house of their own—out of the best located parts of the city," others responded that zoning in Seattle would "remove social barriers in cities and give the poor man, and particularly the foreign-born worker an equal opportunity to live and raise his family according to the most wholesome American standards, in contentment and safety and in a detached house of his own rather than in a tenement."[25]

So out of touch were these early planners that it may not have occurred to them that poor people couldn't afford to live in nice single-family homes in any kind of neighborhood. Nor that the sort of nuisance cases brought by rich people might well have been to stop apartment buildings occupied by poor people from being built in rich people's neighborhoods.

Other than a few builders and real estate interests, there was no political support for more tenement construction. That was especially true when the helter-skelter construction of high-density, low-income housing combined with newly built tall office buildings might depress the value of existing neighborhoods and office buildings. Moreover, the future residents in these tenements were an inchoate political force that usually consisted of politically ineffectual, disunited, and widely loathed immigrant populations. They and any future commercial building tenants were no match for the entrenched self-interested residents and owners who desperately wanted to maintain the status quo—a status quo that could be codified with a zoning code.

On top of that, as Professor Revell noted, some believed that a city-wide zoning code, by separating single-family residential uses from the "strange mix of tenements, factories, offices and apartment buildings" found in Manhattan would encourage more homes built in the outlying boroughs, thus relieving pressure for even more density in Manhattan.[26]

The advocates of zoning were lucky because they could point to some recent favorable legal cases that seemed to upend the old order. For example, the Supreme Court upheld a ban on horse stables in residential areas of Little Rock and let stand a Los Angeles ordinance banning a brickyard (which involved much smoke) in a residential neighborhood.[27] Both cases were decided under variations of a public nuisance theory. These cases built upon a much earlier Supreme Court decision upholding Kansas's ban on distilling alcoholic beverages long before the national prohibition became a reality.[28] But the planners also knew that despite these precedents, they needed to be careful. In prior years, the same Court also struck down a safety regulation banning wooden laundries because the law was squarely aimed in a discriminatory fashion against the Chinese.[29] And a year before the laundry case, the Court found that cigar making in tenements was not a serious health risk and could not be banned.[30] Cigar making in tenement homes was a substantial cottage industry in the late nineteenth century. The tobacco leaves smelled, and some neighbors complained. But underlying this law was some fairly blatant discrimination against immigrants and the Supreme Court saw through the public health veil and struck down the law.

After the usual back and forth of political jockeying, the city adopted its new code in 1916. Unlike a height limitation here, or a specific ban on a noxious use there, this code regulated down to the block level what could or could not be done on the land: residential uses here, business uses there, and unrestricted uses elsewhere. With each use various height and setback standards were imposed. As Professor Revell put it, "By carefully balancing incidental private losses against greater public benefits, the meticulous work of the planning bureaucracy—Bassett, Whitten, safety experts, fire marshals, physicians—ensured that a comprehensive ordinance was a proper exercise of the police power."[31] Or so they had hoped. As with any such code involving extensive line-drawing, there were winners and losers. And wherever there are losers, lawsuits will fly like pigeons on a city landmark. But while the code survived local challenges, no case from New York City managed to reach the Supreme Court. That would take a bit longer.

The popularity of New York–style ordinances soon spread across the nation like wildfire. It made sense. While the severity of the tenement crisis was rarely as bad in the rest of the nation as it was in New York City, no town wanted those problems—or all those immigrants. This was an era of a newfound faith in the power of government to solve all manner of social and economic problems. As summarized by Professor Michael Allan Wolf, cities across the United States copied

New York City and adopted their own zoning ordinances upon the convergence of four factors:

> (1) The shortcomings of traditional, common-law methods for regulating land use; (2) the growing influence of planning ideas and the planning profession in urban America; (3) the importation of zoning ideas from New York City and from the model act circulated by the US Department of Commerce; and (4) the prevailing social and political ethos of the Progressive Era, during which great faith was placed in expert-based governmental solutions to social and economic problems.[32]

To put it simply, the influence of the early progressive movement was gaining momentum. Above all, the progressives called for more judicial deference to legislative bodies when they relied on the police power to enact laws and regulations for the public good—even when those laws curtailed individual rights.

In one classic case, the Supreme Court upheld a ban in Los Angeles of a brickyard near a developing residential neighborhood. Justice McKenna's holding went beyond the mere elimination of nuisances. It was about progress trumping private interests: "There must be progress, and if in its march private interests are in the way they must yield to the good of the community."[33] Such a sentiment would have been anathema to most Supreme Court justices in earlier generations. But such an approach to the law in 1916 and beyond made it possible for cities across the nation to embrace zoning schemes that might have been inconceivable only a few decades earlier.

Chapter 4

Zoning Arrives in Euclid, Ohio, and Travels to the Supreme Court

Whether all this new-fangled zoning was legal wouldn't be decided in New York City. Rather, zoning went up against the Constitution in the small unassuming town of Euclid, Ohio. As described by the Supreme Court, the village of Euclid was a suburb of Cleveland with a population "between 5,000 and 10,000, and its area from 12 to 14 square miles."[1] Although it lived in the shadow of industrial Cleveland, it was not beset with the degree of urban ills that plagued New York City, or even in Cleveland. But as was the case in a lot of suburbs, there was fear. There was fear that the village would be subsumed by its larger neighbor. Most of all, there was a fear of being overrun by the "immigrant hordes," changing the character of the small town forever. All told, there was little that was either special or unique about Euclid. But as unremarkable as Euclid may have been as a suburb, it is where zoning met its greatest test before the Supreme Court.

The zoning scheme adopted by Euclid was modeled after New York City's. As described by the Court, "On November 13, 1922, an ordinance was adopted by the village council, establishing a comprehensive zoning plan for regulating and restricting the location of trades, industries, apartment houses, two-family houses, single family houses, etc., the lot area to be built upon, the size and height of buildings, etc."[2]

In the town of Euclid, the idea for a zoning plan to emulate New York City's arose out of concern that Cleveland's industrialization was creeping toward Euclid. Some landowners, like Ambler Realty, fully embraced that prospect and bought property in anticipation, hoping to capitalize. Others who already owned less intensely developed properties wanted to stop the process in its tracks for fear that Euclid's semi-developed semi-rural charm would be lost, that their property values might be lowered, and that their quality of life would be diminished.

One of the leading advocates for zoning was a Cincinnati attorney named Alfred Bettman, who was a member of a variety of state and national associations dedicated to advocacy of modern planning. When questioned about the constitutionality of such schemes, he wrote:

> A comprehensive city plan, based on a thorough, expert study and upon the promotion of the health, safety, and comfort of the whole community, will surely sooner or later—and probably sooner—be upheld by the supreme court of the United States as a modern form of the regulation of the use of private property for the promotion of general public safety, health, comfort, and welfare; especially as it can be demonstrated, if the ordinance is based upon a thorough study of the situation, that the effect of a city planning ordinance will tend to be toward the stabilizing of values, rather than destroying or diminishing values.[3]

This was the template followed in Euclid. After much study and some debate, it adopted its own comprehensive zoning plan on November 13, 1922. The proponents argued that zoning was needed to stop the march of industry, that the rural character of the town must be preserved, and that the water supply was inadequate to support industry or multi-family housing. During the public debate on the ordinance, there was strenuous opposition from William Ambler, whose family owned sixty-eight acres that he believed would be dramatically reduced in value by the ordinance. After all, his land was across the street from the behemoth Cleveland Tractor Company. Who would want to live across the street from a giant smoke-belching factory? Homes there wouldn't sell nearly as well as commercial development.

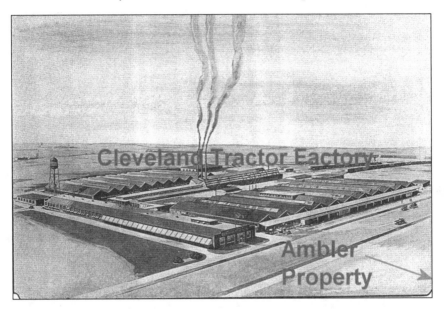

Figure 10. Cleveland Tractor Company, Euclid Ohio, 1921.[4]

Neither the opposition nor the supporters of the ordinance were overtly racially motivated; there were no merchants clamoring to stop Jewish sweatshops as in New York City, and there was no outright zoning by race as in Baltimore and Louisville. But what was not perhaps well understood at the time was that the ability to restrict apartments in favor of sprawling residential neighborhoods would in time contribute to the forces that confined minority populations to urban ghettos. Apparently oblivious to those concerns, and despite the opposition from the real estate industry, the plan was unanimously adopted six to nothing.

The landowners were determined to fight back. While most lawsuits against local towns or villages are filed in state court, the prospect of filing a lawsuit against zoning in state court was unpromising. The state's trial courts had been upholding other Ohio towns' zoning limits on apartment buildings and the like. One trial court described in particular the "evils of apartment houses, the rapaciousness of landlords, and the health dangers posed by overpopulation."[5] In a passage that turned out to be prescient to the Supreme Court's ultimate diatribe against apartment buildings in *Euclid*, the trial court here found, "The number of apartment houses, terraces and tenement blocks in Cleveland, Lakewood and East Cleveland, and the rapidity with which their construction is increasing, is appalling. They may be numbered by the thousand."[6] Nationally, similar challenges to zoning had been filed in the state courts to a very mixed reception. Some states, like Massachusetts, upheld the ordinances. But other states, like New Jersey, found them to be unconstitutional.

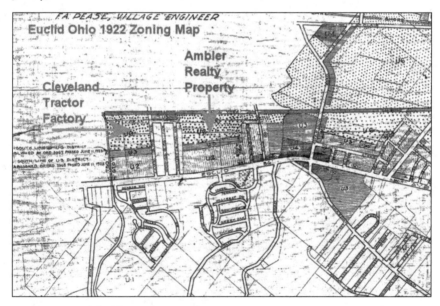

Figure 11. Euclid, Ohio, 1922 zoning map.

In Euclid, fifteen landowners joined forces and hired Newton Baker, an extraordinarily successful and expensive attorney who at one time had served as President Woodrow Wilson's Secretary of War. But he was in it for more than the money. He also had a strong personal aversion to zoning based on both his respect for private property and his representation of a Jewish-run orphanage that was prohibited from opening a facility due to a racially motivated enforcement of a local zoning law. As Baker once wrote, the town's "so-called zoning committee" denied the project "because they did not think it would be good for the village to have a large number of Jewish children in it."[7] That was not an isolated incident. As Professor Wolf wrote, "there was an undercurrent of anti-Semitism in several of the struggles to implement and defend zoning in Metropolitan Cleveland."[8]

Recognizing the perils of filing another suit in state court, Baker took a new tack: In May 1923, he filed in federal court. He hoped he would be less likely to be "hometowned" by local parochial interests. Local state court judges are often dialed into the local political establishment and are often loath to rule against their friends. Moreover, they face reelection challenges, and the force of what has become known as NIMBYism ("Not-in-My-Backyard"-ism) can be a powerful motivator in the electorate. Federal judges, on the other hand, have lifetime appointments and are thought to be less swayed by political necessities and more attuned to federal constitutional imperatives. (Certainly, this was the case in the Southern states in the 1960s desegregation battles.)

Filing a lawsuit challenging zoning in federal court was a bit unusual, as evidenced by the series of lawsuits across the nation that had already been filed in state courts. That made sense. Many attorneys then, as now, are uncomfortable with the more formal and intimidating nature of federal court litigation and prefer the venue they know: state courts. But Baker probably realized federal court was his best shot, and a shot that could very well land before the United States Supreme Court.

At that time, to get into federal court, Baker had to allege that Ambler Realty, the landowner chosen to lead the charge, had suffered over three thousand dollars in damages and that the zoning law violated the federal Constitution. Suing in federal court isn't a matter of right. A plaintiff must be able show enough of an injury to prove it meets the constitutional requirement of a "case or controversy." Without that, there is no jurisdiction in federal court and the case will be dismissed. Here, the injury claim was the three thousand dollars in reduced property value and the controversy was the existence of the unconstitutional zoning ordinance.

But Ambler was clear that it wasn't seeking damages—it was seeking to have the law declared unconstitutional so it couldn't be enforced. That meant that the case would be tried directly before a judge without a jury.

Euclid's first response was to alter the law so its financial impact on Ambler Realty was diminished—to cause Ambler to lose jurisdiction in federal court. James Metzenbaum took up the defense for the town and moved to dismiss the case, arguing that the impact on the property owner wasn't all that significant. Baker had a stroke of luck, however. The federal judge assigned to the case was D. C. Westenhaver, who had been a mentor to Baker and his former law partner.[9] The case was not dismissed.

Next, the parties engaged in extensive factual hearings, arguing over the impact of the ordinance to Ambler Realty and the pros and cons of the zoning ordinance. Litigation of this sort can generally follow two paths: "as-applied" or "facial" challenges. An as-applied challenge will not argue that the challenged law is always unlawful—but that it is unlawful or unconstitutional in the way it is applied to the plaintiff bringing the lawsuit. A facial challenge makes a larger argument—which is that the law is virtually always unlawful or unconstitutional no matter who or what it is applied against.

At first, Baker and his supporting friends of the court (or *amici*, meaning nonparties with an interest in a case) seemed to go both ways, hinting that the ordinance might be okay overall—but not in the way it applied to Ambler Realty. At other times, and in the later stages in the suit, Baker argued that the zoning law was facially unconstitutional. This mattered because it was relevant to the degree to which the parties needed to argue how the area zoning of Ambler's property affected the use and value of the property—devaluing it from ten thousand to twenty-five hundred dollars per acre. If the ordinance were to be challenged facially, it didn't matter so much as long as Ambler could show it met the minimum three thousand dollar threshold for being in federal court. However, if this was an as-applied challenge, the details mattered a lot because Ambler had to prove how unreasonable and harmful the ordinance was when applied to its specific property.

So, while Ambler Realty ultimately argued that the facts mattered less than the unconstitutional nature of the ordinance, the counsel for the town argued the facts—and that they proved Ambler wasn't much hurt by the law. The town even argued that Ambler was better off because zoning helps everyone by creating a better community. It was essentially saying that zoning was like a rising tide that lifted all boats. Except Ambler didn't agree. It was losing value. The town's argument was almost derailed when one of the *amici* that was supporting the town conceded that the ordinance would substantially harm Ambler Realty.[10] Metzenbaum convinced his supporter to withdraw the concession.

But in the end, it did not matter. Judge Westenhaver's ruling, which came down on January 14, 1924, wasn't based on the precise amount of harm to the property owners. He brushed that dispute off, saying "there is no substantial denial that this damage is not only in excess of the jurisdictional amount [of three thousand dollars] but is substantial."[11] He also dismissed the concerns over water, putting the blame for any water shortage on the town itself: "the police power of the village . . . cannot be enlarged by its failure or refusal to perform its fundamental duty of providing an adequate water supply."[12] Instead, Judge Westenhaver found the ordinance to be facially unconstitutional. It was a remarkable decision.

The core of the ruling was the judge's statement that, "Nor, in my opinion, can it be doubted that the ordinance is void because its provisions are in violation of . . . [the] Constitution of Ohio . . . of section 1 of the Fourteenth Amendment to the Constitution of the United States, which provides, 'Nor shall any state deprive any person of life, liberty, or property, without due process of law.'"[13]

Westenhaver began his analysis with an examination of prior building codes, land-use laws, and rent regulations that had been previously upheld, finding that some (such as the rent regulations) were only temporary and none of them went as far as the Euclid ordinance.[14] He next turned to decisions where land-use laws had been overturned, in particular one of the first modern regulatory takings cases, *Pennsylvania Coal v. Mahon.*[15] In that decision, the Supreme Court struck down a Pennsylvania law that prevented a mining company from mining its coal. It was the first twentieth-century case invoking the doctrine of regulatory takings, meaning that when a regulation so degrades the use and value of property that the government has effectively taken that property and must pay for it. In Euclid, the judge surmised that the impact on Ambler Realty would be similar if the law were upheld.

Then Judge Westenhaver turned his attention to *Buchanan v. Warley.* He began with some praise of Louisville's racial zoning ordinance. In a passage that is a stunning reflection of the prejudice of the times, he wrote:

> Compare . . . *Buchanan v. Warley* . . . in which an ordinance of the city of Louisville, held by the state Supreme Court to be valid and within the legislative power delegated to the city, districting and restricting residential blocks so that the white and colored races should be segregated, was held to be a violation of the Fourteenth Amendment and void. It seems to me that no candid mind can deny that more and stronger reasons exist, having a real and substantial relation to the public peace, supporting such an ordinance than can be urged under any aspect of the police power to support the present ordinance as applied to plaintiff's property.

He next explained how popular racial zoning ordinances would be across the nation: "And no gift of second sight is required to foresee that if this Kentucky statute had been sustained, its provisions would have spread from city to city throughout the length and breadth of the land."

He then concludes the paragraph with an astonishing justification for extending racial zoning to zoning that would keep immigrants out of residential neighborhoods:

> And it is equally apparent that the next step in the exercise of this police power would be to apply similar restrictions for the purpose of segregating

in like manner various groups of newly arrived immigrants. *The blighting of property values and the congesting of population, whenever the colored or certain foreign races invade a residential section, are so well known as to be within the judicial cognizance.*[16]

In other words, according to Westenhaver, in *Buchanan* the Court struck down a law that was so popular and beneficial that similar laws would have spread across the land, not only to segregate by race, but also to keep immigrants out of nice White neighborhoods, as well. The judge thought that if a law such as Louisville's racial zoning law with its supposedly worthy goal of segregating property by race could not be upheld by the Supreme Court, then neither could Euclid's with its less important goals. Somewhat ironically, as will be shown, when the Supreme Court got a hold of the *Euclid* case on appeal, it would turn back the clock—justifying Euclid's law with an appeal to racial and ethnic prejudice.

The *Buchanan* Court reached the result that it did based on its recognition of the importance of the affected property interests and because no relevant exercise of the police power could justify the harm to the property the law would cause. Likewise, Judge Westenhaver, after citing extensively from *Buchanan's* discussion of property, concluded,

A law or ordinance passed under the guise of the police power which invades private property as above defined can be sustained only when it has a real and substantial relation to the maintenance and preservation of the public peace, public order, public morals, or public safety. The courts never hesitate to look through the false pretense to the substance.[17]

As for the actual purpose of the Euclid law, the judge spelled it out in terms of class segregation. In a passage that resonates with very recent criticisms of zoning laws, the judge saw what Euclid was trying to do in "furthering class tendencies":

The plain truth is that the true object of the ordinance in question is to place all the property in an undeveloped area of 16 square miles in a strait-jacket. The purpose to be accomplished is really to regulate the mode of living of persons who may hereafter inhabit it. In the last analysis, the result to be accomplished is to classify the population and segregate them according to their income or situation in life. The true reason why some persons live in a mansion and others in a shack, why some live in a single-family dwelling and others in a double-family dwelling, why some live in a two-family dwelling and others in an apartment, or why some live in a well-kept apartment and others in a tenement, is primarily economic. It is a matter of income and wealth, plus the labor and difficulty of procuring adequate domestic service.[18]

That last line about "adequate domestic service" clearly is more a reflection of the judge's class background prejudices than any constitutional insight.

With hindsight, we understand today that it is zoning that has helped confine the poor, minorities, and immigrants to often overcrowded inner cities. As Westenhaver seemed to understand, zoning would divide classes as never before. What not even he understood, and certainly what none of the proponents of zoning realized, was that their creation would lead to the present housing crisis with its obscenely inflated prices and exceedingly limited supply of affordable homes. Indeed, his words lay the seeds of future challenges to restrictive land use laws. As Professor Wolf wrote, "Today, long after its author's passing, Westenhaver's one, key paragraph could serve as a primer for law students interested in finding successful theories to be employed by property owners who choose to attack government regulation of land."[19]

The judge wrapped it all up, stating, "My conclusion is that the ordinance involved, as applied to plaintiff's property, is unconstitutional and void; that it takes plaintiff's property, if not for private, at least for public, use, without just compensation; that it is in no just sense a reasonable or legitimate exercise of police power."[20] A respect for private property rights was the cause of death for the ordinance.

The town, however, may have been defeated but it had not yet lost. It would appeal. In 1924, any federal constitutional case could be appealed directly to the Supreme Court. The rules did not allow the Court to turn down cases that were properly filed, unlike today when the Court refuses to hear almost 98 percent of the petitions brought to its attention. The history of the town's appeal, however, was messy, convoluted, and eyebrow-raising by today's standards.

The first salvo in the appeal came when James Metzenbaum filed what he called a "short and concise" 140-page brief for the town. It focused on the facts and several key legal arguments. After arguing that the facts of the case supported the town because of the minimal impact of the zoning on Ambler Realty, he argued for an expansive and "very wide" understanding of the police power. This was a key element of his argument: he didn't think that the existing under-standing of the police power was adequate to justify zoning and thus the concept of the police power must be expanded in light of modern conditions. As he put it, the towns and cities adopting these ordinances, "have felt that the Police Power necessarily must keep step with and must keep pace with the new and daily problems pre-sented by the complexities of modern civilization, transportation and conditions."[21]

As noted in the discussion of *Lochner* and racial zoning, the police power of a state refers to its authority to protect the health, safety, and welfare of its citizens. The power doesn't have to be spelled out in detail in a state's constitution because it is an inherent power that makes the state sovereign a sovereign. It includes much more than maintaining a police force to stop crime. It may also include a state's power to set working conditions, to provide for the welfare of its poor and elderly, and to regulate the professions. What was unclear at the beginning of the twentieth century was whether the police power included the abil-ity to zone land uses in advance. (It should also be noted that because it is limited to only those powers expressly set out in the United States Constitution, the federal government does not have the police power—its authority to regulate must be found within those powers specifically enumerated—such as the power to regulate interstate commerce that is spelled out in the Commerce Clause.)

Under a section he labeled the "Philosophy of Zoning" Metzenbaum sought to distinguish the sort of aesthetic regulations that courts had struck down from the comprehensive type of zoning pioneered in New York City and followed in Euclid. Next he urged that courts defer to the judgments of legislative bodies, meaning that since the town concluded that the zoning law here was necessary and within its police power, the courts should not second-guess such decision-making. Metzenbaum also pointed to all the state court cases that had upheld local zoning and other land-use laws over the previous several years.

As a backup, he argued that because Ambler Realty had not even applied for a building permit it could not prove any injury and had no right to file a complaint in federal court.

Lastly, Metzenbaum, channeling the sentiment against multi-family housing and those who occupy such homes, quoted from Herbert Hoover before the National Association of Real Estate Boards where the future president exclaimed, "Nothing is worse than an increased tenantry and landlordism in this country." To stop it, the "municipalities through the enactment of zoning laws should cooperate."[22] But this was only a hint of what was to come.

Years later, Metzenbaum elaborated on the importance of the arguments he made in the case, suggesting that at stake was whether "the Constitution was meant so to hamper and restrict the American people, or was intended to protect them in their right to make their cites, large and small, livable and tenantable for the present as well as for the coming generations."[23]

Newton Baker, with his partner Robert Morgan, responded that industrial development was highly suitable for Ambler Realty's property and that the zoning "erects a dam to hold back the flood of industrial development," which would be contrary to "the operation of natural economic laws" and thus "destroys value without compensation to the owners."[24]

Moreover, the zoning regulation here was not to prevent any nuisance, but instead was focused on "mere questions of taste or preference." Finally, Baker concluded by saying,

> That our cities should be made beautiful and orderly is, of course, in the highest degree desirable, but it is even more important that our people should remain free. Their freedom depends upon the preservation of their constitutional immunities and privileges against the desire of others to control them, no matter how generous the motive or well intended the control which it is sought to impose.[25]

Shortly after the briefs were filed, the Court held oral argument on January 27, 1926, before eight of the nine justices. Justice Sutherland was off vacationing that week in the South. Baker was a brilliant and polished advocate; Metzenbaum was not. And he knew it. Although there is no transcript of the argument, we know that Metzenbaum was disturbed enough by the visual picture that Baker painted of the damage the ordinance caused, that he decided that he must file an additional reply brief. On his way home from Washington, his train was caught in a snowstorm, preventing him from returning to his office in time to send a telegram to the Court asking for permission to file a new brief. As Metzenbaum told the story years later, he hand-wrote the request on the train. And then,

> As the train slowed down along a siding where a great string of freight cars were being shoveled out of the snow, I opened the door of the car in which I was riding, leaned out from the car platform and shouted to one of the men who was engaged in the work of shoveling, wrapping the money around the telegram and tossing it to him. I saw it light on a great bank of snow. This was done with the trust that the man would understand what was wanted.[26]

Apparently, it worked. Chief Justice Taft gave permission to both parties to file additional briefs. This also gave time for both sides to solicit *amicus*, or friend of the court, briefs.

Baker solicited and received *amicus* support from George Simpson on behalf of several Minnesota corporations that were concerned over the impact that zoning could have on their ability to grow. Simpson emphasized that zoning was fraught with corruption as local politicians, noted for their "incompetency and dishonesty," tended to favor their cronies by making their land the most profitable. On top of that, the very notion of zoning was alien to the "*Anglo-Saxon* conception of the *right of the owner* to *own, use, and enjoy* his or her property." Indeed, Simpson argued, it was an attempt "to import into this country the European view that government is one of men and not of law."[27]

Before the first oral argument, Alfred Bettman, the chief advocate of zoning from Cleveland, attempted to file a friend of the court brief on behalf of the National Conference on City Planning, the National Housing Association, and other pro-planning groups from Ohio and Massachusetts. However, he made a blunder of the sort only made by novice attorneys: He missed the filing deadline by two weeks. But, with the new briefing underway, he had another opportunity to file a brief. His brief, which diverged significantly from the strategy taken by Metzenbaum, is widely considered to have been crucial to the ultimate outcome. The differences revolved around the government's inherent ability to regulate to protect public health and safety—the so-called "police power."

Where it was widely recognized that the police power could be used by government to abate nuisances, there was concern that zoning went well beyond merely preventing nuisance use of private property. To get zoning within the police power, there were two choices. First, the police power itself must be expanded to go beyond merely preventing nuisances. Alternatively, the understanding of how to contain a nuisance must be modernized.

Metzenbaum argued the former. In the section of the brief titled "The Philosophy of Zoning," he told the Court that the conception of the police power had to be expanded in order to encompass zoning. If the police power were expanded to include improving the general welfare, then zoning could be within that power. This was an implicit admission that zoning went beyond the traditional mere abatement of nuisances. The danger in that argument was that an otherwise conservative court might be reluctant to invent a whole new police power for the sake of Euclid's desire to keep industrial uses out of the town in favor of maximizing residential areas.

Bettman, however, argued that zoning was well within the existing conception of the police power. By crafting a comprehensive plan written by experts, the zoning plan fit together like the pieces of a jigsaw puzzle all designed to best prevent the use of property from becoming a nuisance. It was just a modern way of keeping nuisances from happening. As Professor Power notes, the members of the Court were upper class and acutely aware of the threat posed by the masses:

> Zoning regulations . . . had a social dimension. They were well-conceived to put everything, and everybody in the appropriate place. Smokestacks, slaughterhouses, and stables were placed on the other side of the railroad tracks, and apartment flats and row houses that accommodated second class people (including colored people and foreigners) were not permitted in such first-class neighborhoods.[28]

However, there was a danger with Bettman's argument as well. A legal regime designed to exclude minorities directly or even indirectly might sit uneasy with a Court that had outlawed racial zoning in *Buchanan* only a decade earlier. But if the racist motivations could be buried, albeit shallowly, with euphemisms and the patina of expert analysis, then the scheme was just another way of stopping traditional nuisances. Moreover, the *Buchanan* Court's *primary* rationale was the adverse impact on private property rights, not its impact on African Americans.

Bettman was careful to distinguish the zoning from mere aesthetic regulations, a key criticism made by Baker and Morgan for Ambler Realty. Zoning was for health and safety: "When we put the furnace in the cellar rather than the living room, we are not actuated so much by the dictates of good taste or aesthetic standards, as by the conviction that the living room will be a healthier place in which to live and the house a more generally healthful place."

Likewise, for "the man who seeks to place the home for his children in an orderly neighborhood, with some open space and light and fresh air and quiet."[29]

So with Metzenbaum arguing that the impact on Ambler Realty was manageable, and with Bettman claiming that this was just a modern exercise of the traditional nuisance prevention police power, the pair—although not in agreement on the rationale—managed to cobble together a powerful justification for zoning.

The second oral argument was held on October 12, 1926. Over the years there has been speculation as to why the Court decided to hold a second oral argument. The most likely reason is that with only eight justices at the January argument, there was no consensus for the result. A four-to-four tie vote would mean the lower court's opinion would stand without setting any national precedent. Others say the re-argument was engineered by the absent Justice Sutherland who was truly conflicted. One story by a former clerk is that Justice Sutherland had originally decided to rule against Euclid. It was only after he was talked out of this by Justice Stone that he switched sides and voted to uphold the ordinance in the opinion that he wrote for the Court. Debate continues to this day whether any of this is true.[30]

Oral argument for Metzenbaum was, according to one witness, "quite a disaster," with Metzenbaum spending an inordinate time attacking trial Judge Westenhaver. Baker, on the other hand, was described as being "magnificent and . . . extraordinary."[31] But there is an old adage among attorneys: cases can only be lost at oral argument, not won. It would take a bit over a month for the Court to explain which tactic prevailed.

On November 22, 1926, the Court issued its long-awaited opinion. Apparently, the Court was inclined to uphold the zoning scheme, and Metzenbaum's poor showing wasn't enough to reverse course. It was a resounding victory for Metzenbaum, Bettman, Euclid, and exclusionary zoning everywhere. Justice Sutherland began the decision with a thorough description of the zoning scheme, describing the various districts and listing what could be built where—including a detailed description of where apartment houses were banned.

The Court then proceeded to explain that while the erection of a particular building might be perfectly innocuous in one location, it could be a nuisance in another. Taking up Bettman's "furnace in the cellar rather than the living room" analogy, the Court provided a much more loaded analogy:

> Thus the question whether the power exists to forbid the erection of a building of a particular kind or for a particular use, like the question whether a particular thing is a nuisance, is to be determined, not by an abstract consideration of the building or of the thing considered apart, but by considering it in connection with the circumstances and the locality. . . . *A nuisance may be merely a right thing in the wrong place, like a pig in the parlor instead of the barnyard.*[32]

To make the meaning of this analogy plain, Justice Sutherland added later in the opinion a passage that reflects a patrician antipathy toward apartments and presumably those who inhabit them. While more refined than the language used by Jacob Riis to describe the tenements, the meaning is the same:

> With particular reference to apartment houses, it is pointed out that the development of detached house sections is greatly retarded by the coming of apartment houses, which has sometimes resulted in destroying the entire section for private house purposes; that in such sections very often the apartment house is a mere parasite, constructed in order to take advantage of the open spaces and attractive surroundings created by the residential character of the district.

But the problem, as Sutherland saw it, wasn't with just one parasitic apartment house. It was with everything that follows—from the lack of sunlight to the loss of quiet play areas for children:

> Moreover, the coming of one apartment house is followed by others, interfering by their height and bulk with the free circulation of air and monopolizing the rays of the sun which otherwise would fall upon the smaller homes, and bringing, as their necessary accompaniments, the disturbing

noises incident to increased traffic and business, and the occupation, by
means of moving and parked automobiles, of larger portions of the streets,
thus detracting from their safety and depriving children of the privilege
of quiet and open spaces for play, enjoyed by those in more favored localities—until, finally, the residential character of the neighborhood and its
desirability as a place of detached residences are utterly destroyed. Under
these circumstances, apartment houses, which in a different environment
would be not only entirely unobjectionable but highly desirable, come very
near to being nuisances.[33]

Clearly, Justice Sutherland would not have welcomed affordable housing in *his* neighborhood. The lawfulness of zoning was now the law of
the land.

The ramifications of the Court's decision reached far beyond this
ordinary suburb. The language used by the Supreme Court in affirm-
ing Euclid's zoning ordinance turned out to be a gateway drug to
bigoted exclusionary zoning laws far and wide for decades to come.
Though this was not bigotry with an iron fist, it was a more subtle
bigotry that wore a velvet glove while writing and defending the pages
of the nation's zoning codes. What was born in Baltimore, and died in
Louisville, would be reincarnated in Euclid.

When it comes to the transfer of the control over established rights
in property and wealth, nothing has come close to the revolution engen-
dered by the widespread adoption of zoning and land-use controls in
the United States. Once, land-use decisions were exclusively made by
owners of the land, subject mostly only to the proscriptions against
creating common-law nuisances. Today, these decisions rest in myriad boards, commissions, and regulatory agencies at the neighborhood,
local, state, and federal level, all of whom have one or more hands in
the decision-making process. This curtailment of an individual's liberty to choose how to use one's property is the functional equivalent of
the impressment of various easements and negative covenants on the
property. Thus, while neighbors once could have voluntarily negotiated
the terms of neighboring land uses through easements containing, for

example, height or density restrictions, in the new zoned America these same restrictions are imposed on a broader scale by political bodies. And as will be shown in later chapters, these governmental bodies can and often do use this power not only to regulate the use of land but also to extort money and real property from owners to government.

Chapter 5

Judicial Impotence, Complicity, and Zoning Challenges

O ver time, comprehensive planning has become known as "Euclidean zoning," named not after the geometry of the ancient Greek mathematician, but after the town where it survived its first major constitutional challenge. Such zoning is characterized by arbitrary line-drawing that attempts to confine certain uses to defined geographic areas. The lines are usually drafted to accommodate political pressure and can lack any measure of economic, demographic, or market reality. When local politicians face pressure from voters to limit or stop growth, they task the professional planners to draw neat lines on large colored maps. One zone may allow light industrial, another residential at one home per quarter acre, while another zone may limit homes to one per five, ten, forty, or even larger acre lots. On top of these zones, there may be protective overlays for riparian zones, animal habitat, public recreation corridors, and so on. Plans will sometimes encourage jobs, especially high-tech clean jobs, but usually not the housing needed to accommodate the workers. They can commute in from elsewhere, adding to a region's job-residence imbalance as seen most starkly today in places like California's Silicon Valley.

As will be shown later, it is doubtful whether such zoning is all that effective in doing anything but raising costs, enhancing the power of local politicians, and making it more difficult for the poor and working classes to leave the ghettos.

Of course, purveyors of contemporary zoning declare that today, zoning is better than it used to be because it doesn't as rigidly segregate land uses in order to prevent apartments or commerce from invading residential areas. Planners and zoners call it "smart growth" because there are more mixed-use zones in some modern plans, where apartments are again allowed to be built on top of ground level retail stores, just like in the old days. There is also more emphasis on "walkable" developments, where people are supposed to be able to walk to their jobs and shopping, or at least to a bus or transit stop.

How many people will actually walk or bike to do their grocery shopping or commuting, especially in bad weather, is an open question. In any event, the impetus to limit new housing growth, especially multi-family affordable housing, remains strong. The NIMBY anti-growth movement has not been tempered by modern zoning codes, no matter how smart they purport to be.

Moreover, zoning advocates today have adopted the mantle of a new moral imperative that is greater than simply preserving existing residential neighborhoods from change. Today, they lay claim to an ethic that will save the planet. Zoning now seeks to preserve environmental amenities such as wetlands, habitat, and open space. It can reduce traffic impacts—including those related to climate change. Zoning can be used to keep agricultural lands in agriculture as well as preserving the value of residential neighborhoods. But what these noble goals manage to do in practice is often little different from what the old-style zoning laws tried to do explicitly: keep the poor people out of the neighborhoods of those people agitating for zoning laws. But to better understand what zoning is today, it is useful to understand what happened after *Euclid*.

Despite his general acceptance of zoning, Justice Sutherland did have limits. In *Euclid*, he endorsed the concept of comprehensive

zoning in the abstract and refused to strike down the town's ordinance
wholesale. He did suggest, however, that there might be some cases
where the real-world application of a zoning law to a specific piece of
property might be too unfair to stand:

> when, if ever, the provisions set forth in the ordinance in tedious and min-
> ute detail, come to be concretely applied to particular premises, including
> those of the appellee, or to particular conditions, or to be considered in
> connection with specific complaints, some of them, or even many of them,
> may be found to be clearly arbitrary and unreasonable.[1]

Two years later the Court had the opportunity to explain what that
meant in *Nectow v. Cambridge*.[2] Like so many other cities, Cambridge,
Massachusetts, adopted its own ambitious comprehensive zoning ordinance. But it was too ambitious. The plaintiff in this case owned a
mostly vacant 140,000 square foot lot. On a portion of the lot there
was a brick factory building and a house, both of which were in the
process of being replaced with a warehouse when Cambridge adopted
its ordinance. When the zoning caused the owner to lose the ability
to sell a 29,000 square foot portion for industrial uses, he lost $63,000
and he cried foul. Specifically, he sued and argued that putting his lot
into a residential zoning district made no sense. After all, the lot was
surrounded by a six-story Ford automobile factory, a foul-smelling soap
factory, and a few older residences that had seen much better days. It
was no place to build new homes.

The trial court agreed, finding that "no practical use can be made of
the land in question for residential purposes, because among other reasons herein related, there would not be adequate return on the amount
of any investment for the development of the property."[3] Moreover,
"the districting of the plaintiff's land in a residence district would not
promote the health, safety, convenience, and general welfare of the
inhabitants of that part of the defendant city."[4]

But this was not enough to convince the Massachusetts Supreme
Court that the law was unfairly applied to Nectow's property, calling

it a close case but not one on which the Court felt inclined to sec-ond-guess the city's judgment.[5] After all, the United States Supreme Court had refused to strike down the Euclid ordinance, so why should Massachusetts strike down something similar in Cambridge?

The state court noted that if "there is to be zoning at all, the divid-ing line must be drawn somewhere. There cannot be a twilight zone. If residence districts are to exist, they must be bounded. In the nature of things, the location of the precise limits of the several districts demands the exercise of judgment and sagacity."[6] It wasn't the court's role to sec-ond-guess the city's judgment and sagacity. Or was it?

In an opinion by Justice Sutherland, the Supreme Court said that in this case, it was. The Court began by emphasizing the rightness of its *Euclid* decision, explaining that the judgment of the town officials should not be lightly overturned, "unless it is clear that their action 'has no foundation in reason and is a mere arbitrary or irrational exercise of power having no substantial relation to the public health, the public morals, the public safety or the public welfare in its proper sense.'"[7]

To the Court, putting Nectow's property that was obviously good for only commercial or industrial use into a residential zone was arbi-trary and irrational and did "not bear a substantial relation to the pub-lic health, safety, morals, or general welfare."[8] Thus, only two years after embracing comprehensive zoning in *Euclid,* the Court found that Cambridge had gone just too far. One would think that with these directions, the courts would embark on a rigorous review of otherwise reasonable-sounding zoning laws whose implementation was anything but reasonable. Moreover, one might think that the high Court would, from time to time, weigh in to better establish the distinction between reasonable and arbitrary. But one would think wrong.

In the decades since *Nectow,* there had been only deafening silence from the Supreme Court. Cases where the courts deigned to take on zoning ordinances and rule in favor of property owners have been almost as rare as socialist success stories.

Instead, unfettered by judicial restraints, cities and towns across the nation embraced Euclidean economic segregation. Apartments and their working class, immigrant, and minority residents would be shunted to one part of town—if they were allowed at all. Large lot suburban residential zoning, into which it was usually economically impossible for "lower class" workers to rent or buy a home, predominated.

Of course, there were other impediments to minorities, especially Jews and African Americans, that kept them out of the suburbs. As Richard Rothstein explains, a combination of federally mandated discriminatory lending (known as redlining) and restrictions in property deeds forbidding the resale of homes to Jews and Blacks, sometimes combined with state-sanctioned violence, kept what was White always White, and what wasn't yet built out also White:

> Racial segregation in housing was not merely a project of southerners in the former slaveholding Confederacy. It was a nationwide project of the federal government in the twentieth century . . . Scores of racially explicit laws, regulations, and government practices combined to create a nationwide system of urban ghettos, surrounded by white neighborhoods.[9]

This is a legacy that continues to this day. Except for the aberration of *Nectow*, during the century following *Euclid*, the Court has turned a blind eye to large-lot exclusionary zoning, especially its implications for the less affluent. A few examples are in order, starting with California's exclusion by election scheme.

* * *

After World War II had concluded, the federal government turned some of its attention to subsidized low-income housing, relying on a law passed in 1937 but ignored during the war years. With the newly available federal money, local housing authorities embarked on plans to build subsidized housing for the poor. But that didn't set well with established communities that were afraid that an influx of poor people would bring crime, delinquency, and miscegenation.

Voters in some California counties attempted to use elections to stop federally funded low-income housing projects. The state's supreme court, however, ruled that local voters could not reject housing projects. Californians rebelled. Signatures were collected for a state constitutional amendment. Advocates argued that, "Time after time within the past year, California communities have had public housing projects forced upon them without regard either to the wishes of the citizens or community needs."[10]

Six months later, on November 7, 1950, California voters amended their constitution to require a vote for government-subsidized affordable housing. The new Article 34 said in part, "No low rent housing project shall hereafter be developed, constructed, or acquired . . . until a majority of the qualified electors . . . approve such project by voting in favor thereof at an election."

Poor and Black residents of San Jose and San Mateo counties sued, arguing that the new constitutional provision violated the federal Constitution's Equal Protection Clause because it discriminated against those "who are poor" and "those who are Negro."[11] They explained that "the major method by which laws against open discrimination are evaded is by making most housing in San Mateo County economically beyond the means of most members of racial minority groups."[12] Since the poor and ethnic minorities were excluded by local housing policies, the only way they could live in decent housing in their communities would be through federal subsidies. Moreover, if the voters could veto a low-income housing project, "the primary issue [was] the admission or exclusion of racial minority groups."[13]

The federal district court agreed, finding that the new Article 34 "makes it more difficult for state agencies acting on behalf of poor people and minorities to get federal financial assistance."[14] The court concluded that while "the law on its face treats Negro and white, Jew and gentile in an identical manner, the reality is that the law's impact falls on the minority. The majority needs no protection against discrimination."[15]

The United States Supreme Court reversed. In an opinion by Justice Black, the Court noted that the new provision didn't *explicitly* single out minorities. Therefore, the Court blithely dismissed the trial court's concerns: "Provisions for referendums demonstrate devotion to democracy, not to bias, discrimination, or prejudice."[16] Justice Black and the majority were either naïve or willfully blind to the realities of Article 34's purpose and effect.

In California, only the voters can repeal a constitutional amendment. Attempts to repeal Article 34 have appeared on the California ballot three times: in 1974, 1980, and 1993. All three were resoundingly rejected, with close to 60 percent of the voters opposing. After several more failed attempts, and most likely due to the resurgence of attention paid to issues of racial justice issues in the early 2020s, the legislature voted in 2023 to put yet another repeal provision on the November 4, 2024 ballot.[17]

Whether this vote will fare any better is anybody's guess. Voters will suggest that their opposition to subsidized housing isn't racially motivated. Rather their objection arises out of their negative perceptions of public housing projects as being poorly built and managed, which creates the very real effect of bringing blight into their neighborhoods. These fears are often warranted by experience. Rather than scattering small, subsidized projects across a region, too often governments build very large projects in already distressed neighborhoods—concentrating the poor further. These projects have often understandably added credence to negative views of public housing.

As will be discussed in the coming pages, federally subsidized housing programs, where they have been approved, have hardly been a panacea. Riddled with poor planning and worse mismanagement, many have been disappointments. Others have been outright disasters. Community distrust of federal projects is understandable. But to some extent, communities that complain about federal housing programs have brought this upon themselves. With large lot zoning, redlining, and deed restrictions, minority exclusion has become an open wound on the American soul that is poorly remedied by the band-aid of public housing subsidies.

There have been a few examples where a town's rejection of a public housing project for overt racial animus has run afoul of the

Constitution and the courts.[18] But without proof of racial animus, it is impossible to challenge a land-use law or decision based on its disparate impact on minority populations alone. That was made clear in 1977 by the Supreme Court in *Village of Arlington Heights v. Metropolitan Housing Commission.*[19] There, beginning in 1971, a developer sought to build integrated affordable housing in a Chicago suburb. That would have been a dramatic change because, according to the 1970 census, only twenty-seven of the sixty-four thousand residents were Black. The application to rezone the property to allow the development was denied by a six-to-one vote in the wake of strong community opposition. Much of the opposition raised public concerns over density, crowding, and the impact on property values. But others implicitly or overtly expressed concerns over the "social" problems that might ensue—a code word for a different class and color of the residents.

The opposition voiced by the potential project's neighbors was animated by an inextricable combination of fear and prejudice—both of the influx of poor minority neighbors and what those neighbors would do to property values. The concern about property values may have been real but based more on assumption than empirical fact. Studies have shown a very mixed impact of low-income projects on neighboring properties. The effects range from positive to negative and depend on the size of the project, the nature of what was on the land before the project (e.g., green space or existing dilapidated housing), the project management, and the character of the existing community.[20] One study, looking at projects in Minneapolis ranging in size from four to eighty-six units and averaging twenty-one units, concluded, "In summary, we find none of the supposed negative effects on neighborhood vitality of subsidized housing that is developed by nonprofit [Community Development Corporations.]"[21] However, the Arlington Heights proposal was larger than those in the typical studies, clocking in at 190 clustered townhomes on fifteen acres.

That, however, would have been far fewer than in disasters like the Pruitt-Igoe public house project in St. Louis that, in 1955, tried to cram

2,870 apartment units onto fifty-seven acres. The thirty-three apartment towers were eleven stories tall and surrounded by green space. Pruitt-Igoe was a product of an elitist construct where the animating idea was that thousands of poor people would be better off if their inner-city homes were demolished and replaced by giant towers. The poor could be concentrated in a few brand-new city blocks rather than being scattered in existing neighborhoods.

No expense in design and construction was spared. The chief architect was the renowned Minoru Yamasaki, who would later design the World Trade Center and other public buildings around the world. The modernist concrete towers of Pruitt-Igoe were replete with such impractical social engineering conceits like elevators that stopped only at every third floor, not only to save money but also to better encourage poor people to take the stairs and socialize in common corridors with their neighbors while getting some exercise.[22]

The architectural style was stark, barren, and uninviting. It was the sort of architecture first espoused by the likes of Le Corbusier, the famous twentieth-century French architect, author of the highly influential *The Radiant City,* who once famously said "the plan must rule . . . the street must disappear." He favored concrete behemoths where function was the only aesthetic. It was the style that is epitomized by the old Soviet-era housing projects . . . and federal projects in the United States like Pruitt-Igoe. Regional variations and old-style architecture must surrender to modernist sameness. As Le Corbusier also once said, "Oslo, Moscow, Berlin, Paris, Algiers, Port Said, Rio or Buenos Aires, the solution is the same."[23] All in all, under the influence of Le Corbusier's philosophy, fifty-seven acres of homes and businesses were torn down and redeveloped into densely packed concrete monstrosities.

At first, Pruitt-Igoe was a roaring success.[24] The residents loved their new "penthouses for the poor." It seemed to have solved the problem of housing poor people in St. Louis. But behind the happy façade, the seeds of Pruitt-Igoe's destruction had already been sown. Underneath the new paint, the construction was shoddy. Doors were thin and easily breakable. Windows rotted out and let the rain in. Cabinets were made of shoddy plywood and soon began to fall apart.[25]

While lots of money was spent to build the complex, little was left to maintain it. And there was a demographic time-bomb buried in the foundations of both the project and the city.

Pruitt-Igoe, in fact, was originally supposed to be *segregated*, building by building, with some buildings for Whites and some for Blacks. But with *Brown v. Board of Education*, integration was the new federal policy. As Blacks moved into *all* the buildings, the Whites fled, leaving it a de facto segregated project. With suburbanization, Whites moved out and the city's population began to decline. Just like in other cities across the nation, federal financial incentives made it cheaper for the White middle class to move to the suburbs. Those suburbs, like Black Jack outside of St. Louis, or Arlington Heights outside of Chicago, were places where apartments were banned, and federal policy discouraged any sort of integration. With a population in decline, and especially with the better-off residents of all races in Pruitt-Igoe moving to the suburbs, trouble wasn't far behind.

As jobs followed the Whites into the suburbs, there were fewer tenants in urban projects like Pruitt-Igoe with income available to pay the sort of rents needed to maintain the projects. With maintenance deferred or ignored and security absent, the buildings began to deteriorate. Vandalism went unchecked. The stairwells were dominated by gangs and the floors without elevator stops were the first abandoned by most families.

As historian Amity Shlaes described the chaos:

> The elevators, which stopped only every few floors, were muggers' traps. Poor maintenance meant the elevators often jammed, leaving gangs' victims in with them for long extra minutes. The gangs lurked in the halls and made tenants "run the gauntlet" to get to their doors. Young men threw bricks and rocks at windows and street lamps; the activity was a regular sport. There were no good playgrounds. Because there were no toilets on the ground floor, children had accidents there, and the elevators gradually

became public toilets. The community area was a sorry joke; its only function ultimately was as a place for collecting Housing Authority rents. No
one seemed able to stop the decay.[26]

Resident anger led to rent strikes and demands for maintenance. But
it was too late. Heating and plumbing failed. Residents abandoned
their apartments and drug dealers and squatters moved into the derelict structures that the police rarely if ever visited. And, when they
did, they were often pelted by objects thrown from the upper floors.
In a few years, the project had descended into Hell and people fled if
they could. The city surrendered. Then, on the national news in 1976,
Americans watched the disaster being deliberately blown up by a demolition crew.

Figure 12. Pruitt-Igoe's 2,870 units were demolished in 1976, a testament to the
failure of warehousing the very poor on the cheap.

Pruitt-Igoe wasn't the only such disaster. In Chicago, the Cabrini-
Green public housing development consisting of fifty-five two- and
three-story apartment buildings was built in 1942. In 1950, an extension consisting of high-rises was built—up to nineteen stories tall. Like
Pruitt-Igoe, Cabrini-Green started out as a model, but soon enough
with poor construction and lack of maintenance the project turned into
a crime-ridden nightmare. The high-rises were demolished between
2000 and 2011.

Figure 13. A partly demolished tower at Cabrini-Green in 2006.[27]

Privately run but publicly financed housing can also be problematic. In 2023, a paper in Willamette, Oregon, ran a piece about yet another subsidized complex plagued by crime, drugs, and chaos with this headline: "A $28 Million Low-Income Apartment Complex Descends into Chaos in Just Two and a Half Years."[28] While this disaster isn't run by a public housing agency, it was built with public money and bonds. Apparently, it was also built and is being run without accountability.

The looming disaster of Pruitt-Igoe may have factored into the Court's decision in *Valtierra* that upheld the public veto over subsidized housing projects. Indeed, the lawyers defending California's Article 34 at oral argument were quick to remind the justices of "the housing in St. Louis, which was an absolute fiasco."[29] The subsequent demolition may have been very fresh in the minds of the justices as they pondered the *Arlington Heights* appeal. Today, all that remains of Pruitt-Igoe is forest-covered rubble.[30]

After the Village of Arlington Heights denied the application for low-income housing, the developer and prospective minority tenants sued. They didn't argue that the denial violated the *Euclid* arbitrariness standards that had been raised in *Nectow*. Instead, they argued that the refusal to rezone discriminated against racial minorities in violation of the Fourteenth Amendment. The Fourteenth Amendment was adopted after the Civil War and has been the source of this nation's antidiscrimination laws. It had been, unfortunately, neutered for many years with the doctrine of separate but equal that had allowed Jim Crow to rise in the South. With the repudiation of that doctrine in *Brown v. Board of Education* in 1954, and the rise of the Civil Rights Movement in the 1960s, it became a robust source for challenging discrimination. The question in *Arlington Heights* became what to do when a government action, such as a zoning denial, has a disparate impact on minorities but where there are no obvious expressions of racial animus by the decision makers.

In a five to three decision, the Court held that impact without intent cannot give rise to a violation of the Fourteenth Amendment. Justice Powell wrote for the Court: "Proof of racially discriminatory intent or purpose is required to show a violation of the Equal Protection Clause."[31] He continued that, "Determining whether invidious discriminatory purpose was a motivating factor demands a sensitive inquiry into such circumstantial and direct evidence of intent as may be available."[32] While a number of factors may be relevant to the inquiry, such as impact, a pattern of discrimination, history, and sequence of events, in *Arlington Heights* those factors did not add up to a showing of discriminatory motivation. The trial court, the court of appeals, and the Supreme Court all agreed that the decision to deny the rezoning was not based on any intent to discriminate. Even if that was the effect.

Ever since *Buchanan* and *Euclid*, there has been widespread public opposition to locating dense or low-income housing in middle and upper-class neighborhoods. State and local governments understand that political opposition. Thus, government subsidized housing usually has been built in existing slums because they were often the only places that lacked the political will and organization to oppose it. The desire to replace old slums with new ones was in part motivated by the availability of federal funds for such redevelopment. It was free money, after all, so why not spend it on getting rid of slums—even (or especially) if they were often vibrant neighborhoods filled with the urban poor. Moreover, the federal government was further complicit in creating segregated suburbs through its early explicit prohibitions against integrated housing, its redlined financial guarantees, and its demands that low-income housing be confined to existing segregated neighborhoods.

While the California referendum in *James v. Valtierra* and the *Arlington Heights* decision were not explicitly racial, the underlying public sentiment often has been. And savvy politicians have capitalized on this fear of "those people" moving into our neighborhoods.

None other than Jimmy Carter, while a candidate seeking his party's nomination in 1976, made it clear where he stood with this dog-whistle: "I have nothing against a community that is made up of people who are Polish, or who are Czechoslovakians, or who are French Canadians or who are blacks trying to maintain the ethnic purity of their neighborhoods. This is a natural inclination."[33]

Thus, he said he was opposed to housing programs designed, as one critic put it, "to inject black families into a white neighborhood just to create some sort of integration."[34] While he was forced to walk his statement back, he said it, and he knew what he was saying. This book's author predicted, correctly, that the remark would not hurt Carter's candidacy.[35] Jimmy Carter clinched the Democratic nomination a few weeks later.

* * *

The Court has also had a mixed record when it has come to narrower land-use laws that have the effect of limiting *who* can live in a town. While families love to send their children to college, they don't want college kids to move in next door. To keep out college students, the village of Belle Terre, New York, adopted an ordinance prohibiting more than two unrelated persons from occupying a single-family home. The town's zoning ordinance expressly prohibited a "lodging house, boarding house, fraternity house, sorority house or multiple dwelling" in a single-family zone.[36] In other words, it prohibited some of the most affordable housing available.

In the 1970s, there were 220 homes in the small Long Island town, and Edith and Judith Dickman owned one of them. Trouble came when the Dickmans decided to rent their home to six unrelated college students. The mostly older students liked the arrangement because it was cheap and kept them out of the dorms. The first problem arose when the town refused to give a beach permit to two of the students because they were not lawful residents. Next the village ordered the Dickmans to remedy the violations, meaning they had to kick out four of the students. If they refused, they could be subject to daily hundred dollar fines and up to sixty days in jail.[37] Rather than breaking their lease and throwing out the students, and instead of going to jail, the Dickmans and several of the students sued, claiming that the town had violated their civil rights of association and privacy.

The trial court rejected their claim, saying: "A one-family dwelling zoning district limited to families made up essentially of parents and their children needs no apologia."[38] The federal court of appeals did not agree. It noted: "The effect of the Belle Terre ordinance would be to exclude from the community, without any rational basis, unmarried groups seeking to live together, whether they be three college students, three single nurses, three priests, or three single judges."[39] Concluding, the court ruled that: "The discriminatory classification created by the Belle Terre ordinance does not appear to be supported by any rational basis that is consistent with permissible zoning objectives."[40] One judge dissented, saying he didn't see anything discriminatory about the ordinance. That was enough to give the town enough hope to ask the Supreme Court to take a look. But the hope was a long shot. After all, the Court hadn't taken up a case that was strictly about zoning since its *Nectow* decision in 1928.

But the village's hopeful gamble paid off. In *Village of Belle Terre v. Boraas*,[41] Justice Douglas, a liberal icon of the Court, wrote the opinion. He found that there was nothing wrong with the ordinance because if the town thought that excluding nontraditional families would be for its own good, it wasn't the proper role of any court to question the town's judgment. In sum, the village had the right to enforce zoning that it thought would achieve a "quiet place where yards are wide, people few, and motor vehicles restricted are legitimate guidelines in a land-use project addressed to family needs."[42] The ordinance may have been more anti-student than anti-minority and as such there was nothing overtly racist about it. Nevertheless, the implications of a legal regime that aspires to keeping yards wide and people few can have only an adverse impact on the affordability of housing, especially for the economically challenged. Thus, while the legal holding may have been consistent with precedent, the policy implications of ordinances of this nature are troubling.

The prohibition against boarding house arrangements continues to this day, a half century later. As Travis Chapman from Monroe, Georgia, told the *Atlanta Civic Circle*, "All of a sudden, I heard a cracking sound." The newspaper continued, the door to Travis's bedroom "burst open, spraying wood shards across the floor, and in walked two fire marshals from the Morrow Fire Department. They were there to evict him."[43] His crime? He was living in an unpermitted boarding home run by the internet startup "PadSplit," which essentially operates like Airbnb for long-term renters, turning existing single-family homes into boarding homes. A lawsuit is pending.

On the other side of the country, another startup entrepreneur is trying to capitalize on San Francisco's housing shortage with a novel, if not dystopian, solution: Twin-sized Ikea bed "pods" that rent for seven hundred dollars a month. After SFGATE, a local online media outlet, wrote a story about the pods, the city got wind of the scheme and commenced an investigation.[44] Within a day, the city cracked down, citing the complex as unpermitted, unsafe, and illegal.[45]

To the extent that a city deems boarding houses to be unlawful, courts will generally not interfere, despite the impact on the owners of the property and any potential tenants. Courts should not base their decisions on the personal policy preferences of judges. That is the province of the legislators and those who elect them. But when a land-use law has a substantial negative effect on constitutionally protected property rights, when it has the motivation of exclusion, and when it has the effect of broader exclusion, then that law is not one we should countenance.

But even the Supreme Court has limits to what it will tolerate. Three years after *Arlington Heights*, the Court met those limits when the city of East Cleveland tried to separate a grandmother from one of her grandsons. East Cleveland, a town only about a dozen miles southwest of Euclid, prohibited family members from living together if they were not closely related enough. In an exercise of municipal tone-deafness, it prosecuted and criminally convicted Inez Moore, a sixty-three-year-old grandmother, because her family consisted of one of her sons, Dale, one of her grandsons, Dale Jr., and another grandson, John, who came to live with them after his mother died.[46] Under the town's ordinance, John was an "illegal occupant" and had to go. Mrs. Moore refused, and she was duly convicted and sentenced to five days in jail and a twenty-five dollar fine.

When Mrs. Moore's appeal reached the Supreme Court in *Moore v. City of East Cleveland*, the city naturally cited *Belle Terre*, arguing that it was none of the Court's business how it regulated who could live with whom.[47] But this was more than the Court could swallow. This was a matter of family, not just a convenient living arrangement. The Court noted that "freedom of personal choice in matters of marriage and family life is one of the liberties protected by the Due Process

Clause of the Fourteenth Amendment," and that the precedent of *Belle Terre* was simply irrelevant here.[48]

Moreover, unlike the college students in *Belle Terre,* this case had a more obvious impact on racial minorities, an element that made East Cleveland's prosecution of a grandmother all the more unpalatable to some members of the Court. In his concurring opinion, Justice Brennan, who had dissented in *Belle Terre,* spelled out the discriminatory impact of family restriction: "In today's America, the 'nuclear family' is the pattern so often found in much of white suburbia."[49] Moreover, "black citizens, like generations of white immigrants before them, have been victims of economic and other disadvantages that would worsen if they were compelled to abandon extended, for nuclear, living patterns."[50] While this did not imply a racial motivation, it did highlight its impact on minority populations.

No attempt was made by the Court to elevate the need, described in *Belle Terre,* for quiet places, wide yards, or the absence of people over the needs of Inez Moore's family.[51]

Figure 14. *Piqua Daily Call,* June 1, 1977.
Mrs. Moore and her grandchildren.

* * *

As if exclusionary zoning were not pernicious enough, California cities and counties have adopted another cruel twist: ballot box zoning. In California, NIMBYism is as sacred as the trees and spotted owl. In some regions NIMBYism has evolved into BANANAism, a.k.a. "Build-Absolutely-Nothing-Anywhere-Near-Anyone" and the dark humor acronym NOPEism or "Not-on-Planet-Earth."

While state law requires towns and counties to adopt general land-use plans, which are backed up by specific zoning ordinances, that is often not good enough because somebody somewhere might figure out a way to build something. Worse, a local government may grant a variance to do something not within the strict confines of a zoning plan.

In the beginning of the twentieth century, Californians were getting fed up with the power of the railroad barons. All politics, it seemed, led to the railroads. They owned the trains, the tracks, and often the legislators themselves. Californians had had enough. In the midst of an anti-railroad progressive-populist wave, Californians amended their constitution in 1911, putting the state at the epicenter of citizen initiatives in the United States. With a relatively modest number of signatures, Californians employ ballot measures to pass statutes, amend their constitution, and recall unpopular politicians. It is justly famous for its forays into direct democracy that include the tax-limiting Proposition 13, its ban on governmental polices based on race and sex with Proposition 209, a ban on mountain lion hunting, and the approval of a now much-regretted high-speed rail project. There are myriad others, state and local, that appear on the ballot year in and year out. And, of course, it was a recall election that put political neophyte Arnold Schwarzenegger into the governor's chair.

In the 1990s, the marriage of NIMBYism with direct democracy spawned the California love child of ballot box zoning. The concept is simple. Citizens in a community bothered by the thought of growth can band together and pass an initiative that freezes the local land use status quo. Zoning is frozen in time and place. Any hopeful landowner or developer who wants to develop something beyond existing allowed uses must go to the voters for a community-wide approval. And because just about any kind of intensive development is prohibited under existing zoning, the only way to unfreeze it is with an election. But mounting an election campaign for a small subdivision can be expensive and uncertain. Mounting a campaign for a large subdivision, or one with affordable housing, can be futile. In other words, neighbors are given a de facto veto over new development.

The city of Napa was the first city in California that tried this experiment in local citizen control of land use. But this was not the first time a local government had attempted to give the public a de facto veto. An earlier version was tried in Seattle at the turn of the last century.

Caroline Rosenberg Kline Galland was a wealthy Seattle widow with no children who "devoted her time, money and energy to helping the poor."[52] Born in Bavaria in 1841, it was said she "never turned down a request for help from anyone."[53] In 1905, as described by the Washington Supreme Court, Caroline Galland left a will that established, with the princely sum of $1.4 million, the "Caroline Kline Galland Home for Aged and Feeble Poor." The will provided that those admitted to the home should be aged and feeble men and women, and the intent was that it should be managed in such a way as to bring to the inmates the greatest degree of contentment and happiness in their declining years.[54]

Figure 15. Caroline Rosenberg Kline Galland.[55]

The original home was a converted wooden mansion on five acres overlooking Lake Washington that could accommodate fourteen elderly residents. In 1926, when the managing trust sought to tear it down and replace it with a more suitable and more fireproof brick home that could accommodate thirty residents, the trust learned how unpopular group homes are in residential neighborhoods. That the home would cater to Jewish residents surely didn't help.

Three years earlier, the city had adopted a zoning ordinance, and the home was now located in a single-family residential district. It was possible to build an old-age home, but only after an unusual condition could be met. As the ordinance stated: "A philanthropic home for children or for old people shall be permitted in the first residence district when the written consent shall have been obtained of the owners of two-thirds of the property within 400 feet of the proposed building."[56]

While the existing mansion's use as an old-age home was grandfathered in, it was unsafe and unsuitable for their plans to serve more elderly residents. They had to replace the structure. But when the trust could not secure the two-thirds written permissions, it sued.

The Washington Supreme Court was unmoved. After noting that in *Euclid* the Supreme Court had found apartment buildings to be the right thing in the wrong place: "We think it must be readily conceded that an apartment house would be far more desirable than a charitable institution in a residential district."[57] Yes, if there is one thing worse than an apartment building, it's a building filled with old people.

The United States Supreme Court reversed in *State of Washington ex rel. Seattle Title Tr. Co. v. Roberge.*[58] The Court began its analysis with an endorsement of the owner's property rights, noting: "The right of the trustee to devote its land to any legitimate use is property within the protection of the Constitution."[59] Of course, the Court acknowledged that a community may zone a neighborhood, but giving final veto power to neighbors who "are free to withhold consent for selfish reasons or arbitrarily and may subject the trustee to their will or caprice . . . is repugnant to the due process clause of the Fourteenth Amendment."[60] The home won and has been expanding its services to the elderly ever since.

Over a half-century later, the citizens of Napa County, California, tried something that had the same effect, although the policy was less direct than in *Roberge*. In 1990, using California's populist initiative process, Napa County voters adopted "Measure J" that, with minor exceptions, froze all land use in place for thirty years, or until 2020. Eighteen years later, the voters extended the freeze until 2058.[61] There was an exemption: Property owners and builders could seek approval from the county's voters in an election. Presumably, the bucolic character of the valley had to be preserved from more homes and apartments.[62]

The measure is distinguishable from *Roberge* because Napa didn't just allow the neighbors to veto a project. Instead, the county's voters had to approve it in an election—a prospect likely even more daunting than dealing only with one's neighbors. Only the existing residents of the valley can vote on whether newcomers will be allowed in. Measure J was NIMBYism on steroids.

The measure was unprecedented in California, and home builders didn't like it. They sued to stop the measure in *DeVita v. County of Napa*.[63] However, the developers avoided making constitutional arguments, perhaps recognizing that the passage of time made the *Roberge* rationale less compelling, especially in the California courts where the right of the citizen initiative was near sacrosanct. Instead, the developers based their legal claims on California land-planning law. They argued that the zoning and planning process belonged to the local governments and could not be altered by citizen initiative. The California Supreme Court disagreed, saying that the people's right of initiative was too important to stand in the way of ordinary zoning and planning laws.

The court didn't address Measure J's impact on the supply of affordable housing, saying only that the measure "is, in short, an attempt to manage growth so as to protect both Napa County's environment and its economically productive resources in accordance with the county's unique local conditions."[64] That's a complicated way of saying the voters wanted to protect their "quiet place where yards are wide [and] people few." The court justified its ruling by explaining how important the initiative process is in California and by saying that "it is the duty of the courts to jealously guard this right of the people."[65]

In reality, this citizens' initiative measure is nothing but a cruel hoax: the "people" who most need housing in Napa are those who spend long hours commuting into the valley every day to work in the hotels, restaurants, and vineyards. Because they don't, and can't, live in the valley, they have no vote.

Other communities in California have followed suit with similar no-growth ballot box zoning initiatives. And as these towns make it more difficult to grow, that growth is pushed elsewhere. And when growth is pushed elsewhere, the inevitable cry of "too much" is heard, and new building becomes increasingly difficult. Supply diminishes, demand increases, prices rise, and people suffer.

Chapter 6

New Jersey Courts Take on Exclusionary Zoning

In time, it became apparent that the cumulative effect of zoning laws, especially those mandating large lot single-family home subdivisions, was destroying the ability of the working class to inhabit the suburbs. By 1976, the New Jersey Supreme Court had had enough when it took up a challenge to zoning brought by the NAACP in a Philadelphia suburb, Mount Laurel Township in New Jersey. In the 1960s, Mount Laurel was a town of about twenty-two square miles undergoing a transition from rural to suburban, much like Euclid had been more than a half-century earlier. And like Euclid, its people wanted to keep the riffraff at bay. With limited exceptions, nowhere in the town could anyone build townhouses, apartments, or place mobile homes. The few apartments that could be built were designed to attract childless couples as severe restrictions were imposed on the number of bedrooms and the number of children per bedroom.

Ethel Robinson Lawrence had a small and modest dream—to help the poorer people in her town to be able to live in decent homes. She was one of eight children whose slave ancestors first settled in Mount Laurel in the nineteenth century when it was a stop on the Underground

Railway. She grew up going to a segregated
school, earned a college degree, and taught
preschool while raising nine children of her
own. Lawrence was also a pianist for her local
church when she and her fellow parishioners
became concerned about the lack of affordable housing in Mount Laurel.

Figure 16. Ethel Robinson
Lawrence, the "Rosa Parks
of affordable housing".[1]

At that time, of the 11,200 residents
of Mount Laurel, roughly 350 were Black
and some could trace their ancestry to
the Revolutionary era, long before the
Underground Railway brought Lawrence's
ancestors to town. Yet, too many of the Black residents were living
in deplorable housing. With suburbanization, many more realized
that their children would never be able to afford to live in their
centuries-old community. They needed new, sanitary, and affordable
housing. Starting in the 1969, a group led by Lawrence obtained a
federal grant and sought to build thirty-six affordable garden apartments on thirty-two acres.[2] To accomplish this, the residents needed
to rezone the thirty-two acres because the town prohibited family
apartments. While they knew the increasingly prosperous suburban-
izing town was concerned about its tax base, they thought they had
a chance. They had submitted their plans to the town and, after
several revisions, were awaiting a response. It was not what they had
hoped for.

Sixty members of Lawrence's church, the African Methodist
Episcopal Church, gathered in Jacob's Chapel on a hot October Sunday
morning in 1970 to hear the verdict from Mayor William Haines. The
church had a long and storied history. It was established in 1859 and
was used as a church, school, and most notably, as a sanctuary stop for
escaped slaves such as Lawrence's ancestors.

Figure 17. Historic Jacob's Chapel, established 1859.[3]

Haines was blunt. He told his audience that "the township council would never approve the community group's request."[4] The town didn't want more poor people in their town, especially from nearby communities. Just to make sure they heard, he explained—to families, some of whom had lived in the town for well over two centuries—"If you people can't afford to live in our town, then you'll just have to leave."[5]

That insult turned Ethel Lawrence and the sponsors of the modest housing plan into activists who would embark on a fifteen-year legal battle that changed the course of housing in New Jersey and would influence jurisdictions across the nation. It was a difficult battle for Lawrence. As recounted by one of her daughters, "My mother received threats; I can't tell you how many times we changed our phone number. . . . She feared for her family, she feared for her children, she feared for herself. But she always said, "right is right." It was also a battle that earned Ethel Lawrence the sobriquet "the Rosa Parks of Affordable Housing."[6] The racism was palpable. Neighbors spat obscenities in Ethel's face. One zoning official told her that low-cost apartments shouldn't be built because the town's sewage system would be overloaded because Blacks used the bathroom more than whites.[7]

The NAACP decided that it had to file a test case because the single-family zoning excluded the poor, the working class and, concomitantly, minorities. But the NAACP realized that federal court precedents were not on their side. So, hoping that the New Jersey Supreme Court might be more politically sympathetic, the lawyers filed in state court and based their arguments on the New Jersey state constitution. The trial court agreed with the plaintiffs and held that the zoning was unlawfully exclusionary. The township filed an appeal that changed the state's history.

The New Jersey Supreme Court began it decision with a statement that belongs in the "more things change the more they stay the same" file:

> There is not the slightest doubt that New Jersey has been, and continues to be, faced with a desperate need for housing, especially of decent living accommodations economically suitable for low and moderate income families. The situation was characterized as a 'crisis' and fully explored and documented by Governor Cahill in two special messages to the Legislature-A Blueprint for Housing in New Jersey (1970) and New Horizons in Housing (1972).[8]

To the court, there was no mystery why there was a crisis: "the effect of Mount Laurel's land use regulation has been to prevent various categories of persons from living in the township because of the limited extent of their income and resources."[9] Giving the township officials the benefit of the doubt, it assumed there was no proof of any unlawful discriminatory intent: "In this connection, we accept the representation of the municipality's counsel at oral argument that the regulatory scheme was not adopted with any desire or intent to exclude prospective residents on the obviously illegal bases of race, origin or believed social incompatibility."[10]

In response to the lawsuit, the township protested that even if had been practicing economic (and non-racial) discrimination, it had the right to do so to protect the fiscal interests of the town. Put bluntly, it wanted newcomers only if they could pay a lot of taxes and would not need much in the way of services. In other words, the welcome mat was out for the rich and upper middle-class. Others need not apply.

As in *Euclid*, the township argued it that had broad authority under the police power to enact regulations designed to promote the "public health, safety morals or the welfare" of the town in any way it saw fit, and it wasn't for a court to second-guess a town's police power decision.[11] The court, however, found that there must be a change in such a deferential judicial approach, "as mandated by change in the world around us." In other words, we've learned something since *Euclid*—that zoning can create a housing crisis and then make it worse.

And this wasn't just a circumstance unique to this particular suburb because the same conditions could be found in "any number of other municipalities of sizeable land area outside the central cities and older built-up suburbs of our North and South Jersey metropolitan areas."[12] As the court continued,

> This pattern of land use regulation has been adopted for the same purpose in developing municipality after developing municipality. Almost every one acts solely in its own selfish and parochial interest and in effect builds a wall around itself to keep out those people or entities not adding favorably to the tax base, despite the location of the municipality or the demand for varied kinds of housing.[13]

Accepting at face value the town's protestations that its motives were pure, and even if everyone else was acting in the same manner, the court held the zoning needed to be made more inclusive:

> We conclude that every such municipality must, by its land use regulations, presumptively make realistically possible an appropriate variety and choice of housing. More specifically, presumptively it cannot foreclose the opportunity of the classes of people mentioned for low and moderate income housing and in its regulations must affirmatively afford that opportunity,

at least to the extent of the municipality's fair share of the present and prospective regional need therefor.[14]

The court based its decision striking down the exclusionary zoning in
Mount Laurel on the state constitution's General Welfare Clause, finding that such zoning was incompatible with the general welfare. While
the result may have been necessary and just, it was a highly creative
interpretation of the constitution's text, one easily branded as judicial activism. There was no basis in precedent or in the history of the
state's constitution to support the use of the General Welfare Clause
to strike down exclusionary zoning. Perhaps a better strategy would
have been to go back to the property rights theory used to strike down
the race-based zoning in *Buchanan*. Recall that the Court there didn't
strike down the zoning simply because it discriminated; it struck it
down because of its impact on the rights of property owners. But in the
1970s, judicial respect for property rights had long been dormant. The
NAACP didn't take the *Buchanan* path and the New Jersey Supreme
Court had to find some other way to reach the result that it did.

The court may have thought it was compelled to act boldly simply
because the legislature had failed to act at all. It may have thought
that its ruling would cause the township and similar municipalities to
remove regulatory barriers to affordable housing. It may have thought
its ruling would pave the way for the Mount Laurel activists and others
to build more affordable housing. It thought wrong.

After losing, the township adopted the Southern states' strategy
toward the United States Supreme Court's civil rights rulings: compliance "with all deliberate speed," meaning no speed at all. After almost
a decade of slow-walking reforms, Mount Laurel Township ended
up back at the state supreme court. The town had made virtually no
progress, "After all this time," the court wrote in a 125-page follow-up
opinion,

Mount Laurel remains afflicted with a blatantly exclusionary ordinance. . . .
Papered over with studies, rationalized by hired experts, the ordinance at

its core is true to nothing but Mount Laurel's determination to exclude the poor. Mount Laurel is not alone; we believe that there is widespread non-compliance with the constitutional mandate of our original opinion in this case.[15]

This was more than a mere reduction of regulatory restraints; it was the imposition of an affirmative duty to do something proactive. The court established a procedure that was essentially "build first, ask questions later." Recognizing this was an extraordinary remedy, it noted that it meant to put an end to the municipal stalling: "Municipalities will not be able to appeal a trial court's determination that its ordinance is invalid, wait several years for adjudication of that appeal, and then, if unsuccessful, adopt another inadequate ordinance followed by more litigation and subsequent appeals."[16]

If the original *Mount Laurel* decision was activist, this one was turbo-charged activism. The court simply shrugged off any concerns over being too activist: "here being a constitutional obligation, we are not willing to allow it to be disregarded and rendered meaningless by declaring that we are powerless to apply any remedies other than those conventionally used."[17]

Despite this rebuke, the town's then-current mayor, Andrew August, was somewhat contemptuous of the court's ruling, telling the *New York Times*, "That's pretty harsh. Nobody ever sat down and said we should be exclusionary to any group of people. We'd just like to see our town develop in a nice way. We should have the right to run our own town."[18]

But the mayor spoke in coded contradictions: to be a "nice" town meant exclusion of the poor. He was indignant that this activist court was meddling in the town's traditional affairs and right to zone however it pleased. None of this would have been necessary if towns like Mount Laurel had resisted the lure of exclusionary zoning, or if the United States Supreme Court had itself resisted blessing schemes that stifled the right of property owners to build to meet demand, rather than conform to a town's prejudices.

The court's two rulings were hardly the end of the matter. While the legislature adopted a fair housing law to implement the *Mount Laurel* holdings, opponents to growth for environmental and other reasons have steadfastly opposed affordable housing developments. They claim it's not about excluding poor people, but something else. It's always something else. Even as late as 2017, the state supreme court was still at it, decrying the failure of the state to implement "fair-share" regulations that would direct municipalities on how much affordable housing they must have.[19] In this decision, the court concluded "that municipalities have a constitutional obligation to use their zoning power in a manner that creates a 'realistic opportunity for the construction of [their] fair share' of the region's low- and moderate-income housing."[20] Because of the failure by the state and municipalities to implement a meaning-ful fair-share housing program, the court disbanded the derelict state agency that was supposed to oversee the fair-share law. Instead, the court put the whole mess into the hands of the trial courts to resolve, municipality by municipality. The judges would now be responsible for upzoning and implementing affordable housing mandates. This is judicial activism at warp speed.

Despite the halting progress made by New Jersey, that state has at least recognized the severity of the problem of exclusionary zon-ing. Other states have paid varying degrees of lip service to the prob-lem. California law, for example, requires cities and counties to adopt their own fair-share obligations. But enforcement has largely proved to have the ferocity of a paper tiger. And, as in New Jersey, the mandates are fairly worthless against the onslaught of environmental and other NIMBY litigation designed to maintain the status quo.

In a time characterized by new attention to racial justice as epito-mized by the national disgust with the George Floyd murder, we have yet to move beyond exclusionary zoning. In 2019 and 2020, bills were introduced in California that would override local exclusionary zoning so apartment buildings could be constructed in areas served by mass transit. The proposals were soundly defeated in the democratically con-trolled legislature. While Los Angeles is famous for its liberal politics, every member of its city council and every state legislator from LA opposed these bills. This is in a city where African Americans constitute 8 percent of the population but 42 percent of its street homeless.[21]

It's the same story in Seattle. A modest measure to allow accessory dwelling units, also known as granny flats, in single-family neighborhoods is being opposed by upscale homeowners who have filed an environmental challenge. Changes to single-family exclusionary zoning have likewise been opposed by the progressives from Cambridge, Massachusetts to Denver, Colorado to Berkeley, California, and many places in between. As one Denver councilmember put it, "I hate when people call me a racist . . . Just because I value zoning doesn't make me a racist."[22] Of course it doesn't. It simply means you like minorities just fine so long as they're kept in their proper place—meaning places other than those nice neighborhoods where yards are wide and minds are narrow.

Ethel Lawrence died in 1994. But three decades later, one of her daughters fulfilled her mother's dream when she completed and dedicated the Ethel R. Lawrence Homes.[23] Where Ethel Lawrence dreamed of building thirty-six units, the path she pioneered led thirty-seven years later to 140 such homes in Mount Laurel. It was a long road, but one still not travelled by most suburbs in the United States. In the years that followed, over sixty thousand affordable housing units have been built in New Jersey, thanks to the work pioneered by Ethel Lawrence and the decisions of the New Jersey Supreme Court.[24]

Figure 18. Some of the 140 affordable homes in the Ethel R. Lawrence Homes, Mount Laurel, New Jersey.

Chapter 7

An End to Single-Family Zoning
as We Know It?

There has been a push in several cities and in California to end or modify single-family zoning. In 2018, Minneapolis allowed duplexes and triplexes in land zoned for single-family homes.[1] Similarly, Oregon passed a bill restricting single-family zoning in designated urban areas, as did Arlington, Virginia.[2]

In 2020, Portland, Oregon, went further and adopted an ordinance that allows more duplexes, triplexes, fourplexes, and accessory dwelling units on land zoned for single-family residential.[3] Even greater density is allowed for affordable units. The bill passed the city council by a three-to-one vote, with the only "no" vote from the only city council member who owned a home.

Most dramatic, and controversial, in 2021 California adopted SB 9 and SB 10, two bills designed to limit the force of single-family zoning statewide. SB 9 mandates ministerial approval of development of no more than two residential units within single-family residential zones. There are several caveats. The new units cannot displace existing low-income housing as recorded by deed or covenant or rent control or occupied by tenant for more than three years, the new development cannot replace more than 25 percent of existing walls, and the area cannot be designated as historic. Most significantly, the California Environmental Quality Act will not apply to SB 9 approvals.

SB 10 allows local governments to zone any parcel for ten units per parcel if it is located near transit or an urban infill site. It requires a two-thirds vote of the legislative body if the ordinance supersedes any zoning restriction adopted by local initiative.

Previously, California adopted laws permitting the development of accessory dwelling units (ADUs) on single-family parcels. There has been some pushback and resistance from local governments, who have attempted to adopt permitting roadblocks to new ADUs.[4] These have been met with litigation.[5]

SB 9 and SB 10 may have a particularly large impact on California's suburbs, where single-family zoning is the norm. A study from the University of California at Berkeley estimated that 78 percent of Southern California neighborhoods don't allow apartments.[6] As researcher Stephen Menendian put it, "An inordinately large amount of residential land—in fact, all land in the region—is restricted to large-lot, detached single-family homes. What this means is that apartments, condos and other housing options are simply impossible to build . . . and the consequences are profound."[7]

For the poor and working-class populations, housing supply is inelastic. As noted by the National Bureau of Economic Research, "policies and regulations that raise rents by creating artificial shortages in housing supply . . . may have particularly concerning distributional consequences."[8] In other words, slight impacts on housing supply may cause large price impacts for already struggling Americans. But SB 9 and SB 10 have been especially ill-received. Suburban NIMBY groups like "Livable California" have joined with the uber-left-leaning AIDS Healthcare Foundation (AHF; which sponsored two hugely expensive and unsuccessful initiatives to adopt statewide rent control) to fight the implementation of SB 9 and SB 10, calling them paths to gentrification and, ironically, harmful to people of color. First, the AHF and its affiliate "Housing is a Human Right" took out full-page ads to oppose passage.[9] When that effort failed, AHF sued, arguing the measures interfere with the right of the voters to establish zoning via the ballot box.[10] To date, the AHF litigation has failed.

However, on April 22 2024, in a suit brought by Redondo Beach, a superior court ruled that SB 9 did not apply to 121 charter cities—essentially all the larger cities in the state—because SB 9 was about lot splits, and they are not a matter of statewide concern. Under California law, the legislature cannot overturn local charter city law unless it is a matter of statewide concern.[11] Because the bill's proponents believe all things affecting housing supply are a matter of statewide concern, an appeal is expected.

AHF is also bankrolling an initiative to overturn these measures.[12] So far, the referendum has failed to gather enough signatures to get onto the ballot. The Foundation claimed that 71 percent of Californians opposed the new laws.[13] Yet, according to a LA Business Council Institute/*Los Angeles Times* poll, 55 percent of California voters support the new laws, while 27 percent are opposed.[14]

The fear of gentrification expressed by these opponents is real. However, gentrification comes in different flavors. First, the most extreme example is urban redevelopment wherein affordable units are destroyed to make way for tax-generating development. In *Berman v. Parker*,[15] discussed in a later chapter, the Court upheld an urban redevelopment project that displaced thousands of low-income residents while building only a relative handful of affordable units.[16]

Next is the kinder and gentler redevelopment that is the classic model of gentrification. Here is the repurposing of existing lower-income housing into more expensive market-rate housing. In his history of the Yes-in-My-Backyard (YIMBY) movement, Conor Dougherty describes one such instance from North Fair Oaks, California, an impoverished suburb halfway between San Francisco and San Jose. There an investment company purchased an apartment building where the typical rent for a three-bedroom apartment was $1850 per month. After largely cosmetic improvements and yuppie-attractive amenities like Nest thermostats, the new owners raised the rents to $2750 per month.[17] This is the sort of gentrification that occurs when investors with capital seek to meet a tremendous unmet demand for housing. When the only low-hanging fruit for new market-rate housing is in undercapitalized, lower-income neighborhoods, there will be gentrification. But if more housing were allowed to be built elsewhere, this low-hanging fruit wouldn't be nearly as attractive. It's only in demand for gentrification because there's no place else to put investment money for housing.

Another type of gentrification occurs when commercial and industrial properties are repurposed for new housing. While such developments don't directly displace existing lower-income tenants, such developments can change a neighborhood's character with an influx of richer residents. This can be good for owners, but not so good for renters if the new development attracts more demand for market-rate housing in the area—which in turn can lead to the privately financed redevelopment of existing apartments and eviction of existing tenants.

In any event, the exclusionary suburban enclaves have not taken SB 9 and SB 10 sitting down. The Bay Area town of Woodside attracted worldwide attention (and derision) when it attempted to designate the entire town as a critical habitat for the mountain lion.[18] The state's attorney general put a kibosh on that, despite protestations from town leaders that they had only the best of intentions.[19] Woodside Mayor Brown explained it simply, that it's "not the Woodside way" to value housing over preserving the environment. "We love animals. Every house that's built is one more house taken away from habitat. Where are they going to go? Pretty soon we'll have nothing but asphalt and no animals and no birds."[20] One could always ask the opposite: If homes aren't built, where are the people supposed to go? Do we have enough tents to put on our existing asphalt?

Of course, it seems a wee stretch to assert that subdividing an existing residential lot, which is all that SB 9 allows, will have much of an impact on mountain lion habitat—unless an existing homeowner keeps mountain lions in the family home's backyard.

Portola Valley residents tried another work-around. They requested that the city use another exception to SB 9 by delegating permitting authority to the Woodside Fire District—which could deny subdivision permits if there is a danger of wildfire.[21] It goes without saying that most of suburban California is subject to some degree of wildfire risk, not to mention earthquakes, flooding, drought, and various other horsemen of the apocalypse. If all housing must be risk free, there will be neither risk nor housing.

Pasadena passed an urgency ordinance designating large swaths of the city as "landmark districts," thus falling under yet another one of SB 9's exceptions.[22] State Attorney General Bonta responded by calling the ploy illegal, because the SB 9 exception applies only to individual landmarks, not entire districts.[23] Not to be outdone, the high-end town of Palo Alto is taking advantage of the exception in SB 9 by designating 130 homes as "historic."[24]

That's not to say that increasing density is a panacea, especially if it is accompanied by restrictions on "greenfield" development—that is new housing developments on land previously used for ranching, farming, or open space. There is only so much density to go around, and when regions have tried to force *all* development into a small urban-defined footprint, there have been negative consequences. As described next, Portland, Oregon, is a prime example.

With increased density and no escape valve outside of urban areas, increases in density result in increases in crime, traffic congestion, and pollution.[25] Economist Randal O'Toole studied the severe urban limit lines imposed by the State of Oregon in the 1970s. On land outside the lines, new homes are allowed only on lots in excess of 160 acres that are actively farmed and produce significant revenues.[26] In 2001, O'Toole wrote that only about one hundred landowners per year had been allowed to build homes on their farms.[27] O'Toole concluded:

> The urban-growth boundary and restrictions on new single-family housing have turned Portland from one [of] the nation's most affordable markets for single-family zoning in 1989 to one of the least affordable since 1996. Since 1990, the cost of an acre of land available for housing has risen from $20,000 to $200,000.[28]

By 2017, that figure had risen to over $300,000 for an acre.[29]

Urban limit lines and similar rules have had a devastating effect on housing affordability, but they have been difficult to challenge. Because they do not deprive land of all its use and value, such rules are not susceptible to easy challenges under a claim of regulatory takings (a topic to be addressed in a later chapter.)

Drawing geographic lines is always an exercise in arbitrary power, but courts are loathe to strike down such line drawing—presumably because such lines are permissible under the police power, they "must" be drawn somewhere, and courts are reluctant to second-guess such legislative actions.

SB 9 and SB 10 do not create urban limit lines and do not prevent development outside of existing cities (although there are plenty of other policies in place in California that do prevent greenfield development.) But they do attempt to allow more building in already developed areas, which will have some impact on density.

The extent to which either SB 9 or SB 10 will cause new units to be added into existing lots or cause the replacement of existing single-family homes with more expensive duplexes, triplexes, and quads, remains to be seen. Ultimately, increasing the supply of housing will reduce the price appreciation on a regional scale. But for those particular neighborhoods where more market-rate housing moves in and displaces existing lower-income housing, the local effects may include some amount of gentrification.

Chapter 8:

The Economic Impact of Zoning and Land-Use Regulations Has Been Devastating

In 1991, President George H. W. Bush created a commission to study America's housing crisis. It began by noting a depressing lack of progress: "In the past 24 years, no fewer than 10 federally sponsored commissions, studies or task forces have examined the problem. . . . In the decade since 1981, the regulatory environment has if anything become a greater deterrent to affordable housing, regulatory barriers have become clearly more complex, and apparently more prevalent."[1]

Later, the report concluded: "Millions of Americans are being priced out of buying or renting the kind of housing they otherwise could afford, were it not for a web of government regulations."[2]

That was thirty-two years ago, and we could replace the number twenty-four with fifty-six and repeat the same grim assessment, word for word.

Not only do excessive zoning and other land-use regulations deliberately exclude the poor, when combined with building regulations, but they have also raised prices for everyone else. Multiple studies by economists have demonstrated the relationship between zoning and other land-use regulations and housing costs. For example:

- In 1980, the relationship between growth control and costs was apparent. Lawrence Katz and Kenneth T. Rosen wrote for the Center on Real Estate and Urban Economics that: "Land-use and environmental regulations can have important impacts on almost every component of housing costs" and "Growth moratoria and growth control plans have raised prices between 18–28 [percent] in those San Francisco communities where they are present."[3]

- In 1988, Cynthia Kroll and others with the Center for Real Estate and Urban Economics wrote that growth caps in San Diego "will have significant housing and income impacts on some segments of the population without resolving the county's very serious problems of traffic congestion and infrastructure constraints."[4]

- In 1996, economist Stephen Malpezzi concluded, "Our results suggest that regulation raises housing rents and values and lowers homeownership rates."[5]

- In 2003, economists Edward L. Glaeser and Joseph Gyourko reached the remarkable conclusion that "America is not facing a nationwide affordable housing crisis. In most of the country, home prices appear to be fairly close to physical costs of construction. . . . Only in particular areas . . . do housing prices diverge substantially from the costs of new construction." Where the prices were excessive, they wrote, "Zoning, and other land use controls, are more responsible for high prices where we see them. . . . Measures of zoning strictness are highly correlated with high prices."[6]

- In 2006, Edward L. Glaeser and Bryce Ward concluded that "each extra acre of minimum lot size decreases new construction by roughly 40 percent and increases housing prices by roughly 10 percent."[7]

- In 2014, Joseph Gyourko of the Wharton School estimates that excessive zoning has pushed real house prices a staggering 56 percent above real construction costs.[8]

- In 2018, Glaeser and Gyourko estimated that in the most regulated areas, housing prices are about three times as high as they would be without regulations.[9]
- In 2019, economists Chang-Tae Hsieh and Enrico Moretti, using data from 220 metropolitan areas, concluded that exclusionary zoning had lowered aggregate US growth by 36 percent from 1964 to 2009.[10] In 2022, after methodological errors were brought to their attention, they admitted that the impacts were even higher than they had calculated.[11]
- In 2022, the National Association of Homebuilders estimated that the cost of regulation of the development of multifamily dwellings added 40.6 percent to the total cost.[12]

The most comprehensive study was performed by Professor Bernard Siegan in his classic 1972 book, *Land Use Without Zoning*.[13] Professor Siegan compared Houston, which had rejected zoning when first suggested in 1962, with other cities such as Chicago and Dallas, which had adopted zoning ordinances. In both cases, Professor Siegan found that land-use patterns were essentially the same. But while Houston was built on market forces and voluntary agreements, Chicago had a top-down zoning infrastructure. Instead of the market dictating what could be built where, Dallas had a bureaucracy that controlled every aspect of land-use development. In the end, however, the biggest differences were costs: housing cost roughly 30 percent more in Chicago than Houston—an increase Professor Siegan attributed to the bureaucratic inefficiencies of Chicago's system. One lesson that Siegan took away from his study was that: "The most measurable influence of nonzoning in Houston is its effect on multiple-family dwellings. If Houston had adopted zoning in 1962, this would probably have resulted in higher rents and a lesser number and variety of apartments, and, in consequence, some tenants would have been priced out of the new-apartment market."[14]

The impact of zoning does not fall evenly. Because it excludes poorer residents, those who already own homes in cities where supply is constrained by zoning often see greater appreciation of their property values. More specifically, Siegan continued, "In Houston, it appears that financially the imposition of zoning controls would have benefitted the most affluent homeowners, and would have most adversely affected the renters. There might also have been detrimental effects on the less affluent homeowners. It seems most difficult to justify such public policy."[15]

Houstonians seem to understand the exclusionary nature inherent in zoning better than residents of any other city. Led by opposition from working-class and minority neighborhoods, Houston voters have rejected proposals to introduce zoning repeatedly in 1948, 1962, and 1993.[16]

In more recent times, others have noted the problems caused by zoning. Consistent with Siegan's groundbreaking work, Jason Furman, chair of the Council of Economic Advisers under President Obama, put it this way:

> While land use regulations sometimes serve reasonable and legitimate purposes, they can also give extra-normal returns to entrenched interests at the expense of everyone else . . . Zoning regulations and other local barriers to housing development [can] allow a small number of individuals to capture the economic benefits of living in a community, thus limiting diversity and mobility.[17]

Economist Jonathan Rothwell posited that, "A change in permitted zoning from the most restrictive to the least would close 50 [percent] of the observed gap between the most unequal metropolitan areas and the least, in terms of neighborhood inequality."[18] Noting the disparities in education quality between rich and poor neighborhoods, and commenting on Rothwell, Richard Reeves adds that, "Loosening zoning regulations would reduce the housing cost gap and by extension narrow educational inequalities."[19]

A subtler way that zoning drives up housing costs is by forcing the housing that is built to be of a higher quality than residents might otherwise require, through policies such as minimum lot sizes or minimum parking requirements. Beyond these written prohibitions and mandates, zoning often raises housing costs simply by adding an onerous and unpredictable layer of review to the permitting process.[20] For example, in Canada, the Victoria Transport Policy Institute estimated that requiring one parking space per unit increases moderately priced housing by 12 percent and two spaces increases it by 25 percent.[21] In 2016, the Journal Housing Policy Debate estimated that parking requirements increase rents by 17 percent, or an additional $142 per month.[22] Other researchers have indicated that parking requirements discourages the construction of smaller (which are presumably cheaper) units.[23]

The understanding of the ills caused by zoning and other land-use restrictions cuts across the political spectrum. Echoing the report from President Bush's commission issued in 1991, President Obama's White House said pretty much the same thing: "Local policies acting as barriers to housing supply include land use restrictions that make developable land much more costly than it is inherently, zoning restrictions, off-street parking requirements, arbitrary or antiquated preservation regulations, residential conversion restrictions, and unnecessarily slow permitting processes."[24]

In remarks he made to the US Conference of Mayors, President Obama said, "We can work together to break down rules that stand in the way of building new housing and that keep families from moving to growing, dynamic cities."[25]

Adding to the bipartisan chorus, President Trump, who had some experience as a developer, issued an Executive Order stating:

> It shall be the policy of my Administration to work with Federal, State, local, tribal, and private sector leaders to address, reduce, and remove the multitude of overly burdensome regulatory barriers that artificially raise the cost of housing development and help to cause the lack of housing supply. Increasing the supply of housing by removing overly burdensome regulatory barriers will reduce housing costs, boost economic growth, and provide more Americans with opportunities for economic mobility.[26]

Yet, the Trump Administration's commitment to opening exclusive suburban enclaves to affordable housing has been decidedly mixed in light of his decision to dismantle his predecessor's housing policies. Toward the end of his administration, former President Obama issued the Affirmatively Furthering Fair Housing (AFFH) policy, which required communities to prepare an "Assessment of Fair Housing."

There has been much dispute over whether AFFH required anything more than mere information gathering. Opponents to the Trump Administration's revocation of the rule argue that the Obama rule "does not mandate specific outcomes for the planning process."[27] But more conservative commentators suggest that while the "specific" means of changing the planning process weren't mandated, the end results effectively were.

Part of the confusion stems from the language in the Obama rule indicating that the gathered information would "identify factors" that could help "establish fair housing priorities and goals."[28] Moreover, the administration's "AFFH Fact Sheet" stated that the AFFH and the Fair Housing Act "imposed a duty to affirmatively further fair housing" and would take "meaningful actions . . . that overcome patterns of segregation and foster inclusive communities."[29] "Meaningful actions" meant "significant actions that are designed and can be reasonably expected to achieve a material positive change that affirmatively furthers fair housing by, for example, increasing fair housing choice or decreasing disparities in access to opportunity.[30] According to the *Washington Post*, "the rule required more than 1,200 communities receiving billions of federal housing dollars to draft plans to desegregate their communities—or risk losing federal funds."[31] All these mandates imply more than information gathering.

Indeed, for nearly a decade the federal government and the city of Rochester, New York, were at each other's throats over that city's zoning. In its assessment submitted to the Department of Housing and Urban Development (HUD), the city insisted that its zoning did not contribute to racial bias, but HUD did not buy it. As a result, HUD withheld five million federal dollars from the city. Rochester tried to comply by building low-income housing, but that was not enough. HUD continued to maintain that the city's assessment was inadequate. Rochester sued. Ultimately, a federal appellate court said HUD couldn't force the city to change its zoning laws in order to get the federal money. However, the court also said HUD could withhold the money if HUD deemed the assessment was inadequate. But once the city dropped a statement in its plan that said its zoning was without bias, HUD relented and approved the plan—after the change in administration.

Because of the perception that the federal government was interfering with local decision making, the Obama rule was not well-liked by local governments, especially in some of the more exclusive suburbs. Like Rochester.

Capitalizing on this dislike, the Trump Administration first decided not to enforce the new rule. Then, on August 16, 2020, the president announced that his administration would reverse

> an Obama-Biden regulation that would have empowered the Department of Housing and Urban Development to abolish single-family zoning, compel the construction of high-density "stack and pack" apartment buildings in residential neighborhoods and forcibly transform neighborhoods across America so they look and feel the way far-left ideologues and technocratic bureaucrats think they should. . . .
>
> HUD used the threat of withholding federal money to pressure it to raise property taxes and build nearly 11,000 low-income, high-density apartments.[32]

With no attempt at subtlety, President Trump explained on September 1, 2020 to Fox News's Laura Ingraham that abolishing the Obama rule would protect suburban women from crime. As the president elaborated,

> They want low-income housing and with that comes a lot of other problems including crime . . . You have this beautiful community in the suburbs, including women . . . they want security. I ended where they build low-income housing projects right in the middle of your neighborhood. I ended

it. If Biden gets in, he already said it's going to go at a much higher rate than ever before. You know who's going to be in charge of it? Cory Booker. That's going to be nice.[33]

In their August 16, 2020 *Wall Street Journal* opinion piece on the rule rescission, the president and Secretary of Housing Ben Carson preemptively suggested: "As usual, anyone who dares tell the truth about what the left is doing is smeared as a racist."[34] But what exactly is the specter of air-dropping low-income housing projects, managed by the Black senator from New Jersey, into beautiful suburban neighborhoods filled with frightened women supposed to imply? At least the president didn't imply that Biden would put Silas Lynch in charge.[35]

After he was elected, President Biden gave some indication of agreement with the need for zoning reform in a White House fact sheet issued on March 31, 2021 that accompanied the rollout of his infrastructure bill. The fact sheet includes this aspirational passage:

> Eliminate exclusionary zoning and harmful land use policies. For decades, exclusionary zoning laws—like minimum lot sizes, mandatory parking requirements, and prohibitions on multifamily housing—have inflated housing and construction costs and locked families out of areas with more opportunities. President Biden is calling on Congress to enact an innovative, new competitive grant program that awards flexible and attractive funding to jurisdictions that take concrete steps to eliminate such needless barriers to producing affordable housing.[36]

Regardless of the degree to which the Obama rule was or any future Biden rule will be an incursion on local autonomy, and regardless of the motivations of President Trump in rescinding the rule, the ineluctable fact remains that suburban land-use patterns discourage working class and minority populations. And yet it is just as inescapable a fact that suburban constituencies like just fine the status quo of quiet places where yards are wide and poor people few.

By limiting the supply of new housing, the price of existing homes rises because the restricted supply cannot meet market demand. Existing homeowners benefit from the appreciated prices—at least until their children need to find homes. As such, in addition to maintaining the status quo of uncrowded, open-space-rich suburbs, the increase in home values gives existing owners a source of capital for discretionary spending. In other words, they have little incentive to support an influx of new and perhaps more affordable housing in their existing neighborhoods.

Economist William Fischel wrote extensively on this phenomenon in *The Homevoter Hypothesis*[37] where he explained that since the home is the primary and largest asset of most homeowners, they have every reason to vote for politicians and policies that will best preserve the value of their homes—whether that policy be good schools, robust municipal services, or restrictive land-use policies that favor the status quo over new development. As Fischel put it in describing Washington State's failure to allow adequate metropolitan growth, its statewide "smart growth" planning law known as the Growth Management Act "has little to recommend it so far. It seems to act more like a cartel for those already in possession of suburban homes than as a rationalizer of metropolitan development patterns."[38]

Other economists have a different explanation: voter ignorance and economic illiteracy. The *LA Times* poll cited in this book's introduction is certainly evidence that many voters don't understand the connection between housing supply and prices. If that is correct, then the likelihood that they vote for NIMBY outcomes out of self-interest may be incorrect. Another explanation might be at play.

Going beyond the *LA Times* poll, three economists recently conducted an extensive and sophisticated study of the public's understanding of the relationship between housing supply and costs. They concluded that "supply skepticism" among renters and homeowners is a more thorough explanation of public opposition to new housing.[39] Put simply, while renters understand how the law of supply and demand affects other commodities, they are not convinced that building more homes will lower rents. The researchers found, for example, that "about 30 to 40 [percent] of Americans believe, contrary to basic economic theory and robust empirical evidence, that a large, exogeneous increase in their region's housing stock *would cause rents and home prices to rise*."[40] Moreover, only 30 to 40 percent predict that a large increase in housing stock would cause prices to fall.[41] For many, the law of supply and demand in housing markets is too abstract and too attenuated when compared to more local effects. As the authors put it,

> Somewhat paradoxically, then, both homeowners and renters may oppose housing projects on the basis of neighborhood- or block-level price effects, with homeowners, who live in neighborhoods that are "higher quality" on average, fearing that local home values will go down, and renters, who live in neighborhoods that are "lower quality" on average, fearing that local rents will go up.[42]

In other words, the fear is of lowered property values for those with a lot and gentrification for those without. Even beyond local effects, "most renters disbelieve that even a large, *region-wide* increase in the number of new homes would put downward pressure on rents."[43]

Whatever the explanation for NIMBYism's sway over elected officials, it remains true that the losers in this state of affairs are those who cannot afford decent housing. People who cannot move into an area until either new homes are built or existing owners die or move have zero political force to encourage new housing. And for those already in the community, they too often see no advantage to an increase in housing supply.

To be sure, some types of homes may be more appropriate in some locations than others. Homes to be occupied by the working class should ideally be near transit, jobs, and shopping that can best meet their needs. Under more ideal circumstances a free market and a savvy developer community would combine to build what is needed where it is needed. We wouldn't need to think about artificial market Band-Aids, such as building subsidized affordable housing in upscale neighborhoods, because we wouldn't have the crisis of inadequate and unaffordable housing supply in the first place.

Despite the near universal acknowledgment by economists and policy wonks of the negative consequences of zoning on housing affordability, it is the proverbial third rail of suburban politics. Voters are passionate in their desire to protect their property values and the status quo. Politicians fully recognize the dangers inherent in courage. Thus, we can study the problem until the end of time, and we can quantify the economic and social costs of the politics of suburban exclusion until we run out of numbers, but unless we change the motivations and legal consequences of preventing people from using their land and resources to build new housing, the problems will remain.

PART II

Eminent Domain and the Destruction of Working-Class Housing

Zoning wasn't the only government policy that limited housing options for the poor. When abused, the power of eminent domain can be terribly destructive of working-class neighborhoods. Indeed, the solution to the tenements that so bothered Jacob Riis in How the Other Half Lives *was often their destruction. As noted in* **chapter 2***, the infamous tenements of New York's Mulberry Bend were razed and replaced by Columbus Park. Portions of Central Park were built on the remains of a neighborhood owned by African Americans. Even in more recent times, the choice of where to route our interstate highway system has very often coincided with the location of minority neighborhoods not simply because that's where land was cheap but because it was a way to eliminate troublesome minority-occupied slums or at least separate them from "better" neighborhoods with an impenetrable four or six lane barrier of concrete and fast-moving cars.*

Most profoundly, the use of eminent domain, called the despotic power by the Supreme Court in 1795,1 creates tremendous tension between the government's power to condemn and the people's right to own and use private property, unmolested by government.

Chapter 9

The Modern Rise of Eminent Domain and the Destruction of Existing Housing

On May 8, 1959, Los Angeles deputies dragged a thirty-seven-year-old World War II widow named Mrs. Aurora Vargas out of her home at 1771 Malvina Avenue in Chavez Ravine and detained her. Her mother threw rocks at the deputies. Children cried. The rest of the family was escorted out. Then, the waiting bulldozers were fired up and the home smashed to pieces minutes later. Her family's home had been taken by involuntary eminent domain so her Latino neighborhood could be razed. The first plan for the site was for public housing. Although the residents were to be given first dibs on the new housing, many objected. The people had deep ties to their neighborhood, which had been established in the 1840s and was home to over a thousand families.[2] As Aurora's father recounted, "My family and I fought every way we knew how to stay in our home in Chavez Ravine. Police had to carry my daughter, Aurora Vargas, from our house . . . we lost our home and our land, but we didn't lose our pride because we fought with everything we had."[3]

The displaced families were never fully compensated.[4] The three lots and two homes owned by Aurora's father and extended family, for example, had been appraised at $17,500, but a judge lowered the offering price to a mere $10,050.[5] But the family didn't want to sell for any price. For a week following their eviction, the family camped out at the ruined site of their former home. But nothing changed. They were never to move back home.

To add insult to injury, instead of public housing, Vargas's home and neighborhood became Dodger Stadium.[6] Aurora Vargas lost her husband to the World War II Battle of the Bulge. She lost her home to the LA Dodgers. The downfall of the public housing plan came when it was discovered that its chief proponent was a communist and a new mayor killed the project. Today, it is estimated that the homeless *students* in California could fill Dodger Stadium five times over.[7]

Figure 19. Mrs. Aurora Vargas being carried out of her home in Chavez ravine, May 8, 1959; Source: Hugh Amott, *Los Angeles Times*.[8]

* * *

A half-century later, Suzette Kelo and her neighbors faced a similar threat. The City of New London, Connecticut, had a plan. All it had to do was destroy a neighborhood so that multinational Pfizer Pharmaceutical could move in and create high-paying jobs and pay big tax dollars. But, after the city bought eighty-three homes, the remaining residents resisted.

Figure 20. Chavez Ravine after; note lack of affordable housing at Dodger Stadium. According to a UCLA study, this stadium could be filled five times with California's homeless students and still have an overflow into the parking lot.

Suzette Kelo was a registered nurse who bought her dream home in the Fort Trumball neighborhood of New London, Connecticut in 1997. The house was a mess, and the yard was filled with weeds. She restored what became known as a "little pink house," and planned to spend the rest of her life there. But on the day before Thanksgiving in 2000, the New London Development Commission posted a notice on her door, saying she was being evicted and had four months to leave.[9]

Kelo and her neighbors fought back. Represented for free by the Institute for Justice, they argued that the evictions and takings were not for a "public use" as required by the Constitution. The case eventually made its way to the Supreme Court. Dozens of "friend of the court" briefs were filed by people across the nation (including one by Pacific Legal Foundation.) At oral argument, some of the justices understood what was at stake. Referring to an elderly widow in the neighborhood, Justice Scalia responded to the argument that the residents were being paid: "Yes, you're paying for it, but you're giving the money to somebody who doesn't want the money, who wants to live in the house that she's lived in her whole life. That counts for nothing?"[10]

Unfortunately, it did count for nothing. In a great disappointment to advocates for limits on eminent domain, a divided court upheld the taking. The Court found that because the redevelopment furthered a "public purpose," the Constitution's requirement that there be a "public use" was satisfied. A vigorous dissent by Justice O'Connor rued that the "specter of condemnation hangs over all property. Nothing is to prevent the State from replacing a Motel 6 with a Ritz-Carlton, any home with a shopping mall, or any farm with a factory."[11]

A few years later a movie was made about the case, *A Little Pink House*. After a screening, Suzette Kelo said of the city, "the heartbreak, the pain, and suffering, they caused us. . . . They destroyed us . . . they destroyed our families and they ripped our hearts out, and they killed the elderly, and it was pretty bad."[12]

In November 2009, nine years after the city pinned the notice on Suzette Kelo's door, Pfizer announced it was moving out, taking the tax revenue and fourteen hundred jobs with it.[13] The Kelo property was never redeveloped. The weeds have returned to Kelo's now-vacant lot.[14] The final cost to the city was $78 million and the destruction of an entire neighborhood—all for no lasting jobs or tax revenue.

* * *

When employed as designed, the institutions of private property should serve to protect the interests of the working and middle classes as much as anyone else. If constrained by its constitutional limits, the power of eminent domain would pose only a limited risk to the rights of individuals. That is because government would take private property only when the legislature declares it necessary for public use—as the Fifth Amendment commands. But that is not the case with modern eminent domain practices, where poor and minority households are at greater risk from eminent domain—especially eminent domain employed to further urban redevelopment.

Figure 21. Suzzette Kelo and the little pink house from *Kelo v. New London, Connecticut,* July 1997.[15]

Figure 22. The Kelo Neighborhood in 2010, a year after Pfizer walked away from New London.[16]

It is not a coincidence that the expansive notions of state power espoused by the progressives came into prominence at the same time as the constraints on the power of eminent domain were loosened.[17] With government taking on the role of a provider of goods and services, there has been a vast expansion in the definition of what constitutes "public use." As one writer put it, "now all behavior was seen as having public ramifications justifying government control, to serve the 'popular will.'"[18]

The use of the sovereign power of eminent domain to condemn private property has been the most visible manifestation of government's tendency to harness private property for the private good of government-favored special interests. While often couched in terms of improving the lives of the poor, the reality has been the dispossession of the poor from their homes and the destruction of their neighborhoods.

As the very meaning of private property has become more and more malleable in the hands of government actors, it has become more of a target of the entrenched political class for the benefit of that class. Such crony capitalism has not been kind to the owners of modest holdings of private property, and the public has suffered. And, as will be shown, the property owners who have suffered the most have been those with the least—the working class, the poor, and minorities. Put simply, the erosion of rights in property has hurt those with the least property far more than those with the most.[19] Or, as Professor Kanner puts it, eminent domain for redevelopment means using the "coercive power of government to redistribute wealth from the deserving middle class and the few poor who own modest dwellings . . . to the undeserving rich."[20]

Thus, working-class homes are condemned for shopping centers and factories for the ostensible purpose of creating public amenities or jobs or increasing tax revenues. In reality, condemnation is often for the purpose of enriching favored developers and multinational business enterprises. For example, the working-class and mixed ethnicity Poletown neighborhood in Detroit was taken for a General Motors Factory.[21] Likewise, Suzette Kelo's little pink house was condemned for a corporate headquarters.[22] These are not aberrational examples; they are part of the standard lexicon of government abuse.[23]

Kelo is a particularly emblematic case because it awakened many ordinary Americans to the reality of eminent domain gone wild. In 1959, few cared about Vargas's neighborhood in Los Angeles's Chavez Ravine. They were just poor minorities in a run-down neighborhood. But when the City of New London, Connecticut, decided to revitalize itself by bringing in a major corporation to locate its headquarters there, things changed. Suzette Kelo's neighborhood wasn't blighted. It reminded many middle-class Americans of their very own neighborhoods. *Kelo* brought home the fact that today, middle-class and poor homes alike, private businesses in nice areas and private businesses in bad areas alike, can all be taken for the benefit of whatever multinational corporation waves a lot of money in front of the noses of local officials.

Even entire neighborhoods of "undesirables"—the poor, the ethnic minorities, and those least able to mount meaningful political resistance—can be condemned in order to revitalize their neighborhoods. But this sort of revitalization simply disperses and displaces the powerless for the benefit of the powerful. The poor are shunted elsewhere, out of sight and out of mind. Once vibrant neighborhoods can become sterile office parks, while new highways can tear asunder the social fabric of communities of color.

One critic, Eric Avila, recounts with mordant humor this reflection on eminent domain and highways: "If future anthropologists want to find the remains of people of color in a post apocalypse America, they will simply have to find the ruins of the nearest freeway."[24] This follows from the Avila's assertion that "as far back as the 1930s, federal blueprints for urban expressways presumed a racial hierarchy of spaces."[25] He continues that in cities like "Columbia and Kansas City, Missouri; Charlotte, North Carolina; Atlanta and New Orleans, federally funded highways were instruments of white supremacy, wiping out black neighborhoods with clear but tacit intent."[26] "Through both malicious intent and benign neglect," he concludes, "interstate highways tore into the heart of African American cities across the nation."[27]

Other ethnic communities were targeted as well. As Avila says, "Across the nation, highway construction leveled Jewish neighborhoods, Little Italys, Germantowns, Poletowns, and Irish neighborhoods."[28] Avila isn't the only researcher who makes these types of claims. The National Association of Realtors recently issued a study that concludes that "the negative ramifications of pursuing [highway] infrastructure projects without taking a holistic, community-centric approach are still visible in many cities today in hyper-segregated neighborhoods of concentrated poverty."[29]

A popular metaphor during the Vietnam War was that the Americans "had to destroy a village in order to save it."[30] Apparently, the same logic applies to our slums.

After decades of such marginalization of the poor for the public good, the broader public had an epiphany with *Kelo*: Condemnation can happen anywhere and to anyone. It is not only the so-called blighted neighborhoods of the urban poor, but also the blight-free White neighborhoods like Mrs. Kelo's that can be targeted.[31] In other words, *Kelo* took the reality of eminent domain abuse out of the poor and minority neighborhoods and thrust it into the consciousness of white middle-class Americans.

A common justification for the destruction of working-class homes and neighborhoods is that they are blighted. Some state laws even require that a targeted home or neighborhood be blighted before it can be taken and destroyed. But blight has never been much of an impediment to a redevelopment taking. Just about anything can be declared blighted due to factors as varied as a diversity of ownership to peeling paint.[32] And even with many post-*Kelo* reforms, not much has changed with blight justifications for eminent domain, because the chasm between what the public considers to be blight and what the takers consider to be blight is vast. After all, if the reader lives in a single-family suburban home surrounded by other individually owned homes, there is "diversity of ownership," which is a factor used for determining blight. And heaven forbid a neighbor has too many wet leaves on her tennis court, even if that neighbor is a member of

Congress from Naglee Park, an upscale San Jose neighborhood that was apparently swept up in the city's zeal to designate one-third of the city as blighted. This was despite the objections from the neighborhood's residents who didn't want or need any "help" from the city to alleviate its non-existent blight.[33] For most urban working-class neighborhoods, however, when blight is used as an excuse for redevelopment and gentrification, it is only a short step from a neighborhood being blighted to one becoming whited.

In the United States, there is something of a backlash. Once seen as a benevolent tool of social improvement, resistance to eminent domain is growing. Long-simmering resentments by minority communities have become more visible and have spilled into nonminority territory. Judicial and legislative skepticism of the motivations of condemning authorities is growing. With the Supreme Court's decision in *Kelo*, sporadic efforts to contain the abuses of eminent domain became a movement.[34] But will that movement last? Despite reforms, there is an inexorable tendency for condemning authorities and their cronies to again seek the power to take.[35] The role of private property as a bulwark of individual liberty is not yet secure.

The Fifth Amendment in the United States Constitution says, "No person . . . shall be deprived of life, liberty, or property, without due process of law; nor shall private property be taken for public use without just compensation."[36] In theory, confining the use of condemnation to those projects that serve a public use, combined with the payment of just compensation, should limit the ability and incentives of government actors to abuse the power of eminent domain. In practice, a potent combination of ambitious government actors, politically connected developers, and a willingly complicit judiciary has called into question the effectiveness of these constitutional limitations. As will be shown, the term "public use" has been transformed into a mere aphorism that has little to do with the "public" and sometimes not even much to do with "use." All the while, government condemners have striven mightily to put the prefix "un" in front of "just compensation."[37]

* * *

The stories are legion of eminent domain being used to destroy working-class neighborhoods to make way for all manner of dubious projects. In addition to Aurora Vargas from Chavez Ravine and Suzette Kelo from New London, other stories include the following:

- To stop the condemnation of private homes for a Hollywood museum, one landowner tried "to prove that the Hollywood Museum [was] merely a front of some kind under the guise of eminent domain and under the guise of a public body to put up a private enterprise . . ." The proof was not allowed. Although the land was condemned and the owner removed by alleged trickery, the museum was never built.[38]
- The Poletown community in Detroit was taken and razed for a General Motors automobile plant that never yielded the promised number of jobs and was eventually shuttered.[39]

Figure 23. Poletown before condemnation.

Figure 24. One hospital, 6 churches, 140 businesses, and 1,300 homes for 4,200 people in Poletown being razed as a gift to General Motors so it could build a plant that it eventually closed and abandoned.

- Vera Coking fought the condemnation of her home by then-real estate mogul, Donald Trump, so it could be razed for a casino limousine parking area. According to the future president, his casino guests were "staring at a terrible house instead of beautiful fountains . . . that would be good." It was only because the Institute for Justice heard her story and gave her free legal assistance that she staved off the condemnation and remained in her home for the remainder of her life, in the shadow of the casino.[40] After Vera Coking's death, mega-investor Carl Icahn, who had acquired the casino and the Coking property, tore down the home on November 14, 2014. Ironically, by that time, the casino had fallen on hard times and had been shuttered two months earlier. In a spectacularly appropriate show of smoke and noise, the Trump Plaza was imploded on February 17, 2021.[41] Vera Coking was very lucky. Most homeowners don't have the good fortune of finding free legal representation to fight off the bulldozers.

Figure 25. Thanks to litigation brought by the Institute for Justice, Vera Coking spent the remainder of her life in her home, despite the wishes of Atlantic City and a famous developer who would become president and complained that his guests had to look at "a terrible house instead of beautiful fountains . . . that would be good."

Figure 26. Trump Plaza implosion. Where is the public use?

Sometimes after the neighborhoods are destroyed, the projects fail or never even get built in the first place.[42] These condemnations lead to a vexing question: where is the public use in privately owned factories, stadiums, and museums, especially those that never get built?

Chapter 10

The Transformation of "Public Use" into "Politically Useful"

The *Kelo* decision was not the Supreme Court's first evasion of the "public use" limitation on the power to condemn private property. That happened many years prior.[1] But it was the most visible manifestation of the Court's chicanery and the one that managed to capture the public's attention when the press discovered the plight of elderly widows and pensioners who were being thrown out of their homes for some vaguely defined benefit of a multinational pharmaceutical conglomerate.

The public was justifiably outraged at a practice that many of us in the business of defending landowners have known about for a long time. As Professor Somin noted, "Polls showed that over 80 percent of the public disapproved of the Court's ruling, and it was also denounced by politicians, activists, and pundits from across the political spectrum."[2] There were a few exceptions to the outcry, such as Representative Pelosi, who said of the opinion that it "is almost as if God has spoken."[3] But overall, the public learned that crony capitalism was alive and well in city halls, county offices, and state bureaucracies across the land.[4]

It didn't begin this way. In the early years of the republic, the notion of a forced-government transfer of land from one private owner to another private owner was unthinkable and something of an anathema. Probably the earliest American case dealing with private takings is *Giddings v. Brown*, a Massachusetts decision from 1657 in which the Colony's Supreme Court held that "the right of property is . . . a fundamental right. In this case the goods of one man were given to another without the former's consent. This resolve of the town being against the fundamental law is therefore void, and the taking was not justifiable."[5]

In the late eighteenth century, when the United States Supreme Court was new, it heavily criticized the suggestion that property could be taken from one private individual for the benefit of another in two cases: *VanHorne's Lessee v. Dorrance*[6] in 1795 and *Calder v. Bull* three years later.[7] Particularly memorable was Justice Samuel Chase's admonition in *Calder*:

> A law that takes property from A. and gives it to B: It is against all reason and justice, for a people to entrust a Legislature with SUCH powers . . . . To maintain that our Federal, or State, Legislature possesses such powers, if they had not been expressly restrained; would, in my opinion, be a political heresy, altogether inadmissible in our free republican governments.[8]

A few decades later, the well-respected Justice Joseph Story wrote for the Supreme Court in *Wilkinson v. Leland*:[9]

> That government can scarcely be deemed to be free where the rights of property are left solely dependent upon the will of a legislative body without any restraint. . . . We know of no case in which a legislative act to transfer the property of A to B without his consent has ever been held a constitutional exercise of legislative power in any State of the Union. On the contrary, it has been consistently resisted as inconsistent with just principles by every judicial tribunal in which it has been attempted to be enforced.[10]

These early cases involved *uncompensated* takings,[11] a fact that has led some to question whether the "A-to-B" prohibitions in these cases should apply to *compensated* takings. But the principle against A-to-B transfers was extended to a compensated transfer in the 1848 case of *West River Bridge v. Dix.*[12] In *Dix*, a private bridge was condemned for free public use. Concurring, Justice McLean wrote, "It is argued, that, if the State may take this bridge, it may transfer it to other individuals, under the same or a different charter. This the State cannot do. It would in effect be taking the property from A to convey it to B. The public purpose for which the power is exerted *must be real, not pretended.*"[13]

But what is real and what is pretend when it comes to public use never proved to be an effective standard. As the needs of industrialization came to the fore, this ethic of keeping it real began to crumble. First came the new industrial mills that required dams on private property for waterpower. Even if the mills were privately owned, some courts saw a public use in them. And then came the railroads that were to stitch the nation together on steel rails. For these purposes, the mills and railroads needed land, and not just any land, but land in very particular places. Mills had to be in favorable spots next to rivers. And railroads had to get from point *A* to point *B*, preferably in a straight line with a minimum of twists and turns.

While some mills and railroads made deals and bought land from willing sellers, others were either less patient or less willing to negotiate a fair price with the landowner. To be fair, some holdout landowners asked for more than fair market value. And, if they were in a particularly strategic place, they could ask for a lot more money. Local and state governments—which were often controlled by the railroads or other land-hungry industrial concerns—were willing to accommodate those industrialists who wanted other people's land without the bother and risk of the free market. In this era, the prohibition of private A-to-B transfers began to erode. The meaning of public use became more elastic.

One justification for allowing railroads to benefit from the power of condemnation was that the lines would be open for *use* by all members of the *public* who could pay the freight. Thus, for example, in *Hairston v. Danville & W. R. Co.*,[14] the Court held: "The uses for which the track was desired are not the less public because the motive which dictated its location over this particular land was to reach a private industry, or because the proprietors of that industry contributed in any way to the cost."[15]

Some states and state courts were more receptive to these private takings by railroads and mills than others. But the trend was toward a more fluid interpretation of the Public Use Clause in order to facilitate industrial development.[16]

The coup de grâce for the Public Use Clause as a meaningful check on the government's power to effect A-to-B transfers came in the 1954 decision of *Berman v. Parker*.[17] That case involved an effort at so-called slum clearance in Washington, DC. The plan was to remove the dilapidated tenements and crumbling infrastructure and replace them with a planner's vision of utopia—shiny new office buildings, public squares, and perhaps some new housing for the poor. Well, actually, perhaps not for the last of those three.

To accomplish this nirvana on earth, entire city blocks had to be acquired, razed, and rebuilt into a new shining city on the hill by private developers. But the owner of a department store objected. He claimed that his building was perfectly fine; it was not a tenement and not a slum. In fact, while there were some dilapidated buildings, much of the condemned neighborhood was a perfectly nice working-class *integrated* neighborhood of twenty-three thousand people. As one scholar recounted:

> The two cases [that became *Berman v. Parker*] were brought by Max Morris, the owner of a department store, and Goldie Schneider, who owned a hardware store down the street. Both stores were located on 4th Street, which was then a lively commercial area with various shops and stores, and neither of the buildings was considered to be substandard or deteriorating. Fourth Street at the time was a hub of black and Jewish life, and one of the few areas in the city, then segregated, that displayed a measure of racial harmony. It was the site of the city's first integrated parade, and the mostly Jewish stores on 4th Street relied on business from black residents.[18]

Figure 27. Block targeted for redevelopment in *Berman v. Parker.*[19]

How could the city take these properties and turn them over to a private developer and call that public use? The case eventually made its way to the Supreme Court.

That was where the Supreme Court manifested its peculiar brand of genius. In a decision written by the very progressive and very liberal Justice William O. Douglas, the Court held that public use really meant the public purpose.[20] In other words, the public did not have to actually use the taken property in any literal sense, so long as the public's "purpose" was served by the project. And what could have been more in the public interest than slum clearance?

But this was not the only left turn taken by the Court. The Court essentially said that the government's eminent domain power was coterminous with police power, which is the power to regulate. In other words, whatever the government could regulate, it could take. This was an important conflation of power because it also meant that the courts should not second-guess decisions to condemn any more than they should second-guess the details of day-to-day regulations. By 1954, in the post-New Deal era, it had already been well established that the courts would defer to government decisions pertaining to regulations of economic affairs.[21] This standard of deference meant that a court would overturn an economic regulation in only the most extraordinary of circumstances. And so it was in *Berman*, where Justice Douglas put forward an aphorism that was breathtaking both in its degree of condescension and its surrender to government power:

> We do not sit to determine whether a particular housing project is or is not desirable. The concept of the public welfare is broad and inclusive . . . . The values it represents are spiritual as well as physical, aesthetic as well as monetary. It is within the power of the legislature to determine that the community should be beautiful as well as healthy, spacious as well as clean, well-balanced as well as carefully patrolled. In the present case, the Congress and its authorized agencies have made determinations that take into account a wide variety of values. It is not for us to reappraise them. *If those who govern the District of Columbia decide that the Nation's Capital should be beautiful as well as sanitary, there is nothing in the Fifth Amendment that stands in the way.*[22]

All that was missing was a reference to wide yards and few people. And to remove any doubt about the degree to which the Court was determined to remove the judicial branch from any meaningful oversight of the Public Use Clause, the Court established a standard of review of extreme deference:

> Subject to specific constitutional limitations, when the legislature has spoken, the public interest has been declared in terms well-nigh conclusive. In such cases the legislature, not the judiciary, is the main guardian of the public needs to be served by social legislation, whether it be Congress legislating concerning the District of Columbia . . . or the States legislating concerning local affairs. . . . This principle admits of no exception merely because the power of eminent domain is involved. The role of the judiciary in determining whether that power is being exercised for a public purpose is an extremely narrow one.[23]

With *Berman*, it was all over, except for the details.

The next time the Court focused on the Public Use Clause was in *Hawaii Housing Authority v. Midkiff.*[24] At a time when land reform was all the rage in Latin America and supported there by the United States,[25] the State of Hawaii had its own version of land reform. Rather than helping any landless peasants in Hawaii, this land reform was aimed at helping middle-class homeowners who were leasing the land under their homes from the Hawaiian land trusts.

In Hawaii, much of the land is owned by the Native Hawaiian land trusts whose purpose was to benefit Native Hawaiians. Private homeowners often do not own the land under their homes but lease it from the trusts. Under Hawaii's Land Reform Act of 1967, homeowners were given the right to take the ground under their homes from the land trusts. In fact, as Professor Kanner explains, "The property owner in this case, the Bishop Estate-Kamehameha Schools was a charitable trust (holding the lands of Bernice Pauahi Bishop, the last member of Hawaiian royalty) operating for the benefit of native Hawaiian children educated by the Kamehameha schools."[26] In other words, this was really a sort of anti-public use, taking land from a charitable trust without votes and giving it to the not-so-deserving homeowners with votes. Following the precedent of constitutional minimalism set down in *Berman*, the Court refused to find this private-to-private land transfer unlawful. Instead, in *Hawaii Housing Authority v. Midkiff*, the Court said that so long as there was a public purpose behind the scheme, it would not interfere.

The Court knew its decision would be controversial. Indeed, while he was visiting Hawaii on other matters, Justice Blackmun asked Justice O'Connor to withhold issuing the decision until he was safely out of the state, saying, "I run into enough flak as it is these days, and I think it would be better if I were out of the State by the time the decision comes down."[27]

What the Court did not know was what a failure the scheme would be. At first, the state thought it could get away with paying less for the land leases than they were worth by ignoring the full value of the land. This would have meant that there was a public use in robbing

Peter to pay Paul. A lower court put a stop to that, saying that the land trusts must be paid fully. And then, after paying off the trusts, the state offered the land to the homeowners—but many of them could barely afford it. What happened next was truly bizarre.

A wealthy Japanese investor, later dubbed Honolulu's "worst neighbor," went from house to house from the back of his limousine, with his agents going to the homes and offering cash—whether or not the home was for sale. Many owners sold and moved elsewhere in Oahu, pushing up the prices of other Honolulu homes. This in turn created an inflationary spiral, and land prices doubled in the five years after the Supreme Court decided *Midkiff*.[28] When the power of eminent domain is abused, there can be some very unintended consequences.

And then there was *Kelo*.[29] The condemned in *Kelo* were not the mere ethnic Jewish shop owners of *Berman*. The Kelo homeowners didn't own department stores. They weren't giant Hawaiian land trusts. They were simply middle-class homeowners who lived in ordinary little homes in a very ordinary (and unblighted) neighborhood.[30] But, alas for them, they didn't happen to own a multinational pharmaceutical concern that could dangle politically advantageous dreams of economic revitalization before the politicians of New London, Connecticut.[31] New London was undoubtedly a tired little city that had seen better days. Its unpretentious circumstances clearly didn't match the ambitions of those in charge. It was difficult for the city to resist Pfizer's beguiling promises. After all, all that stood between New London becoming a city headquarters for a major international player and its economically distressed status quo was a neighborhood of some expendable middle-class residents.

The decision in *Kelo* was not any sort of radical change in the doctrine that had evolved from *Van Horne's Lessee* and *Calder* to *Berman* and *Midkiff*. What set *Kelo* apart was that it could no longer be denied that the Public Use Clause was worth less than the parchment on which it was written. The pretense was gone. The public was outraged because it was not as familiar as lawyers were with the manner in which the courts can build one small doctrine-eviscerating precedent on top of another to ultimately transform the meaning of one thing to something completely different.[32] And so, with *Kelo* the veil was lifted, and everyone knew that "public use" meant "public interest," which meant whatever damn-fool thing the politicians thought was a good idea to do with other people's homes and lives at an opportune moment.

Chapter 11

The Public Use in Removing the Poor from Cities

It didn't take long before the idealistic notions of *Berman*, that eminent domain could be used to make cities "sanitary" and "spiritual," led to a perverse understanding that the best way to beautify a city was to remove that which was ugly. And not to put too fine a point on it, but what was ugly was not White and upper middle class. By the time of *Kelo*, the criticisms of eminent domain were becoming widespread.[1] It finally began to dawn on people that urban redevelopment had turned from a salutary mechanism for societal improvement to something more sinister. In her *Kelo* dissent, Justice O'Connor, the author of *Midkiff*, noted that if eminent domain could be used for mere economic development, then the weak and politically powerless would become victims of progress, not its beneficiaries.[2] Justice Thomas likewise noted that the poor were unable to "put their lands to the highest and best social use [and] are the least politically powerful."[3]

As a recent report from the National Academies of Science puts it:

Unfortunately, the urban renewal programs it authorized often destroyed more housing than was created. . . . Its use of public housing to serve the displaced households, who were generally minorities, and creation of a

Federal Housing Administration (FHA) mortgage program to finance
suburban housing available only to whites helped to entrench poverty and
segregation in America's cities, particularly for people of color.[4]

Indeed, poor and minority communities had borne the brunt of redevelopment pain before and since *Berman.*[5] In the late nineteenth and
early twentieth centuries, the poor were removed from New York City
tenements by the tens of thousands, with the notion that they would
"self-relocate." As Joel Schwartz puts it, "Among reformers it also was
axiomatic that the toiling classes had no special claim to the inner city,
but belonged somewhere else and would self-relocate."[6]

In fact, Justice Thomas noted that of the families displaced by
the urban renewal rush blessed by *Berman* between 1949 and 1963, 63
percent were racial minorities.[7] Commentators have noted the same.
Wendell Pritchett wrote that "blight was a facially neutral term infused
with racial and ethnic prejudice."[8] Sometimes even in the absence of
an intent to remove minorities, it is the inevitable result of supposedly
race-neutral redevelopment because today's redevelopment cannot be
divorced from the policies that led to urban concentrations of minorities in the first place. As Leland Saito wrote:

> Economic redevelopment and the demolition of a building or neighbor-
> hood take place within a history of explicit racial inequality. This inequal-
> ity manifested itself as racial exclusion, which created concentrations of
> racial minorities in residential and commercial areas. . . . urban renewal
> efforts that disproportionately destroyed minority communities, policies
> of racial steering by real estate agents that support racial segregation, and
> historic preservation policies that ignore the social history of minorities. . . .
> As a result, race-neutral policies are only one part of a long chain of events
> that contribute to racialized consequences.[9]

Indeed, urban renewal had become pejoratively known as "Negro
removal."[10] African American author and social critic James Baldwin
criticized urban renewal as nothing more than "move the Negroes

out."[11] It was a time when there was a massive urban renewal project in the African American Hunter's Point neighborhood in San Francisco. As Baldwin recounted on public television:

> A boy last week, he was 16, in San Francisco, told me, on television, thank God we got him to talk . . . to listen, he said, "I got no country, I got no flag." He was only 16 years old. And I couldn't say, "You do." I don't have any evidence to prove that he does. They were tearing down his house, because San Francisco is engaging—as most Northern cities now are engaged—in something called urban renewal, which means moving the Negroes out. It means Negro removal, that is what it means.
>
> And the federal government is . . . an accomplice to this fact . . . Now this . . . We're talking about human beings, there's not such a thing as a monolithic wall or some abstraction called the "Negro problem." These are Negro boys and girls who at 16 or 17 don't believe the country means anything it says . . . [or that] people have any place here.[12]

Thus, whether or not urban redevelopment was a "public use," it certainly had the effect of transferring what little wealth some minority communities had to more politically favored interests. With eminent domain, the progressive dream of improvement had been exposed as a concrete example of systemic racism.

At least with *Berman*, there was the pretense that those removed from the redeveloped neighborhood would be able to move back into new public housing. That, at least, could have been relevant to the Court and planners, who figured that only 1,345 families would be displaced to make way for the DC mall redevelopment project, that there was other adequate housing in the city, and that five hundred new units would be built nearby.[13] Lavine noted that of the four thousand residents in one particular area, 97 percent were Black, and no more than thirty-six hundred were supposed to be housed in the new development.[14] As Professor Kanner recounted,

Unfortunately, for the residents, the low-income housing did not material-
ize. The housing actually built there, instead of bettering the lot of the slum
dwellers whose plight figured so prominently in Justice Douglas's opinion
as justification for the taking, turned out to be aesthetically sterile and so
pricey that by 1969 it inspired a rent strike by affluent tenants.[15]

The original residents were instead forced to move into "worse slums
elsewhere in the District of Columbia that commanded higher rents."[16]
Of the fifty-nine hundred new residences built in the area, all of 310
were "affordable."[17] Nor did subsequent redevelopments in a host of
cities do anything positive for the residents who were thrown out of
their homes.[18]

Chapter 12

Tax Increment Financing and the Perversion of Incentives

Even assuming that the original motivations of urban planners were benevolent, this state of affairs didn't last. Why not? The planners of the early to mid-twentieth century had an organic view of social improvement. If the "blight" could be removed from a city, that city would prosper, just like a plant could be restored to health if the dead, dying, and infected leaves were removed. The problem is that these planners, coming from the upper echelons of society, didn't fully grasp that when they saw threatening blight, others saw functioning neighborhoods with often vibrant communities.[1] As Professor Pritchett explained,

> Several studies have shown how urban elites promoted redevelopment to reorganize urban areas and to protect and enhance their real estate investments. These scholars have studied the rise of "growth coalitions"—groups of business and political leaders that promoted renewal—and they have examined the political debates over post-war housing policy. Other works have documented the impact of urban renewal in intensifying racial segregation and limiting the mobility of African Americans.[2]

Those "blighted" communities may very well have been poor, and dark, and burdened with unfamiliar tongues and strange cultural traditions. But that didn't make them the equivalent of an agricultural blight that must be excised from the community like fungus-infested trees near an apple orchard.[3]

It takes more than a profound ignorance of the value of poorer communities to explain the headlong conversion of urban redevelopment from being a tool for community improvement into an instrument of neighborhood destruction. It took something called "tax increment financing." With tax increment financing, redevelopment agencies get to keep any increases in tax revenues for themselves. Thus, if a neighborhood is improved so it generates more taxes, the agency gets to keep the increase—not the city, not the schools, and not the people who have been displaced.

Let's say a working-class neighborhood generates $200,000 in property taxes in a typical year. The local redevelopment agency draws up some plans and has four alternatives:

1. It could maintain the status quo generating $200,000 in annual property taxes, yielding no increase in its budget.
2. It could build brand new affordable housing that might generate $300,000 in taxes, yielding a $100,000 larger budget.
3. It could build high-end luxury apartments that will generate $750,000 in taxes, giving it a $550,000 budget increase.
4. It could build an office and retail complex that might bring in a cool million dollars in taxes a year, yielding an $800,000 windfall.

Which will it choose? More often than not, the answer is obvious. Redevelopment agencies do not improve their own bottom line by spending money on the poor or keeping their neighborhoods filled with poor people. Put bluntly, if the poor can be replaced with tax-paying businesses and upper-income residents, a redevelopment district's books will look a whole lot better. And no self-respecting, empire-building bureaucracy will prosper if saddled by slums. This isn't higher mathematics; it's basic arithmetic.

With the incentive of increasing the tax base, it was inevitable that the redevelopment districts would give birth to the redevelopment industry—builders and developers that specialize in acquiring "underutilized" property on the cheap. Through eminent domain, a neighborhood filled with poor people can be condemned and then turned over to the redeveloper for far less than it would cost on the open market. Then, the condemned homes, stores, and apartments can be converted into higher tax-generating businesses.

Since it's not easy to alleviate the suffering of the poor, why even suffer the poor if you can have office complexes, high-end housing, shopping malls, and automobile factories? And if you throw into the mix the usefulness of routing highways through inner city slums at the behest of the highway-building lobby, it only makes sense that poor, urban neighborhoods are targeted for saving through destruction.

For private developers not subsidized by the mechanics of redevelopment, it might not make a lot of sense to build a shopping center or office complex in a former slum based on "build it and they will come" optimism or assurances of "build it and they will subsidize."[4] Private unsubsidized developers generally don't like to lose money.[5] Moreover, no sane redeveloper actually *guarantees* the success of a project developed with other people's money.

The redevelopment industry is often more sophisticated than the agencies they use for their projects. Redevelopment agency staff often cannot recognize a white elephant until it tramples them. The pretty drawings and scale renderings can be all that it takes to launch a redevelopment project. Reality can wait.

As a result, the landscapes of American cities are littered by failed redevelopment projects, defunct shopping centers, empty office buildings, and rusting hulks where factories once loomed.[6] No landscape is more littered by failure than the very heart of the New London experiment: Today, Pfizer has abandoned New London, and where the homes once stood is not a field of dreams, but a field of weeds inhabited by feral cats.[7] The redevelopers make their money, the poor are gone, and the cities are left with less than they had before.

To be fair, even without the redevelopment agencies, poor neighborhoods are often attractive targets for infrastructure projects simply because the land is cheap, and the projects can be accomplished before the displaced residents figure out how to mount a challenge—or even pay for the challenge. After all, why even try to build a highway through a collection of stately upper-class homes when the same highway can plow through a slum, giving rise to a project that both clears a slum and builds a highway, a power plant, or a dump?[8] And, as Richard Rothstein pointed out, even aside from eminent domain, land-use planning

> attempted to protect white neighborhoods from deterioration by ensuring that few industrial or environmentally unsafe businesses could locate in them. Prohibited in this fashion, polluting industry had no option but to locate near African American residences. The first contributed to creation of exclusive white suburbs, the second to creation of urban African American slums.[9]

But even if the Public Use Clause has been stretched, even if condemnation serves an uglier side of America's intolerance of the poor and minority populations, and even if there are perverse economic incentives to displace the poor from their neighborhoods, then at least there is the requirement to pay just compensation to make everybody whole again.

But being made whole is in the eyes of the beholder.

Chapter 13

The Unjust Compensation Gambit

Exactly what is just compensation? We can be pretty sure we know what compensation is. But what is "just"? Compensation is a real and pressing concern for a legion of condemned across the land. No government wants to pay more for property than it is worth, nor should it. But more than a few seem happy to save taxpayer money and pay less for property than it is worth.[1]

The Supreme Court put compensation in terms of fair market value, and what a willing buyer would pay to a willing seller.[2] But these aphorisms give rise to more questions. What is fair? What exactly does willing mean? And why should justice always be defined by the market?[3]

To many owners, their homes have great intrinsic value that cannot be captured by comparative sales of similar properties. How do you measure the value of the kitchen wall on which you measured your kids' growing height year after year? How does an elderly widow measure the worth of the bedroom where she said goodbye to her husband? How does a government check make up for the forced diaspora of a community of longtime friends and neighbors? Emotional attachment, intrinsic value, and other purely subjective measures of worth cannot be divorced from justice.

Philosophers have tried to define the meaning of justice for centuries. St. Thomas Aquinas, for example, wrote that "the act of justice in relation to its proper matter and object is indicated in the words, 'Rendering to each one his right,' since . . . 'a man is said to be just because he respects the rights [jus] of others.'[4] Is the taking of the home of one person for the benefit of a corporation or a town's tax collectors in accord with respecting the rights of others?

As James Madison put it in Federalist No. 51, "Justice is the end of government. It is the end of civil society. It ever has been and ever will be pursued until it be obtained, or until liberty be lost in the pursuit."

At minimum, government should exercise the despotic power of eminent domain sparingly if for no other reason than to avoid the sort of nonmonetary hardships that are inherent in involuntary condemnations. It may be too much to ask government to put a value on one's emotional attachments to a home, but at least it should avoid unnecessary takes and the sort of under-compensation games that will be described.

While it may not be realistic that all manifestations of emotional attachment can be given value, the failure to make any attempt can be dispiriting when property is condemned, especially when it is condemned solely for the purpose of making someone else rich. At oral argument in *Kelo*, Justice Scalia put it this way:

> What this lady wants is not more money. No amount of money is going to satisfy her. She is living in this house, you know, her whole life and she does not want to move. She said I'll move if it's being taken for a public use, but by God, you're just giving it to some other private individual because that individual is going to pay more taxes. I—it seems to me that's, that's an objection in principle, and an objection in principle that the public use requirement of the Constitution seems to be addressed to.[5]

Mrs. Kelo and her neighbors did not want to trade their homes for cash. Period. Their subjective needs were not being met, and they instinctively did not think the process or outcome was fair.

Professor Gideon Kanner argued that because appraisers are instructed by courts to look only at "fair *market* value," real intrinsic value is ignored, and landowners are undercompensated.[6] Kanner continued that judicial focus on comparable sales-based fair market values "inherently omits from consideration a variety of economic losses suffered by persons evicted from their homes and businesses. These include moving expenses, the cost of finding and renovating substitute premises, the loss of favorable mortgage financing, the loss of rents . . . the owners' . . . expectations of gain, ... the cost of litigation . . . [and] business losses."[7] As Professor Thomas W. Merrill, put it, "The most striking feature of American compensation law—even in the context of formal condemnations or expropriations—is that just compensation means incomplete compensation."[8] Likewise, Professor Klein wrote, "Despite its origin in principles of natural justice, despite the declared object of making the victim whole, despite the generally broad understanding of the term 'just compensation' itself—it is clear that only a bare minimum of the effects of a taking become the subject matter of financial awards."[9] Moreover, he continues, with eminent domain "American courts do not give redress to one seeking recovery for grief, pain and suffering, mental anguish, loss of comfort, any other . . . emotional and psychological injuries."[10]

While there are statutes like the federal Uniform Relocation Assistance Act that provide a mechanism for the compensation of some of these costs, the Act, in Professor Kanner's words, "can be a 'toothless tiger.'" Because the limits on awards are "grossly inadequate to acquire even a modest replacement business, or even to renovate new premises,"[11] "decision law has it that a condemnor may simply seize private property and say to its owner, 'sue me.'"[12]

Moreover, even if fair market value is paid for each individual home, that payment does not capture the added value created when the lots are combined for a large-scale project. For example, if ten homes on a block are worth $100,000 each, then the entire block is worth $1 million. But if the homes are razed for an office building or industrial park, the land itself might be worth much more, say $2 million.[13] Yet, when such a neighborhood is condemned, the individual homeowners are paid at most only $100,000. All the "profit" from consolidation is captured by the town or its redeveloper cronies.[14] The Supreme Court has accepted this state of affairs when it has held that compensation is measured by what the owner has lost, not what the taker has gained.[15]

This breaks the social contract. When landowners are paid fairly for their homes before they are taken for an obvious community benefit and public use, such as a school or road, the former homeowners may grumble, but the social contract is intact. But when the taking is mostly for the private benefit of politically connected private redevelopers, the contract has been torn to shreds.

This is not the worst of it. Government condemnors are notorious for paying as little as they can get away with. This is not even fair market value, it is the "how-little-can-we-get-away with" value. Government condemnors exploit the fact that most small landowners lack the wherewithal to fight back. Indeed, Professor Gideon Kanner published a "lowball watch" for decades.[16] He cataloged numerous examples in which condemning agencies have offered to landowners only a fraction of what those landowners were able to acquire after trial. But most small landowners cannot afford a trial. After all, only a few states will reimburse landowners for their attorneys' fees, and even then, only if the landowner prevails by obtaining a significant increase over the government's offer. Sadly, it is common practice in some jurisdictions for condemning authorities to make one lowball offer, then threaten to withdraw that offer and replace it with a lower one if the landowners resist.[17] Such gamesmanship should have no place in the halls of government. But it prevails at all levels of government.

At one time, the scrubland between Miami and the Everglades was largely occupied by hundreds of rural landowners who had small farms, orchards, and some livestock. Their land was coveted by conservationists who wanted to expand the boundaries of the Everglades National Park. While a national park expansion fits within the definition of public use, the National Park Service and the Department of Justice employed a multipronged approach to underpay.[18]

First, the Park Service visited the local towns where they hoped to acquire land for the future park expansion and persuaded the towns to downzone the land in order to make it less valuable. Then, when it came time to condemn, the Park Service argued that the property was not worth very much because it had been downzoned by the towns.

Next, rather than taking the properties one at a time, the Park Service grouped various landowners together so they could all be condemned in a combined proceeding before a commissioner—who is essentially a federal bureaucrat who oversees government taking of property. Unlike condemnations by state and local authorities, there is no right to a jury trial when the federal government condemns land.[19] Most of the rural landowners couldn't afford a lawyer and didn't even understand how important it was to have one. In fact, if any landowner hired an attorney, the federal government would pull that landowner out of the case. Most of the landowners were not sophisticated enough to know how to object to faulty appraisals, properly raise legal objections (such as to the downzoning gambit), or hire independent appraisers. It was rural folks up against very sophisticated government attorneys. The rural folks were uniformly underpaid.

But the real kicker came next. After the federal government got through with the landowners who hadn't hired attorneys, it then went after those landowners who had. But by this time there was a history of lowball prices paid for the properties belonging to the folks without lawyers. And the government then used those lowball values to establish "fair market value." The landowners with lawyers weren't even able to object to those lowball figures. Their own appraisers and evidence were deemed mostly irrelevant, and value was based on what had been paid to those who had been previously screwed.

Seeking full value for taken property can be difficult and expensive, even if the deck isn't already stacked. Landowners must hire attorneys who must hire appraisers and experts to make their case. This is often beyond the means and sophistication of working-class homeowners in urban neighborhoods or rural farmers in the hinterland. What makes the Florida case unusual is that not only were the landowners who were unable to retain attorneys undercompensated, but so too were those who were savvy or well-off enough to hire lawyers.

In other circumstances, landowners are often drastically under-compensated when an ongoing and successful business is taken. Many states simply refuse to compensate for the value of the ongoing business.[20] For example, if a baker owns a successful bakery with lots of local loyal customers, that customer base can be of great value—known in the trade as "business goodwill." If the baker retires and sells to another baker, the buyer is getting more than a storefront and some ovens—the buyer is getting a neighborhood of loyal customers. There's value in those customers, and the new baker will pay much more for a successful bakery than for just an empty store and some ovens without customers. But in many jurisdictions, the business owner is paid only what the land and building are worth. The business goodwill is ignored.[21] This can be devastating for the small business owner unable to find or utilize available property in the same neighborhood.

In one particularly egregious recent example, a successful soil excavation business was condemned in order to improve the levee system. That may well be a legitimate public use, but the landowner was compensated only for the raw value of the land, not for its business value.[22] Even more galling, the landowner was charged by the levee district for the dirt that he had excavated before the condemnation but not removed until after. In other words, the district took the property so it could become the sole beneficiary of the business—without paying the business what it was worth.

As Professor Kanner concluded, "The reverse Robin Hood process of displacing indigenous (usually lower middle-class or poor) populations in redevelopment project areas under conditions of under-compensation, in order to enrich private redevelopers, or for that matter, to enrich the community, does not withstand moral or economic scrutiny."[23] This state of affairs is a long way from any recognizable measure of justice. After all, if property is a fundamental right, and a man's home is his castle, the forced loss of ownership cannot be cured by shoving an inadequate fistful of dollars into the homeowner's hands so the castle can be demolished for a Walmart, Costco, or Pfizer headquarters.

Chapter 14

Reform of Eminent Domain at the State Level and What Must Be Done

T he reaction to *Kelo* was swift. Many states enacted reforms that attempted to limit the power of redevelopment. Some states actually adopted meaningful reforms.[1] Florida, for example, banned all economic redevelopment takings of private property without a three-fifths vote of each house.[2] California, however, had a series of failures from ill-conceived reforms. An early attempt at reform was a ballot initiative brought by an individual who was unfamiliar with California law and that was written, for all practical purposes, for the State of Nevada. Another effort tried to package eminent domain reform with a ban on rent control.[3] Finally, by the time the reform advocates got their act together, the redevelopment industry had mustered its own countermeasure, a "reform" that contained a few cosmetic but meaningless protections for homeowners while at the same time enhancing the power of redevelopment agencies.[4] But then, in something of an "only-in-California" move, Governor Jerry Brown proceeded to abolish redevelopment agencies in order to grab the tax increment financing money to help solve one of the state's periodic fiscal crises.[5] But rest assured, the power is being restored, one measure at a time.[6]

State supreme courts have done better. Even before *Kelo*, the Supreme Court of Michigan reversed *Poletown*, a case where the same court previously upheld the condemnation of a working-class neighborhood to make way for a General Motors factory that would eventually fail:

> To justify the exercise of eminent domain solely on the basis of the fact that the use of that property by a private entity seeking its own profit might contribute to the economy's health is to render impotent our constitutional limitations on the government's power of eminent domain. Poletown's [economic development] rationale would validate practically any exercise of the power of eminent domain on behalf of a private entity. After all, if one's ownership of private property is forever subject to the government's determination that another private party would put one's land to better use, then the ownership of real property is perpetually threatened by the expansion plans of any large discount retailer, "megastore," or the like.[7]

And after *Kelo*, there was a spate of state court decisions taking reform seriously.[8] But, so long as the Supreme Court of the United States fails to reverse *Kelo*, the temptation of states to backslide will be strong.

The constitutional limitations on the government's power of eminent domain, when adhered to, redound to the benefit of all classes of Americans. The framers of the Constitution were deeply moved by the intellectual tension between John Locke and Thomas Hobbes. Locke believed that the proper role of government is to protect the inherent property and rights of the people; Hobbes thought the role of government was to control the people, doling out rights when necessary. The framers took the Lockean view that the best way to preserve liberty is to restrain government power rather than limiting the inherent rights of the people.

As both Locke and Hobbes understood, a society without government would lead to the powerful taking advantage of the powerless.[9] Government serves to mediate the Hobbesian "war of every man against every man"[10] by controlling the instincts and abilities of some to take advantage of others. Remove that government mediation, and the result is war on the powerless. Make government an ally of some people in their war against other people, and the oppression becomes palpable. Nowhere is this more evident than when the constitutional limits on eminent domain are lifted.

The American experience has been that when the power of eminent domain is unchained, it will attack the most vulnerable: the poor, the working class, and minorities. The advantage will go to those who are rich, powerful, politically connected, and white.

The ability to use the political process for self-advantage lies with those with the strongest economic incentive to drive the politics. Redevelopment agencies and aligned developers have much to gain from private takings of the politically less organized. It is but one more classic example of rent seeking, where laws can be crafted to favor those with a definable and large economic advantage in a political outcome (such as redevelopers) at the expense of those small, unorganized individuals with small, individual stakes, such as working-class homeowners.[11]

As a result, we have witnessed the transmogrification of the late "Public Use Clause" into the "Politically Useful Clause." With their embrace of "judicial deference," the courts have abdicated their authority to judge the fairness and constitutionality of corrupt condemnations. What we have here is not only a failure to compensate fully but also the destruction of the social contract. The constitutional limits on the taking of private property for private gain have been eviscerated, and it has not been the rich who have suffered. Post-*Kelo* reform has given hope to some. But unless and until the underlying causes of eminent domain abuse are rooted out, any respite may be but a temporary pause.

PART III

Using the Environment to Destroy Property Rights and Housing Opportunities

Government action clothed in moral imperative is a most dangerous force. Zoning was first justified as a tool to maintain our quality of life—by keeping immigrants and racial minorities away from nice neighborhoods. Later and today it simply keeps the less affluent from straining local government infrastructure and resources. Eminent domain in the employ of the beneficent forces of urban renewal has more often been used to destroy working-class and minority neighborhoods with the blunt force of bulldozers than it was ever used to improve them.

The 1960s brought with them a new moral imperative: saving the environment from a manmade apocalypse. Now, we're no longer focused on our neighborhoods. Our attention must be on the planet. As with other great moral awakenings, to achieve our goals the rights of individuals must yield to the greater good. Indeed, in some formulations that take on a quasi-religious orthodoxy rooted in an ethic of neo-Calvinism, mankind itself is at the heart of the problem, and to reach a true environmental salvation we might be better off without our species. That, of course, could be the ultimate answer to the housing shortage.

On the eve of the first Earth Day in 1970, the propaganda machine was in full swing. The earth was in decline. Paul Ehrlich told us that the world's population was headed toward a massive famine of apocalyptic dimensions.[1] We learned from Rachel Carson that our air and water were poisoned and the birds were dying.[2] The great animals were on a fast train to extinction, and Noah was absent, his God having recently died.[3] A mock documentary on public television portrayed two greedy capitalist developers in the near (?) future shaking hands as the last square foot of land in America was paved under. It wasn't subtle, but it was effective.

In order to stave off the coming calamities, Congress and the Nixon White House lurched into action. In the space of a few short years, Congress passed the National Environmental Policy Act of 1969,[4] and the Clean Air Act of 1970,[5] turned relatively ineffectual water pollution laws into the powerhouse of the Clean Water Act in 1972,[6] and, in what turned out to be a true wolf in endangered megafauna's clothing, passed the Endangered Species Act (ESA) in 1973.[7]

In addition, in order to combat toxic waste, Congress passed the Toxic Substances Control Act in 1976 (TSCA)[8] and the Resource Conservation and Recovery Act of 1976 (RCRA).[9] A few years later, in response to a perceived toxic waste calamity at Love Canal,[10] Congress passed the Comprehensive Environmental Response, Compensation, and Liability Act (CERCLA or "Superfund") of 1980.[11] There are other federal statutes as well.[12]

These statutes changed everything, and everything was changed in ways that were mostly unanticipated by those in Congress who passed them. If there is one truism about the combined weight of these statutes, it is that they went way beyond Euclidean zoning in their ability to convert the *right* to develop and use property into a *privilege,* where the ultimate decision-making powers were wrested from the owners and given to the public, the bureaucrats, and the courts. The enactment of each one of these statutes, combined with the associated regulations and enforcement actions, has served to reduce the freedom of individual landowners to utilize property as they see fit. And that's only on the federal level. To varying degrees, the states have met or exceeded these regulatory constraints.

With rising environmental consciousness, traditional zoning schemes designed to provide reciprocal economic and aesthetic benefits to existing landowners were replaced by overarching environmental controls. At first, environmental land-use regulations were benign enough, derived from a utilitarian ethic that valued the conservation of nature for the benefit of people and their future generations. For example, a justification for setting aside the national forests in the early twentieth century was to preserve the supply of timber and to protect the watershed. Gradually, however, many environmental regulations were the result of a "deep ecology" ethic that sought to preserve the environment for its own sake. Thus, the Wilderness Act of 1984 exalts land that is in a most non-utilitarian conceit—"untouched by the hand of man." And the ESA became a law less concerned with preserving species for humanity's sake than it is in using those species to stop human economic activities for nature's sake. In some cases, the public's thirst for environmental amenities has given way to expressions of classic NIMBYism and even into cooption by those who harbor the misanthropic dreams of deep ecology.[13]

And yet, despite the profound changes wrought by environmental regulations to the nature of property rights, the question of how much individual freedom has been sacrificed in pursuit of an environmental utopia has seldom been asked. We are living in the fifth decade of robust environmental regulation. It may be time to consider what we have wrought.

Chapter 15

The Endangered Species Act—Humans Need Not Apply

The Endangered Species Act[1] is the most powerful of all environmental laws.[2] In the early 1970s, public angst over the fate of charismatic megafauna such as the bald eagle, trumpeter swan, peregrine falcon, various whales, grizzly bears, and other animals, led to a clamor for federal protection. With the ESA, species received federal protection. But we also got a whole lot more than virtually anyone anticipated. The Act directs the Fish and Wildlife Service to identify species that are endangered or threatened, and then makes it illegal to "take" a member of that species without federal permission. To "take" a species means just about anything, including harassing, harming, pursuing, hunting, shooting, wounding, killing, trapping, capturing, or collecting.[3] And that doesn't mean that one has to actually touch a species to violate the prohibition against a take—destroying a species' habitat by cutting trees or farming in its habitat can be enough, even if the animal doesn't presently occupy those trees or fields.[4] The reach of the Act is not confined to large animals and plants (also known as megafauna.) Instead, the Act covers virtually every plant and animal, including many that Congress never considered in its wildest collective imagination as deserving federal protection. Nor is it likely that Congress appreciated that species would be protected, "whatever the cost."

That "whatever the cost" language came out of the famous (or infamous) 1978 snail darter case, *Tennessee Valley Authority v. Hill.*[5] There, after Congress had appropriated funding for the Tellico Dam, and after the dam was largely built and ready to be operated, environmentalists sued, claiming that the dam threatened one of the last populations of the snail darter—a small, insignificant-looking fish that lived in a few streams in rural Tennessee.

Now, the merits of the dam were controversial in some quarters, with its opponents arguing that it was an indefensible government boondoggle that would cost roughly 78 million pork barrel dollars and achieve very little in terms of flood control or economic benefits to the state. But the project was strongly supported by those who rarely saw a government construction project they didn't like, boondoggle or not.

To the environmental community, the dam was about to destroy a largely pristine rural environment. While they'd tied up the dam in litigation for years, they were about to run out of options. The litigation was drawing to an end, and they didn't have the political muscle to persuade the state's powerful political establishment to stop the project, which was already 80 percent completed.

But then the environmentalists found their salvation in a little fish. They were able to make a fairly persuasive argument that the snail darter would be driven into extinction by the dam. As the Secretary of the Interior admitted, "the proposed impoundment of water behind the proposed Tellico Dam would result in total destruction of the snail darter's habitat."[6] This was, the environmentalists claimed, a violation of the Endangered Species Act.

The public and politicians were taken aback. They had largely assumed that the Act was passed to protect more publicly popular critters like grizzly bears, bald eagles, and trumpeter swans. Not some tiny little fish that nobody knew the first thing about, nobody fished for, and which served no apparent useful purpose.

Such an attitude, however, was antithetical to the environmental ethic in which all creatures, great and small alike, are essential parts of the vast interdependent web of life. The words of the Endangered Species Act made no distinctions: all animals were equal, and no animals were more equal than others—unless they could be used to stop a project.[7]

And stop it they did. At least for a while. When the case reached the Supreme Court, Chief Justice Burger wrote for the majority that the "plain intent of Congress in enacting this statute was to halt and reverse the trend toward species extinction, *whatever the cost.*"[8] People were either shocked or elated by the ruling. Some were elated because the environment had been elevated over all other priorities. Others were shocked for the same reason.

Congress stepped in with a few safety-valve amendments that have proven largely illusory. For example, it allowed for the convening of a special super-committee of agency heads with the power to reverse the listing of a species as endangered. This so-called "God squad" has never delisted a species.[9]

Congress also passed a special exception for the dam, which Jimmy Carter signed in 1979. The dam was completed, the flood gates were closed, and the valley was flooded, taking a population of the snail darter with it. The political imperative was simply too great. Fortunately for the fish, other populations of the snail darter were found elsewhere after the dam was built. But the fish had served its purpose well—while it did not permanently stop the Tellico Dam, the case did pave the way for a multitude of future challenges to all kinds of projects across the land. Highway construction, timber harvesting, fishing operations, farming, home building, and virtually anything else requiring a federal permit were now in the cross hairs of the Endangered Species Act.

The ESA has become a useful tool for those wishing to stop things. As one commentator wrote,

> Groups and individuals who petition to list a species often do not have any
> interest in the species itself, but rather, seek to erect the ESA's substantive

prohibitions to serve the group's or individual's own goals. For example, many special interest environmental groups, for reasons independent of any concern for a specific species, seek to control or eliminate resource development and land use activities. Local decisionmakers do not always share these environmental views, but unfortunately, many federal wildlife officials do. In light of the substantive provisions of the ESA, listing provides a powerful means by which resource and land use decisions can be controlled or eliminated.[10]

Nowhere has this been truer than with the *Strix occidentalis curina*, a.k.a. the northern spotted owl.

For generations, some of the best-paying and steadiest blue-collar jobs in California and the Pacific Northwest could be found in the forests. The resulting timber, especially the coveted rot- and insect-resistant redwood, could be found in homes across the nation. But cutting trees had its costs. Aesthetically, it grated on people who preferred natural vistas that were temporarily lost until new growth replaced what was taken out. And if done wrong, timber cutting could have adverse impacts on watersheds and the local ecology. Most professional foresters cared about the sustainability of the forests and did what was necessary to protect the land and water.

For the environmental opponents of logging, salvation came in the form of a "medium-sized, dark brown owl with a barred tail, white spots on the head and breast, and dark brown eyes."[11] The northern spotted owl lived in old growth forests and was thought to be dependent on those forests, meaning that it couldn't thrive anywhere else. Best of all, the Fish and Wildlife Service determined that the owl was threatened or endangered in California, Oregon, and Washington State—meaning that it was in danger of extinction.[12] If the loss of old growth habitat caused by timber harvesting could be blamed for the endangerment of the owl, then that harvesting could be stopped.

It was a brilliant and devastating strategy. As Andy Stahl from the Sierra Club Legal Defense Fund (in)famously put it when describing the owl's role in stopping logging in old growth forests: "Thank goodness the spotted owl evolved in the Northwest, for if it hadn't, we'd have to genetically engineer it. It's the perfect species for use as a surrogate."[13]

It proved to be a success beyond everyone's wildest dreams. Not only was the owl's image the source of endlessly profitable sales of owl-themed tchotchkes and fund-raising, but it was an indomitable force to lay waste to the timber industry. Within a few years, lawsuits to "save" the spotted owl began to succeed.[14] The ESA, the National Forest Management Act, and NEPA all played a vital part. Loggers protested en masse, reporters descended upon the woods, and chicken dishes rebranded as "Spotted Owl Souffle" became a staple in local restaurants. But for all the *Sturm und Drang*, the law was the law, and it was inexorable. The loggers lost.

When the chainsaws stopped, silence descended on the forests, and timber mills were shuttered. Loggers faced massive unemployment and welfare dependency. Many left. Those who remained found themselves in dying timber towns that faced decades of hard times (except where illegal and environmentally damaging pot farming moved into the abandoned forests).[15]

It is not without reason that the ESA has been called the pit bull of environmental laws. The Tellico Dam snail darter and the northern spotted owl are but two of a long list of species that have been drafted to stop economic activity. There are over thirteen hundred species listed as threatened or endangered by the federal government.[16] Most of these have some impact on the ability to engage in economic activity.

For example, in the Central Valley of California, litigation over another small fish, the delta smelt, resulted in severe irrigation water cutbacks. Based on a biological opinion from the Fish and Wildlife Service on the delta smelt, water destined for farmers instead remains in the streams and rivers for the benefit of the smelt. This has been the cause of what farmers have called regulatory drought—meaning farmers have had to fallow hundreds of thousands of acres of farmland and farmworkers have experienced much higher levels of unemployment.[17] Some of the small farmers, represented by attorneys from Pacific Legal

Foundation, brought their own lawsuit and argued that the water cut-backs were illegal because they ignored the economic impacts of the cutbacks. The trial court agreed and struck down the Fish and Wildlife Service's biological opinion. On appeal, however, the Ninth Circuit disagreed, and the Supreme Court declined to hear the case.

In the Klamath Basin along the California–Oregon border, there have been severe water cutbacks to save salmon. This has caused severe economic distress to many farmers whose long-held water supplies were cut off.[18] In the Intermountain West, protections for grizzly bears and the reintroduction of wolves—over the bitter opposition of ranchers—has caused a rise in livestock killings to the economic detriment of local economies. [19] Elsewhere, home building has been halted or made more expensive by species ranging from the wood stork in Florida to the golden cheeked warbler in Texas hill country to the California gnat-catcher along the California coast.

Beyond all these examples of economic impact, the ESA has worked more fundamental changes. First, along with the Clean Water Act described in the next chapter, the ESA has provided the federal government with the authority to wrest local land-use decision-making powers from local and state governments (those are the powers that belonged to landowners in the pre-*Euclid* days). While nowhere does the ESA explicitly usurp local land-use decision-making powers, it has that practical effect.

A local government may, for example, zone fifty acres to be used for environmentally friendly, affordable working-class housing conveniently located near mass transit, shopping, and businesses. But if an endangered or threatened plant or critter is found on the property, the owners may be required to obtain a federal "incidental take permit" before disturbing any ground in order to avoid running afoul of the ESA.[20] Moreover, if any federal permits or actions are required (say for the filling of a wetland or the use of federal low-income housing grant moneys), then the federal agencies responsible for the permits or grants must themselves comply with another part of the ESA, potentially requiring extensive studies and mitigation. Failure to comply can result in civil or criminal penalties.[21] Most troubling to local governments, however, is that a local government official who grants a building or other permit for an activity that results in a violation of the ESA may be individually guilty of violating the Act.[22] Local officials now would much rather deny a building permit than risk being charged with violating federal law. Clearly, with the overlay of the ESA, local land-use regulation is not what it used to be.

With the enactment and enforcement of the ESA, the federal government now holds a de facto conservation easement over private lands that contain endangered plants or animals. In the circumstance of a private easement, one party can buy an easement over the land of another. That could be for access to another parcel or merely an agreement not to block a neighbor's view. One neighbor can sell such an easement to another neighbor for cash money, and the easement can be enforced like any other land contract in court. But with the ESA, there is often little or no notice to the landowner that the federal government has acquired authority over the property preventing the owner from using the property—whether it be for farming or home building. There is no payment to the landowner. And most distressing to a landowner, the easement can be enforced with massive fines or imprisonment. It is no wonder that some landowners have become bitter over the legacy of the ESA and sometimes resort to the eliminating the specis' habitat before it becomes occupied.

Owners of southern pine plantations are thought to be harvesting trees early before the trees are mature enough to develop cavities that red-cockaded woodpeckers are wont to interpret to be an "open house" invitation.[23] Owners of meadows likely to attract the endangered preble's meadow-jumping mouse have taken similar actions.[24] Worse, there is the direct elimination of a protected species with the "shoot, shovel, and shut-up" trifecta.[25] This is a sardonic way of describing what some landowners allegedly do when they encounter an endangered species on their property. Rather than losing the economic value of the land, they might shoot the animal, bury it, and say nothing. This is no way to encourage the development of housing on private land.

Nor does it do much to protect the species.

Chapter 16

The Clean Water Act and Wetlands

I f the ESA is the pit bull of environmental statutes, the Clean Water Act is the swamp monster that devours housing projects large and small.

Trying to demonstrate his commitment to the environment, President H. W. Bush encouraged the Corps of Engineers to crack down on people who were filling wetlands. Meanwhile, a small contractor named Ocie Mills decided to build a small cabin for his son Carey on two small lots next to a coastal waterway near the Florida Panhandle town of Navarre. After beginning to prepare the lot with clean building sand, Mills received a letter from the Corps of Engineers telling him to stop because he was filling wetlands. Ocie was skeptical, and he asked the Florida Department of Environmental Regulation—which was using the same office building as the Corps—to show him where the wetlands were supposed to be. The state helpfully came to the property and showed Ocie where the wetlands were—along a line parallel to the waterway. Ocie recommended his work on the upland side of the line. Oddly, to him, he received another letter from the Corps, ordering him to stop. Ocie responded with a letter explaining, somewhat unartfully, that a "line had been drawn in the sand" and that the Corps would have to prove otherwise. Not hearing from the Corps for a couple of months, Ocie and his son recommended work for a third time.

The next visit from the federal government was in the form of federal marshals who arrested Ocie and his son. Ocie was convinced that all he had to do was explain to the court what had happened, and the case would be dismissed. So, he represented himself in federal court. That was a huge mistake. No one, not even a lawyer, should attempt to self-represent when facing federal criminal charges in federal court. The judge was unsympathetic, and Ocie made some serious errors—mainly he failed to properly introduce evidence that could have exonerated him. He lost and, in 1989, he was sentenced, along with his son, to twenty-one months in federal prison plus a year of supervised release.

After they were released from prison, Ocie and his son were ordered to remove the sand they had previously placed on their property. They complied, but not to the satisfaction of the EPA, which sought to enforce the removal order in federal court. This time, Ocie and Carey hired a local criminal defense attorney who persuaded a new judge to visit the site to see for himself the so-called wetlands. After reviewing the history of the lots and visiting the site, the judge concluded that the lots probably didn't contain wetlands to begin with and found that the Millses had no further obligations to restore the site.[1]

Even though they had served their time, Ocie and Carey were determined to reverse their federal convictions. They went back to court, arguing that because the lots weren't wetlands, they should have their convictions expunged. The trial judge, while sympathetic, could not agree. Because the Millses had not been allowed to introduce evidence at their original trial that their property was uplands, it was too late. But the judge was obviously distressed, writing,

> This case presents the disturbing implications of the expansive jurisdiction which has been assumed by the United States Army Corps of Engineers under the Clean Water Act. In a reversal of terms that is worthy of Alice in Wonderland, the regulatory hydra which emerged from the Clean Water Act mandates in this case that a landowner who places clean fill dirt on a plot of subdivided dry land may be imprisoned for the statutory felony offense of "discharging pollutants into the navigable waters of the United States."[2]

Represented by the author at the Eleventh Circuit Court of Appeals, the Millses appealed, but were unsuccessful. The Court said it was too late to correct any errors the Millses made at the original trial.[3]

Figure 28. The author in 1994 with Ocie Mills on his *Alice-in-Wonderland* wetlands that landed him and his son in federal prison for twenty-one months.

While Ocie and Carey weren't trying to build enough homes to relieve any housing shortages, and a single cabin by itself would have had no significant impact on supply, their story is one of many in which landowners have been discouraged, threatened, and prosecuted for trying to use land that they didn't think contained wetlands. After all, who would want to take on the federal government when it can threaten prison time or millions in fines—for something as insignificant as trying to build a home on a residential lot? In Priest Lake, Idaho, one couple had been under threat for nearly two decades.

In 2005, a small contractor named Mike Sackett and his wife Chantell decided to build a small home for themselves in rural Priest Lake, Idaho. They purchased a modest 0.63-acre residential lot a couple of blocks away from Priest Lake, a navigable waterway.[4] Mike was an experienced local contractor and knew the implications of wetlands well. He also thought he knew a wetland when he saw one. But alas, identifying a wetland can be notoriously difficult—and subject to widely divergent opinions.[5]

In the spring of 2007, shortly after the Sacketts began clearing their lot to build their single-family home, they received a visit from an EPA officer who told them to stop. Shortly thereafter, the EPA sent them a compliance order. In a nutshell, the order demanded that the Sacketts restore their lot to the status quo ante, plant it with native vegetation, and fence it off for three years. After several years, if the Sacketts still wished to build, they could then apply for a wetlands permit, which the Corps and EPA may or may not grant. Only then, the EPA said, could the Sacketts appeal the basic question of whether their land contained any wetlands at all.

The Sacketts consulted wetlands experts, who agreed with them that the property was not in fact wetlands. Yet there was nothing the Sacketts could do. Every day that they failed to restore their "wetlands" meant another day of violating the compliance order and a fine of $37,500 per day plus an additional fine of $37,500 per day for violating the Clean Water Act. But there was no telling when or if the EPA might bring an enforcement action. It could be the next day or never. But for every day the Sacketts resisted the order, it could be another $75,000 in fines.[6] Worse, they had no way of appealing the EPA's conclusion that there were wetlands on their property. Logically, one would think that a couple in the predicament of the Sacketts could challenge the compliance order in federal court to argue that there were no wetlands on the property.

But for nearly five years, they were told they could not. Represented by attorneys from Pacific Legal Foundation, they sued for the right to challenge the wetlands ruling. The Ninth Circuit ruled against them, holding that neither the Clean Water Act nor the Administrative Procedures Act allowed an appeal of the compliance order. The only remedy, according to Ninth Circuit, was to wait until EPA brought an enforcement action against the Sacketts for violating the order, or for the Sacketts to restore the so-called wetland, wait a few years, and then apply for a permit. Only if the permit were denied or if it contained unreasonable demands could the Sacketts challenge the EPA's finding that their land contained wetlands. The Sacketts didn't want to risk going to federal prison or spending years and untold expense trying to get a permit. Instead, they appealed, and the Supreme Court took their case.

In a unanimous decision in 2012, the Supreme Court reversed the Ninth Circuit's holding. The Court held that people like the Sacketts had every right to challenge a wetlands designation before spending years in administrative hell. But that's not the end of the story. The Sacketts then spent the next decade in federal court trying to prove that their land contained no wetlands. The EPA spent a few years gathering more data to prove its case.

After the trial court sat on the case for several years, it finally decided in 2019 that there was a small patch of wetlands on the property. Two years later, the Ninth Circuit affirmed. The Sacketts then appealed to the Supreme Court. They argued that even if there was a small damp spot on their property, the EPA lacked authority over it because the damp spot had no meaningful connection to a navigable waterway—a prerequisite for federal authority.

A critical problem with all this is that no one is quite sure what is a wetland subject to federal jurisdiction and what is not. It is notoriously unclear, and even experts disagree. If experts cannot agree, what are ordinary landowners like the Millses and Sacketts supposed to do? As

Justice Alito pointed out in a concurring opinion in the first *Sackett* case, "real relief requires Congress to do what it should have done in the first place: provide a reasonably clear rule regarding the reach of the Clean Water Act."[7]

Figure 29. Chantell and Mike Sackett on their home site. Where are THE WETLANDS?

All the Sacketts were trying to do was build a modest single-family home in the middle of a residential subdivision.[8] The developer of a subdivision, small or large, faces even greater hurdles. Simply put, America's housing crisis is not going to be solved so long as home builders face the prospect of prison and millions of dollars in fines for violating a statute where the experts cannot even agree on what a wetland is or where federal jurisdiction begins and ends.

The federal government has only the powers given to it in the Constitution. One of the most important powers is the federal government's power to regulate commerce. Traditionally, this has included such things as the regulation of roads and vehicles, waterways and boats, and other matters of interstate commerce. It is under the government's authority to regulate navigable waterways that Congress passed the Clean Water Act in order to protect the quality of those navigable waters. In a series of court decisions interpreting the Clean Water Act, courts included tributaries to navigable rivers and wetlands in the federal scheme. But landowners like the Sacketts have argued that even if their land did contain some wetlands, those wetlands were too far and disconnected from any navigable stream or lake to give the federal government the authority to demand a permit. These arguments came to a head when the federal government tried to send John Rapanos to prison for filling wetlands. Rapanos, represented by Pacific Legal Foundation attorneys, took the case to the Supreme Court.

As described by the Supreme Court in *Rapanos v. United States*:

> In April 1989, petitioner John A. Rapanos backfilled wetlands on a parcel of land in Michigan that he owned and sought to develop. This parcel included 54 acres of land with sometimes-saturated soil conditions. The nearest body of navigable water was 11 to 20 miles away. . . . Regulators had informed Mr. Rapanos that his saturated fields were "waters of the United States," . . . that could not be filled without a permit. Twelve years of criminal and civil litigation ensued.[9]

Figure 30. John Rapanos faced time in federal prison for filling this alleged wetland, many miles from a navigable waterway.

Similarly, in a companion case to *Rapanos*, *Carabell v. United States*, June and Keith Carabell tried to build 112 condominium homes on nineteen acres of alleged wetlands that were connected to a navigable lake only by a manmade ditch, and even then only when water over-topped an impermeable berm. In both cases, the landowners protested that the federal government lacked jurisdiction because the connection between the wetlands and a navigable waterway was too remote. After all, they argued, neither the Clean Water Act nor the Constitution's Commerce Clause gave the federal government unlimited power to regulate land that had no impact on "waters of the United States."

The Supreme Court agreed with the landowners, sort of. While a majority of the justices agreed that the federal government had gone too far in trying to regulate wetlands that had no obvious connection to navigable waters, they couldn't agree on how much of a connec-tion would be enough. Justice Scalia and three other justices wrote that there had to be a "continuous surface connection" to a navigable waterway.

But Justice Kennedy, in a lone concurring opinion said that the federal government could regulate a wetland that by itself or with other wetlands would have a "significant nexus" to navigable waters, which would "significantly affect the chemical, physical, and biological integrity of" navigable waters. For years, no one was sure which test to apply: Justice Scalia's "continuous surface connection" test or Justice Kennedy's "chemical, physical, and biological integrity" test. Logically, one would think the test with the most winning votes would prevail. But logic is often in short supply in the courts.

Prodded by environmental groups, the EPA, and the Corps of Engineers, most courts chose the Kennedy test. But the problem with that test is that no one knows what it is supposed to mean, or how to apply it in the real world. No one knew what a "significant nexus" meant. This sort of ambiguity is a regulator's dream—a bureaucrat can just make stuff up to get the desired result.

There are two types of wetlands permits: individual permits for larger projects and an expedited "nationwide" type permit such as for all homes built under a certain size. Both are time-consuming and expensive. When it decided the *Rapanos* case, the Supreme Court noted that the "average applicant for an individual permit spends 788 days and $271,596 in completing the process, and the average applicant for a nationwide permit spends 313 days and $28,915—not counting costs of mitigation or design changes."[10] So what is a landowner thinking about building some houses supposed to do? Assume that there are no wetlands and face years in prison if the assumption is wrong? Or spend hundreds of thousands of dollars on permit costs (fees, expert studies, etc.) and wait years for a permit? True, landowners can hire experts and try to get the Corps to buy off on an opinion that there are no wetlands, but that too is costly and risky.

Even members of the Court admit there is no clear understanding of what a wetland is. Justice Alito lamented at oral argument in the 2012 *Sackett* case that the Clean Water Act is "notoriously unclear." Justice Kennedy even suggested it could be "unconstitutionally vague." Which is ironic since he's the one who conjured up the vaguest of vague tests.

Finally, in 2023, the Court mostly cleaned up the mess when the Sacketts came back to the Supreme Court. After languishing for years in the lower courts after their 2012 victory, the Sacketts (still represented by Pacific Legal Foundation pro bono) now argued that, damp spot or not, the EPA lacked jurisdiction because there was no surface water connection to Priest Lake. They expressly asked the Supreme Court to disavow Justice Kennedy's "significant nexus" test. The EPA responded that it had control over the Sackett's property because rainwater might seep from the damp spot on their lot northward under a thirty-foot-wide paved road into another wetland and then into a ditch and a few thousand feet later, into a small stream that eventually flows south into Priest Lake. That, supposedly, was a significant enough nexus.

In a nine-to-nothing decision, the Supreme Court put a kibosh on the EPA's fantasy. The Court tossed out the "significant nexus" test in favor of the late Justice Scalia's "surface water connection" test. If a wetland isn't connected directly to navigable water via a surface water connection, then the federal government needs to butt out. That's not to say a state or local government can't regulate the property, but it's a local—not federal—matter.

Finally, the Sacketts can build their home and be free of ruinous fines. If only. During this epic decade and a half battle the Sacketts went into bankruptcy. It's uncertain whether they will ever be able to build their modest dream home.

Moreover, the EPA and Corps of Engineers must now craft a new regulatory definition of what a wetland is based on the Court's decision. Given their track record, it is uncertain how faithful the agencies will be to the decision. Even with the favorable decision in *Sackett*, the federal government will still wield vast power over millions of acres of wetlands—where the jurisdiction is unambiguous. Moreover, the proposals that have come out of Washington so far have been criticized by some as being "overly broad, unduly burdensome, and insufficiently certain."[11] Even if the new regulations are somewhat faithful to the new *Sackett* test, as sure as the sun will rise tomorrow, more lawsuits will follow. Unless and until Congress adopts clear laws that comport to constitutional limits, the wetlands morass will continue.

With the federal government's expansive reach in defining navigable waterways, the Clean Water Act represents another shift in the ownership of property rights away from the individual and toward the federal government. In essence, with Section 404, the federal government has obtained an easement over a vast acreage of property in the United States, where homebuilding can be done only with the permission of the federal government. Our housing crisis is not going to be solved if landowners must spend hundreds of thousands of dollars on permitting costs—or risk huge fines and prison time if they don't— just to build much-needed housing. We need to limit the reach of the federal agencies, and we need to streamline the permitting process for those who need permits.

Chapter 17

The Special Case of California Environmental Land-Use Permitting

California has always been notorious for being the first juris-diction to sustain extreme municipal regulations. Practitioners in other states have joked about why a developer would sue a California community when it would cost a lot less and save much time if he simply slit his throat.[1]

While all the states have their own set of environmental regu-lations, California is unique in the ferocity of its law, the California Environmental Quality Act, or CEQA. When Governor Reagan approved the law in 1970, few in their wildest dreams thought CEQA would unleash the equivalent of the bubonic plague on California housing development. Unlike the National Environmental Policy Act, which requires projects to be studied for their environmen-tal consequences but still allows a project to move forward once its impacts are known, CEQA demands that environmental impacts be minimized or eliminated before a project can proceed. What's more, virtually anybody can sue to stop a project—whether that person is genuinely affected by the project, a NIMBY neighbor just trying to stop it, or a labor union trying to hold a project hostage pending a favorable labor agreement with the developer. All these interests can and do sue, adding years to a project's lifespan while putting many developments over the financial edge, resulting in their abandonment.

Take the saga of Tejon Ranch, which won approvals in late 2021 for 19,300 "zero-emission" homes on 6,700 acres about seventy miles north of Los Angeles, with 3,500 units being "affordable." While that sounds like a success, it's not.[2]

- The ranch first proposed developing a larger project on its 270,000 acres in 1999.
- The developers were immediately sued for a host of environmental reasons relating to sprawl under the California Environmental Quality Act, among other causes of action, by the Sierra Club, Audubon California, the Natural Resources Defense Council, and others.
- Tejon Ranch settled with most of the environmentalists in 2008, promising to set aside 240,000 acres for open space, leaving 30,000 acres for 34,780 homes and commercial development.[3] The homes were to be divided into three separate developments: the Grapevine Project (12,000 homes), Tejon Mountain Village (3,450 homes), and the Centennial Project (19,300 homes).
- The 21,000-page environmental impact report was completed in 2009. It comprised "14 notebooks, 13 of them 5.5 inches thick, two others adding four more inches, plus two rolls of large maps. They add up to a tower nearly six feet tall."[4]
- Much litigation has been filed by the Center for Biological Diversity, an organization that is dedicated to stopping all development on undeveloped land. To accomplish this, according to one of its founders, "we will have to inflict severe economic pain."[5] No doubt, they have accomplished at least that at Tejon Ranch.
- In 2009, the Center for Biological Diversity sued to stop the Tejon Mountain project, alleging inadequate environmental review and concerns with Chumash Indian sites, air quality, and

traffic. They lost in 2010 in trial court and in 2012 in the court of appeal.[6]

- In 2009 the Kawaisu Tribe sued, claiming an interest in portions of the ranch. That claim was ultimately rejected by the Ninth Circuit in 2015.[7]

- In 2013, the Fish and Wildlife Service approved a 5,200-page Habitat Conservation Plan for the developments to protect the California condor, among other species.

- In 2016, Kern County approved the Grapevine Project. The Center for Biological Diversity sued and stopped the project in 2018 for allegedly inadequate environmental review. More environmental review was conducted, and, in 2019, the Grapevine Project was again approved. Once more, the Center for Biological Diversity sued. That suit was lost in January 2021.[8]

- In 2019, the Center for Biological Diversity sued the US Fish and Wildlife Service, alleging that a proposed golf course would impact the habitat of the California condor. Because the condor is allegedly a Native American "cultural artifact," the development violates the National Historic Preservation Act. A trial court rejected those allegations in December 2020. On February 2, 2021, the Center announced an appeal.[9] The Center dismissed the appeal in October 2021.[10]

- Another pair of lawsuits were filed in 2019 by Climate Resolve, the Center for Biological Diversity, and the California Native Plant Society—none of whom were not part of the original settlement. This suit stopped the Centennial Project in early 2021 over allegations that the environmental review did not fully address grassland wildfire danger and that the homes were not net zero. (The developer asserted that the law did not require net zero.)[11]

- On December 2, 2021, the parties settled after the developers agreed to install 30,000 charging stations and provide incentives for 10,500 electric cars, buses, and trucks. Additionally, the developers agreed to ensure that 3,500 of the units would be "affordable." A total of 19,300 homes will be built on 6,700 acres. No doubt, the remaining units will be commensurately less affordable. Or, as put by a ranch spokesperson, "These measures will come at a cost, which makes it increasingly difficult to build houses that people can afford, which is at cross purposes with other state priorities."[12]

- On January 14, 2022, the trial court revived the CEQA litigation brought by the Center for Biological Diversity, which alleged that the approvals failed to adequately consider the fire danger and impact on climate change.[13] In March 2023, a trial judge ordered the County of Los Angeles to set aside its approvals of the project.[14]

If they are ever built, the carbon-neutral homes will be surrounded by lovely open space, but at what cost? There is a problem when third parties can drag out a substantial housing project for over twenty years while California is experiencing an ever-worsening housing crisis. While Tejon Ranch has had the assets to fight through two decades worth of lawsuits, it is no wonder then that so many other less capitalized landowners and developers are forced into bankruptcy, abandon projects, or look to opportunities in other states. This is no way to build out of the housing shortage.

There have been thousands upon thousands of instances of CEQA being used to slow and stop housing projects since it was enacted in 1970. With each round of litigation, the gauntlet through which home builders must run gets tighter and tighter. Here are just a few more recent examples:

- In 2016, a Bay Area suburb, Redwood City, approved a twenty-unit affordable housing project downtown and near transit lines. The project promoted by Habitat for Humanity was stopped dead by Geoff Carr, an attorney who didn't like the impact on the view from his office located in a two-story home. He sued under CEQA and related laws alleging the additional residents would increase traffic and block his view.[15] The case eventually settled in 2018, but only after the cost increased by millions of dollars.[16] The same lawyer boasts that he stopped dead another nearby project with ninety-one condominium units.[17] And because he got into the CEQA game late, he laments that he was able to reduce another project by only one-story.[18] Carr was not alone in his NIBMY opposition. In a series of Facebook posts, residents said such things as "I'm all for affordable housing but I am against any particular person or group making decisions for others . . . . [and robbing] people of their natural source for Vitamin D"; "Next up: tenements!"; "The crisis is not Redwood City's alone to solve"; and "The ugly has to stop somewhere!"[19]

- In 2019, led by a prominent property attorney, opponents of a proposed homeless shelter to be located on a San Francisco parking lot formerly used for busses started a GoFundMe drive to raise $100,000 in order to file a CEQA lawsuit to stop the shelter.[20]

- Likewise, residents near Venice Beach in Los Angeles filed a suit—for which they raised $220,000—to stop a proposed shelter.[21]

- Just as CEQA is used to stop small projects, it and other environmental laws are used to stop larger ones. In 2015, the California Supreme Court halted the Newhall Ranch project, which would have provided 20,885 homes for over 58,000 residents to be developed over twenty years. The CEQA analysis, which was one of several prepared and shot down since the first one was approved in 1999, hadn't adequately studied the project's impact on greenhouse gas emissions.[22] By 2021, however, the developer began to build homes after agreeing to make them net zero, subsidize electric vehicles, and build charging stations. Most bizarrely, as the CEO of one of the projects claimed that "We went all the way to Africa and, as we speak, replaced tens of thousands of cooking stoves to mitigate for greenhouse gas."[23] (similar to what Tejon Ranch eventually capitulated to).

- CEQA is an equal-opportunity destroyer of housing projects. Just as it has been used to stop homeless shelters and afford-able housing, it has also been employed against luxury homes. In 2019, after a fourteen-year battle based on CEQA and other California environmental statutes, a five-home luxury home project on 155 acres in the hills above Malibu that was the brain-child of David Evans, a.k.a. "The Edge" from U2, was scuttled over a jurisdictional defect. Evans gets to start over again with the promise of many more CEQA challenges ahead.[24] This is after spending $10 million on sixty lawyers and seventy technical reports for a plan that initially called for a dozen homes until it was scaled back to five.

- On October 7, 2021, a superior court stopped a housing proposal at Otay Ranch for 1,119 homes because it did not fully consider fire dangers and greenhouse gas emissions.[25]

- Despite the housing crisis, CEQA-based denials of housing projects are unabated. On March 3, 2022, in another case brought by the Center for Biological Diversity, a California superior court judge ruled that a proposal for three thousand homes near San Diego could not go forward because it failed to consider how an influx of new residents could affect the region's fire risk.[26]

Under California's law, environmental documents must study over one hundred different "environmental" topics.[27] Any person may anony-mously challenge a project in court under CEQA grounds at little cost and have about a fifty-fifty chance of stopping the project—requiring it to be restudied from scratch, modified, or abandoned. If a court orders new studies, the results of those studies can be stopped in new litigation ad infinitum. There are many cases in which dozens of law-suits have been filed over the span of two or more decades. But the pri-mary targets of CEQA lawsuits are not the usual suspects of industrial development or developments on pristine land, but of residential development within already developed cities—so-called "infill development. In fact, over 80 percent of CEQA lawsuits in the Los Angeles area target housing and other projects in existing cities and towns, as opposed to open spaces.[28] In fact, such litigation is a contributing factor in pushing new development into undeveloped areas where there are fewer neighbors with a penchant to sue—a pattern CEQA expert Jennifer Hernandez calls "Green Jim Crow."[29]

The targets are the same as those in Baltimore in 1910, Louisville in 1917, Euclid in 1926, and a century's worth of large-lot exclusionary zoning: poor and working class people that need to live in housing that is affordable, such as townhomes and apartments; that is, the "pig in the parlor instead of the barnyard," as Justice Sutherland put it in *Euclid.*[30] As Hernandez has written, "Another inconvenient truth is that LA CEQA housing lawsuits disproportionately target new housing in whiter, wealthier, healthier communities."[31] This means that poor and minority home buyers will be shunted to existing poorer neighborhoods, maintaining segregated housing patterns.

Picking up on Richard Rothstein's thesis in *The Color of Law*, Hernandez continues to note that CEQA is a powerful tool in the hands of those wishing to keep the status quo of land-use patterns—and that those patterns are the direct result of overtly discriminatory government policies that reigned for most of the twentieth century. In other words, more often than not, CEQA is used to maintain, in the twenty-first century, the racism in land use against any change that might break the suburban color barrier. In Hernandez's words, "The core legal structure of CEQA, which measures 'environmental' impacts against the existing setting, protects the existing characteristics of those neighborhoods and thus perpetuates land use practices founded in race and class discrimination."[32] Moreover, "CEQA lawsuits are uniquely anti-democratic, and uniquely vulnerable to being hijacked for racist and other discriminatory objectives . . . that would be abhorrent and unlawful if openly acknowledged."[33] Lastly, Hernandez concludes that "CEQA lawsuits put a sword in any opponent of change, motivated by any reason, including but by no means limited to protecting housing patterns rooted in race and class discrimination."[34]

To be sure, there are other impediments to building in California. In San Francisco, for example, even projects that fully meet local zoning codes can take years just to go through a series of permitting processes and neighborhood appeals. One study points out that if neighbors are opposed to a project, they can demand, over the space of several years, a dozen public hearings and delays.[35] As the same study notes, "At each of these hearings, publicly elected or appointed officials are held in thrall to the demands of oppositional neighbors. Many of these public hearings will in fact involve multiple hearings in front of boards and the public before a final decision is rendered. One developer said they had to engage in over 100 community meetings for a single project."[36]

While some in the environmental community argue that CEQA is only one of many factors that limit the supply of housing in California,[37] those who actually try to build housing tend to counter that, while permitting is bad in California, CEQA makes things much worse. And the statistical evidence based on suits filed and projects delayed or denied makes it plain that until there is meaningful reform of CEQA—as well as other uniquely California legal impediments to homebuilding—housing will continue to be in short supply, and the crisis will continue in the Golden State.

There is also the very special case of the California Coastal Commission. It has a veto power over practically all land use decisions along the California coastal zone—which can include land five miles from the ocean.[38] Since it was established in 1978, it has denied permits for likely thousands of homes, condos, apartments, and hotel rooms, discouraged builders from even trying to seek permits for many thousands more, and buried the rest in paperwork. For example, in 2024, it prepared a 129-page environmental staff report on a single "granny flat," or small accessory dwelling unit.[39] Its former director often bragged that his measure of success was all the homes that never got built—and was credited for making "coastal residency a practical impossibility for working Californians."[40] Astonishingly, a few years ago, the Commission suggested that the city of San Clemente had to get a Coastal Development Permit for a homeless camp on city property.[41] Again, this is a recipe for a housing shortage.

PART IV

Rent Control Isn't the Answer

The crisis in the supply of affordable housing is the result of government meddling with the housing market, primarily the determination by many communities to keep affordable housing at bay, the condemnation of poor neighborhoods, and other government regulatory actions that maintain economic and racial segregation. But as with so many government-created or at least government-augmented problems, the proffered government solutions only stand to make things worse. And of the asserted solutions, rent control is the worst of the worst.

In the years after World War I, temporary rent control measures were adopted by the cities of New York and Washington, DC, in order to alleviate an emergency housing shortage caused by returning soldiers. During World War II, the federal government did the same to accommodate the many workers needed to support the war effort. New York City adopted new controls when the federal controls expired. However, the roots of rent control in the United States are older than that. They can be found in the years that followed the Civil War.

Chapter 18

The Early History of Rent Control in the United States

Before the Civil War, Chicago had become a center for grain distribution from farms across the upper Midwest. After a half-decade of one of the bloodiest conflicts this nation had ever experienced, our reunited nation was moving forward again. We got back to work growing crops and creating the means necessary to feed and clothe ourselves. Nowhere was the synergy between agriculture and industry more apparent than in Chicago. The expanding and modernizing farms of the Midwest became the granaries of the nation. Before that grain could reach the nation's cities, much of it had to travel through Chicago. And along the Chicago waterfront was the heart of this burgeoning economic system: the grain warehouses, known as grain elevators, because they lifted the grain from street level into giant storage facilities.

The grain elevators didn't just take grain from individual farmers and sell it to individual bakers. Instead, after the farmers sent their grain by rail to Chicago, the elevator operators graded and sorted it according to quality. They then combined grain from all over the upper Midwest and shipped it out on steamships across the Great Lakes to wholesalers in the cities on the East Coast, who in turn sold it to bakers and retail distributors. The prices for these transactions were set by the railroads and elevators, not the farmers. And because there was a monopolistic cartel system, the railroads and elevators bought low and sold high.

These elevators and railroads became the linchpins of a vast infrastructure, and they had a lock on key segments of the economy. So long as there was competition and few barriers to entry, the system should have worked well. But the tendency toward cartelization and monopolization is always present. If the owners of the elevators could cooperate, exclude competition, and collude on prices, the gains could be enormous—especially in the early days of America's industrial economy, when statutes against monopolies didn't exist. Likewise for the railroads that served the granaries. In fact, the elevators and railroads were closely intertwined, with the former often leasing land from the latter, and the latter deciding which elevator would receive which shipments of grain.[1] While they were intertwined, they were often fiercely at odds with one another, jockeying for position and ultimately seeking help in the legislature for one side or the other.[2]

The farmers were none too pleased. To reverse their relative political impotence, they banded together across the upper Midwest after the Civil War in what became known as the Granger movement. Every state eventually had its own state grange—a voluntary organization of farmers that agitated for political protection from the monopolies. In only a few years, in 1870, the movement bore political fruit in Illinois with the adoption of a state constitutional provision that allowed the state to set the maximum rates that the elevators could charge.[3]

Ira Y. Munn and George L. Scott were the influential and somewhat corrupt owners of the "North-Western Elevator" that was leased on land owned by the Northwestern Railroad. Munn was a player on the Chicago Board of Trade and was deeply immersed in the elevator cartel and the cartel's setting of rates. Munn's credibility was damaged after a warehouse fire, when he filed an insurance claim for grain that was supposedly lost in the fire. His insurance company demanded the right to inspect his operations. After dragging his feet, Munn consented to a warehouse inspection, which determined that there was no missing grain and that Munn had false bottoms constructed in the bins.

It was against the backdrop of powerful competing and corrupt interests, that the State intervened with a constitutional reform. Article XIII, Section 1, of the revised 1870 Illinois Constitution began by declaring that "All elevators or storehouses where grain or other property is stored . . . are declared to be *public* warehouses." These private warehouses now had a public character making them susceptible to direct government regulation—something not previously applicable to purely private enterprises. With statutes adopted the following year to implement the constitutional revisions, there was now a body of law establishing a scheme for elevator licensing, inspections, and maximum rates.

But this was not an anti-monopolist consumer protection bill, as we might envision such things today. It was a classic example of sausage making. As the poet John Godfrey Saxe once wrote (in a line often misattributed to Otto von Bismarck), "laws, like sausages, cease to inspire respect in proportion as we know how they are made." The constitutional amendments and related statutes were the product of raw political jockeying in which the elevators lost more than they gained. But the politics was not about keeping grain prices reasonable; it was about dividing the spoils of the system of grain distribution between the railroads, the elevators, and the farmers.

But if nothing else, the rate-setting law here set an important precedent for extensive government interference in the market, albeit a corrupt and monopolistic market. With this sort of government interference, was rent control far behind? Some thought not.

Munn and Scott resisted the law. They refused to obtain a license, and they charged the cartel's rates, not the prices established by the statute. As a result, they were criminally charged with violating the licensing and rate mandates. They took their case to the United States Supreme Court, arguing that, among other things, the law deprived them of property without due process of law.

In *Munn v. Illinois*,[4] the Court did not agree that there had been any deprivation. Instead, the Court noted that the grain elevators had a "virtual monopoly." Moreover, their business was "affected by the public interest" because it was devoted to use by the public. This, "in effect, grants to the public an interest in that use, and must submit to being controlled by the public for the common good."

To the dissent, this was a breathtaking incursion on private property. Justice Stephen Field began his dissent by complaining that the enterprise was a *private* business, not a public one: "The defendants were no more public warehousemen . . . than the merchant who sells his merchandise to the public is a public merchant, or the blacksmith who shoes horses for the public is a public blacksmith . . . so they could be brought under legislative control."[5]

Justice Field then had a warning:

> If this be sound law, if there be no protection . . . against such invasion
> of private rights, all property and all business in the State are held at the
> mercy of a majority of its legislature. The public has no greater interest
> in the use of buildings for the storage of grain than it has in the use of
> buildings for the residences of families. . . . ***According to the doctrine
> announced the legislature may fix the rent of all tenements used for
> residences, without reference to the cost of their erection.***[6]

He thought that the very notion of residential rent control was inconceivable and used it as a bogeyman to illustrate the very worst—and most unconstitutional—thing that could follow from the Court's majority decision. Because the majority's decision made rent control possible, he was convinced that the decision was wrong. It took forty years and a world war for Justice Field's worst fears to be realized.

* * *

During World War I, the federal government expanded greatly. New federal employees flocked to Washington, DC, and a housing shortage developed. Rents rose, often substantially, and there was a clamoring, especially among nascent socialists, for Congress to do something about it. Congress responded by authorizing the district to impose rent control for two years during the wartime emergency. The Food Control Act and the District of Columbia Rents Act were Congress's answer to wartime shortages of food, fuel, and housing.[7] Tucked inside a bill designed to criminalize the profiteering of food and fuel supplies during the war, the new law, echoing the old *Munn* decision, declared that "all rental property and apartments and hotels are affected with the public interest." It then required President Woodrow Wilson to appoint three commissioners who would oversee the terms of rental agreements in the city. According to the statute, its provisions were "made necessary by emergencies growing out of the war with the Imperial German Government, resulting in rental conditions in the District of Columbia dangerous to public health and burdensome to public officers and employees." It had a two-year expiration date.

Likewise, many soldiers returning from the war moved to New York City, causing a post-war housing shortage. New York City imposed its own version of rent control in 1920. Landlords in both Washington, DC and New York City sued, and their cases made it to the Supreme Court in two cases, *Block v. Hirsh*[8] and *Edgar A. Levy Leasing Company v. New York*.[9]

On November 17, 1919, Louis Hirsh purchased a building in downtown Washington, DC, with the intention of taking over and using the first floor and basement. Julius Block occupied that first floor and basement. His lease was set to expire on the last day of 1919. Two weeks prior to the expiration of the lease, Hirsh notified Block that he needed to leave by December 31. Citing the new rent control law, Block refused to move out. He argued that the law extended existing leases such as his, and that the law required a minimum thirty-day notice of eviction. Hirsh sued in federal district court and won, with the trial court holding the law to be unconstitutional because it violated Hirsh's constitutional due process rights since the new law did not advance any legitimate purpose. In this case, Hirsh's right to move into his property was restricted in favor of another private party, Julius Block. The district court reasoned, "nor can Congress, by a mere legislative declaration, convert a private use into a public use; nor, by such a declaration, create an arbitrary exercise of the police power, or make an act constitutional which otherwise would be unconstitutional."[10]

Block appealed to the Supreme Court. There, in an opinion written by Justice Holmes, the Court reversed the lower court's decision. Holmes began by dismissing the lower court's concerns over imbuing a private activity with the public interest. After noting that billboards and coal mines had been regulated, Justice Holmes pronounced, "Housing is a necessary of life. All the elements of a public interest justifying some degree of public control are present."[11] But a rhetorical flourish is not enough for a sound legal argument. Just because other things were regulated doesn't mean everything else should be. And just because housing is important doesn't mean that, at the snap of the judicial or legislative fingers, the law allows for price controls on private businesses.

Avoiding the fundamental question of the legitimate reach of government, Justice Holmes then pivoted by reframing the case with a simpler and vaguer question: "The only matter that seems to us open to debate is whether the statute goes too far. For . . . it may be conceded that regulations of the present sort pressed to a certain degree might amount to a taking without due process of law." Of course, "too far" is a standard-free standard that depends on whether a judge likes the law in question enough to avoid even considering the effectiveness of the law. Holmes also used the "too far" standard in a classic regulatory takings case, *Pennsylvania Coal v. Mahon,* discussed in a later chapter. Justice Holmes's predilection for vague, "too far" standards has confounded judges and lawyers for decades.[12]

Here, Justice Holmes embraced the notion that the courts should defer to legislative bodies in questioning the constitutionality of statutes. "We have no concern of course with the question whether those means were the wisest, whether they may not cost more than they come to, or will effect the result desired."[13] This is too deferential. It may be appropriate for judges to defer to legislative pronouncements in the ordinary course of judicial review where little is at stake. But when fundamental constitutional rights and liberties are in play—as in the case of the right to own and use private property—the courts have a duty to ensure that those rights are not being destroyed on behalf of a foolish legislative whim or a purely political calculation.

It gets worse. Justice Holmes concluded his analysis by noting, "It is enough that we are not warranted in saying that legislation that has been resorted to for the same purpose all over the world, is futile or has no reasonable relation to the relief sought."[14] But since when do we measure our liberties by practices "all over the world?" For a nation that takes pride in an origin story based on individual liberty and the escape from European tyranny (and ultimately our own tyranny over minority populations), we should be wary of sanctioning and adopting liberty limiting laws from nations whose embrace of freedom has been more tenuous.

Four justices, led by Justice McKenna, dissented. The dissent was unimpressed by Justice Holmes's argument: "Houses are a necessary of life but other things are as necessary. May they, too, be taken from the direction of their owners and disposed of by the government?"

As for the justification that the war made the restrictions on liberty necessary, Justice McKenna quoted from a civil war era case where a civilian from Indiana was sentenced to death by a military tribunal: "'the Constitution of the United States is a law for rulers and people, equally in war and in peace . . . [and none] of its provisions can be suspended during any of the great exigencies of government.'"[15]

A year after *Block v. Hirsh* was decided, the Court was confronted with New York City's wartime emergency rent control law. In *Edgar A. Levy Leasing Co. v. Siegal*, Jerome Siegal signed a two-year lease starting October 1, 1918, for an apartment at $1,450 per year, payable in monthly installments. In June 1920, Siegal signed a new lease for two more years, this time at $2,160 per year, an increase of nearly sixty dollars per month. When it came time to pay the higher rent in October, Siegal refused. Levy Leasing sued to evict Siegal. But Siegal claimed that he was coerced into signing the lease under threat of eviction. Moreover, he argued that the higher rent was unfair and violated New York City's emergency rent control law, which had just been adopted that year.

Levy Leasing responded by arguing that the rent control law was "unconstitutional, in that it impairs the obligation of the contract of lease . . . deprives the plaintiff of its property without due process of law; denies to it the equal protection of the law . . . and takes private property for a private use without compensation."[16] A month before *Block v. Hirsh* was decided, the New York Court of Appeals upheld the law.[17] Unsurprisingly, on appeal and a year after *Block v. Hirsh* was decided, the owner lost again. The Supreme Court of the United States found that the public interest in alleviating the problems and abuses caused by the city's housing shortage outweighed any constitutional objections:

> All agree: That there was a very great shortage in dwelling house accommodations in the cities of the state to which the acts apply; that this condition was causing widespread distress; that extortion in most oppressive forms was flagrant in rent profiteering; that, for the purpose of increasing rents, legal process was being abused and eviction was being resorted to as never before; and that unreasonable and extortionate increases of rent had frequently resulted in two or more families being obliged to occupy an apartment adequate only for one family, with a consequent overcrowding, which was resulting in insanitary conditions, disease, immorality, discomfort, and widespread social discontent.[18]

The Court never considered whether rent control would remedy any of these problems because it didn't think that was its job. As in *Block v. Hirsh*, the Court just accepted at face value the government's justifications for rent control. But there was not then (nor today) any evidence that rent control cures in any way "insanitary conditions, disease, immorality, discomfort, and widespread social discontent." If a legislative body wishes to tax all of its citizens (and voters) to try to solve these problems, so be it. Likewise, if a city wishes to establish health and safety standards, that too can help. If fact, there had already been housing regulations imposed in New York City to put a stop to the construction of the lightless and ventilation-free tenements that had proliferated during the nineteenth century.[19]

Voters can decide easily enough whether the money has been well-spent. But when the costs of such programs are borne not by the general public but by the distinct minority of people who own rental housing, then it behooves a court to take a careful look at whether impact on the rights of that minority comports with the constitutional standards.

The framers of our Constitution were acutely aware of the potential for majoritarian overreach and the danger that a democracy could turn on those with more wealth than the majority. As James Madison warned in the Federalist Papers, an unchecked democracy can lead to "a rage for paper money, for an abolition of debts, for an equal division of property, or for any other improper or wicked project."[20] For many years following the ratification of the Constitution, judges understood their role to render unconstitutional laws unenforceable.

But there were, at least in the early part of the twentieth century, *some* limits to the Supreme Court's deference to the wartime justification for rent control. After the two-year emergency law ended in Washington, DC, the act was extended again in October 1919 and then again in May 1922. By this time, the Great War had joined all prior wars between the pages of the history books. Its effects on the lives of Washingtonians had faded. Nevertheless, tenants in an apartment building successfully petitioned the rent board for a roll-back of a post-war increase in rents. The apartment owner sued, and when the Supreme Court got the case, it held that with the emergency clearly over, the time for deference had expired. Justice Holmes's opinion began by noting that "a Court is not at liberty to shut its eyes to an obvious mistake, when the validity of the law depends upon the truth of what is declared." The opinion continued, saying that "a law depending upon the existence of an emergency or other certain state of facts to uphold it may cease to operate if the emergency ceases or the facts change even though valid when passed."[21] The Court sent the case back down to the district court for a factual determination of whether there was still an emergency.

The New York rent control laws died a slower death, but a death of natural economic causes. To alleviate the lack of housing, New York

City declared a decade-long tax holiday for new housing construction and exempted new units from rent control. New construction took off like Lindbergh's airplane. By 1929, vacancy rates approached 8 percent. Rent control in New York was abolished. It wasn't necessary or useful anymore. The lesson is simple: Removal of government disincentives to building housing will result in more housing and more affordable prices. Free markets work.

It took another world war to forget the lesson and for rent control to be resurrected from its peacetime crypt.

* * *

World War II threw the economy into high gear, and the federal government's New Deal era penchant for planning was put on steroids. In 1943, the federal government adopted price controls, including controls on rents because it anticipated housing shortages. With sixteen million Americans serving the war effort, and with millions of those overseas, the war itself probably did not cause a housing shortage except in those local areas in the states that had geared up manufacturing to serve the war effort.

By the end of 1946, over seven million soldiers had returned to civilian life.[22] Whatever crisis there may have been, it had dissipated enough that Congress let the 1943 Emergency Price Control Act expire, replacing it with the Federal Housing and Rent Act, which kept price controls only on buildings built before 1947. In 1950, the federal act expired. However, rent control proved to be incredibly sticky in New York.

New York City

Rather than consign rent control to the dustbin of history, New York City carried on the federal program with its own local legislation. As a result, unless they have been converted into condominiums, many non-luxury apartments built in New York before 1947 have remained under some sort of rent control ever since. Newer buildings had to wait until 1969 before they were to fall under a kinder and gentler form of rent control: so-called rent stabilization. This form of rent control refers to a more recent approach, that has some flexibility to allow for inflation-based rent increases. In theory, this less drastic type of rent control is less likely to result in abandoned and derelict rental apartments, and it seemed to work—abandonments decreased. In New York City, "rent stabilization" covers those regulated rental units built before 1974 in buildings with six or more units. Rents may increase only in accordance with city guidelines. However, new legislation adopted in 2019 by the State of New York severely limits the ability of landlords to raise rents to recover costs invested in apartment improvements. There are new limits on the amount of money that can be spent, and costs can be recovered only over a period of thirty years. These and other changes bring rent stabilization a lot closer to the rent control of old and highlight the danger of adopting any form of "rent control lite" because it is only a gateway to the harder drug of punitive rent control.

Rent stabilization in New York was adopted in 1969 under the premise that the low-vacancy rates had created a housing "emergency." But the low vacancy rates were actually fairly normal for a big-city market like New York. There was no "emergency" like there was in wartime. And if the rates were low, it was only because the city made it so difficult to build new apartments. Year after year, the city has since renewed its declaration of an emergency—until deciding to end the charade in 2019 by passing straight-up punitive rent control. But what is an emergency? A world war can create an emergency. A flood in the process of inundating a city is an emergency. But a forever war that lasts decades is no longer an emergency that can justify broad restrictions on civil liberties—if it ever could. And water that covers a city for fifty years is no longer an emergency—it's a lake. With the rise of progressive pressure for more rent control across the nation, this lake is drowning an increasing number of cities and states.

Landlords brought several challenges to the New York City 2019 rent control provisions. In October 2023, the Supreme Court turned down one appeal from apartment owners who claimed the law was unconstitutional. Another appeal brought by a different set of owners was turned down in February 2024. Justice Thomas agreed that the case should be rejected, but wrote that he would grant review if the case had been better developed.[23] Another petition to the Supreme Court in yet another case was filed on April 23, 2024.[24]

California

Independent of the New York rent control saga, and following his activist anti-war days, Tom Hayden of Chicago Seven[25] fame spearheaded a tenants' rights movement in California, which led to rent control being adopted by a number of cities, including Los Angeles, San Francisco, San Jose, and Hayden's political base, Santa Monica. In total, twenty-one California jurisdictions adopted some form of rent control. Their terms varied widely.[26] Some of the existing ordinances, for example, limit rent increases to a *fraction* of the Consumer Price Index, meaning that rents will not keep up with inflation.[27] Some regulate apartments only, and others mobile homes only. Landlords complained loudly that their investments were being destroyed—especially in those jurisdictions where rent increases could not keep up with expenses or inflation.

They brought a number of lawsuits and had only a mixed record of success.

Recognizing the danger to the housing supply, the legislature introduced a bill named after its bipartisan sponsors Jim Costa and Phil Hawkins, that limited rent control to older buildings. The purpose was to encourage investors to build more apartments in California—something they were reluctant to do where there was rent control. It was successful, but only mildly so because of all the other restrictions on building in California. Nevertheless, in 2018 tenant advocates led by the AIDS Healthcare Foundation put Proposition 10 on the ballot. If passed, it would have repealed *Costa-Hawkins* and allowed local governments to impose rent control on nearly all rental units. It failed by a nearly twenty-point margin after $97 million was spent by both sides.[28] Ignoring the voters will, however, the legislature adopted limited statewide rent controls in 2019.

Believing the statewide law to be inadequate, and using profits from the ability to buy AIDS drugs wholesale and resell them to public programs at retail,[29] AHF bankrolled another ballot measure in 2020. The measure lost by the same margin after both sides spent over $124 million.[30] Still undeterred, another measure is slated for the 2024 ballot.[31] Landlord groups are fighting back, this time seeking to ban AHF from spending its profits on anything other than patient care.[32]

Massachusetts

Cambridge and Boston adopted rent control in 1969 and 1970. However, in a rare victory for common sense, Massachusetts voters repealed rent control in the entire state in 1994. The repeal had a significant positive effect on housing supply and value. The National Bureau of Economic Research has estimated that from 1994 to 2004, property values in Cambridge rose in value by $1.8 billion, which included $1 billion in spillover value added to never-controlled rental units.[33] According to the study's conclusion:

> Under any reasonable set of assumptions, increases in residential investment stimulated by rent decontrol can explain only a small fraction of these spillover effects. Thus, we conclude that decontrol led to changes in the attributes of Cambridge residents and the production of other localized amenities that made Cambridge a more desirable place to live.[34]

More recently, there has been a push to repeal the ban. In fact, in progressive cities across the nation there is a renewed effort for rent control, not only at the local level but at the national level. In fact, two prominent politicians have been pushing for their own versions of rent control.

Federal

New York Congresswoman Alexandria Ocasio-Cortez submitted the A Just Society: A Place to Prosper Act of 2019.[35] The law would apply to owners with five or more units, or mobile home park owners with two or more parks. The proposal would, among other things, impose nationwide rent caps with annual increases tied to the consumer price index or 3 percent, whichever is greater. It also has vacancy controls, forbids discrimination against Section 8 voucher holders, provides standing to tenants to sue, and overrides any arbitration clause leases. Evictions may not commence until a tenant is two months behind in rent, and there will be a national program of free legal counsel to tenants facing evictions, with a fund of $6.5 billion annually to pay for the attorneys. It provides that state attorneys general may sue to enforce the Act. The bill also would amend the Civil Rights Act to include people who receive income such as Section 8 vouchers to be a "protected class," meaning landlord discrimination against a tenant with such income would be actionable under federal law in either state or federal court.

Another element of the proposal would require owners with over a thousand units nationwide, or a hundred units in a metropolitan area, to disclose for a public database, information about their business practices, including statistics on evictions, rents, code violations, standard leases, and details on corporate ownership.

Senator Bernie Sanders's Housing for All[36] plan would do many of the same things as the AOC plan. It would spend $1.4 trillion to restore and build new government housing, end discrimination against Section 8 recipients, impose a national rent cap of 3 percent or 1.5 times the consumer price index (whichever is higher) "to help prevent the exploitation of tenants at the hands of private landlords," implement just-cause eviction laws, allow states to adopt more stringent laws, and provide $2 billion for attorneys for tenants facing evictions. There are a host of other restrictions on house flipping, inclusionary zoning, and a tax on vacant homes.

None of this was passed in the 116th or 117th Congresses, the latter of which ended on January 3, 2023.

Eviction Bans

On top of the push for rent control, it has become unnecessary for those tenants unable or unwilling to pay rent in the COVID-19 era.

With eviction bans adopted in many states in the wake of COVID-19, many tenants enjoyed a de facto rent reduction or even a total rent holiday. Legal challenges to a federal eviction moratorium issued by the Centers for Disease Control and Prevention (CDC) resulted in the moratoria being struck down by the Supreme Court as an unconstitutional exercise of power because Congress never gave the CDC the authority to restrict rents.[37]

However, numerous state and local challenges to COVID-19 eviction bans have thus far proven unsuccessful with one notable exception. In 2022, the Eighth Circuit ruled in favor of a challenge to Minnesota's eviction ban in *Heights Apartments v. Walz*.[38] The court explained that "a state's authority to impose restrictions is not unlimited and judicial deference, even in an emergency or crisis like the COVID-19 pandemic, 'does not mean wholesale judicial abdication.'"[39] The court continued that the apartment owner had stated a cognizable claim that its right to contract had been infringed upon and that its property had been taken.[40] But other challenges in California, Washington State, and other jurisdictions have thus far failed. If local governments can succeed in imposing eviction bans, where some tenants have gone for years without paying rent, builders will be far less likely to build new apartment buildings.

Rent control may provide a nice short-term solution for high rents, but the damage it can do to the long-term housing supply is severe. As will be shown next, economists rarely agree about much, but they seem to be in near-universal agreement that rent control makes housing shortages worse.

Chapter 19

Rent Control Makes Housing Worse
and More Expensive

In many cases rent control appears to be the most efficient technique so far known for destroying cities—except for bombing.[1]

The Americans couldn't destroy Hanoi, but we have destroyed our city by very low rents. We realized it was stupid and that we must change policy.[2]

Economist Assar Linbeck and North Vietnam's Foreign Minister Nguyen Co Thach agree: Rent control destroys cities. Outside of war and natural disasters, there is no force more destructive to cities than unconstrained rent control. In a 1981 book by the Fraser Institute, there is a series of fifteen black and white photographs of post-apocalyptic urban landscapes with the caption *Bomb Damage or Rent Control?*[3] One must go to the index for the answer because it is otherwise impossible to tell. Comparing a block in the South Bronx to one in Nagasaki or Hiroshima may seem fatuous, but photographs (at least back then) don't lie: rent control is terribly destructive.

Figure 31. This photo shows how eerily similar the South Bronx—the epicenter of New York's rent control—was to war-torn regions.

To be sure, most of these photographs illustrate the effects of old-style rent controls, where absolute ceilings were placed on rents—often arbitrarily determined by rent boards and with little understanding or consideration of owner costs and profitability. The effects of more modern rent controls—which generally seek to limit the magnitude and frequency of rent increases—are more subtle but can be just as damaging in the longer term.

We've come a long way from the nineteenth century, when Joseph Ris explained high rents: "Rents were fixed high enough to cover damage and abuse from this class, from whom nothing was expected, and the most was made of them while they lasted."[4]

Today we have a more nuanced understanding of pricing. Indeed, owners of rental property are like the rest of us: If they own a lot of rental properties, they want to earn a living from managing and renting them. If they own just a few units, they are doing it to supplement their incomes. The vast majority of landlords want to do the right thing—give their tenants clean and decent homes in exchange for rent. The small "mom and pop" owners of a small rental building often put a large chunk of their life savings into their apartments so they can have some sort of equity in their retirement. And as much as they may sympathize with tenants who are stretched thin by rising prices, these landlords are small business owners. They are not charities.

When rent control gets out of hand, the owners of rental properties cannot keep up with expenses. Taxes must be paid, always. Boilers break, roofs leak, and some tenants damage apartments. All that and more takes money to fix. But when regulated rents cannot keep up with those expenses, something must give. Either the property is converted to a non-rental use, maintenance gets deferred, or the money-losing investment is abandoned: "Abandoned city blocks . . . begin with one or two individual apartments struck by fire and vandalism, then an entire floor, then the whole building, and then the next. The steady process gradually devastates entire neighborhoods."[5]

This is the genesis of the question: *Bomb damage or rent control?*

Because of rent control, the apartments that once provided stable housing are no longer available. With a lousy residential rental investment climate, they are not rebuilt. Supply shrinks, and the price of unregulated housing rises. Then, the housing of choice for the economically distressed becomes some far-away elsewhere, old automobiles, or the streets, parks, and back-alleyways of rent-controlled cities.

As much as some politicians might try, no one has figured out a way to repeal the law of supply and demand. There can be no repeal, only workarounds. In some of the old (and current) communist states, the workaround was mass starvation. That lessened demand. Starvation, combined with political repression, staved off collapse. Venezuela has made conditions so miserable that millions have resorted to the workaround of mass emigration, leaving those in charge the masters of a much-diminished nation. And cities in California have had their own workaround: effectively putting the casualties of its housing policies into moving vans or onto the streets. But long term, the law of supply and demand is inexorable: if you restrict prices, supply will diminish and demand will find substitutes, whether it be the streets, emigration, or death.

Rent control in response to a housing crisis is like pouring hot soup over a hungry person shivering in the freezing cold. At first it feels great. There's lots of warmth and soup. Then it cools off. The cold penetrates the soup-soaked clothing, and everything feels much colder than before. The food is wasted, the hunger is greater, and the cold is more bitter.

In a 1990 survey designed to gauge how much economists agree with one another, researchers asked 1,350 US economists of all political persuasions whether they agreed with forty statements of economic theory; 464 responded.[6] When presented with the statement: "A ceiling on rents reduces the quantity and quality of housing available," 93 percent agreed. There was more agreement on that statement than for any of the other thirty-nine propositions.

In a more recent survey of forty-one economists, only 2 percent agreed with the statement that "Local ordinances that limit rent increases for some rental housing units, such as in New York and San

Francisco, have had a positive impact over the past three decades on the amount and quality of broadly affordable rental housing in cities that have used them."[7]

A few younger economists steeped in the leftist tradition of academia have suggested that newer, more flexible rent control is the answer. But there is no empirical evidence to back that claim. A review of the recent economic literature studying newer versions of rent controls concludes that "it is not clear why it is desirable to tax such a narrow base as landlords" and that "the clearest finding of this review is the need for empiricists to develop more direct tests of the 'new' theoretical literature of the last two decades."[8]

Even left-leaning economists like Paul Krugman have written about the perils of rent control, calling it "predictable" that in a rent-control environment there will be "sky-high rents on uncontrolled apartments, because desperate renters have nowhere to go—and the absence of new apartment construction, despite those high rents, because landlords fear that controls will be extended."[9]

Economists continue to publish on rent control, and they agree: it doesn't work. One study from 2019, concluded:

- "These results highlight that forcing landlords to provide insurance against rent increases can ultimately be counterproductive. If society desires to provide social insurance against rent increases, it may be less distortionary to offer this subsidy in the form of government subsidies or tax credits. This would remove landlords' incentives to decrease the housing supply and could provide households with the insurance they desire."[10]
- "Thus, while rent control prevents displacement of incumbent renters in the short run, the lost rental housing supply likely drove up market rents in the long run, ultimately undermining the goals of the law."[11]

As noted previously, when Massachusetts repealed rent control, property values increased.[12] That in turn created incentives to build more housing. More of something is the ultimate solution to a shortage of that something. Housing is no different other than its emotional hold on otherwise rational policy makers.

In contrast to the Massachusetts experience, recent expansions of rent control in Oregon, New York, and California are already having adverse economic impacts and causing a marked decline in property values.

Because of its rent control and restrictive zoning laws, Oregon now boasts the lowest rate of residential construction it has had in decades:

> Oregon's population grew by nearly 400,000 between 2010 and 2019. But the state added a mere 37 housing permits for every 100 new residents, according to a report released last week by the Oregon Office of Economic Analysis. Economist Josh Lehner found that "while much of the attention is paid to rising housing costs, we know they are the symptom and not the cause of the disease. The chief underlying cause is the ongoing low levels of new construction this decade."[13]

In New York, it is the same. According to the *Wall Street Journal*, there have been drastic devaluations of rental property in New York City because of the new laws. Two months after passage of the new, much-more-restrictive law in 2019, the *Journal* reported, "Two New York landlords with large portfolios of rent-regulated apartments are behind on payments on more than $200 million in real-estate loans, a sign that new state rent laws are starting to hurt investors."[14]

As reported in the *Wall Street Journal*, "The biggest beneficiaries of rent regulation in New York aren't low-income tenants across New York City, but more affluent, white residents of Manhattan."[15] For example, in an article lauding the rent control life, the *New York Times* celebrates the good fortune of a woman who has lived in a rent-stabilized apartment for *thirty* years—starting at $250-a-month which was a quarter of what she had been paying in 1994.[16]

The implications of the new law are stark. In a *Wall Street Journal* article, several brokers and investors reported that "the new laws could cause the values of rent-stabilized apartment buildings to drop 20 [percent] to 45 [percent], depending on their current rent rolls. . . . That would leave many properties worth less than their mortgages and put building owners at risk of default."[17] Similarly, sales of apartment buildings have plummeted, and, as a result of the depressed values, some landlords are reportedly falling behind on loan payments.[18] After a few years under the new law, an increasing number of landlords have gone bankrupt.[19]

Likewise, the *Journal* also reports that with the advent of increased rent control in New York, rental apartment building sales fell by 51 percent in late 2019.[20] Instead of dealing with rent control, "investors are shifting to parts of the country that face little or no restrictions on rising rents."[21] By reducing investments, this will only make supply shortages worse. As the head of one investment firm put it, "We're not producing enough housing in this country . . . that continues to drive up rent levels."[22]

What's more, while the value of rent-controlled units has plummeted, the value of buildings free from rent control has risen. Six months into the new law, the *Wall Street Journal* recounted, "The near collapse of rent-regulated-building sales also produced some anomalies in residential sales. . . . because of the decline in regulated-building sales, sales of more valuable buildings with market-rate units predominated . . . driving up the average price per square foot tabulated in market reports."[23] In other words, some prices (and rents) are increasing more than they otherwise would, making the overall merit of rent control on steroids elusive.

Because New York's rent control makes it impossible for landlords to recoup expenses of over $15,000—and that over a decades-long amortization period—landlords today are taking units off the rental market when tenants move out. It's just too expensive to do the necessary repairs and upkeep. The city's housing agency estimates that there were in 2021 over 88,000 rent-stabilized apartments off the market.[24] Many of those are because landlords would lose money renting them. In fact, there are roughly 20,000 fewer rent-regulated apartments available than there were before the rent control law was tightened.[25]

But the recent New York experience should not surprise. New York City should have already learned that the best way to encourage more housing is to remove rent control. Not unlike the more recent experience in Massachusetts, when the World War I rent controls were removed in New York, there was a massive increase in the construction of new housing:

> The 1920s produced a volume of new housing which has never again been equaled, quantitatively or qualitatively. Between 1921 and 1929, 420,734 new apartments, 106,384 one-family houses, and 111,662 two-family houses were constructed. The total of 658,780 new dwellings averaged 73,198 units per year, a figure unmatched even in the 1960s, also a period of substantial growth. In the most prolific year, 1927, 94,367 dwellings were built, compared with 60,031 in 1963, the peak year since.[26]

Moving to California, there was a recent study out of San Francisco by economists at Stanford that found that, while rent control may help those who live in the rent controlled units, and it may help maintain some diversity in those units, overall rent control has caused a decline in rental housing stock. Moreover, rents in unregulated buildings have increased—making housing costs higher overall than they otherwise would have been. The authors found

> that rent control led to a 15 percentage point decline in the number of renters living in treated buildings and a 25 percentage point reduction in the number of renters living in rent-controlled units, relative to 1994 levels. This large reduction in rental housing supply was driven by both converting existing structures to owner-occupied condominium housing and by replacing existing structures with new construction.[27]

As a result, the authors concluded that: "rent control contributed to the gentrification of San Francisco, contrary to the stated policy goal. Rent control appears to have increased income inequality in the city by both limiting displacement of minorities and attracting higher income residents."[28]

When prices of any good are forced to be below the market price, the demand for the price-controlled good increases, but the incentive to supply that good decreases. A shortage develops. It's what economists call a disequilibrium in the market. It's a lot like trying to squeeze Jell-O. You can squeeze prices all you like, but soon enough, there's nothing left between your fingers.

If it doesn't work, and if it causes more harm than good, why do we still have rent control? Are politicians so venal that they will pander to their constituency just to get elected? Or do they actually think rent control works?

Clearly, the advocates of rent control think it will work—at least for them, at least for a while. It certainly can help those tenants who are lucky enough to live in a rent-controlled apartment (so long as the apartment doesn't deteriorate too much). But it is a myth to say that these tenants are mostly poor.

The language in many rent-control ordinances in California expressly says that rent control is necessary to help the poor, minorities, the elderly, and those otherwise socially and economically disadvantaged. To put this to the test, Pacific Legal Foundation hired Michael St. Johns, an economist, to compare renters in rent-controlled jurisdictions with those in neighboring communities without rent control.[29] According to the tenant advocates, rent control should allow those renters of fewer means to stay in their apartments. But in reality, in every comparison, the people living in rent-controlled apartments were on average richer, whiter, healthier, younger, and better employed. This is to be expected. Those with greater economic and social stability in their lives have the ability to stay in one location longer and thereby take advantage of rent control for a longer period of time. Put another way, with or without rent control, the poor are forced to move more often and lack the stability to take advantage of rent control in the longer term.

Based on this data, Pacific Legal Foundation represented a small landlord in a challenge to Santa Monica's rent control law. The landlord's attorneys argued that because the rent control ordinance had the opposite effect of its stated purpose, the law "failed to substantially advance a legitimate governmental interest" and was, therefore, an unconstitutional regulatory taking. While a state court of appeal agreed and found Santa Monica's rent control law to be unconstitutional, that holding was reversed by the California Supreme Court.

The court ruled that the courts shouldn't be second-guessing legislative determinations (even when they impinge of the rights of property owners) and, besides, the court said, without evidence, the rent control ordinance served the public purpose of keeping rents low. While even that conclusion is questionable in light of rent control's impact on the housing supply, the court would not entertain further analysis. The United States Supreme Court declined to take up the case.[30]

The California and New York experiences are fairly typical: when there is an episode of escalating rents, there is a movement to do something about it. Increasing the housing supply is a more difficult and longer-term solution than the obvious quick fix of rent control. Those who advocate for rent control often do so out of a combination of well-meaning concern for renters and a great deal of political or personal self-interest. But whatever the motivations may be, the end result is a less-free market in housing. It is one thing to accede to the idea of some government regulation of rental property, such as minimum health and safety standards or judicial mechanisms for resolving landlord-tenant disputes. But it is quite another for government to take over the pricing mechanisms in ways that harm tenants, landlords, and other private homeowners in the same housing market.

A recent Brookings Institute study concluded:

> New research examining how rent control affects tenants and housing markets offers insight into how rent control affects markets. While rent control appears to help current tenants in the short run, in the long run it decreases affordability, fuels gentrification, and creates negative spillovers on the surrounding neighborhood.[31]

But these lessons are never learned. In 2021, voters in St. Paul, Minnesota, imposed a 3 percent annual rent increase, with no exceptions for ownership status or inflation. As the *Wall Street Journal* reported, investors and developers immediately pulled out of the St. Paul market.[32] Two economists from the University of Southern California studying St. Paul's new rent control ordinance found that the ordinance "caused property values to fall by 6–7 [percent] for an aggregate of $1.6 Billion." More disturbingly, they concluded "that the tenants who gained the most from rent control had higher incomes and were more likely to be white, while the owners who lost the most had lower incomes and were more likely to be minorities"[33] and "in contrast to the law's intended goal . . . the benefits of rent control are enjoyed by relatively higher income tenants, while the burden of rent control is borne by relatively lower income owners."[34]

Rent control, whether it is the traditional type or the more flexible version of rent stabilization, isn't designed just to establish minimum living standards. It is directed toward wealth redistribution that favors a politically active constituency. Where it has been adopted, it has only been effective in the short term. It lowers rents for some. But because it also discourages the only practical means of alleviating high housing costs—an increase in supply through new free market construction— it ends up doing more harm than good.

PART V

Affordable Housing Mandates— Unworkable, Unaffordable, Unproductive, and Unconstitutional

Recognizing that there is a shortage of housing, politicians refuse to adopt policies that might solve the crisis. Very little has been done to undo exclusionary zoning. Permitting schemes remain fraught with delays. And raising taxes to subsidize housing, even if it was a good idea, is a political nonstarter. Instead, the solution du jour is to force those who build and buy new homes to subsidize affordable housing for others. This is an increasingly popular but terrible idea, because it only raises the cost of housing and unfairly creates a newcomers' tax on new home buyers—usually younger families with little in the way of extra resources. Such programs, sometimes euphemistically called "inclusionary zoning," are unworkable, unproductive, and unconstitutional.

Chapter 20

Extorting Developers and Home Buyers to Pay for Subsidized Housing

Where once government was closely constrained to increase the freedom of individuals, now property ownership is closely constrained to increase the power of government. Where once government was a necessary evil because it protected private property, now private property is a necessary evil because it funds government programs.[1]

Seventy-two-year-old George Sheetz is not a rich man. He is not a greedy developer. But to El Dorado County in California, he is an ATM. In July 2016, he applied for a permit to place a modest 1,854 square foot manufactured home for his family on a ten-acre lot on Fort Jim Road, a rural road in El Dorado County, which is just east of Sacramento, California. The county gave him a permit—but demanded that he pay $23,420 for traffic mitigation. The fee is based on a formula and not tied to any particular traffic impacts caused by the Sheetz family living in their new home. Indeed, the fee is supposed to go toward such things as helping build a new interchange on Highway 50, a major East–West arterial that is four miles away by the nearest road.

Sheetz paid under protest, built his home, and sued to recover the fee. Represented in part by Pacific Legal Foundation,[2] his case came before the Supreme Court in early 2024. But his case is hardly unique. It is just the latest case to reach the Supreme Court in a long line of cases where local governments have used their permitting power to demand money and property from people seeking to build homes.

To understand why Sheetz is protesting, and whether he might win, we must understand the magnitude and history of land-use permit extortions.

Figure 32. George Sheetz at his home.

A typical example of such history occurred a few years ago when, to build a single-family home in Elk Grove, south of Sacramento, the city demanded over a quarter-million dollars so the city could reconfigure a traffic intersection and install a traffic light. It took a lawsuit, with attorneys from the Pacific Legal Foundation, to halt the demand. But these cases are just the tip of the iceberg.

To build one single-family home in California in 2018, homebuilders had to pay development fees that ranged from a little more than $20,000 per home to more than $157,000, depending on the city.[3] For homes, on a per-bedroom basis the fee ranged from $6,000 to nearly $45,000, while apartment fees ranged from $11,500 to over $50,000 per bedroom.[4] Such fees can have the impact of making the construction of multi-family housing more expensive than it already is. In fact, impact fees alone add 6 to 18 percent to the cost of new homes.[5] Moreover, such huge fees have a distinct exclusionary impact, if not an actual exclusionary intent.[6] The higher the fees, the fewer middle-income people will be able to afford the higher-cost housing. Unless they are very poor and qualify for the limited supply of subsidized units, they are out of luck.

Government-imposed fees are a leading and direct cause of our housing affordability crisis. These fees are as damaging to affordability as are the typical cost-raising exclusionary zoning practices such as large-lot zoning or prohibitions on apartments. They are a direct cost levied on homebuilders that translates into a combination of reduced homebuilder profits and higher home costs. The higher the demand is for housing, the more of that cost will be borne by the new home buyers.[7] In other words, in California, the burden is on the shoulders of buyers. Moreover, as the cost of new housing skyrockets from fees, the cost of existing homes will follow suit.[8] How did we get to this point?

The demands on modern government are many. They include the pleas from people for government to do far more through the regulation of property than simply prevent nuisances and similar obvious external harms. Thus, we not only have area-wide use restrictions, height restrictions, and density restrictions, but we also have aesthetic-review boards. We have overlays for various endangered and not-so-oendangered species. We have riparian and other ecological setbacks. And we have wetlands, and sensitive-habitat zones, airport corridor restrictions, and a myriad of other land-use restrictions maintaining the status quo. Suffice it to say, many of these land-use restrictions go far beyond the prevention of traditionally understood, nuisance-like impacts that affect neighbors and the community.[9]

Some of these regulations—when they go "too far,"[10] deny all use or value,[11] or cause more economic harm than reasonable[12]—may give rise to a regulatory taking of property for which the government must pay,[13] especially when the regulations are not grounded in a meaningful nuisance-preventing rationale. In fact, the legitimacy of the nuisance-preventing rationale must be emphasized. Simply saying that a particular use of land creates a nuisance does not make it so. Apartments are not nuisances, despite what Justice Sutherland might have said in *Euclid*. Otherwise, as Justice Scalia remarked in *Lucas*, a nuisance-test would come down to a mere test of whether the legislative body had a "stupid staff" that could not concoct a harm-preventing rationale for a land use restriction.[14] However, to the extent that a governmental body can make a plausible case that a land-use permit denial serves a legitimate nuisance-prevention rationale, the denial is likely to be upheld by a deferential court against a takings challenge.

Government regulators, however, have more options than simply denying the offending land use. They can, under the right circumstances, suggest and approve an alternative land use that can meet the landowner's objectives while avoiding harmful impacts to neighbors or the public—impacts often referred to as negative externalities. Or regulators can impose conditions on the land use, including the condition that the permit-seeking landowner reduce or eliminate the project's adverse impacts. To minimize such impacts, government permitting agencies may impose a condition, known as an exaction. Exactions can include giving up property in an easement, restoring wetlands, improving traffic infrastructure, or engaging in habitat restoration.

At the same time that they are regulating to prevent noxious land uses, democratically elected officials are under pressure to provide more goods and services to their voters. It is all the better if the officials can provide these amenities with as few new taxes as feasible. The public wants better roads, affordable housing for all,[15] bigger parks, and prettier communities. The public wants to live in Eden, but it wants someone else to pay the rent.

Thus, there is a match made in heaven for an elected official here: the public's desire for free amenities married to the government's ability to control land use with its concomitant power to demand exactions.

Permit-seeking property owners can be forced to pay for many of the amenities desired by the public. But an elected official's heaven can be a landowner's hell.

Unchecked, excessive regulations can destroy all use and value in a property. It can result in a regulatory taking. If a taking is found, government might have to compensate for the value of the property, plus fees, plus interest, plus, in many cases, attorneys' fees. Similarly, unchecked demands for exactions in place of permit-denying regulations can lead to violations of the doctrine of unconstitutional conditions. Thus, in the context of land use, the doctrines of regulatory takings and unconstitutional conditions are inextricably intertwined. And to avoid a regulatory taking caused by a permit denial, government cannot simply substitute the permit denial with whatever set of exactions it desires. A town's land-use permitting department is not its ATM. There are constraints on the ability of government to demand exactions in exchange for land-use permits.

A governmental body may be tempted to demand some action or something of value in exchange for the receipt of a government benefit. Often, the demand can be legitimate, as when the benefit carries with it certain inherent duties and responsibilities. For example, the grant of an unpatented mining claim carries with it the duty to expend resources on the development of the claim's minerals and to properly register the claim on an annual basis.[16] And, of course, any development of the minerals on the claim must be done by obeying all applicable environmental laws and regulations.

But sometimes the government demands too much—as when the government requires the sacrifice of a constitutional right in exchange for some government benefit or discretionary permit. In one of the earliest cases invoking the "Doctrine of Unconstitutional Conditions," the Supreme Court held that the purpose of the doctrine is to enforce a constitutional limit on government authority:

> [T]he power of the state . . . is not unlimited, and one of the limitations
> is that it may not impose conditions which require relinquishment of

constitutional rights. If the state may compel the surrender of one constitutional right as a condition of its favor, it may, in like manner, compel surrender of all. It is inconceivable that guarantees embedded in the Constitution
of the United States may thus be manipulated out of existence.[17]

In *Perry v. Sindermann*, the Supreme Court considered whether due
process protections would attach to the decision not to rehire a junior
college professor who had criticized the school's administration. The
Court noted,

> For if the government could deny a benefit to a person because of his con-
> stitutionally protected speech or associations, his exercise of those freedoms
> would in effect be penalized and inhibited. This would allow the govern-
> ment to "produce a result which (it) could not command directly." Such
> interference with constitutional rights is impermissible.[18]

Similarly, in *F.C.C. v. League of Woman Voters*, the government conditioned the receipt of federal money on an agreement that public radio
station operators forego their First Amendment right to editorialize.[19]
The Supreme Court found this to be an unconstitutional condition,
noting that the danger posed by "the bewitching power of governmental largesse"[18] could not justify the ban because the statutory scheme
had structural protections against such co-option. Because the danger
inherent in the funding statute was insufficient to justify the ban on
First Amendment expression, the Court held that the "no-editorializ-
ing" condition was unconstitutional.

Nowhere, however, has the danger of the government's unrestrained
ability to demand something in exchange for government permission
been more apparent than in the context of land-use decision-making.

Nollan v. California Coastal Commission Extends the Unconstitutional Conditions Doctrine to Land-Use Permitting

The regulation of land use is not new. As governments developed land-
use–permitting regimes, they also understood the advantages in asking

for something in exchange for those permits. Sometimes such demands were appropriate, at other times they were not. In time, a fairly robust set of standards developed in the state courts for the imposition of an exaction that is a condition for the granting of a permit.[24] But some agencies were outliers, demanding more than could be justified even under the generous standards of their jurisdictions.

By 1987, the California Coastal Commission had raised its ability to leverage its permitting authority to an art form. Since its creation in 1972, the Commission has had the power to require a permit for any kind of development along the coastal zone from the Oregon border to Mexico, 840 miles to the south. And to the Commission, development can include everything from a subdivision to a garden wall to setting off fireworks. They all require permits, and they all provide an opportunity to demand something in exchange.

Patrick Nollan was an assistant Los Angeles city attorney who, for many years, leased with an option to buy a dilapidated one-story bungalow on the beach in Ventura County. To provide a permanent home for his growing family, he bought the property and sought a permit from the Coastal Commission to tear down the old house and replace it with a nicer two-story home. The Commission was happy to give him a permit—so long as he agreed to surrender an easement so the public could walk all over the one-third of his property between his home and the ocean. While none of his neighbors had yet been forced to grant an easement to their beachfront property in exchange for a permit, it was the plan of the Coastal Commission to start demanding a similar easement from anyone seeking any kind of development permit. Then, when one homeowner after another needed a permit to build, improve, fix, or alter their homes, each would be forced to give up an easement, creating one long public beach park along that stretch of the coast. All at zero cost to the taxpayers.

At first, Patrick Nollan reluctantly agreed and handed in the permit before heading into work. Arriving at work, Nollan began his day by opening the local legal newspaper. There he read about a nonprofit public interest law firm, Pacific Legal Foundation, that had had some

Figure 33. The Nollan bungalow, before demolition.

history suing and beating the Coastal Commission. He immediately telephoned a Foundation attorney and asked for help. A Foundation attorney answered the call and told Nollan, "No," the Foundation couldn't take his family's case. It was too late because under California law once you sign a permit and agree to the conditions, you can't challenge those conditions later in court. But Patrick Nollan was undeterred.

During his lunch hour, he went back to the Commission headquarters and told a staffer that he might have made a mistake and asked if he could see the permit again. A staffer found it and handed it to him. Nollan looked at it and said he had indeed made a mistake and asked if could keep the permit. The staffer agreed. Nollan took the permit back to his office, tore it up, and called PLF again. The case was on.

Nollan's main argument was that the demand that he give a third of his property to the state was an unconstitutional taking. But the Commission countered that the easement was necessary to protect the public from losing its view of the ocean. In an administrative hearing, the Commission found that "the new house would increase blockage of the view of the ocean, thus contributing to the development of 'a "wall" of residential structures' that would prevent the public 'psychologically . . . from realizing a stretch of coastline exists nearby that they have every right to visit."[20]

In other words, the motoring public driving along Highway 1 might look over in the direction of the new Nollan home and, because it is taller than before, be psychologically prevented from realizing that the ocean was still out there. According to the Commission, forcing Nollan to hand over one-third of the property would advance the public purpose of "overcoming the 'psychological barrier' to using the beach."[21]

Nollan initially won his case in trial court, only to be reversed by the California Court of Appeal, which said that his legal arguments had no merit. He asked the California Supreme Court to take his case. That court refused. But then the United States Supreme Court agreed.

The Court was not impressed by the Coastal Commission's arguments. In an opinion by Justice Scalia, the Supreme Court pointedly noted that the motoring public's psychological problem wouldn't be remedied by forcing Nollan to give up property between the house and ocean because the public couldn't see that third of his property. The new home was in the way. The Court speculated that if the Commission had demanded that the Nollans provide some sort of "viewing spot" on their property that might be okay. But, said the Court, it "is quite impossible to understand how a requirement that people already on the public beaches be able to walk across the Nollans' property reduces any obstacles to viewing the beach created by the new house. It is also impossible to understand how it lowers any 'psychological barrier' to using the public beaches."[22]

Because there was absolutely no connection, or as the court said, no "nexus," between the demand for the Nollans' property and the public purpose of protecting views, the Commission had gone too far: "In short, unless the permit condition serves the same governmental purpose as the development ban, the building restriction is not a valid regulation of land use but *an out-and-out plan of extortion.*'[23]

The victory for the Nollans was the first use of what is known as the doctrine of unconstitutional conditions in the context of a land-use permit. The Court's bottom line was that unless there was a "nexus" between the harm caused by a potential development and the thing the permitting agency is demanding in exchange for the permit, the condition is unconstitutional.

Figure 34. Patrick Nollan and his son in front of their new home (Pacific Legal Foundation photograph).

But what exactly is a nexus and how significant must it be? The answer to that question came out of Tigard, Oregon.

* * *

Dolan Adds a Rough Proportionality Test to the Nollan Nexus Requirement

John and Florence Dolan owned a hardware store on land next to Fanno Creek in Tigard, Oregon.[24] They sought permission from the city to expand the store and pave thirty-nine parking spaces. Just like in *Nollan,* the city here agreed to give the Dolans a permit—but only upon the condition that they give away a public easement over their riverfront property and build a bicycle path on their land for the public. The Dolans were outraged and fought back. What right, they asked, did the city have to demand that they simply give away their property and build the city a bike path merely because they wanted to expand their store? Their fight took years, and John Dolan passed away before it was over. But on his deathbed his dying wish to Florence was that she continue the fight. She did, and history was made.

According to the city, there was a relationship between these demands and the adverse impacts caused by the project. Because the paving of thirty-nine parking spaces would create an impermeable surface, it could increase the risk of flooding, thus justifying the public easement on the riverfront land. Similarly, a larger store could create traffic impacts, which could be alleviated with the bike path.

The Dolans, however, thought that was ridiculous. Allowing the public to walk across their land wasn't going to hold back floodwaters. And they sold hardware supplies, not things their customers carried off on bicycles.

But since the city had a plan for bicycle paths and a public greenway park along the creek next to their property, it couldn't resist the opportunity presented by the permit request to extort these public goods from the Dolans at no cost to the city.

Represented by a small nonprofit, Oregonians in Action, Florence Dolan eventually got her case to the United States Supreme Court in *Dolan v. City of Tigard.* At oral argument, the city repeated its flooding and traffic justifications for the easement and bicycle path. But Justice Scalia was quite skeptical, saying, "People are going to go to the hardware store on their bike? . . . There are a lot of bike paths around

Washington, and I've never seen people carrying shopping bags on their bikes."[25]

Florence Dolan won. While there may have been some kind of relationship or "nexus," between the alleged impacts of the bigger store and the city's demands, the Court said there must be more. The city had to do more than show just any old connection. Instead, the city had the burden of proving that its conditions were "roughly proportional" to the impacts of the development.[26]

Now asking for a bike trail to ameliorate traffic impacts from a new apartment building might be roughly proportional if the new apartment dwellers were likely to use the bike path for transportation. However, asking for the same bike trail in exchange for a plumbing store expansion might be a path too far under the rough proportionality test.

The Supreme Court sent the case back to the lower court for it to decide whether the city could meet the new burden. It couldn't, and Mrs. Dolan settled with the city. The city paid $1.4 million for the property it wanted to take, paid Mrs. Dolan's attorneys' fees to the tune of $100,000, and—at the insistence of Mrs. Dolan—erected a nice plaque in honor of her and her husband John with a citation to their case and a quote from the Constitution's Takings Clause.[27]

Figure 35. The City of Tigard erected this plaque as part of its settlement with Mrs. Dolan.

But this was hardly the end of government attempts to demand more stuff from landowners seeking permits. When Chief Justice Rehnquist wrote the opinion in *Dolan*, he made a passing remark that governments later tried to use to get around the ruling. In assuring governments that the decision would not affect the general, run-of-the-mill land-use regulations, the chief justice distinguished the *Dolan* facts as follows:

> First, they [acceptable land-use regulations] involved essentially legislative determinations classifying entire areas of the city, whereas here the city made an adjudicative decision to condition petitioner's application for a building permit on an individual parcel. Second, the conditions imposed were not simply a limitation on the use petitioner might make of her own parcel, but a requirement that she deed portions of the property to the city.[28]

Using this language, quite a few government agencies claimed that it was okay to extort property from permit-seeking landowners, so long as the extortion happens through general legislation or ordinances, as opposed to a permit process. As will be shown, it took thirty years for the Supreme Court to put a stop to that nonsense.

On top of that, for a time, government agencies also claimed that demands of money didn't count either because money is a different kind of property.

Landowners were quick to point out, however, that if demands for cash-money were not subject to the limits set out in *Nollan* and *Dolan*, then it would be relatively easy to circumvent the logic of those cases. For example, what if the California Coastal Commission had not asked for the easement over the Nollans backyard, but instead forced the Nollans to give the Commission enough money to pay for the beachfront property in a condemnation action? Or, what if the City of Tigard had demanded that Mrs. Dolan give the city enough money, say $1.4 million, so that the city could turn around and use the cash to condemn and pay her for the riverfront property? Would asking for money instead of interests in land be any different in the constitutional sense?

For some years after *Dolan* was decided, the lower courts were mixed on this question. Some courts actually agreed with government agencies and said money demands were exempt from the rule of *Nollan* and *Dolan.* Other courts found that any demand for any sort of property, including money, was subject to the rule. That was the confused state of the law until the *Nollan-Dolan* doctrine of unconstitutional conditions landed in some swampland in Florida.

Koontz Applies the Unconstitutional Conditions Doctrine to Monetary Exactions

The four-decade saga of *Koontz v. St. Johns River Water Management District*[29] began in 1972 when Coy Koontz Sr. applied for a permit to develop a small shopping center on a portion of a 14.9-acre parcel near the intersection of two major roadways near Orlando, Florida. After obtaining all the necessary permits from the local town, all Koontz needed was a wetlands permit from the St. Johns River Water Management District, which he applied for in 1994.

After some negotiations with staff, Coy Koontz thought he had a deal: in order to develop 3.7 acres, he would give up his remaining eleven acres for wetlands preservation. But when it came time to sign the permit documents, the district suddenly told him it wanted more. Like a car dealer telling a buyer at the last minute that the car will cost more than bargained for, the eleven acres weren't good enough for the suits in district headquarters. Now the district demanded that Koontz finance the drainage improvement of some district-owned property more than five miles away, improvements that could cost up to $150,000. *What the heck,* Koontz thought, *did his 3.7 acres have to do with some poorly managed district property many miles away?* Koontz refused, and the permit was denied.

Like all good ticked-off permit applicants, Coy Koontz sued, arguing that the demand constituted a taking in violation of *Nollan* and *Dolan.* The litigation outlasted Coy Koontz Sr. His son, Coy Koontz

Jr., carried on. The animosity between the district and the Koontz family was palpable. After one heated hearing, Coy Koontz Jr. and his wife Linda found themselves in an elevator with a government official. Coy and Linda asked, "Why don't you just pay for the property you want?" The answer: "Why would we buy the property when we can get it for free?"[30]

After Koontz won at trial, the district appealed. The case then went up and down the courts system like a yo-yo and dragged on for decades. Eventually, Coy Koontz Jr. wound up at the Florida Supreme Court. There, Koontz lost on two grounds. First, the state court found that because the permit had been denied, no condition had actually been imposed. Thus, the court reasoned, it would be premature and counterproductive to subject the denial to an analysis under *Nollan* and *Dolan*. Second, because Koontz was objecting to a demand of money and not one demanding land, *Nollan* and *Dolan* were not relevant.[31]

Put bluntly, the Florida court said the district could get away with the extortionate demand for money because Koontz never accepted the permit and never handed any money over to the district. And even if he had forked over the cash, because cash isn't land, the requirements of *Nollan* and *Dolan*—that government agencies justify the demand—were irrelevant.

Attorneys from Pacific Legal Foundation stepped in and took the case to the United States Supreme Court. After forty years, the Koontz family finally won. All the justices agreed that a governmental body cannot avoid scrutiny under *Nollan* or *Dolan* simply through the expedient of denying a permit when the owner refuses to give in to the demanded exaction. The majority opinion put it this way: "The principles that undergird our decisions in *Nollan* and *Dolan* do not change depending on whether the government *approves* a permit on the condition that the applicant turn over property or *denies* a permit because the applicant refuses to do so."[32]

The Court was especially aware of the tension between the government's ability to exact excessive concessions from permit applicants and the legitimate need to reduce the impacts that property development can cause. It explained in terms of "two realities":

> The first is that land-use permit applicants are especially vulnerable to the type of coercion that the unconstitutional conditions doctrine prohibits because the government often has broad discretion to deny a permit that is worth far more than property it would like to take. . . . Extortionate demands of this sort frustrate the Fifth Amendment right to just compensation, and the unconstitutional conditions doctrine prohibits them.
>
> A second reality of the permitting process is that many proposed land uses threaten to impose costs on the public that dedications of property can offset.[33]

In response to the argument made by the district that money was different and not subject to the analyses of *Nollan* and *Dolan*, a majority found that an exaction of money was just like a demand for any other kind of property. Since Koontz had a constitutional right to keep his property, including his money, he couldn't be forced to give it up in

Figure 36. Coy Koontz Jr. and his wife Linda.

order to get a permit—unless the standards of *Nollan* and *Dolan* were met. To make the point clear, the Court used the word "extortion" five times in the opinion to describe the leverage power government has over landowners.

One issue still loomed large over the application of *Nollan*, *Dolan*, and now *Koontz*: What if a condition is imposed by a legislative body rather than through the ad hoc permitting process? Does it make a difference if the City Council demands the money or land through an ordinance rather than through the building department? The dissent in *Koontz* raised this as a possible way out of the *Koontz* requirement, and some courts bought into this distinction.

This is a curious notion. Traditionally, when courts, including the Supreme Court, have considered the doctrine of unconstitutional conditions, it has mattered little how the condition was imposed—whether by a bureaucrat, an elected official, or a legislative body. Courts have routinely stricken conditions that force people to give up a constitutional right in order to obtain a government permit or benefit.

Nor is there a good reason to treat legislatively imposed exactions with more leniency than those imposed administratively. As Justice Thomas put it in a dissent, "A city council can take property just as well as a planning commission can."[34] What matters is the exercise of government power, not the source of that power. To a landowner being forced to exchange a right for a permit, it doesn't matter who wields the enforcement power. What matters is that power is being wielded to take a constitutionally protected right.

Given this background, legal scholars like Professor David Callies find "little doctrinal basis beyond blind deference to legislative decisions to limit [the] application of [*Nollan* or *Dolan*] only to administrative or quasijudicial acts of government regulators."[35]

Fortunately, George Sheetz helped resolve this argument and put an end to unjustified and unjustifiable permit demands. As described at the beginning of this chapter, George Sheetz is the seventy-two-year-old man who paid under protest $23,400 in "traffic mitigation fees" in order to put a modest 1,854 square foot manufactured home on ten acres in rural El Dorado County. His plan was to spend his retirement years there with his wife and grandson.

The county argued, and the California courts agreed, that the county did not need to justify this demand under the nexus and rough proportionality standards of *Nollan* and *Dolan*. The county pointed to a map that it had adopted a few years back. The map had six zones. Everyone building within one of the zones was assigned a set amount. Sheetz's property is in Zone 6, and according to the map, that meant he had to pay $23,420 for traffic mitigation. Of that, $2,240 was supposed to help improve an interchange on an interstate highway, several miles away. There was no attempt to tie the specific expected traffic to Sheetz's family home and the fee.

Since the fee was approved by the county supervisors and not a permitting bureaucrat, the county argued that it is exempt from the calculus required by *Nollan* and *Dolan*. The county essentially argued that there was a "legislative action exception" to the Constitution's protection of property rights. Unsurprisingly, dozens of state and city governments filed friend of the court briefs, suggesting that when it comes to legislatively imposed permit fees, the operative principle should be "trust us."

But as Sheetz's attorneys pointed out, the demands for land and money in *Nollan*, *Dolan*, and *Koontz* were all based on legislative actions. Moreover, the constitution doesn't give a pass to legislative bodies to take what they want without meaningful judicial oversight, Sheetz's attorneys argued.

Finally on April 12, 2024, the Supreme Court unanimously ruled that El Dorado County was out of line.[36] The Court held that "The Constitution provides 'no textual justification for saying that the existence or the scope of a State's power to expropriate private property without just compensation varies according to the branch of government effecting the expropriation.'"[37] Hopefully, this will put a stop to this sort of extortionate gamesmanship that local, state, and federal government entities have been using to extract millions upon millions of total dollars from homebuilders large and small, which has been crushing the dream of making housing affordable again.

* * *

Affordable Housing Mandates, a.k.a. "Inclusionary Zoning"

One of the goals of Pacific Legal Foundation—which represented the Nollans, Coy Koontz Jr., and George Sheetz, and which filed a friend of the court brief in *Dolan*—is to get a case to the Supreme Court challenging a particularly pernicious legislative exaction. In these cases, local governments are imposing "affordable housing" mandates on new home builders by demanding that builders build or subsidize new low-income housing in order to get building permits to build market-rate housing.

Government officials like to call these schemes "inclusionary zoning" as a way of pretending that they are a solution for their exclusionary zoning policies. But they have nothing to do with zoning. They don't dictate what can be built where, but simply demand subsidies for affordable housing. In short, to quote *Nollan*, they are "an out-and-out plan of extortion."

With inclusionary zoning, developers of market-rate housing are forced to build and sell housing units at subsidized prices and sell them to qualifying lower-income buyers.[38] While the ordinances vary from community to community, they all have some common elements:

- The affordable housing requirements go into effect once a certain threshold is met—usually when a developer seeks to build at least ten to fifteen units of market-rate housing.[39]
- Sometimes, however, an affordable housing fee is imposed on every land-use permit—from large subdivisions to single parcel-lot splits.[40]
- A builder may be required to build an "affordable" unit that roughly matches the size of the neighboring market-rate units.

The affordable units must usually be placed within the same development as market-rate units, although ordinances can have options for placement elsewhere.

- Alternatively, a builder may have the option of paying an in-lieu fee, with the fee set by a formula.
- The units must be sold to buyers who meet certain income criteria, often hovering between 50 and 70 percent of the area's average income.
- The units must be sold at a price that the low-income resident can afford—based on a formula where mortgage payments will amount to roughly one-third of the typical low-income resident's take-home pay.
- The units must have deed restrictions attached—so the low-income owner can sell only to other low-income buyers at a controlled price. Owners cannot sell at market rates or take any "excess profits." (As a policy matter these restrictions remove any incentive for these home buyers to invest more than the bare minimum for the maintenance and improvement of their homes. They are essentially "renters with title" responsible for taxes and their own maintenance.)
- The affordable housing mandates are imposed by a legislative body such as a city council, removing some discretion from the planning and building departments.

Home builders have objected to the substantial increase in the costs for market rate homes caused by these affordable housing mandates. These mandates not only reduce the builders' profits, but they also make housing more unaffordable. They are simply an attempt to create the public benefit of subsidized housing without higher taxes on the voters. Because the costs are borne by builders and new residents who don't yet vote in a community, there is little political pressure to stop these mandates. By making some units more expensive and others cheaper, on average, they do nothing to alleviate the overall cost of housing but only create a disincentive for new construction.

Moreover, economists are skeptical that inclusionary zoning, or IZ, does anything to alleviate the shortage of affordable housing. As economist Emily Hamilton put it,

> As legal scholar Robert Ellickson explained in 1981, IZ is a tax on the construction of new housing units and a price ceiling on the units that must be set aside at below-market rates. Both of these factors can be expected to reduce the quantity of housing supplied, resulting in higher prices for units that are available at market rate.
>
> . . . the body of research attempting to measure the causal effect of IZ on house prices and new housing construction provides some evidence that IZ increases house prices and reduces housing supply.[41]

When challenged under the theory that the mandates violate the doctrine of unconstitutional conditions, the California courts have resorted to the subterfuge of saying that the doctrine is irrelevant. Because the exactions were imposed via a legislative act or formula, the California Supreme Court said, they are merely land-use or zoning regulations, not subject to *Nollan*, *Dolan*, or *Koontz*. Until now, the United States Supreme Court has declined to accept such cases for review.[42] With *Sheetz*, that may change and courts may finally put a stop to situations like the one from San Jose described next.

* * *

California Building Industry Association v. City of San Jose[43]

The City of San Jose demands all developers of fifteen or more residential units to set aside ten percent of their units for a subsidized sale to low-income buyers, with a price based not on costs but on the buyer's ability to afford mortgage payments. Alternatively, developers can pay several hundred thousand dollars per unit into a low-income housing fund. The city has ignored the doctrine of unconstitutional conditions and has never attempted to prove that building new homes creates an increased need for subsidized homes.

When challenged, San Jose simply claimed the demands that home builders build or subsidize low-income housing are simply zoning mandates and, because they were *legislative* actions, they were not subject to *Nollan, Dolan,* or *Koontz.* In other words, they don't force landowners to give up any rights in order to build; they simply required builders to conform to their residential zoning requirements, which include price controls and a mix of market rate and subsidized housing. The California Building Industry Association (CBIA) sued.

The California Supreme Court upheld the ordinance that required developers to build affordable housing units. The state court found that the *Nollan, Dolan,* and *Koontz* standards for unconstitutional conditions did not apply

> because there is no exaction—the ordinance does not require a developer to give up a property interest for which the government would have been required to pay just compensation under the takings clause outside of the permit process. This condition does not require the developer to dedicate any portion of its property to the public or to pay any money to the public. Instead, like many other land use regulations, this condition simply places a restriction on the way the developer may use its property by limiting the price for which the developer may offer some of its units for sale.[44]

The court surmised that the program did not impose an exaction but was simply a type of zoning ordinance with price controls and that municipalities have "broad discretion to regulate the use of real property to serve the legitimate interests of the general public and the community at large."[45] We've come a long way from the time when folks were concerned that the Euclid zoning ordinance might be unconstitutional. In *Euclid,* the Supreme Court upheld a prohibition on apartments; here it is making builders subsidize homes and apartments. In no way is San Jose's subsidy mandate anything like Euclid's zoning ordinance.

But demanding money or forcing the sale of some units at below-market prices is not the mere regulation of "the use of real property," as the California Supreme Court intoned.[46] Just saying "this is not an exaction" doesn't make it "not an exaction." Owners are forced to give up money or the right to sell homes at full price in order to get a permit. This is not the sort of land-use law described in *Dolan* as "essentially legislative determinations classifying entire areas of the city."[47] There, the Court was referring to regulations such as standard zoning, height restrictions, and the like. It was certainly not contemplating the forced construction or creative financing of low-income housing, even if those exactions were imposed via ordinance rather than the planning department's permitting desk. They have nothing to do with zoning or land-use planning.

The difference between forcing Coy Koontz to spend money to fix district property and forcing San Jose developers to spend money to subsidize lower-income housing is elusive at best. What matters is that the property owner is being forced to sacrifice property in exchange for a permit to develop. It does not matter if the means to accomplish the forced sacrifice is through a zoning bureaucrat following local law or a city council enacting local law. The rights are violated just the same.[48]

The United States Supreme Court did not take the *San Jose* case. The Court never explains why it declines to take cases, but here it might have been because the case was largely litigated before *Koontz* was decided, and so the trial attorneys weren't able to raise arguments based on *Koontz* until the case was well underway. The Supreme Court may have decided it would be better to take a different case in the future where the *Koontz* arguments were front and center.

While agreeing with the Court's refusal to take up *San Jose*, Justice Thomas noted that the treatment of legislatively imposed exactions remains unresolved:

> For at least two decades, however, lower courts have divided over whether
> the *Nollan/Dolan* test applies in cases where the alleged taking arises from

a legislatively imposed condition rather than an administrative one. That division shows no signs of abating. The decision below, for example, reiterated the California Supreme Court's position that a legislative land-use measure is not a taking and survives a constitutional challenge so long as the measure bears "a reasonable relationship to the public welfare."

I continue to doubt that "the existence of a taking should turn on the type of governmental entity responsible for the taking."[49]

San Jose is not the only locality to demand money for subsidized housing from builders. Perhaps the most outrageous case involved Dartmond and Esther Cherk who owned a three-acre residentially zoned lot in Marin County, just north of San Francisco. They wanted to divide the property in two so they could sell one lot and use the proceeds to build a retirement home on the other.

After nearly twenty years of battling with the county, the county relented—so long as the Cherks agreed to pay almost $40,000 for the county to spend on affordable housing. The county never felt the need to explain why adding another buildable lot where another home could be built in any way made the housing crisis worse. Of course, it couldn't because there is no math where adding to the supply of building lots causes the price of housing to rise. Represented by Pacific Legal Foundation attorneys, the Cherks sued.

Sadly, the California courts rejected the Cherks' claim that the fee violated *Nollan*, *Dolan*, and *Koontz*. The state court said the demand for money was a mere land-use regulation and not the kind of extortionate demand seen in those other cases. There is no logic to this, only an excuse to evade the holdings of the Supreme Court. In late 2019, without explanation, the Supreme Court denied the Cherks' petition for further review.

But the future landscape for these types of cases may have changed with the decision in *Sheetz*. George Sheetz beat the County of El Dorado because area-wide traffic impact fee zones weren't immune from the Constitution. Neither should so-called inclusionary zoning schemes. If state legislatures don't ban the practice, homebuilders will

Figure 37. Dartmond and Esther Cherk.

have to return to the Supreme Court, this time armed with *Nollan*, *Dolan*, *Koontz*, and now, *Sheetz*.

PART VI

The Great Emptying of the Mentally Ill onto Our Streets

Stop fuc*ing with me, you motherfuc*er.[1]

Chapter 21

Unhousing the Mentally Ill

I remember well my first trip to a mental hospital. It was early evening in late September 1972. Marcy State Hospital was a sprawling complex of two- and three-story red brick buildings in upstate New York. I traveled there in a blue Hamilton College van where I was a freshman undergraduate. We drove down a driveway and into the parking lot. As I got out of the van, I looked up at an entrance that may have reminded more than few patients over the years of Dante's line, "Abandon hope, all ye who enter here." Once inside the wide double exterior doors, a guard with a rattling ring of keys unlocked the interior doors to the wing on the right-hand side. He ushered me in and locked the door behind me.

In a room the size of a small basketball court, there was an assortment of institutional green vinyl chairs and couches. The ceiling was low and, instead of basketball hoops, there were two blaring black and white televisions hanging from the ceiling on either end. The air was heavy with smoke from the patients' hand-rolled cigarettes. The guards or wardens mostly stayed in their station. Most of the men were older. Some appeared physically okay, but others shook from various palsies, and displayed odd drooling and tongue-thrusting—symptoms of a condition called tardive dyskinesia, a side-effect of some psychotropic drugs that they lined up to take twice a day. That could make rolling cigarettes with their shaking, yellow-stained hands tough, but they had lots of practice. It's not as if they had anything else to do all day.

I sat down on one of the couches and introduced myself. The residents began to tell me their limited life stories.

Most of them had been in the institution for a very long time. Most had never experienced a significant adulthood outside the walls of an institution. A typical story went roughly like this: "When I first arrived here in 1945, I was put in Building C. I used to help in the kitchen. Then for a few years, I delivered the mail between buildings D and E. And I washed dishes for a while at building A. My last job was to sweep the floor here in this building. But that stopped a little while ago because of the judge."

There were many variations on this theme. Between cigarettes they would all tell me pretty much the same thing: they had a series of menial jobs in the different buildings that had recently ended when a judge said they had to stop. None of them really understood what had happened, but they knew that instead of having something to do, they now had all the time in the world to do nothing. Except eat, sleep, watch television, take their medications, and smoke cigarettes.

The judge they were referring to was District of Columbia Circuit Judge Aubrey Robinson Jr. and the case was *Souder v. Brennan.*[2] That case involved a demand from self-appointed patient advocates that the US Secretary of Labor issue an order that mental hospital patients who performed jobs be treated as employees under the Fair Labor Standards Act. In other words, they had to be paid minimum wage. This upended the treatment model employed by psychiatric hospitals across the nation. Before the ruling, patients who could work were given jobs that they could handle to give them something to do all day while instilling in the patients a sense of worth and self-discipline. Also, quite frankly, the patient labor helped ease the costs of running these large institutions. While much of the work performed by the patients was necessary, there was redundancy, make-work, and inherent inefficiencies with some of the patients who had limited mental faculties.

Patient labor, therefore, was an integral part both of the structure of the patient's lives and of the economic structure of the institutions. As one hospital administrator said, "The economy of a mental hospital is based on 'patient labor.' . . . [W]ithout it the hospital . . . would collapse."[3]

Judge Robinson wasn't troubled by the impact of his ruling on the therapy model, writing that

> The fallacy of the argument that the work of patient-worker is therapeutic can be seen in extension to its logical extreme, for the work of most people, inside and out of institutions, is therapeutic in the sense that it provides a sense of accomplishment, something to occupy the time, and a means to earn one's way. Yet that can hardly mean that employers should pay workers less for what they produce for them.[4]

That organized labor, the American Federation of State, County, and Municipal Employees, joined in support of the suit only furthers a sense of cynicism. Rather than unpaid patient labor, the work would have to be performed by well-paid union members.

With the *Souder* decision everything changed. The institutions could not afford to pay the patients minimum wage when they could employ more capable members of the outside community to perform the same tasks. And, of course, many of the tasks fell by the wayside. By having to pay employees to perform these tasks, every psychiatric hospital that relied on work-therapy now found its budget in tatters.

Certainly, a patient may attach a greater value to work when he is paid for his labor than when not. As one researcher wrote, "Nothing appears to be a greater stimulus to engage in activities that reflect health instead of illness than to be paid for the product of those activities."[5] But what I saw at Marcy State Hospital was not paid work, or unpaid work, but no work at all.

The judge may have been well-intentioned but was dismissive of such concerns. He had taken a special interest in the humane treatment of the mentally ill, and over his career, he issued many rulings trying to improve their condition. But the immediate result of his ruling was the enforced idleness of hundreds of thousands of patients nationwide. Their work-therapy over, and the budgets of the institutions strained, what happened next was inevitable.

The advocates advancing *Souder* had no plan other than to tear down the existing system while hoping that something better might come along. Destruction of one system without a concrete plan, budget, and financing for a replacement is a dangerous exercise in hubris. For the mentally ill, that hubris led to a disaster that has been playing out on the streets for nearly a half-century.

Chapter 22

From the Courtroom and
Hospitals to the Streets

For four years I continued my volunteer work trying to help socialize the patients at the hospital, and I ran the volunteer program during by junior and senior years. Our goal was to interact with the patients. As members of the community who were neither their doctors nor their keepers, the residents could have normal conversations with normal people. People they could trust.

Starting in late 1975 and early 1976, the patients began to excitedly tell me some good news. One after another, they told me that by the end of 1976 they were going to be transferred to a halfway house.

One said, "Jim, I'm going to Albany and will stay in a halfway house for six months."

Another, "Jim, I'm going to Schenectady where they'll be putting me in a halfway house."

I'd ask for how long.

"Six months."

"Six months."

And so on. It was always "six months."

Then I asked, "Where will you go after six months?"

Every time, I received a blank stare, a quizzical look, or "I don't know."

"They haven't told me yet."

That's because "they" hadn't figured it out yet.

As one commentator has alleged, "The *Souder* case has proved one of the most destructive to patient welfare of all the cases brought by the mental health bar." Moreover, in other writings, the legal advocates, made clear that their real goal was to empty institutions, not improve the way they were run.[1]

It was the beginning of the great emptying of the state-run psychiatric hospitals in New York and across the nation. From 1955 to 1994, the population in state mental hospitals had declined from 558,239 to 71,619 patients.[2] Liberal Democrats loved the idea because it meant freedom for people, many of whom had long since ceased to be a threat to themselves or others. And with medications, everyone could lead a normal life.

If only.

And the Republicans and fiscal conservatives loved it because emptying out the institutions would save bucket-loads of real money—especially after *Souder* altered the fiscal dynamic.

Who would have thought that comprehensive out-patient and group-home treatment might not be a great money saver? Unless the out-patient and group-home treatments never fully materialized.

What could possibly go wrong?

It was one of the cruelest hoaxes of self-deception in American history. We've since learned that after the halfway houses, there was often nothing but the streets. And this was for hundreds of thousands of people who had never lived on their own. Outpatient treatment facilities were woefully inadequate. For patients who had enough trouble with a regular medication regimen inside the walls of an institution or halfway house, regular medication became well-nigh impossible when there were no walls at all. And for the great majority, there was still no work.

Of course, the psychiatric hospitals were far from perfect. There were horror stories that were more real than *One Flew Over the Cuckoo's*

Nest. Geraldo Rivera gained fame by using a stolen key to sneak his camera crew into Willowbrook State School, a locked New York City institution for 5,230 mostly younger, developmentally disabled patients. For the whole world to see, Rivera found and recorded the young people in horrific conditions, uncared for, sometimes naked, and frequently wallowing in their own filth.[3] Rivera described New York's attitude toward its charges as treating them like "human vegetables in a detention camp."[4] It was blindingly apparent that state-sponsored mass neglect was not an appropriate standard for treating the mentally ill.

Nor was it constitutional. After his father surmised that Kenneth Donaldson had "delusions," he tried to get help for his son. A Florida court ruled that he had been suffering "paranoid schizophrenia" and committed Donaldson to a state mental hospital in Chattahoochee starting in 1957.[5] Despite his protestations that he was neither insane nor a danger, Donaldson remained locked up for fifteen years—*without treatment*. After he was released, he sued for damages under the Civil Rights Act. In 1975, the Supreme Court ruled in favor of Donaldson.

The Court held that it was a violation of the Due Process Clause to confine someone unless the person is a danger to himself or others.[6] And, in words relevant to the plight of the mentally ill on the streets today, the Court acknowledged the argument that hospital confinement may provide a superior living standard: However, the court found that "the mere presence of mental illness does not disqualify a person from preferring his home to the comforts of an institution."[7] That was before the "comforts" of home consisted for many of nylon tents and hard sidewalks. The Court also held that public discomfiture with the mentally ill cannot justify their confinement, stating that "Mere public intolerance or animosity cannot constitutionally justify the deprivation of a person's physical liberty"[8] After all, said the Court, people cannot be confined just because they are "physically unattractive or socially eccentric."

Four years later, the Supreme Court confronted the case of Frank O'Neal Addington, who had been repeatedly, but temporarily, confined for various infractions while in the grip of his mental illness.

After he threatened his mother, the State of Texas involuntarily confined Addington for an indefinite period. On appeal, the Supreme Court clarified the *Donaldson* decision, finding that if a jury finds by "clear and convincing evidence" that a person is a danger he can be indefinitely confined "for his own welfare and protection, or the protection of others."[9] These decisions, for humanitarian reasons no doubt, substantially raised the bar a state must reach before a mentally ill person can be involuntarily confined to a state mental hospital.

Judicial intervention and Rivera's exposé led to reform efforts. The megahospitals were doomed. Financially they were unsustainable. Legally, they were doubtful. Legislatively, they were done with. The great emptying was about to begin.

Even assuming there is space today in a hospital, no one can be confined for more than a few days unless they are proven to be a danger to themselves or others. That's a standard that was born in humanity but was the bane for decades of families who fail in their desperate attempts to get help for their loved ones. If they can't prove the standard, in-patient treatment is unavailable. The spouse, child, or other mentally-ill family member must go back home, or if that's impossible, onto the streets. Once on the streets there is the added stress from fear, hunger, physical deprivation, abuse, and isolation. On the street, the line between being mildly ill and seriously ill is easy to cross.

The most recent and credible estimate suggests that over three-quarters of the street homeless are mentally ill.[10] The old state-run mental hospitals of yore have been replaced by our streets and prisons. Prisons, where between 10 and 35 percent of inmates are mentally ill, have become the new de facto formal institutions for the ill.[11] The streets are the informal institutions.

The great emptying has not only emptied the psychiatric institutions of their patients, but apparently also our collective moral responsibility for their plight. If we are to solve the homeless crisis, we must once again take on that responsibility.

We've tried gigantic institutional warehouses. Today, we're trying the prisons and streets, with a nod here and there to community treatment. But pervasive community treatment is the only method that we haven't fully tried. In his 1972 documentary, Rivera also showed alternative community treatment programs in California. That was a good start in 1972, but a half-century later it clearly isn't enough.

While the courts have occasionally beaten back the NIMBY resistance, neighborhoods still resist the thought of housing the mentally ill nearby. It's time to embrace much more community treatment, not shuck off the problem to someone else's streets or prison cells.

Of course, it's an expensive proposition. But it's way more expensive than it ought to be because the price of housing is too high in many areas. We also need more inexpensive individual housing for the mentally ill once they leave community housing. To the extent that the mentally ill can live independently, the stress of unaffordable housing can only make a bad situation worse. So, to solve the problem of housing the mentally ill, we must also solve the national housing crisis. To do that, we must begin to build again, and build more, and build until supply meets demand.

Marcy State Hospital is no more. Its patients are dead or dispersed. The nation's mentally ill are now everywhere, without adequate medical care, food or shelter.

PART VII

Property Rights—A Way Out of the Housing Crisis

We have already seen that a defense of property rights played a key role in overturning racial zoning in Buchanan v. Warley, *and how property rights were mostly ignored in the Court's consideration of the zoning scheme in* Euclid v. Ambler Realty. *To fully appreciate the role of private property in American jurisprudence, we must consider the meaning of the rights people have in property and how those rights secure our liberties. Under any traditional understanding of the law of nuisance, building homes should rarely, if ever, be considered a nuisance-like activity that can trump the property rights of the owners. After a strong beginning, this nation gradually lost its respect for private property rights, and it became increasingly difficult to build enough homes. The Takings Doctrine promises to restore some of the vitality to property rights by providing a remedy to owners whose property rights have been unnecessarily curtailed.*

Chapter 23

A Short History of the Rise, Fall, and Rise of Private Property

The poorest man may in his cottage bid defiance to all the forces of the Crown. It may be frail; its roof may shake; the wind may blow through it; the storm may enter; the rain may enter; but the King of England cannot enter—all his force dares not cross the threshold of the ruined tenement![1]

Private property creates for the individual a sphere in which he is free of the state. It sets limits to the operation of the authoritarian will. It allows other forces to arise side by side with and in opposition to political power. It thus becomes the basis of all those activities that are free from violent interference on the part of the state. It is the soil in which the seeds of freedom are nurtured and in which the autonomy of the individual and ultimately all intellectual and material progress are rooted.[2]

To understand the role of private property in the development of housing, one must first begin at the beginning and ask "what is property?" This is not a simple question. Nor is there a simple answer. Books on top of books have been written on the origins of, and even the legitimacy of, private property. Scholars have spent lifetimes contemplating and arguing over the meaning of property. Politicians have built careers on supporting or opposing notions of property. Wars and revolutions have been fought over the ownership of property. However, there are some basic and universal principles that can be easily understood:

1. Government does not create property but is formed to protect it.

Which came first, government or property? That question engaged seventeenth-century philosophers for some very practical reasons. In an era in which the king claimed absolute authority over his subjects and their land, many of his subjects resisted. In doing so they developed a revolutionary idea that the people and their property did not exist to serve their king, but instead the king's power derived from the need for there to be a government to protect the people and their property. In other words, the king serves the people.

One of the first great explications of modern property theory came early in the seventeenth century from the Dutch legal philosopher Hugo Grotius. In his 1625 *The Rights of War and Peace*, he concluded, "Thus property, as now in use, was at first a creature of the human will. But, after it was established, one man was prohibited by the law of nature from seizing the property of another against his will."[3]

A half century later, in 1689, Enlightenment English philosopher John Locke put it this way in his *Second Treatise of Government*:

> [Man] seeks out, and is willing to joyn in Society with others who are already united, or have a mind to unite for the mutual *Preservation* of their Lives, Liberties and Estates, which I call by the general Name, *Property*.
>
> The great and *chief end* therefore, of Mens uniting into Commonwealths, and putting themselves under Government, *is the Preservation of their Property*.[4]

Thus, property came first, and government was created to protect it. Locke wrote this *Second Treatise* to refute the more monarchist (now called statist) view of Thomas Hobbes and others. In 1651, Hobbes wrote *The Leviathan*. His purpose was to provide intellectual support for the theory of absolute monarchy. Most of England understood that there was a severe threat to the power of the king. Indeed, *The Leviathan* was published in the midst of a century that saw one civil war that led to the execution of Charles I in 1649 and a second civil war that ultimately resulted in a dictatorship by Oliver Cromwell in 1653. After Cromwell died of natural causes in 1658, the Crown was restored under Charles II in 1660—at which point Cromwell's bones were dug up, hung, and tossed into a pit—except for his head, which was stuck onto a pole outside Westminster Hall. Clearly, the question of the power of the king was in hot debate.

Hobbes argued in *The Leviathan* that man had formed government only for his self-preservation, and in doing so assigned all rights to all things to the government, thus giving free reign to the government to grant to the people as much, or little, liberty and property as necessary:

> Without a common power to keep them all in awe [i.e., the power of government] they [the people] are in that condition which is called war; and such a war as is of every man against every man . . . and the life of man [is] solitary, poor, nasty, brutish, and short.
>
> . . . .
>
> [Thus, it is] necessary, to lay down this right to all things; and be contented with so much liberty against other men as he would allow other men against himself.
>
> [It] is annexed to the sovereignty the whole power of prescribing the rules whereby every man may know what goods he may enjoy, and what actions he may do, without being molested by any of his fellow subjects: and this is it men call propriety.[5]

This is very much the opposite of what John Locke argued several decades later in his *Second Treatise*. Locke understood well that his refutation of Hobbes and his supporters could be personally dangerous under a powerful monarch. Indeed, when Locke first published *The Second Treatise,* he did so anonymously. After all, in the years after the civil wars, the dictator Cromwell, and the Restoration of the monarchy, England had not yet returned to normalcy.

When Charles II was succeeded by his Catholic brother, James II, in 1685, more trouble ensued. Fearing the re-imposition of Catholicism, Parliament rebelled in the Glorious Revolution of 1688. That bloodless revolution led to King James's exile to France. In his place, Parliament recruited from Holland William II and his wife Mary to be the new English monarchs in 1689—but on the condition that William and Mary would agree to and abide by the newly drafted English Bill of Rights and acknowledge that the monarch's power derived from Parliament and not from any unchallengeable Divine Right of kings.[6]

So, it was in this context that Locke published *The Second Treatise*—a work that challenged the notion of an absolute monarchy and that supported the new understanding from the Glorious Revolution that the king derived his authority from the people and their Parliament. These ideas would profoundly affect the future course of England, and years later provided support for another revolution against another British king on the other side of the Atlantic.

That was in 1776, less than a century later, when Locke's words were used to justify the American Revolution. Compare the passage from *The Second Treatise* about why men "joyn in Society . . . for the mutual preservation" of their property with this language from the Declaration of Independence:

> We hold these truths to be self-evident, that all men are created equal, that they are endowed by their Creator with certain unalienable Rights, that among these are Life, Liberty and the pursuit of Happiness.—That to secure these rights, Governments are instituted among Men, deriving their just powers from the consent of the governed.

An earlier draft of the Declaration described these rights as "Life, Liberty, and Property." Various theories have been put forth over the years for the substitution. One holds that since property can be sold, it is in fact "alienable" and thus makes no sense in this context. Another is that the pursuit of happiness is pretty much the same as the acquisition of property, or that property is an essential element of happiness. Or that there is more literary consistency with a second use of the word "happiness" a bit later in the text. Whatever the reason, the Lockeean influence on the Declaration is irrefutable.

2. Government must protect property, not threaten it.

Locke and the drafters of the Declaration both justified the shaking off of a government that failed to protect the rights of its people. Consider this passage from *The Second Treatise*: "Whenever the legislators endeavor to take away, and destroy the Property of the People . . . they put themselves into a state of War with the People, who are thereupon absolved from any further obedience."[7]

Compare that to this identical sentiment in the Declaration: "That whenever any Form of Government becomes destructive of these ends, it is the Right of the People to alter or to abolish it, and to institute new Government, laying its foundation on such principles and organizing its powers in such form, as to them shall seem most likely to effect their Safety and Happiness."

In 1787, the drafters of the new United States Constitution likewise believed that a central purpose of government was to be a protector of private rights and liberties, including and especially, rights in property. In arguing for the adoption of the new Constitution, James Madison, Alexander Hamilton, and John Jay published a series of essays from 1787 to 1788 explaining how the new constitution and government were supposed to work in practice. These eighty-five Federalist Papers compared various governments from ancient Greece to the eighteenth century, pointing out the faults and virtues of each one. Most importantly, the essays explained how the new Constitution of the United States would best avoid past mistakes and ensure that the new government would be one that preserved liberty rather than slipping into tyranny.

In Federalist No. 10, James Madison emphasized the duty of government to promote and preserve those conditions that allow for citizens to acquire property: "The diversity in the faculties of men, from which the rights of property originate, is not less an insuperable obstacle to a uniformity of interests. The protection of these faculties is the first object of government."[8] He continues later in the essay to explain that the new government's structure of dispersed authority and interests provides some assurance against government actions that destroy property, such as calls for "paper money, for an abolition of debts, [or] for an equal division of property."[9]

A government that becomes an instrument for the destruction of its citizens' property, or that allows lawlessness to descend on a populace such that it cannot protect the safety and property of its people is one that has failed to justify its very existence.

3. Property and freedom are inseparable.

A chief reason why it is important for government to protect property and the conditions that allow it to be created is that property is essential to freedom. The ownership and control over property are essential to providing a barrier between people and the outside world, including the government. The English people understood that their ability to own property created a sphere of independence. As the great eighteenth-century jurist William Blackstone wrote, "There is nothing which so generally strikes the imagination, and engages the affections of mankind, as the right of property; or that sole and despotic dominion which one man claims and exercises over the external things of the world, in total exclusion of the right of any other individual in the universe."[10]

One of the most influential early British jurists was Lord Coke, who wrote in one case that "the house of every one is to him as his Castle and Fortress as well for defence against injury and violence, as for his repose."[11] In this case, Lord Coke made it plain that a homeowner had as much a right to protect his home against thieves and intruders as against a sheriff if the sheriff was not following proper procedures. This sentiment would be repeated time and again in opposition to government usurpations of property rights.

A decade before the American Revolution, there was debate in the British Parliament over the application of revenue laws that allowed British officers to enter the homes of colonists at will to look for violations. British Statesman William Pitt, the earl of Chatham, was opposed and in 1763, he spoke at the House of Commons against the usurpations of the colonists' property rights with this famous passage: "The poorest man may in his cottage bid defiance to all the forces of the Crown. It may be frail; its roof may shake; the wind may blow through it; the storm may enter; but the King of England cannot enter—all his force dares not cross the threshold of the ruined tenement!"[12]

This speech resonated with the colonists. Indeed, there are towns and counties named after the Earl of Chatham throughout the East Coast. Moreover, as will be shown, the same sentiment was employed in the colonial courts to challenge the British search and seizure laws.

More recent scholars have described the ownership of property in a similar vein. Property, they write, contributes to our sense of "personhood": "To achieve proper self-development—to be a *person*—an individual needs some control over resources in the external environment. The necessary assurances of control take the form of property rights."[13]

But there is more to property than its sense of individual personhood or creating an inward-looking domain that excludes the external world. Property is also critical for protecting the freedom of individuals against the world and the government.

In more prosaic renderings of this strand of thought, it can be asked whether there could be a free press if the government owned the presses? Could there be freedom of religion if the government owned the houses of worship? Could citizens be at liberty to criticize their government if employment and the means of production were all controlled by the government? What would happen to the ability of renters to challenge government bureaucrats if governments were the landlords over all housing?

Perhaps the best summation of the importance of the relationship between liberty and property came from Arthur Lee. Lee was an American diplomat who represented American interests during the Revolutionary War era. He was also a delegate from Virginia to the Continental Congress—and one of the few who publicly opposed slavery. In a 1782 speech to the Congress, he said, "The right of property is the guardian of every other right. And to deprive a people of this, is to deprive them of their liberty."

4. There are limits to the government's ability to take private property.

Clearly, the founders of this nation were profoundly influenced by John Locke's vision of government, liberty, and property. They knew their Locke and their Blackstone. As Blackstone wrote, "So great moreover is the regard of the law for private property, that it will not authorize the least violation of it; no, not even for the general good of the whole community."[14]

To be fair, even Blackstone recognized the exception of eminent domain. But he cautioned:

> If a new road . . . were to be made through the grounds of a private person, it might perhaps by extensively beneficial to the public; but the law permits no man, or set of men, to do this without consent of the owner of the land. . . . the legislature alone, can [compel only] . . . by giving him a full indemnification and equivalent for the injury thereby sustained. . . . All that the legislature does is to oblige the owner to alienate his possessions for a reasonable price; and even this is an exertion of power, which the legislature indulges with caution, and which nothing but the legislature can perform.[15]

The Fifth Amendment limits the government's ability to take private property to those cases in which there will be a "public use" of the property and where just compensation is paid: "nor shall private property be taken for public use, without just compensation." As discussed in a prior chapter, in recent years this guarantee has been honored more in the breach than in reality.

5. The role of the courts is to protect property.

There is also, however, a critical reality to the nature of government that is common to all forms of government not run by angels: those in power take advantage of those who are not. And in the context of land-use regulations and the exercise of the power of eminent domain, the advantage taken is often private property. To avoid abuse of any power wielded by the government—either by the executive or the legislature—the judiciary is supposed to mediate. The judiciary is given the authority to act as a neutral arbiter between government and individuals. This judicial power to interpose between individuals and their governments is the key to liberty.

It was an essential epiphany to those involved in the struggles for power between the monarchy, the parliament, and the judiciary of seventeenth-century England that not even the king could command his subjects or pass judgment upon them without the law adopted by Parliament and the interpretation of that law by independent judges.[16] With the elimination of the monarchy's own prerogative courts (what we would call administrative agency tribunals today) such as the much-hated Star Chamber, an *independent* court system—with the ability to say no to the Crown—became an essential element of the British Constitution, and, ultimately, many state constitutions and the Constitution of the United States.[17] As Professor Philip Hamburger put it, "The cardinal achievement of the English in their constitutional struggles was to subdue the Crown under the law, particularly under the English constitution."[18] Thus, the courts have had a long and storied tradition of protecting the liberties of the people against all manner of attempted usurpations.

The liberty of property is no different. Indeed, one of the first great attempts to assert the liberties of the American colonists against British usurpations came in the famous challenge by James Otis in 1761 to the Crown's Writs of Assistance. These were the hated laws that allowed

British officers to ransack private homes on the merest pretext that the home might have evidence of a violation of the customs laws—for example, goods imported from France for which no duties had been paid.

James Otis was a powerful and well-connected lawyer who at one time was the Advocate General of the Admiralty Court in Boston. But when the Crown sought to enforce the despised Writs of Assistance, he instead defended the colonists against them. In a five-hour defense, he excoriated the Crown's position as being against the sacred right of private property:

> A man's house is his castle; and whilst he is quiet, he is as well guarded as a prince in his castle. This writ, if it should be declared legal, would totally annihilate this privilege. Custom-house officers may enter our houses when they please; we are commanded to permit their entry. Their menial servants may enter, may break locks, bars, and everything in their way; and whether they break through malice or revenge, no man, no court can inquire. Bare suspicion without oath is sufficient.
>
> This wanton exercise of this power is not a chimerical suggestion of a heated brain.[19]

Although Otis lost the case that day, his argument had a profound effect on the colonists. This defense of private property stirred the colonists to reconsider their relationship with the tyrannical forces of the Crown. As John Adams wrote many years after observing the argument as a young man, "the child independence was then and there born, every man of an immense crowded audience appeared to me to go away as I did, ready to take arms against writs of assistance."[20]

Private property rights deserve an equally forceful protection by the judiciary from the government's power of eminent domain. In the case of eminent domain, government officials are not just entering and "break[ing] locks, bars, and everything in their way."[21] They are *taking* the locks, bars, and everything in their way, as well as the house itself and the very land upon which the house sits. The Constitution limits such power only to instances where the property taken is to be put to public use, and it tasks the judiciary with ensuring that the power of eminent domain is exercised only within constitutional limits. And yet, in the context of the forced transfer of property from those without power to those with it, that process fails because the judiciary defers too much to those who are doing the taking. And in recent times that process has failed badly because "judicial deference" has taken on an exalted status in the nation's courthouses.[22]

The United States, however, was not founded upon principles of deference. The structure of the government was instead designed to establish vigorously competing branches of government. Moreover, each branch is imbued with an interest in preventing the undue arrogation of power by the other branches. Such a check on the amassing of power was seen to be the best guarantor of liberty, and property, for the people. As Madison wrote in *Federalist No. 47*, "There can be no liberty where the legislative and executive powers are united in the same person, or body of magistrates."[23]

As for the role of deference, it was to be limited. Alexander Hamilton put it this way in *Federalist No. 78*:

> the courts were designed to be an intermediate body between the people and the legislature, in order . . . to keep the later within the limits assigned to their authority. The interpretation of the laws is the proper and peculiar province of the courts. A constitution is in fact, and must be, regarded by the judges as a fundamental law. It therefore belongs to them to ascertain its meaning.

In other words, when government entities adopt laws that exceed their limits, and which infringe upon the rights of the people—and that includes land use laws that destroy private rights in property—it is the duty of the courts to intercede. It is not their duty to defer.

6. To understand the role of property in protecting liberty, we must understand what freedom and property are.

If the regulatory state poses a threat to freedom, it must be asked: freedom to do what? Freedom to stand up to the government bureaucrats who hold the keys to the regulatory kingdom? Freedom to earn a living from the use of privately owned property? Freedom to use property and property-derived wealth to challenge the government itself? Freedom is universally considered a good thing to have—in varying degrees at any rate. Even those states unwilling to allow it to flourish in the classical liberal sense have often adopted the Orwellian tactic of providing freedom to the state's citizens after redefining what freedom means. Thus, some states are in the habit of defining freedom to be the availability of whatever the government provides for its citizens—jobs (freedom from want), security (freedom from fear), and food (freedom from hunger). Other states have an even more paternalistic way of suggesting to their citizens that they have all the freedom they will ever need—conservative religious-based dress codes for women provide freedom from male harassment. Where there is a state religion, prohibitions on preaching an unapproved religion provides freedom from the conversion of the young. In other states restrictions on "hate speech" can provide citizens with freedom from intolerance of one's race, religion, or gender orientation. And by limiting the freedom of one set of owners to utilize their property, zoning may provide freedom from unwanted neighborhood land uses.

Generally, however, freedom in the tradition of Western democracies means not the positive provision of goods and services, and not even the protection from the insults, trigger words, or microaggressions lobbed by fellow citizens. Instead, it means the freedom *from* government itself, as spelled out in the Bill of Rights when it says what government *cannot* do. For example, the government *shall not* restrict free speech,[24] the government *shall not* infringe on the practice of religion or the beliefs of its citizens, the government *shall not* take property except in limited circumstances and only after the payment of just compensation, the government *shall not* deprive one of his life or liberty without due process of law, the government *shall not* search a person's home or effects without a warrant, and so on.[25]

This sense of freedom permits one to speak for or against the government and for or against a particular religious belief without fear of being punished. It permits one to believe any legitimate or cockamamie philosophy one likes without being locked up.[26] It permits one to worship whatever deity one wishes—whether that be the God of Abraham, Vishnu, the Devil, Gaia,[27] some Really Big Trees,[28] the Great Pumpkin,[29] or even no god at all—all without the benefit or impediment of government sponsorship or persecution. At the same time, freedom in the classical liberal tradition permits the Greta Garbos of the world to exercise their freedom to be let alone.[30]

Moreover, just because a protected right isn't detailed in the Constitution, government still cannot infringe upon an unenumerated freedom. When the idea of the Bill of Rights was being debated, some people argued that it shouldn't list those freedoms that the government couldn't take away, because anything not listed would be fair game. As Representative Theodore Sedgwick put it during the debate over the First Amendment, if the committee had to list all the rights protected, "they might have gone into a very lengthy enumeration of rights; they might have declared that a man should have a right to wear his hat if he pleased; that he might get up when he pleased, and go to bed when he thought proper."[31]

The drafters didn't think that was necessary. Instead, they adopted the catch-all Ninth Amendment: "The enumeration in the Constitution of certain rights shall not be construed to deny or disparage others retained by the people."[32]

Exactly what those "other" rights retained by the people are has been subject to debate ever since. But there has been no question that the drafters of the Bill of Rights thought that private property should be protected. The Fourth and Fifth Amendments both protect property, with the former from unreasonable searches and seizures, and the latter from takings for public use without the payment of just compensation.

The Bill of Rights fulfilled the promise of James Otis's rhetoric from decades earlier. As Otis's remarks made clear, property, like the home of even the poorest person, provides a refuge into which the government cannot normally enter. If an individual may utilize property as a means to a livelihood, as a cushion against economic want, and as a physical place to be free from the prying eyes of officious government employees, then the essential relation between property and freedom is apparent. But if property cannot be used without obtaining an assortment of arbitrary permissions from a multitude of officials, if the right to earn a living from property is made dependent on the good will of others, and if property may be routinely entered and inspected as a condition of its use, then the hallmarks of a free society are diminished.

Thus, the freedoms embodied in classical liberalism cannot be considered in isolation. They are not hermetically sealed off from one another, and there are common threads running through them all. In the views of the Founding Fathers, first and foremost of the common threads was the right to own and use property. In his *Essay on Property*, James Madison took a generous view of property, explaining that property and personal human rights are one and the same,

> This term [property] in its particular application means "that dominion which one man claims and exercises over the external things of the world, in exclusion of every other individual."
>
> In its larger meaning, it embraces every thing to which a man may attach a value and have a right; and which leaves to every one else the like advantage.
>
> In the former sense, a man's land, or merchandize, or money is called his property. In the latter sense, a man has property in his opinions and the free communication of them.
>
> He has a property of peculiar value in his religious opinions, and in the profession and practice dictated by them.
>
> He has a property very dear to him in the safety and liberty of his person.

He has an equal property in the free use of his faculties and free choice of the objects on which to employ them.

In a word, as a man is said to have a right to his property, he may be equally said to have a property in his rights.

Where an excess of power prevails, property of no sort is duly respected. No man is safe in his opinions, his person, his faculties, or his possessions.[33]

Madison continued: "If the United States mean to obtain or deserve the full praise due to wise and just governments, they will equally respect the rights of property, and the property in rights: they will rival the government that most sacredly guards the former; and by repelling its example in violating the latter, will make themselves a pattern to that and all other governments."[34]

7. Modern understandings of property have regressed.

But this fundamental vision of the proper role of government began to decay over a century ago. Government power, instead of being the chief protector of the liberties and property of the people, transformed into the chief guarantor of the general welfare of the people, even if that meant that liberty and property had to step aside.[35]

Thus, for example, President Franklin D. Roosevelt put the "freedom from want" and "freedom from fear" on an equal footing with the freedom from government interference with speech and religion. With that, the freedoms in the Bill of Rights requiring government to *refrain* from infringing upon our liberties, as in "Congress shall make no law," or "the right . . . shall not be infringed," or "nor shall . . ." become mandates for government to *provide* positive benefits to its people. However, with a government mandate to provide material goods and comfort to its citizens, there must be the simultaneous rise of the regulatory state to manage all these benefits. And with the rise of the regulatory state there is a decline in the rights of the individual.

Some argue that the institution of private property, and the protections given to private property, serve only to protect the haves against the have-nots. As a pair of influential nineteenth-century philosophers put it, "Modern bourgeois private property is the final and most complete expression of the system of producing and appropriating products, that is based on class antagonisms, on the exploitation of the many by the few."[36]

Marx and Engels were not the first to question property rights. Jean Jacques Rousseau lamented the nature of private property:

> The first man, who, after enclosing a piece of ground, took it into his head to say, "This is mine," and found people simple enough to believe him, was the true founder of civil society. How many crimes, how many wars, how many murders, how many misfortunes and horrors, would that man have saved the human species, who pulling up the stakes or filling up the ditches should have cried to his fellows: Be sure not to listen to this imposter; you are lost, if you forget that the fruits of the earth belong equally to us all, and the earth itself to nobody![37]

There have been many successors to Rousseau. Marx and Engels were especially adept at creating a pseudo-scientific basis for their redistributive instincts. In one passage from the Communist Manifesto, they wrote:

> August von Haxthausen discovered common ownership of land in Russia, Georg Ludwig von Maurer proved it to be the social foundation from which all Teutonic races started in history, and, by and by, village communities were found to be, or to have been, the primitive form of society everywhere from India to Ireland. The inner organization of this primitive communistic society was laid bare, in its typical form, by Lewis Henry Morgan's crowning discovery of the true nature of the gens and its relation to the tribe.[38]

Anthropologically speaking, this is considered utter nonsense today. Historian Richard Pipes responds that: "The notion of primitive communism has no basis in fact: it is simply the ancient—and, apparently, indestructible—myth of the Golden Age dressed up in modern pseu-do-scientific language. Anthropology has no knowledge of societies ignorant of property rights."[39] Nonsense though it may be, it has sup-ported an antipathy toward property rights that has caused the death of millions in the old Soviet Union, Mao's China, and Pol Pot's Cambodia and that continues to spawn human misery today from North Korea to Cuba to Venezuela.

From Marx to Lenin to Mao, many scholars and political leaders have had little use for a philosophy of rights that elevates individuals above their governments and that attempts to justify and cement the inequalities that inevitably arise in a system of laws that distributes property and wealth on principles other than total equality. Rousseau also presaged a more modern attack on private property—the notions of deep ecology that animate a core ethos within the environmental movement. In his *Discourse on Inequality*, he posited that without civ-ilization and all its accoutrements, men would be in a state of perfect health and bliss: "Man therefore, in a state of nature where there are so few sources of sickness, can have no great occasion for physic, and still less for physicians . . ."[40]

Moreover, a government that sees individual rights in property as an obstacle to good government is not one that will be shy about using the power of eminent domain. That the ideals of progressivism and individual liberty were considered to be mutually incompatible can be seen, for example, in the writings of Woodrow Wilson. In 1887, as a professor at Princeton University, he wrote:

> [A]ll idea of a limitation of public authority by individual rights be put out of view, and that the State consider itself bound to stop only at what is unwise or futile in its universal superintendence alike of individual and of public interests. The thesis of the state socialist is, that no line can be drawn between private and public affairs which the State may not cross at will; that omnipotence of legislation is the first postulate of all just political theory.

> . . . must not government lay aside all timid scruple and boldly make
> itself an agency for social reform as well as for political control?[41]

Later, while campaigning for the presidency, Wilson said, "that property as compared with humanity, as compared with the vital red blood in the American people, must take second place, not first . . . ."[42] As president, Wilson also infamously instituted the re-segregation of the federal government and civil service, setting into motion the disastrous employment and housing policies that haunt the nation to this day.[43]

With the rise of progressivism in the United States and the concomitant understanding that government should play a much larger role in promoting collective action for the public good, fealty to principles of individual rights, and especially economic and property rights, began to wane.[44]

Under progressive thought of the sort espoused by Wilson, notions of individualism and private property were seen as impediments to social improvement.[45] But the reformers were sorely mistaken if they believed that the lessening of restraints on government interference with individual rights and property would benefit of the poor and working classes. The result was quite the opposite. The regulation of property under the progressives evolved from regulations designed to protect health and safety to regulations designed to protect established and privileged neighborhoods from excessive development—and infiltration by the poor. Justice Sutherland's tirade against parasitic apartment buildings in *Euclid v. Ambler* was a harbinger of much more to come.[46]

While freedom and property may be inseparable, the temptation to sacrifice one or the other to seemingly more critical societal goals is ever present. And when either one is threatened so is the other.[47] Yet, the temptation to yield to either is an inexorable imperative of those who govern. In the United States, for example, the threat to security in the post-9/11 world has led to the Patriot Act, which some claim intrudes upon the individual liberty and privacy of American citizens.[48] Starting with the rise of progressivism and continuing through the post-New

Deal era and perhaps to the Green New Deal juggernaut, the compulsion to reengineer society for the "common good" has been given free rein, at great cost to originalist understandings of individual rights—especially those based in private property.[49]

Recently, however, there has been some judicial pushback. Most notably, the long-moribund doctrine of regulatory takings was revived in the 1980s and continues to provide one bit of light to those who understand the importance of property rights.

Significantly, the United States Supreme Court began the restoration of property rights in 1972 when it took up a rather ordinary case between debtors and their lender. In the course of deciding that the case should proceed in federal court (the details of which are unimportant here) the Court admonished that

> [t]he dichotomy between personal liberties and property rights is a false one. Property does not have rights. People have rights. The right to enjoy property without unlawful deprivation, no less than the right to speak or the right to travel, is in truth, a "personal" right, whether the "property" in question be a welfare check, a home, or a savings account. *In fact, a fundamental interdependence exists between the personal right to liberty and the personal right in property. Neither could have meaning without the other. That rights in property are basic civil rights has long been recognized.*[50]

Chapter 24

Regulatory Takings—A Way to Protect Property

When government seizes property for a supposed public use, it, at least in theory, must pay for it. But what if government seizes the *use* of the property but denies it has taken it and refuses to pay?

From the end of the Civil War through the 1920s, courts were largely silent on the question of what limits there were on the ability of governments to regulate away the use and value of private property. That changed in 1922, when the Supreme Court revived the moribund doctrine of regulatory takings—the rule that says that if a regulation destroys the use and value of property then the government must pay for it. But after 1922, the Court promptly went to sleep again until the 1980s. Since 1987, however, there has been an explosion of regulatory takings cases at the Supreme Court. Next, a few of the most significant cases are described. It should be apparent that these cases give some hope to a restoration of private property rights and—importantly for the purposes of this book—a way out of the housing crisis.

1. The Supreme Court rediscovers in Pennsylvania Coal v. Mahon that regulations can go too far.

During the nineteenth century, forward-thinking coal barons instructed their land agents to buy up coal rights in rural areas of Midwestern states. Farmers in need of cash had little to fear. To them, a coal mine might be a small pit here and there, or a few underground tunnels, and not much to worry about. And like farmers everywhere, they could use the cash.

But when the nation began to industrialize and its northern cities exploded in size, the nation's appetite for coal became insatiable. As the mines expanded, they literally undermined not only the farms but also the farmhouses and buildings throughout the region. As the mines were worked and abandoned, farmland and farmhouse alike could collapse into what miners call glory holes. When land sank into the coal mines below, it was called land subsidence and became a threat to homes and farms on the surface. It also became a major goal of farmers to support legislation that prohibited the coal companies from causing subsidence. After all, there were far many more farmer votes than votes from the owners of coal companies. The Pennsylvania legislature was more than happy to oblige, and it passed the Kohler Act, which prohibited coal companies from taking out so much coal that the surface would collapse.

But there was a problem with the Act because the coal companies had purchased not only the coal but also the "support estate," meaning they bought the right to allow the surface to collapse after they had mined the coal. As a result, the mine owners sued. Their vindication came in 1922 with *Pennsylvania Coal v. Mahon*.[1] This was the first case in many decades where the Court found government regulation could involuntarily take private property.[2]

Justice Holmes, who was generally very progressive and not much of a friend to business interests, ruled in favor of the coal companies, saying, "The general rule at least is that while property may be regulated to a certain extent, if regulation goes too far it will be recognized as a taking."[3] That's it. There was no in-depth analysis of the Takings

Clause, or the Due Process Clause for that matter. Nor was there much in the way of guidance beyond the test of "too far." But this sentence stands out from the other rhetorical flourishes of the opinion and has come to stand for the beginning of the modern era of takings jurisprudence. It was also the beginning of over a century's worth of debate over how far is "too far."

Figure 38. Coal mine subsidence in England is a feature, not a bug for this inn.

Justice Brandeis dissented from the holding, saying that "the defendant has failed to adduce any evidence from which it appears that to restrict its mining operations was an unreasonable exercise of the police power."[4] This reflected his belief that any valid exercise of the police power could absolve any takings liability. While the doctrine of the police power would be put to great advantage a few years later by advocates of regulation in *Euclid*, Brandeis pointed out its use in 1887 in *Mugler v. Kansas.*[5] That case arose from the early temperance movement, shortly after Kansas prohibited the manufacture and sale of alcoholic beverages. When the owners of a brewery sued, they lost. The Court held that a legitimate exercise of the police power—such as in stopping the nuisance of alcohol—was not a taking because there was no right to engage in such harmful behavior.

In addition, Brandeis, in his *Pennsylvania Coal* dissent, surmised that there might be "an average reciprocity of advantage,"[6] negating any taking. In other words, while a landowner might suffer some harm from a regulation, he might also receive a benefit when everyone is similarly treated. For example, in the context of zoning, a person might lose some value by not being able to build a ten-story apartment house, but everybody's property is enhanced because the neighborhood will retain its nice bucolic environment. But this theory ignores the scale of the loss of the regulated party who filed the lawsuit and ignores the enhanced value that could be realized by an owner who might otherwise be able to replace a home of modest value with an apartment building of great value. Nevertheless, the aphorism of "average reciprocity of advantage" is often used to justify a regulation and negate a takings argument.

For a dissent, this formulation has been given great weight and is often trotted out to deny takings liability for land-use regulations—in other words "reciprocity of advantage" has been a thorn in the side of property owners and has coexisted uneasily with the evolution of regulatory takings doctrine.

From *Pennsylvania Coal* to the 1980s, the idea that a regulation could result in takings liability was more of an academic curiosity than a usable doctrine in the hands of landowners and their attorneys. It was not for want of trying.

A few years after *Pennsylvania Coal*, in 1928, the Court found no problem when the owner of cedar trees was forced to destroy his trees, without compensation, to prevent the spread of blight from the cedar trees to the more valuable apple trees. The case, *Miller v. Schoene*,[7] stands again for the proposition that with regulations there will be winners and losers. In *Mahon*, the coal companies won. In *Miller*, the apple farmers won. To the Court it was simple enough: either the cedar trees would have to be removed (and the timber sold) or the more valuable apple trees would die. The Court found no need to apply or extend a takings or due process theory to these circumstances.[8]

Following the collapsing coal mine case and the case of the dueling trees, nothing much of any significance happened in regulatory takings for the next half-century. In 1960, in a case dealing with a government takeover of some liens, the Supreme Court did manage to explain what the purpose of the Fifth Amendment's Takings Clause was, stating, "The Fifth Amendment's guarantee . . . [is] designed to bar Government from forcing some people alone to bear public burdens which, in all fairness and justice, should be borne by the public as a whole."[9] While that aphorism has been repeated many times, "fairness and justice" has proven to be in the eyes of the beholder.

Beginning in the late 1970s and through the mid-1980s, in one case after another, the Court seemed about ready to take on the doctrine of regulatory takings, only to step aside and avoid deciding. In one instance, the Court accepted a case for review of a takings claim brought by a landowner who wasn't allowed to build any homes on residentially zoned property. But after hearing the argument, the Court almost inexplicably went sideways, finding some reason not to rule on the case.[10] Sometimes the Court set out some tests, saying for example, if the regulation denied economically viable use (whatever that means) or failed to substantially advance a legitimate governmental interest (ditto), there might be a taking. But the Court never actually got around to deciding whether there was a taking. Instead, it found some procedural flaw and avoided making a decision.

That all changed in 1987.

2. In 1987, the Court finally begins to put flesh on the Takings Doctrine with *Nollan v. California Coastal Commission* and *First English Evangelical Lutheran Church of Glendale v. County of Los Angeles.*

What happened next in 1987 was the culmination of good facts, good theories, and a change in the intellectual currents. With the cases through the late 1970s and 1980s, the Court got close to finding a regulatory taking—but not close enough for property owners. At the same time, the academy had begun to stir. Law review articles appeared across the ideological spectrum, with most giving some degree of credence to the idea of a regulatory taking, albeit often in limited terms.[11]

Most significantly, in 1985 Professor Richard Epstein published *Takings: Private Property Rights and the Power of Eminent Domain*. With the popularity of his book, Epstein's libertarian view of regulatory takings reached a wider and more general audience than the academic consumers of law review articles. This book was highly influential, and controversial, in legal circles. But it provided the firmest defense thus far of private property rights and the theory that regulation can take property thus far. By 1987, with *Takings* leaving its mark, the academic foundations had been built that made it possible for the Court to recognize and articulate the doctrine of regulatory takings beyond the amorphous notions of "fairness," "justice," and "too far."

The first case of 1987, *Keystone Bituminous*,[12] was an inauspicious beginning to the 1987 takings cases. In that case, Pennsylvania passed a regulation requiring that coal miners leave some coal in the ground in order to prevent the collapse of the surface. This was, of course, pretty much identical to the facts that animated Justice Holmes's decision in *Pennsylvania Coal*. Nevertheless, the Court distinguished *Pennsylvania Coal* and rejected the regulatory taking claim. Although, the coal operators making the takings argument thought they had some controlling authority in *Pennsylvania Coal*, the passage of time and the public's embrace of environmental values led the Court to reach a different conclusion. When it came to the argument that the regulation would require that twenty-seven million tons of coal be left in the ground, the Court essentially reasoned that there was a lot more where that came from, and the overall economic impact wasn't that great.[13]

But, with the next case, *First English Evangelical Church*,[14] the justices changed course. In California, just as night follows day, floods follow fires. After fires ravaged some canyons outside of Los Angeles, massive flooding destroyed the church's downstream camp for disabled children. Fearing further flooding, the county imposed a moratorium on construction, preventing the church from reconstructing its camp. The church sued. In addition to arguing that the county's cloud seeding was partially responsible for their flood damage, the church also claimed that the prohibition on reconstruction was a regulatory taking, and they were entitled to damages pursuant to the Fifth Amendment's Takings Clause. In other words, the county's building ban had gone too far.

The camp lost in the state courts for a reason that caught the attention of the United States Supreme Court. That was because the state supreme court ruled that even if the church could prove there was a taking, it would be entitled only to have the reconstruction ban tossed out—but it would not receive a dime of compensation.

The Supreme Court took up the church's appeal. Of significance, a few years earlier in one of the cases the Court sidestepped, Justice Brennan had noted with some disgust a common practice in California cities. After having onerous regulations ruled unconstitutional, the cities would simply enact a brand new and nearly identical onerous regulation. Even after winning a challenge, a landowner would have to expend countless additional dollars in permitting costs and new legal challenges. In fact, Justice Brennan quoted from a legal how-to manual in which a city attorney gleefully explained the practice to a meeting of city attorneys:

> IF ALL ELSE FAILS, MERELY AMEND THE REGULATION AND START OVER AGAIN.
>
> If legal preventative maintenance does not work, and you still receive a claim attacking the land use regulation, or if you try the case and lose, don't worry about it. All is not lost. One of the extra goodies contained in . . . [a] recent [California] Supreme Court case . . . appears to allow the City to change the regulation in question, even after trial and judgment, make it more reasonable, more restrictive, or whatever, and everybody starts over again. . . .
>
> See how easy it is to be a City Attorney. Sometimes you can lose the battle and still win the war. Good luck.[15]

Now the California Supreme Court told the Church that it would never get damages, even if the county's building ban were unconstitutional.

The only remedy would be to start over again. And again. This time, the United States Supreme Court had had enough. With Justice Scalia writing the opinion, the Court held that *if* a regulation takes property, even for a short period of time, compensation is due for the period of the taking.[16] This was a shot in the arm for property owners who had been enduring an endless "sue and start over" scenario for decades in California and elsewhere. In other words, after *First English*, landowners could seek compensation, rather than just invalidation, as a remedy for a regulatory taking, giving landowners—and their attorneys—an incentive to sue and governments an incentive not to take.[17]

The most telling victory for property owners in 1987 came with *Nollan v. California Coastal Commission*, the exactions case discussed in Chapter 20.[18] Finally, the tide was beginning to turn. The Court was paying attention to the plight of property owners facing the onslaught of government regulators and takers.

3. The denial of all use and value gives rise to a compensable taking: *Lucas v. South Carolina Coastal Council*

David Lucas bought two residential oceanfront lots on the South Carolina coast. His plan was to build a home on each lot, sell one, and move into the other. The homes were to be pretty much the same size and style as all the previously built houses that already lined the beach. But the South Carolina Coastal Council had other ideas for these last two remaining vacant lots.

Worried about the potential of coastal flooding, the council established a line along the coast. No homes could be built on the seaward side of the line. Unfortunately for David Lucas, his lots were on the wrong side of the line. He could have a picnic on his lots, but he couldn't build a home just like those of his neighbors—whose lots were also on the wrong side of the line. But because the neighbors' homes were built before the line was drawn, they were okay—at least for the time being. (If a house burned or was blown down and had to be rebuilt, that might be another matter.)

Lucas sued and won in trial court. In handing him the win, the trial court noted that the new law "deprive[d] Lucas of any reasonable economic use of the lots . . . eliminated the unrestricted right of use, and render[ed] them valueless."[19] But then he promptly lost on appeal to the state supreme court. The court agreed that there might be a total loss, but said it didn't matter. So long as the regulation was a valid exercise of the police power, the state owed David Lucas nothing for destroying the use and value of his property.

But if this view is correct, what does the Constitution mean when it says that just compensation must be paid when property is taken for a public use? That a regulation is adopted consistent with the state's police power cannot mean that the duty to compensate for a taking goes away; otherwise the Takings Clause would be hollow and empty words. Likewise, if a regulation destroys the use and value of the property, then surely the state has taken the property. That is what Justice Holmes meant in *Pennsylvania Coal* and what has been the foundation of every takings case since *Pennsylvania Coal*.

Lucas appealed his case to the United States Supreme Court. The case generated much interest in both the property rights and environmental legal bars. Attorneys for Pacific Legal Foundation filed a friend of the court brief arguing that Lucas should be compensated for his loss. Opposing amicus briefs were filed by environmental groups that said the environment was more important than property rights, and Lucas should not be paid.

The United States Supreme Court reversed. Writing for the Court, Justice Scalia held that just because a regulation advanced a police power objective didn't mean that the state didn't have to pay for the taking. In a trenchant remark, Justice Scalia found that it was not enough for the government merely to claim the existence of "a harm-preventing justification for its action. . . . Since such a justification can be formulated in practically every case, this amounts to a test of whether the legislature has a stupid staff. We think the Takings Clause requires courts to do more than insist upon artful harm-preventing characterizations."[20]

Indeed, at oral argument, the attorney for South Carolina argued that allowing David Lucas to build his homes could create a nuisance because "portions of homes, even homes themselves during times of great storm events will be blown or washed into houses behind them."[21] To that argument, Justice O'Connor responded, "I guess under your theory South Carolina could require those homes to be removed because it still is the same threat to public safety that exists with respect to allowing new construction on these lots. Isn't that right? Wouldn't your theory take you that far?"[22]

The Court didn't buy it. Only if the regulation prevented what would otherwise be considered a "background principle" of the state's law of nuisance, the Court held, could the state escape the duty to pay. But a background principle had to be a use of property that was never part of the property's title to begin with, not something newly made up by a legislative body. Thus, Justice Scalia continued in the Court's opinion, building a nuclear reactor on a fault zone or a dam that would flood a neighbor's property could be considered a nuisance and be legitimately banned. No compensation would need to be paid. But forbidding the building of homes in a residential neighborhood was something altogether different.

Figure 39. David Lucas's two lots in 1992 (William A. Fischel, Dartmouth College).

While landowners hailed the case as a great victory for property rights, its real-world impact has been less impressive. Unlike the finding in *Lucas*, in most cases, not *all* use and value of property has been taken away by a regulation. There is almost always something leftover. Therefore, it has been only in the most extreme cases in which landowners have received compensation under the *Lucas* precedent.

But at least two professors, one liberal and one libertarian, believe the time is right for a takings challenge to exclusionary zoning.[23] They conclude:

> Both originalism and leading variants of living constitutionalism provide support for judicial intervention to curb exclusionary zoning by using the Takings Clause of the Fifth Amendment. Judicial review is not a complete solution to the problems caused by this pernicious practice. But it can be of great help.[24]

PART VIII

The Future—Speculations and Solutions

The future ain't what it used to be.[1]

It's always easier to talk about the future after it has happened. At present, we know there is a lack of affordable housing. We know that the law of supply and demand persists and that we need to build more homes. We know we need to remove the many existing barriers to the construction of new homes and that many of these barriers are rooted in various governmental policies—some well-intended and some less so.

But we also know that there is much that we don't know. We don't know all of the consequences that will flow from whatever policy decisions we make today. We also don't know how advances in technology, changes in where and how we work, and changes in our lifestyle choices will affect the future of housing.

But we do know that if we are to solve the housing crisis we must change the way many things are being done today. We will need to remove the many government policies that dampen the construction of new housing. We need to make it possible for all Americans to afford decent housing.

This section will address some of the unknowns that may affect housing in the future and some of the things that we know should be done today.

Chapter 25

The Future of Housing in a Post-COVID AI World

In thinking about the many costs of exclusionary zoning, from housing unaffordability, rampant homelessness, and unbearable super-commutes, there may be a new factor to consider: the depopulation of city business centers in the wake of COVID-19 and the rise of working from home. For example, according to the Census Bureau, home-based work caused a decline in Manhattan's commuter-adjusted population by 800,000.[1] Other cities had similar outcomes. At present, we are too early in the post-COVID world to know the persistence of working-from-home routines and their long-term implications. However, some trends may be emerging and some serious questions need to be considered.

First, as some knowledge-based workers have learned, they can work as easily from Sun Valleys of the nation as from the Silicon Valleys, so there have been rising home-price pressures on once out-of-the-way localities. Theoretically, this should at the same time ease the price pressures in areas within commuting distance of urban business centers. So far, there is some evidence of the former, but not so much on the latter. Perhaps that is because the pent-up demand in the inner suburbs remains high and the pressures for price appreciation have been relaxed but not abated. *But wherever we will be located, we will still need more homes to be built where we end up living.*

Second, the benefits may be realized more by the attorneys, code writers, and creative workers rather than by the people who must be at their work stations—the machine operators, cleaning personnel, and hospitality workers—who have traditionally borne the brunt of exclusionary housing policies.[2] Perhaps price pressures will abate, and these traditional workers can live closer to their workplaces in better neighborhoods while avoiding marathon multi-hour daily commutes. But some of these workers may well lose their jobs. We're already seeing the need for fewer restaurants, coffee-shops, and office spaces in downtowns across the nation. Where will the people who staff these businesses find new jobs? Home-workers do not have the same need for professional office cleaning, lunch spots, and parking lot attendants. *But wherever they will be located, both knowledge-workers and support workers will still need more homes to be built where they end up living.*

Third, there is growing pushback from corporate leaders for a full or partial return to the office. Some of this may be coming from bosses who do not trust workers they cannot see. As a ZipRecruiter study claimed, "The number one downside of remote work employers cite is difficulty observing and monitoring employees."[3] But a more lasting concern is the loss of the synergies of collaboration fostered by people working together. This, after all, is why some believe so strongly in the power of cities to foster human potential. Edward Glaeser, the same economist who has written extensively on the costs of exclusionary zoning, is best known for his paean to cities: *The Triumph of the City.*[4] His thesis is that the collaborative effects of urban workplaces have propelled human development for as long as there have been cities. That, he writes, is the very reason for the rise of cities. How much of this are we willing to sacrifice for a convenient commute from the bed to the desk? How will younger workers get effective mentoring from a boss hundreds or thousands of miles away? Aren't Zoom calls great? Or are Zoom calls an evil wrought upon an unsuspecting world? Let's face it: unless and until we install a moving 3D Zoom that trails us through the hallways of our homes, from our desks to the coffee pots, some of the advantages of collaboration will be lost. But heaven forbid that Zoom cameras should one day follow us throughout our work-day! So, will the bosses calling for a return to the office prevail? And if so, what percentage of workers will be affected so that they must leave their rural Shangri-las and trudge back into cities and suburban commutes? *But wherever they will be located, office workers will still need more homes to be built wherever they end up living.*

Fourth, no one fully understands how the rise of artificial intelligence will reorder existing jobs and employment trends. Will some knowledge-based workers become obsolete? Will attorneys who perform routine tasks, editors, and code-writers need to look for something else to do?[5] Will robots take on an increasing number of tasks performed by hospitality workers? Robot screens are already asking if we want fries with our burgers: Why not have them ask us if we have prepared our wills?

What is the future of factory work? Will there be an Elon Musk future without work? While arm-waving pundits have opined on all manner of our potential futures living with AI, no one really has a clue. It could be a dystopian hell. It could be paradise. Or it could likely be somewhere in between—better than now but worse than heaven. In any event, despite all the hullabaloo surrounding AI, people will still need to live somewhere. We will still need to build more homes, even if we don't know what the people living in those homes will do with their time. *But whatever they will be doing, we will still need more homes to be built where people end up living.*

Fifth, as we emerge from the post-COVID world, cities—especially those on the West Coast—are not seeing any reduction in homelessness. The impacts on housing trends caused by where people work and live have been drowned in the urban tsunami of fentanyl. Immigration is contributing as well. Some cities like Portland, Oregon, have seemingly surrendered to hard drugs by decriminalizing their use and possession. But rather than encouraging treatment, the result has been the opposite: more addiction, more homelessness, and more despair.[6] Wherever one finds a homeless camp today, one is likely to find a substantial percentage of users. To the addicted, commuting and the location of jobs matters far less than finding a space to pitch a tent and a nearby supplier. *But wherever they will be located, addicts will still need places to live.*

Finally, technology has always changed the where and how we have worked and lived. Monumental changes are easy to see in hindsight. The rise of farming put an end to the prevalence of the hunter-gatherer lifestyle for most of humanity. The Industrial Revolution gave rise to large cities in ways that no one imagined when the first steam engine was conceived. And the conversion of carbon-based fuels into power and electricity has changed the work and life of virtually every human on the planet.[7] The future, on the other hand, is far less clear. But there are at least two things of which we can be absolutely certain: we won't see or understand the future until well after it happens. And whatever happens, we'll still need places to live. *But wherever they will be located, our future selves will still need more homes to be built wherever we end up living.*

Chapter 26

Respecting Property Rights— The Way Out of Our Housing Crisis

---

The seeds of our current housing crisis were sown in 1910, when Baltimoreans decreed who could live in what neighborhoods. While that particular flavor of racist exclusionary zoning was struck down by the Supreme Court, a newer, more sanitized version of zoning grew up in its place and received the Supreme Court's blessing in *Euclid v. Ambler Realty*. Towns didn't explicitly forbid poor people and minorities from living in nice neighborhoods, but the towns made it economically impossible for them to do so through comprehensive zoning. Land-use regulations are all about people of class and privilege using the power of government to exclude from their neighborhoods people with, in their opinion, less class and privilege.

The command to "love thy neighbor as thyself"[1] isn't a prescription to fill your neighborhood only with ones you think you can love, i.e., those who look like you and earn about what you do. Nor does it mean that you should care only about those who already live in your immediate geographic neighborhood. But there is no other way to interpret America's current state of land-use regulation, except as a rejection of fundamental moral and religious principles.

Moreover, the federal government joined the rush to exclude by making it impossible for minorities to obtain financing to move into the new subdivisions that took over the suburbs.[2] On top of that, the federal government often demanded that racially restrictive covenants be pushed on the subdivisions it helped finance—covenants that the state courts were only too happy to enforce.

The key to rejecting such objectionable policies was seen when the Court threw out Louisville's racial zoning law in *Buchanan v. Warley*. The key in that case was a respect for the property rights of landowners and their right to buy and sell property without government interference. But as the progressives gained authority in the corridors of power and halls of justice, that key was largely forgotten. Property rights took a back seat and were forgotten. They would become, in the words of the progressive President Wilson, "second-place" rights.

Property owners once had the right to determine the fate of their land—what would be built where and when. So long as a use didn't harm their neighbors or the public, they were mostly free to put their property to its highest and best use. However, with zoning and its attendant land-use regulations, the choice of what use an owner can put property to is largely out of the owner's hands.

We take this for granted nowadays. Neighbors and their city and county governments have as much right or even a greater right to decide what can be done with property than do the owners. Fundamental notions of what property is and what rights exist in property have been turned on their head. Owners are not owners; they are mere managers and instrumentalities of a collective will.

Now the regulation of land was not a twentieth century innovation. There were restrictions against unpopular and harmful land uses going back to the colonial era and before. But what the twentieth century did bring that was unprecedented was the combination of two evils: the fulfillment of the majority's worst exclusionary instincts with the enabling power to wield excruciatingly detailed land-use regulations.

Once the need to prevent "pigs-in-the-parlor" apartment buildings became well-entrenched, environmentalism arose to provide even more ammunition to keep the status quo forever, never mind population growth and the need for more housing. Now, not only has property been burdened with ordinary zoning, but it is also burdened by a de facto ecological easement.

There is no longer a free right to develop our property. Instead, it is a right that must be bought through the permitting process at a cost of years of delay and tens to hundreds of thousands of dollars in fees, exactions, and extortions.

As a society, we have been masterful in disguising bad intentions with nobility. We zone to protect "open space" and not to keep out affordable housing. We rally at city councils to stop low-income projects not because we don't think the poor should have a place to live, but because a project might cause harmful traffic and chop down a bird's nest. We don't mean to destroy people's homes, but instead we improve their neighborhoods by replacing them with beautiful redevelopment projects. We need a transportation infrastructure, so we jam highways right through vibrant but poor neighborhoods, hoping those people will take those same highways and move far, far away. We never mean to exclude "those people," but, as Mt. Laurel, New Jersey's Mayor August put it: "We'd just like to see our town develop in a nice way." As a society, we have elevated hypocrisy to an art form.

All the while, with every impediment to building, with every zoning restriction, with every environmental restriction, with every new fee, and with every NIMBY lawsuit, there is less and less land available for housing, homes become more and more unaffordable, and the American Dream is further and further out of reach.

Enough is enough. Over a century's worth of meddling with property rights has come to a very bad end. It is time for a radical reset. If we are to work our way out of the housing crisis, we must put more trust in something we cannot see: Adam Smith's invisible hand. Where there is demand, the market should be freed to meet that demand.

We cannot depend on the government to solve the problems it has created. Government-built and managed housing like the now-demolished Pruitt-Igoe or anything run by New York City's housing department, is as much a disaster as were the nineteenth century slums of New York City; the only difference is that government housing costs us a lot more.

Still, there are advocates from the Left who believe that the answer to the housing shortage is not more housing, but more regulation.[3] Two pundits, for example, note that while the population of San Francisco has increased only 3.85 percent from 1950, the cost of housing has increased 400 percent.[4] Most economists would conclude that the increasing demand to live in the city combined with the lack of new building—as reflected by the stagnant population growth—has driven lower and moderate income people from the city and forced everybody to use more dollars to chase a limited number of housing units. But these pundits, while conceding that two hundred thousand new units would be required to drop prices down to 1981 levels, conclude incongruously that costs have risen independent of population or the number of new units. The solution they suggest is "improving renter protections" (i.e. rent control), "more tightly regulating the mortgage market . . . [to] slow down housing appreciation," "limit foreign investment," and to "reverse the trend of corporations getting into the housing market and reintroduce public land ownership" (i.e. more government-owned housing).[5] Lastly, the authors point to the subsidized housing in the Netherlands as a model, which is ironic because that nation is facing its own housing crisis.[6]

Hoping that more government and more government power will solve the housing crisis is like hoping that giving more axes to an axe-murderer will solve the murder crisis. Real solutions will not be found in more government programs, more government regulations, or more government mandates. *Instead, real solutions will require less—not more—government!*

Thickets of government regulations over land use must be pared away. There is no need, for example, for the federal government, state governments, and the local governments to all regulate the same things, such as wetlands or endangered species. Redundancy on top of redundancy only reduces opportunities for home building. Regulations must focus more in allowing things to be done, not stopping all manner of human activity. Regulations should promote home building, not stifle it. Regulations must protect human endeavor, not stop it. Regulations must make things regular, not make things impossible.

Environmental Regulations Must Be Reformed

Wetlands

Sackett was a good start. But only a start. The role of the federal government is limited by the Constitution. It does not have general police power authority over everything that politicians would like to control. Unless an activity directly impacts interstate commerce, state governments—not unelected federal bureaucrats—have the power to regulate. In *Sackett*, the Supreme Court struck down the federal government's attempt to regulate wetlands that are remote and disconnected from any navigable water. If a wetlands area doesn't touch a navigable stream, lake, or other navigable body of water, then what business is it of the federal government to send people to prison for filling in a lot to build a home? As the Court explained, it's not the business that Congress gave the US Army Corps of Engineers or the EPA when it wrote the Clean Water Act. Nor is it the business that the Constitution permits.

To make this point abundantly clear, so that even the most zealous bureaucrat understands, Congress should reform the Clean Water Act. It should provide once and for all a definition of the type of wetlands that are subject to federal jurisdiction. And that definition should be written so that even a lay person without a string of degrees can understand it. The definition should make it plain that the federal government can regulate only those wetlands that are directly next to and connected to navigable bodies of water, and not one connected in only the most indirect way by unnavigable creeks, tributaries, ditches, and underground hydrological connections. State governments are more than capable of taking over the regulation of those wetlands not connected to interstate waters. If Congress thinks they're not, Congress can always provide resources out of the money it will no longer have to give to the Corps and EPA to meddle in local wetlands.

The Sacketts, whose plight was described in Chapter 16, will receive nothing for their nearly two decades of regulatory Hell. Likewise, Ocie and Carey Mills received not even an apology for the eighteen months they spent in federal prison for putting clean, dry sand on dry land. In the future, if a small landowner or business person beats back a regulatory onslaught from the Corps or EPA, they should be compensated for their expenses and time lost.

Congress should put the responsibility of regulating exclusively into the hands of the Corps of Engineers and only the Corps of Engineers. The EPA has enough already to do. Fifty years of redundancy is enough.

The Endangered Species Act

When Congress adopted the Endangered Species Act, it distinguished between "endangered" and "threatened" species, with the former referring to those that were in present danger of extinction and the latter those that might, or might not, face extinction in the future. For many years, the federal government has treated "endangered" and "threatened" species the same, applying the same strict regulatory regime on both, causing great and largely unnecessary hardships on farmers and other landowners across the nation. The Trump Administration eased the regulatory burdens on threatened species so it could concentrate its budget and restoration efforts on those that were endangered. The Biden Administration reversed this reform. Congress should reinstate the reform and make it permanent.

The listing and regulation of endangered and threatened species is often done without regard to the economic and social impacts of the regulations. While Congress has mandated some cost considerations in some aspects of species regulation, the bureaucrats pay scant attention to those requirements. Congress should mandate that all aspects of endangered species regulation—from listing to habitat restrictions to enforcement—consider both the long-term and short-term social and economic impacts. Failure to do so should give those affected by the economic and social impacts standing to sue.

The California Environmental Regulatory Climate

What happens in California doesn't stay in California. With that state's housing crisis being second to none, skyrocketing prices have forced millions of Californians to leave the state, with a third of Californians surveyed stating they are seriously considering such a move.[7] Nibbling around the edges of reform, such as by allowing a few more granny flats and construction of duplexes isn't enough. These measures won't produce the 2 to 3.5 million homes that the state needs to meet demand.[8] Unless and until California reforms itself, the impact will be felt throughout the nation.

A good start would be to repeal and replace the California Environmental Quality Act. To date, every attempt at meaningful reform has been crushed by the iron triangle of NIMBYs, environmental lawyers, and labor unions. The NIMBYs get to stop development, the environmental lawyers get paid attorneys' fees while their clients get fundraising material, and labor unions "negotiate" for their piece of the action in projects they sue or threaten to sue. The legislature, being captured by the triangle, isn't about to reform any time soon. Only a ballot measure could possibly succeed.

In place of CEQA, there can be reasonable legislation requiring the consideration of environmental impacts before major projects over a certain size are built. But there should no longer be the practical death penalty for home-building projects, caused by endless rounds of litigation and injunctions and demands for million-dollar studies followed by more million-dollar studies. Only people directly affected by a project's environmental impacts should have a right to sue *once*— but only if they put up a bond to cover the costs of delay and attorneys' fees should they lose. And anyone who sues to extract leverage demands unrelated to environmental concerns, such as union contracts, should be summarily barred from suing ever again and required to pay the home builder's costs. Moreover, any attorneys engaged in such a practice should be referred to the state bar for violations of the rules of ethics.

Moreover, California regulators should cease and desist from imposing ever more onerous regulations on new homebuilding. The California Air Resources Board's current push to prohibit projects that increase "vehicle miles traveled," or VMTs, is as misguided as it is onerous. People moving into new homes in California will cause less of a climate impact than if they move to a state with higher costs for heating, air conditioning, and transportation. But draconian restrictions like VMTs are creating an impossible situation for new home builders throughout the state.

Zoning Cannot Continue the Status Quo

Zoning had its beginnings in an overt attempt to keep minorities out of white neighborhoods. After such explicitly racial zoning was outlawed, "comprehensive zoning" had the practical impact, if not always the overt intent, to keep poor and minorities out of the best, better, and not-so-bad neighborhoods. Zoning severely limits what property owners can do with their own property. If there is a huge pent-up demand for more affordable multi-family housing, chances are it cannot be built where it's needed. And where it can be built, chances are that there will be years of delay through permit applications, hearings, denials, and appeals.

Some argue that the only solution is to eliminate zoning.[9] But zoning is hugely popular in the suburban enclaves where, to paraphrase Justice Douglas, the "yards are wide and people (of color) are few." NIMBYs are not about to give up their exclusionary zoning until their lawnmowers are pried from their cold, dead hands. So, what can be done?

There are some relatively noncontroversial steps, such as limiting parking requirements that add tens of thousands of dollars to apartments that lie near transit. If someone wants to park a car, they can pay for it. But people who don't want or need to use cars shouldn't have to pay for parking they won't use.

Other reforms, in order of increasing likelihood of controversy, include:

1. Zoning approvals must be granted absent any significant harm to the public. Zoning boards and city councils should not deny projects simply because of the objections of a vocal minority.
2. Allow more clustered development in open space areas.
3. Allow for more accessory-dwelling units, also known as ADUs or "granny flats," in the yards of existing single-family homes. Likewise, towns that theoretically allow ADUs should not saddle them with excessive fees and conditions that make it economically impossible to build.
4. Allow limited multi-family dwellings in single-family neighborhoods. No one would be forced to build multi-family if they don't want to, but neither should they be forced to build single-family homes if they don't want to. Oregon, California, and Minneapolis have already taken steps to reduce or eliminate single-family zoning in limited areas, making it easier to build duplexes and fourplexes. The rest of the states must follow suit.
5. Allow the conversion of single-family homes into multi-family homes. Of course, health and safety codes should be enforced to make the additional living spaces habitable and safe.
6. Ensure that every locality has set aside areas for multi-family homes to meet the region's fair share of demand for new housing.
7. Urban limit lines such as those that surround Portland, Oregon, and other cities should be eliminated. Such lines create severe market distortions that lead to artificially induced densification with accompanying traffic and crime within cities and a lack of development everywhere else.[10] Likewise, open space corridors and greenbelts should not be used as an excuse to limit the supply of housing.
8. Set a schedule for eliminating large lot zoning. For example, 160-acre and larger minimum lot sizes should be the first to

go, followed by eighty-acres and so on until people can build what they want where they want to meet the demand of what people want to buy. Of course, all building should be able to accommodate or ameliorate adverse nuisance-like impacts caused by growth.

9. Home-builders should no longer be required to get permission from neighbors or the entire town in order to get a zoning variance or permit approval.

To make some of these latter solutions more politically palatable, some local governments may want to follow the Houston model where neighborhoods can band together and agree to limit some types of building for twenty-five years. After twenty-five years, they can renew or decide the time has come to allow denser building. So far, this seems to be working.

Rent Control Must Be Eliminated

Rent control is a temporary fix that makes a long-term problem much worse. It destroys the incentive to build new rental units and serves to discourage mom and pop investments in rental housing, leaving more and more apartment ownership and management to large corporate entities. While it is true that rent-control is addictive, we must still wean ourselves away. Where it is most ingrained, a schedule might be set to eliminate rent control on a gradual basis, with rents being allowed to rise gradually over a five- or ten-year span until market rates are achieved. At that time rent control should be permanently eliminated. With the certainty of the elimination of rent control, builders will build and rents will achieve a more normal and affordable equilibrium. Even better, the Supreme Court should take up a rent control case and restore property rights.

Code Enforcement Must Be Reasonable

Only necessary regulations should be retained. Legitimate health and safety regulations—and the serious enforcement of those regulations—can ensure that lower-income housing is maintained, and that the safety of residents is assured. But code enforcement must not descend into excuses for fining and seizing properties either through eminent domain blight designations or the imposition of fines on those who can least afford them.

Permitting Must Be Streamlined

It should not take years upon years to get a simple building permit. A building bureaucrat should not have the power to demand a never-ending series of studies and reviews just because of a personal hostility toward the building of new homes. If a builder meets the objective requirements of a town's ordinances and regulations, that builder should have an *enforceable* right to a permit—a right that cannot be changed at the next meeting of the city council. Building codes must be modernized. Too often, they are the result of entrenched interests seeking a bigger slice of construction costs, not the result of an objective analysis of how to build homes well and with efficiency.

The Power of the NIMBYs Must Be Constrained

NIMBY neighbors should not have the right to sue a housing project and tie it up in court for years on a mere pretext. NIMBYs should be allowed in court only if they can prove a real physical or economic harm to themselves from a project. A lost view or vague concern for open space habitat should not be enough to stop a duly appropriate and legal project. Neighbors could be given an economic incentive to support infill projects by ensuring that impact fees are actually spent in affected neighborhoods.

Eminent Domain Must Not Be an Excuse to Eliminate Working-Class Neighborhoods

Redevelopment should never target existing neighborhoods or viable businesses. Post-*Kelo* reforms must be extended where they did not take root. Attorneys must press the Supreme Court to reverse *Kelo* and restore the Public Use Clause to its original meaning. If there is a problem with neighborhood blight, fix the problem with hammers, nails, and paint. Not bulldozers.

Local Governments Should Not Treat Home Builders Like ATM Machines

We must recognize that people who build new homes are solving the crisis, not adding to it. New home builders should not be saddled with exorbitant "inclusionary zoning" or affordable housing exactions requiring them to subsidize low-income housing or pay in-lieu fees.

Excessive land-use exactions, or demands for land and money, must be reined in. The *Sheetz* case may help. Towns must wean themselves from dependency on development fees. If the people in a community think something is important enough, they should pay for it through their taxes. If it's not important enough to raise taxes for, then it's also not important enough to put the costs exclusively on new home buyers through extortionate permitting demands.

The demands imposed on builders to pay are like asking a barn full of hens to produce more and bigger eggs by giving the hens less chicken feed and water.

Courts Must Take the Doctrine of Regulatory Takings Seriously

When all else fails, the Takings Clause should be enforced. When government usurps an owner's right to use his or her property, it should be compelled to pay for what it has taken. Cost-free regulation begets only more regulation, and more regulation begets only more abuse of property owners. Requiring the government to share the pain through the doctrine of regulatory takings will cause the government to prioritize and take only that which it needs, not all that it can eat.

Final Word

Our housing crisis didn't just happen spontaneously. It has taken decades of bad government policies to reach the boiling point. This is a crisis of the government's making. This is a crisis borne from the worst prejudicial instincts of our society that government at all levels aided and abetted under the blind eye of a complicit judiciary.

Today, we are paying the price for over a century's worth of mistakes—some demanded by the people, and some imposed upon them. Through progressive politics and the instinct to control what others can do with their own property, we have created a monster of a housing crisis. People cannot afford homes where they want to work or live. Our streets and parks are being overrun by tents and hopelessness. Our children are moving away and facing a sense of resignation that they will never be able to afford what prior generations could. Is this the legacy we want to leave for future generations?

No!

Now it is time to end the crisis. Despite everything, there are still plenty of landowners and builders who want to build more homes and apartments. There are still plenty of people who dream of a home they can afford.

Let builders build! Let people have the homes they need!

And more than anything: Government, get out of their way!

Acknowledgments

There are many people to thank for this book. Among them are:

- First and foremost, my wife, Angela Burling, for her infinite patience for all the time that I have spent over the years reading, researching, and writing. I am truly blessed to share my life with her.
- The many people at Pacific Legal Foundation who have inspired and supported me for over four decades. These include Kate Pomeroy for her help in connecting me with a publisher, Deborah LaFetra for her invaluable early edits, Collin Callahan for tracking down the photographs and their copyrights, Scott Barton for helping get the word out about this book, Steven Anderson and John Groen for supporting me as this project moved forward, and all the staff without whom nothing would be possible.
- The many Pacific Legal Foundation clients who have persevered in what have often been long and draining battles with government to vindicate their fundamental rights.
- The folks at Skyhorse Publishing for believing in this book and especially Caroline Russomanno for her invaluable editing and Tony Lyons and Mark Gompertz for seeing merit in this endeavor.
- And last, two departed giants in the field of property rights: Professor Gideon Kanner, a true mensch whose passion for justice

was second to none. And Toby Brigham, a great lawyer and champion of landowners everywhere, whose humanity touched all who knew him. I am forever in their debt for so much that I have learned.

Endnotes

Foreword

1   United States Congress Joint Economic Committee, "The HOUSES Act: Addressing the National Housing Shortage by Building on Federal Land," August 4, 2022, https://www.jec.senate.gov/public/index.cfm/republicans/2022/8/the-houses-act-addressing-the-national-housing-shortage-by-building-on-federal-land.

2   Jeffrey M. Jones, "Views of U.S. Housing Market Reach New Depths," Gallup, May 16, 2023, https://news.gallup.com/poll/505901/views-housing-market-reach-new-depths.aspx.

Introduction

1   "The New Colossus," National Park Service, https://www.nps.gov/stli/learn/historyculture/colossus.htm accessed April 29, 2024

2   Susan Shain and Aidan Gardiner, "What's Homelessness Really Like?," *New York Times*, February 20, 2023. https://www.nytimes.com/interactive/2023/02/10/headway/homelessness-mental-health-us.html?searchResultPosition=1

3   U.S. Department of Housing and Urban Development, "The 2023 Annual Homeless Assessment Report (AHAR) to Congress: Part 1—Point in Time Estimates of Homelessness in the U.S.," December 2023, 13. https://www.huduser.gov/portal/sites/default/files/pdf/2023-AHAR-Part-1.pdf ."

4   *Id.*, 13.

5   A cursory review of the HUD reports might suggest that there were more homeless people before 2016; but that is a statistical anomaly caused by a rule change and the reclassification of people living in motels or friend's couches. See U.S. Department of Housing and Urban Development, "Expanding Opportunities to House Individuals and Families Experiencing Homelessness through the Public Housing (PH) and Housing Choice Voucher (HCV) Programs, Questions and Answers," September, 2013, https://www.hud.gov/sites/documents/PIH2013–15HOMELESSQAS.PDF. The final rule is at 24 C.F.R. Parts 91 and 578, http://www.gpo.gov/fdsys/pkg/FR-2015–12-04/pdf/2015–30473.pdf.

6   "The 2023 Homeless Assessment," 22.

7   Andy Newman, "Migrants Sleep on the Sidewalk, the Face of a Failing Shelter System," *New York Times*, Aug. 1, 2023, https://www.nytimes.com/2023/08/01 /nyregion/nyc-migrants-homelessness.html.

8   Thomas Fuller and Josh Haner, "Among the World's Most Dire Places: This California Homeless Camp," *New York Times*, December 17, 2019, https://www .nytimes.com/interactive/2019/12/17/us/oakland-california-homeless-camp .html?

9   Anna Gorman and Kaiser Health News, "Medieval Diseases Are Infecting California's Homeless," *Atlantic*, March 8, 2019, https://www.theatlantic. com/health/archive/2019/03/typhus-tuberculosis-medieval-diseases-spread- ing-homeless/584380/; Chuck DeVore, "Typhoid Fever, Typhus & Tuberculosis: Are L.A.'s Medieval Diseases Coming to Your City?," *Forbes*, June 4, 2019, https://www.forbes.com/sites/chuckdevore/2019/06/04/typhoid-fever-typhus- tuberculosis-are-l-a-s-medieval-diseases-coming-to-your-city/#3166ee6610dc; Stephanie Dazio, "Union: LA Officer Gets Typhoid Fever, 5 Others Show Symptoms," *U.S. News & World Report*, May 30, 2019, https://www.usnews .com/news/best-states/california/articles/2019–05-30/lapd-union-seeks-city -cleanup-after-typhoid-fever-diagnosis; Eric Johnson, "Paradise Lost: Homeless in Los Angeles," *KOMO News*, June 19, 2019, https://abc3340.com/news /nation-world/paradise-lost-homeless-in-los-angeles-06–19-2019.

10   A combination of climate change and rats in homeless camps could be the trigger for bubonic plague. David K. Randall, "Op-Ed: Climate change could bring bubonic plague back to Los Angeles," *Los Angeles Times*, May 16, 2019, https://www.latimes.com/opinion/op-ed/la-oe-randall-plague-climate-change -rats-20190516-story.html.

11   Joanne Kenen, "What Covid Taught this Mid-Sized City About Ending Homelessness," *Politico*, February 15, 2022, https://www.politico.com/news /agenda/2022/02/15/covid-taught-mid-size-city-ending-homelessness-00008829.

12   Samuel Braslow, "How the Homeless Ended Up Being Blamed for Typhus," *Los Angeles Magazine*, February 12, 2019, https://www.lamag.com/citythinkblog /typhus-los-angeles-homeless/.

13   *Id.*

14   See e.g. Sam Stanton, "Judge won't order city to leave port-a-potties at Sacramento homeless camp." *Sacramento Bee*, February 10, 2020, https://www .sacbee.com/news/local/crime/article240172248.html.

15   Lisa Hig, "Don't Call Them Bums: The Unsung History of America's Hard- Working Hoboes," *Collectors Weekly*, April 16, 2015, https://www.collectors weekly.com/articles/dont-call-them-bums-the-unsung-history-of-americas -hard-working-hoboes/

16   While the 25% has often been cited over the years, the original source for that number is murky. More recently, the *Los Angeles Times* wrote about the wide-ranging estimates. *See* Doug Smith and Benjamin Oreskes, "Are many homeless people in L.A. mentally ill? New findings back the public's percep- tion," *Los Angeles Times*, Oct. 7, 2019, https://www.latimes.com/california/story /2019–10-07/homeless-population-mental-illness-disability.

17 Similarly, the *Los Angeles Times* notes estimates for the percentage of the homeless with substance abuse range from 14 to 75%. *Id.*

18 Sam Levin, "'We have failed': how California's homelessness catastrophe is worsening," *The Guardian*, March 22, 2022, https://www.theguardian.com /us-news/2022/mar/22/california-homelessness-crisis-unhoused-and-unequal,

19 Thomas Fuller, "A Rising Tally of Lonely Deaths on the Streets," *New York Times*, April 18, 2022, revised June 22, 2023, https://www.nytimes.com/2022/04/18/us /homeless-deaths-los-angeles.html.

20 Moreover, the rule itself is only a crude measure of housing affordability. Higher income families will have more money left over after 50% is spent on housing than some lower-income families who spend only 30% on housing. See e.g. U.S. Dep't of Housing and Urban Development, "Rental Burdens: Rethinking Affordability Measures, *PD&R Edge*," Sept. 22, 2014, https://www.huduser.gov /portal/pdredge/pdr_edge_featd_article_092214.html.

21 McKinsey Global Institute, "A Tool Kit to Close California's Housing Gap: 3.5 Million Homes by 2025," at 4, Oct. 2016, https://www.mckinsey.com/~/media /McKinsey/Industries/Public%20and%20Social%20Sector/Our%20Insights /Closing%20Californias%20housing%20gap/Closing-Californias-housing -gap-Full-report.pdf.

22 Zillow "California Market Overview," https://www.zillow.com/ca/home-val-ues/; See also Liam Dillon, "Experts say California needs to build a lot more housing. But the public disagrees," *Los Angeles Times,* Oct. 21, 2018, https: //www.latimes.com/politics/la-pol-ca-residents-housing-polling-20181021 -story.html, citing Zillow.

23 *Id.*

24 Zillow, "California Market," note 20, *supra.*

25 McKinsey Global, "Tool Kit," note 19, *supra.*

26 Katie Ziraldo, "Median Home Prices by State: 2023 Edition," Rocket Homes, Oct. 1, 2023, https://www.rockethomes.com/blog/housing-market/median-home -price-by-state#:~:text=What%20Is%20The%20Average%20Home,the%20 fourth%20quarter%20was%20%24479%2C500; See also Nicole Feldman, "U.S. Existing-Home Sale Prices Hit a Record of $407,600 in May," *Wall Street Journal*, June 21, 2022, https://www.wsj.com/articles/u-s-existing-home-sale -prices-hit-record-of-407–600-in-may-11655820516?mod=hp_lead_pos2.

27 Joint Center for Housing Studies of Harvard University, "The State of the Nation's Housing 2023," https://www.jchs.harvard.edu/sites/default/files/reports/files /Harvard_JCHS_The_State_of_the_Nations_Housing_2023.pdf.

28 Molly Cromwell, United States Census, "Low-Income Renters Spent Larger Share of Income on Rent in 2021," December 8, 2022 (census.gov).

29 Joint Center for Housing Studies, "Nation's Housing 2023," 5–7.

30 *Id.* at 22.

31 *Id.* at 38.

32 Denny Heck, Stephanie Murphy, Juan Vargas, and Scott Peters, "Missing Millions of Homes, Preliminary Findings of the New Democrat Coalition Housing Task Force," (2018), 6, https://newdemocratcoalition.house.gov/imo

/media/doc/NDC%20Missing%20Millions%20of%20Homes_Housing%20
TF%20Findings%20Report_June%202018.pdf. The statistics are based mainly
on HUD data that are out-of-date.

33 *Id.*at 7, citing to Laurie Goodman and Rolf Pendall. "Housing Supply Falls
Short of Demand by 430,000 Units." Urban Institute, June 21, 2016, https:
//www.urban.org/urban-wire/housing-supply-falls-short-demand-430000-
units." Goodman and Pendall conclude that "in 2015, we estimate that more
than a million new households were created, but only 620,000 new housing
units were completed, creating a shortage of just over 430,000 units." The 6.8
million unit figure comes from Kenneth T. Rosen, David Bank, Max Hall, Scott
Reed and Carson Goldman, Rosen Consulting Group, "Housing is Critical
Infrastructure: Social and Economic Benefits of Building More Housing,
June 2021" at iv., https://cdn.nar.realtor/sites/default/files/documents/Housing
-is-Critical-Infrastructure-Social-and-Economic-Benefits-of-Building
-More-Housing-6–15-2021.pdf.

34 California YIMBY, "Report—Housing Underproduction in California: 2023,"
https://cayimby.org/wp-content/uploads/2023/09/2023-Housing_Underproduction
-compressed.pdf.

35 *See* United States Census Bureau, "New Residential Construction Historical
Data," https://www.census.gov/construction/nrc/historical_data/index.html
and co_cust.xls (live.com). See also Tradingeconomics chart, showing that in
some years in the 1960s there were over two-million housing starts, as opposed
to around a million in recent years, https://tradingeconomics.com/united-states
/housing-starts.

36 *Id.*

37 Although there is some talk about more people leaving parts of California
than moving in, the state's population continues to increase because of internal growth. Compare e.g. Jonathan Lansner, "Los Angeles County suffers
nation's worst population outflow: 98,608 more exits than arrivals," *Los Angeles
Daily News*, June 24, 2019, https://www.dailynews.com/2019/06/24/la-county
-nets-98608-more-departures-than-arrivals-nations-worst-population-outflow
/?fbclid=IwAR36RwHxJoSFDBHkqmYdT4Fs70h_usXYfrmjLMQYHEdDl
rv1qtOcQC_RoJQ with Golden state population trends, ft *Journal*, Oct. 6,
2019, https://journal.firsttuesday.us/golden-state-population-trends/9007/.

38 Rosen et al, Housing is Critical Infrastructure, *supra* note 31 at iv.

39 Rosen, at 4.

40 Mac Taylor, "California's High Housing Costs, Causes and Consequences,"
at 21, *Legislative Analysts' Office,* 2015, https://lao.ca.gov/reports/2015/finance
/housing-costs/housing-costs.pdf; California Housing Partnership, California's
Housing Emergency Update, March 2019 https://chpc.net/wp-content
/uploads/2019/03/CHPC_HousingNeedReport_2019_PRINT_Rev4–5-19
_Hi-Res.pdf. The report relies on data from the National Low Income Housing
Coalition.

41 McKinsey Global, *supra* note 19, at 2–3.

42 *Id.* at 2, note 2.

43   *Id.* at 2, exhibit 2.

44   Thadani, Trisha. "S.F. Spends More than $60k Per Tent at Homeless Sites. Now It's Being Asked for Another $15 Million for the Program," *San Francisco Chronicle*, June 23, 2021, https://www.sfchronicle.com/politics/article/S-F-officials-want-15-million-for-tent-sites-16269998.php?converted=1#photo-20702792.

45   City News Service, "$600K per unit is too much for homeless housing, says LA Controller," *Los Angeles Daily News*, February 22, 2022, https://www.dailynews.com/2022/02/23/600k-per-unit-is-too-much-for-homeless-housing-and-837k-is-definitely-too-much-says-la-controller/; Doug Smith, "$600,000 for homeless housing? Audit suggests spending money on shelters instead," *Los Angeles Times*, Oct. 7, 2019, https://www.latimes.com/california/story/2019–10-07/homeless-housing-bond-measure-audit-shelters-galperin.

46   Liam Dillon, Ben Poston, "Affordable housing in California now routinely tops $1 million per apartment to build," *Los Angeles Times*, June 20, 2022, https://www.latimes.com/homeless-housing/story/2022–06-20/california-affordable-housing-cost-1-million-apartment.

47   Los Angeles Homeless Services Authority, "2016 Homeless Count Results Los Angles Coundy and LA Continuum of Care," May 10, 2016, http://documents.lahsa.org/Planning/homelesscount/2016/factsheet/2016-HC-Results.pdf.

48   LA County Homeless Initiative, "2022 Homeless Count Results, September 8, 2022," https://homeless.lacounty.gov/news/2022-homeless-count-results/#:~:text=The%20results%20of%20the%20point-in-time%20count%2C%20conducted%20over,conducted%20in%202021%20due%20to%20the%20COVID%20pandemic.%29

49   "Los Angeles Housing Market," Redfin, https://www.redfin.com/city/11203/CA/Los-Angeles/housing-market , access April 29, 2024

50   Dillon and Poston, "Affordable housing in California."

51   Liam Dillon, "Experts say California needs to build a lot more housing. But the public disagrees," *Los Angeles Times*, Oct. 21, 2018, https://www.latimes.com/politics/la-pol-ca-residents-housing-polling-20181021-story.html. The USC Dornsife/Los Angeles Times survey asked respondents, "Why is California housing unaffordable?" The answers, with weight given for second answers, were: Lack of rent control, 28%, Lack of funding for low-income housing, 24%, Environmental regulation, 17%, Foreign buyers, 16%, Influence of tech industry, 15%, Too little homebuilding, 13%, Wall Street buyers, 10%, Restrictive zoning rules, 9%. The margin of error was 3%.

52   Thomas H. Kean, Chairman, Thomas Ludlow Ashley, Vice Chairman, Advisory Commission on Regulatory Barriers to Affordable Housing, "'Not In My Backyard'" – Removing Barriers to Affordable Housing. Report to President Bush and Secretary Kemp," (1991) 3, https://www.huduser.gov/portal/Publications/pdf/NotInMyBackyard.pdf.

53   White House, Housing Development Toolkit, September 2016, https://obamawhitehouse.archives.gov/sites/whitehouse.gov/files/images/Housing_Development_Toolkit%20f.2.pdf.

54 "Executive Order Establishing a White House Council on Eliminating
    Regulatory Barriers to Affordable Housing," June 25, 2019, https://trump
    whitehouse.archives.gov/presidential-actions/executive-order-establishing
    -white-house-council-eliminating-regulatory-barriers-affordable-housing/.

55 The White House, "President Biden Announces New actions to Ease the
    Burden on Housing Costs," May 16, 2022, https://www.whitehouse.gov
    /briefing-room/statements-releases/2022/05/16/president-biden-announces
    -new-actions-to-ease-the-burden-of-housing-costs/.

56 Lucie Levine, "Looking back at the Depression-era shanty towns in New
    York City parks," *6sqft New York City*, https://www.6sqft.com/looking-back
    -at-the-depression-era-shanty-towns-in-new-york-city-parks/.

57 National Academies of Science, Engineering, and Medicine, et al, "Consensus
    Study Report, Permanent Supportive Housing: Evaluating the Evidence
    for Improving Health Outcomes Among People Experiencing Chronic
    Homelessness," https://nap.nationalacademies.org/catalog/25133/permanent-
    supportive-housing-evaluating-the-evidence-for-improving-health-outcomes;
    Appendix B, "The History of Homelessness in the United States, Homelessness
    Through the Early 20th Century," Washington, DC: The National Academies
    Press, https://www.ncbi.nlm.nih.gov/books/NBK519584/.

58 Quoted in Greg Rosalsky, "How California Homelessness Became A Crisis,"
    NPR capradio Planet Money, June 8, 2021, https://www.npr.org/sections/money
    /2021/06/08/1003982733/squalor-behind-the-golden-gate-confronting-californias
    -homelessness-crisis.

Chapter 1

1   The story is related in Roger L. Rice, "Residential Segregation by Law, 1910–
    1917," *The Journal of Southern History*, 34, (1968):179; Garrett Power, "Apartheid
    Baltimore Style: The Residential Segregation Ordinances 1910–1913," *Maryland
    Law Review*, 42, (1983):289.

2   Power, "Apartheid Baltimore Style," 298 (citations omitted).

3   Rice, "Residential Segregation," at 180.

4   *Id.*

5   "Petition to the Mayor and City Council, Baltimore City Archives Mahool
    Files, File 406 (July 5, 1910)," as cited in Power, "Apartheid Baltimore Style," at
    298–99.

6   Power, "Apartheid Baltimore Style," at 299.

7   Rice, "Residential Segregation," at 181.

8   All democrats voted in favor, Republicans against. Power, "Apartheid Baltimore
    Style," at 299. While the word "apartheid" has its origins from South Africa in
    the mid-twentieth century, there is no better term for describing an effort to
    create geographical separation of the races through the law.

9   *Id.*

10 *Id.*

11 *Id.*at 300, citing to "Memo from Edgar Allan Poe to Mayor J. Barry Mahool,
    Baltimore City Archives, Mahool Files, File 451 (Dec. 17, 1910)."

12 Power notes that many progressives had come to believe the only solution to what came to be known as the "negro problem" was for blacks to be "quarantined in isolated slums" to prevent their contagion from spreading. *Id.*at 301.

13 "Baltimore Tries Drastic Plan of Race Segregation," *New York Times*, December 25, 1910, https://timesmachine.nytimes.com/timesmachine/1910/12/25/105900067.pdf.

14 Id

15 *Id.*

16 *Id.* Poe compares the Baltimore ordinance favorably to other Jim Crow laws in the South.

17 *Id.*

18 *Id.*

19 See "Celebrating George McMechen, Morgan's first graduate, *WEAA*," https://www.weaa.org/arts-culture/2023–02-22/celebrating-george-mcmechen-morgans-first-graduate . (Photo in public domain.)

20 Power, "Apartheid, Baltimore Style," at 302.

21 *Id.*

22 *Id.* at 303.

23 Power, "Apartheid Baltimore Style," at 304.

24 *Id.* at 307–09.

25 *Id.* at 310.

26 Rice, "Residential Segregation," at 182.

27 *Id.* at 182.

28 *Id.*

29 *Id.*at 184.

30 Rice, "Racial Segregation," at 185, citing the *Baltimore Afro-American*, July 4, 1914.

31 Plessy v. Ferguson, 163 U.S. 537 (1896). In dissent, Justice Harlan prophetically announced that, "In my opinion, the judgment this day rendered will, in time, prove to be quite as pernicious as the decision made by this tribunal in the Dred Scott Case." *Id.* at 559 (Harlan, J., *dissenting*).

32 Plessy, 163 U.S. at 559 (Marshall, Harlan J., *dissenting*).

33 347 U.S. 483 (1954).

34 Students for Fair Admissions, Inc., v. President and Fellows of Harvard College, 600 U.S. 181, 249, n.3 (2023) (Thomas, J. *concurring*).

35 Berea College v. Kentucky, 211 U.S. 45 (1908). The Court decided the case on a narrow technicality of Kentucky corporation law and essentially punted the larger issue of the Equal Protection Clause.

36 Rice, "Racial Segregation," at 185.

37 Buchanan v. Warley, 245 U.S. 60, 70 (1917).

38 Rice, "Racial Segregation," at 186. See notes 31 and 32 and *supra*.

39 Brief for the Plaintiff in Error, page 2, Buchanan v. Warley, https://babel.hathitrust.org/cgi/pt?id=coo.31924032799805&view=1up&seq=7, see also Rice, "Racial Segregation," at 186.

40 198 U.S. 45 (1905).

41 David E. Bernstein, *Rehabilitating Lochner, Defending Individual Rights against Progressive Reform*, (Chicago: University of Chicago Press, 2012), 34–39.

42 *Id.* at 34.

43 *Id.*

44 Paul v. Florida Lime and Avocado Growers, 373 U.S. 132 (1963).

45 For more on rent-seeking and regulatory capture, see Gordon Tullock, "Efficient rent-seeking," in *Toward a Theory of the Rent-Seeking Society*, edited by J. Buchanan, R. Tollison, G. Tullock (College Station: Texas A&M Press, 1980), 97.

46 *Id.* at 37.

47 *Id.* at 40.

48 *Id.* at 40–41.

49 Photo discovered by Professor Josh Blackman, see https://joshblackman.com /blog/2015/10/26/c-span-used-the-image-of-lochners-bakery-i-discovered/.

50 People v. Lochner, 69 N.E. 373, 381 (1904).

51 Lochner v. New York, 198 U.S. 54, 64 (1905).

52 *Id.* at 65, (Holmes, J., *dissenting*). The reference is to Herbert Spencer's laissez-faire philosophy which advocated against government interference in economic relationships.

53 Brief for Plaintiff in Error at 10.

54 *Id.* at 14.

55 *Id.* at 16.

56 *Id.* at 22.

57 *Id.* at 28.

58 *Id.* at 32.

59 *Id.*

60 *Id.* at 73. Citing 1 *Blackstone's Commentaries* (Cooley's Ed.) 127.

61 Buchanan, 245 U.S. 60, 79 (1917).

62 *Id.* at 79.

63 *Id.* at 80, quoting Carey v. City of Atlanta, 84 S.E. 456 (Georgia, 1915).

64 *Id.* at 82.

Chapter 2

1 The best treatment of housing in New York City can be found in Richard Plunz, *A History of Housing in New York City*, Revised Edition (New York: Columbia Univ. Press, 2016), Kindle.

2 Plunz, *History of Housing*, chap. 2 at 21, Kindle. See also Timothy Collins, "An Introduction to the NYC Rent Guidelines Board and the Rent Stabilization System, Updated and Revised by the Staff of the NYC Rent Guidelines Board," February 18, 2018, (discussing early conditions,) https://www1.nyc.gov/site /rentguidelinesboard/about/history-rent-regulation-and-the-rgb.page.

3 Plunz, *History of Housing*, Preface, Kindle location 93.

4 Plunz, *History of Housing*, Kindle location 917, citing Richard H. Shryock, "Origins and Significance of the Public Health Movement in the United States," *Annals of Medical History* 1, no. 6, n 20 (November 1929).

5   Riis, Jacob A., *How the Other Half Lives (Illustrated): Studies Among the Tenements of New York* (New York: Charles Scribner's Sons, 1890,) 11. Reproduced by Annie Rose Books, Kindle Edition.

6   Riis, supra, at note 4, Kindle (quoting a report presented to the Citizens' Association of New York by the Council on Hygiene).

7   Riis, *How the Other Half Lives*, 10–12, Kindle.

8   Riis, *How the Other Half Lives*, 9, Kindle.

9   Plunz, *History of Housing*, 50, at lxiii- lxiv, Kindle (quoting Dr. William P. Buell in Citizen's Association of New York.)

10 Riis, *How the Other Half Lives*, 7, Kindle.

11 Riis, *How the Other Half Lives*, 11, Kindle (quoting city historian Mrs. Martha Lamb).

12 Power, *Apartheid, Baltimore Style*, 301 ("Progressives reformers were not concerned with the plight of Negroes . . . 'Victim blaming' was much less costly than attempting to solve the underlying social problems.")

13 Riis, *How the Other Half Lives*, 45, Kindle.

14 Riis, *How the Other Half Lives*, 46, Kindle.

15 Riis, *How the Other Half Lives*, 50, Kindle.

16 West Virginia v. EPA, 597 U.S. 697, n. 1 (2022) (Gorsuch, J., *concurring*,) (*quoting* W. Wilson, "The Study of Administration," 2 *Pol. Sci. Q.* 197, 212 (1887).

17 Riis, *How the Other Half Lives*, 69, Kindle.

18 Riis, *How the Other Half Lives*, 69, Kindle.

19 Riis, *How the Other Half Lives*, 72–73, Kindle.

20 Pamela Newkirk, "The man who was caged in a zoo," *The Guardian*, Jun 3, 2015, https://www.theguardian.com/world/2015/jun/03/the-man-who-was-caged-in-a-zoo. See also "In the Matter of Nonhuman Rights Project v. Breheny, New York Court of Appeals," 197 N.E. 3d 921, 932, (Wilson, J, *dissenting*) ("The *New York Times* reported that Mr. Benga was 'one of a race that scientists do not rate high in the human scale.'")

21 Aliya Hoff, "Madison Grant (1865–1937)," *The Embryo Project Encyclopedia*, Arizona State University, https://embryo.asu.edu/pages/madison-grant-1865-1937, Hoff notes that Hitler was a great admirer of Grant's book, often quoting from it in speeches and in *Mein Kampf*.

22 Power, *Apartheid, Baltimore Style*, at 302, quoting G. Frederickson, *The Black Image in The White Mind: The Debate on Afro-American Character and Destiny, 1817–1914*, (Harper & Row, 1971), 255.

23 Plunz, *History of Housing*, 52.

24 Joel Schwartz, *The New York Approach, Robert Moses, Urban Liberals, and the Redevelopment of the Inner City*," (Ohio Univ. Press, 1993), 8. PDF download available at https://kb.osu.edu/handle/1811/6273.

25 *Id.* at 313 n. 14. (Quoting Riis, "The Tenement, Curing Its Blight," *Atlantic Monthly*, (July 1899),26–27.)

26 Joel Schwartz, *The New York Approach*, 8–9, 13.

27 *Id.* at 14.

28 Plunz, *How the Other Half Lives*, 54.

29   Central Park Conservancy, "Before Central Park: The Story of Seneca Village," January 18, 2018, https://www.centralparknyc.org/articles/seneca-village; *see also* Wikipedia, Seneca Village, https://en.wikipedia.org/wiki/Seneca_Village; Robert Thomas, *New York City Takings Pilgrimage, Central Park Edition,* September 5, 2017, https://www.inversecondemnation.com/inversecondemnation /2017/09/new-york-city-takings-pilgrimage-central-park-edition.html;. Joel Schwartz describes Seneca Village as a sarcastic name given to the 5,000 "whites and mulattoes" who were displaced. Joel Schwartz, *The New York Approach*, 4.

30   Riis, *How the Other Half Lives*, 15.

31   Riis, *How the Other Half Lives*, 52–53.

32   Plunz, *History of Housing*, 51, quoting Charles Dickens, *American Notes*, 263.

33   Riis, *How the Other Half Lives,* 119.

34   Riis, *How the Other Half Lives*, 7.

Chapter 3

1   Hadacheck v. Sebastian, 239 U.S. 394 (1915) (closing brickyard after residential area grew near it).

2   For a detailed history of early zoning laws, and the efforts to convince the courts to uphold them, see Keith Revell, "The Road to Euclid v. Ambler: City Planning, State-Building, and the Changing Scope of the Police Power," *Studies in American Political Development*, 13, (Spring 1999):50. *Download available at* https://www.researchgate.net/publication/231757611_The_Road_to_Euclid_v _Ambler_City_Planning_State-Building_and_the_Changing_Scope_of _the_Police_Power.

3   Attorney General v. Williams, 174 Mass. 476, 478, 55 N.E. 77, 77 (1899).

4   Welch v. Swasey, 79 N.E. 745, 747 (Mass. 1907). See also Welch v. Swasey, 214 U.S. 91, 103 (1909) (taking was without compensation).

5   Welch v. Swasey, 214 U.S. 91, 106 (1909).

6   Cochran v. Preston, 108 Md. 220, 70 A. 113, 114 (1908).

7   Revell, "The Road to Euclid," 66, quoting Curran Bill Posting & Distributing Co. v. Denver, 47 Colo 221 at 227 (1910). Curran involved a successful challenge to a billboard ordinance.

8   Varney v. Williams (Cal.) 100 Pac. 867, 868 (1909) (a billboard case).

9   These window-mandates remain in place today, long after the invention of modern ventilation. One expert suggests that these mandates have become outdated and are an impediment to converting old office buildings into res-idential apartments. Joshua Benaim, "A Room With a Government-Ordered View," *Wall Street Journal*, Nov. 14, 2021, https://www.wsj.com/articles/room -government-ordered-view-office-space-apartments-new-york-city-zoning -housing-11636921942?mod=Searchresults_pos14&page=5 .

10   The church has a mission of providing housing to the poor. While the tene-ments it built were at one time much better than much existing housing, as standards evolved, they became substandard. But the church did not accept or understand that it had any obligation to make expensive improvements such as providing running water from New York City's fresh water supply.

11   Sarah Zielinski, "Cholera, John Snow and the Grand Experiment," *Smithsonian Magazine*, August 18, 2010, https://www.smithsonianmag.com/science-nature /cholera-john-snow-and-the-grand-experiment-33494689/.

12   Health Dep't of City of New York v. Rector of Trinity Church in City of New York, 145 N.Y. 32, 48–49, 39 N.E. 833, 838–39 (1895). While the court seemed to focus more on cleanliness and using the water to wash, rather than the purity of the supply, this is immaterial. It recognized that public health and safety were advanced by a supply of readily available fresh water.

13   Joel Schwartz, *The New York Approach*, 19.

14   *Id.*at 20.

15   David W. Dunlap, "Zoning Arrived 100 Years Ago. It Changed New York City Forever," *New York Times*, July 26, 2016, https://www.nytimes.com/2016/07/26 /nyregion/new-yorks-first-zoning-resolution-which-brought-order-to-a-chaotic -building-boom-turns-100.html. Berkeley, California, also passed a zoning ordinance in 1916, "to prevent a prominent negro dance hall from locating on a prominent corner," See Jesse Barker, Berkeley, "Zoning has served for many decades to separate the poor from the rich and whites from people of color," *Berkleyside*, March 12, 2019, https://www.berkeleyside.org/2019/03/12/berkeley -zoning-has-served-for-many-decades-to-separate-the-poor-from-the-rich-and -whites-from-people-of-color, citing Marc A. Weiss, Berkeley Planning Journal, 1986. However, from the prominence of the city, New York's ordinance was most influential.

16   Appended Report, Zoning and Districting, Minutes of the Heights of Buildings Commission, June 9, 1913, Heights of Buildings Commission, New York City Municipal Archives, Box 2507, as quoted in Revell, *Road to Euclid*,1.

17   Edward M. Bassett, "Constitutional Limitations on City Planning Power," *New York: Board of Estimate and Apportionment*, 1917.

18   Revell, *Road to Euclid*, 56.

19   Revell, *Road to Euclid*, 72.

20   Revell, *Road to Euclid*, 75, citing Edward M. Bassett, "A Survey of the Legal Status of a Specific City in Relation to City Planning," *Proceedings of the Fifth National Conference on City Planning*, 46, 57 (1913).

21   Revell, *Road to Euclid*, 55.

22   Alfred Bettman, "The Constitutionality of Zoning," 37 *Harv. L. Rev.* 834, 845 (1924).

23   Joel Schwartz, *The New York Approach*, 20.

24   John Infranca, "Single-Family Zoning and the Police Power: Early Debates in Boston and Seattle," 15, 25 *Cityscape 11*, June 28, 2023, quoting "Zoning Plan Ready," *Seattle Times*, April 23, 1922. SSRN: https://ssrn.com/abstract=4494555 or http://dx.doi.org/10.2139/ssrn.4494555.

25   Infranca, "Single-Family Zoning," 17–18, quoting Charles Cheney, "Removing Social Barriers by Zoning," *Survey* 44 (11): 275–278 (1920).

26   Revell, *Road to Euclid*, 57.

27   Reinman v. City of Little Rock, 237 U.S. 171 (1915); Hadacheck v. Sebastian, 239 U.S. 394 (1915).

28 Mugler v. Kansas, 123 U.S. 623 (1887).

29 Yick Wo v. Hopkins, 118 U.S. 356 (1886).

30 In re Jacobs, 498 U.S. 1076 (1885). For more the anti-immigrant bias and home cigar businesses, see David Bernstein, *Rehabilitating Lochner*, 27, and Riis, *How the Other Half Lives*, 64–65, (describing the life of Bohemian cigar making home businesses as not "less healthy than other in-door workers.")

31 Revell, *Road to Euclid*, 95.

32 Michael Allan Wolf, *The Zoning of America, Euclid v. Ambler*, (Lawrence, KS: University Press Kansas, 2008), 17. In this detailed history of Euclid, its zoning ordinance and the legal challenge, Professor Wolf takes an overall sympathetic view towards zoning, though he does recognize its limitations and flaws.

33 Hadecheck v. Sebastian, 239 U.S. at 410.

Chapter 4

1 Village of Euclid, Ohio v. Ambler Realty Co., 272 U.S. 365, 379 (1926). According to the United States census, the population in 1920 was only 3,363. Despite attempts to zone out progress, it steadily rose to 71,552 in 1970. From that time, it has steadily declined to under 50,000. See HomeArea.com, "Euclid City, Ohio - Housing, Employment, Education, More," https://www.homearea .com/place/euclid-city-ohio/3925704/#historical_population. According to the trial court, "If fully built up as a city, it will accommodate a population of several hundred thousand, but its present population is only a few thousand." Ambler Realty Co. v. Vill. of Euclid, Ohio, 297 F. 307, 309 (N.D. Ohio 1924).)

2 Euclid, 272 U.S. at 379–80.

3 Quoted in Wolf, *The Zoning of America*, 26.

4 Photo in public domain. For more illustrations of the case *see* Andrew Kull, Property Visual Syllabus, Village of Euclid .v. Ambler Realty Co., http://property kull.weebly.com/village-of-euclid-v-ambler-realty-co.html.

5 Wolf, *The Zoning of America*, 46, describing trial court opinion in Morris v. East Cleveland (1919).

6 Morris v. East Cleveland, as quoted in Wolf, *The Zoning of America*, 47.

7 Wolf, *The Zoning of America*, 83.

8 Wolf, *The Zoning of America*, 84.

9 Wolf, *The Zoning of America*, 49.

10 Wolf, *The Zoning of America*, 54.

11 Ambler Realty Co. v. Vill. of Euclid, Ohio, 297 F. 307, 308, (N.D. Ohio 1924).

12 *Id.*at 308.

13 *Id.*at 310.

14 The history of these rent regulations is discussed in a subsequent chapter.

15 260 U.S. 393 (1922) (this case will be discussed in more length in a subsequent chapter).

16 Ambler Realty, 297 F. at 312–13 (emphasis added.)

17 Ambler Realty, 297 F. at 314.

18 Ambler Realty, 297 F. at 316.

19 Wolf, *The Zoning of America*, 56.

20 Ambler Realty, 297 F. at 217.
21 Quoted in Wolf, *The Zoning of America*, 60.
22 Quoted in Wolf, *The Zoning of America*, 62.
23 James Metzenbaum, *The Law of Zoning* (2d ed. 1955) Vol 1, 57, as quoted in Garrett Power, "Advocates at Cross Purposes: The Briefs on Behalf of Zoning in the Supreme Court," 2 *Journal of Supreme Court History*, 79, 83–84 (1997).
24 Summaries of the briefs can be found at https://biotech.law.lsu.edu/cases /zoning/euclid.htm.
25 *Id.*
26 Quoted in Wolf, *The Zoning of America*, 70.
27 Wolf, *The Zoning of America*, 85.
28 Power, "Advocates at Cross-Purposes," 85.
29 *See* Wolf, *The Zoning of America*, 88.
30 *See* Wolf, *The Zoning of America*, 76–78.
31 Wolf, *The Zoning of America*, 90.
32 Euclid v Ambler Realty, 272 U.S. 365, 388 (1926) (emphasis added).
33 Euclid v. Ambler, 272 U.S. at 394–95.

Chapter 5

1   Euclid v. Ambler, 272 U.S. at 395.
2   Nectow v. Cambridge, 277 U.S. 183 (1928).
3   Nectow, 277 U.S. at 187.
4   Nectow, 277 U.S. at 187.
5   Nectow v. Cambridge, 157 N.E. 618 (Mass. 1927). The state court also held, mistakenly, that the Fifth Amendment's Takings Clause did not apply to the states.
6   Nectow, 157 N.E. at 620.
7   Nectow, 277 U.S. at 187–88.
8   Nectow, 277 U.S. at 188.
9   Richard Rothstein, *The Color of Law: A Forgotten History of How Our Government Segregated America* (New York, Liverright, , 2017), Preface, Kindle.
10 Brief of Appellees Anita Valtierra, et al, 1970 WL 12210 in James v. Valtierra, 402 U.S. 137 (1970).
11 Valtierra v. Housing Authority of the City of San Jose, 313 F. Supp. 1, 4 (1970).
12 Brief of Appellees Anita Valtierra et al, 1970 W.L. 122010.
13 *Id.*
14 Valtierra v. Housing Authority of the City of San Jose, 313 F. Supp at 5.
15 *Id.*
16 James v. Valtierra, 402 U.S. 137, 140 (1971).
17 This is the awkwardly named "California Remove Voter Approval Requirement for Public Low-Rent Housing Projects Amendment" (2024). Only the voters can repeal a constitutional provision. *See* https://ballotpedia.org/California _Remove_Voter_Approval_Requirement_for_Public_Low-Rent_Housing _Projects_Amendment_(2024).

18   See e.g. cases cited by Justice Marshall dissenting in Village of Belle Terre v. Boraas, 416 U.S. 1, 14, n. 3 (1974.) (Marshall, J., *dissenting.*)

19   429 U.S. 252 (1977).

20   See e.g. Spenser Agnew, "Discussion Paper: The Impact of Affordable Housing on Communities and Households," *Minnesota Housing Finance Agency,* (undated), https://medinamn.us/wp-content/uploads/2014/04/The-Impact-of -Affordable-Housing-on-Communities-MHFA.pdf ,accessed April 30, 2024.

21   Edward G. Goetz, Hin Kin Lam, and Anne Heitlinger, "There Goes the Neighborhood? The Impact of Subsidized Multi-Family Housing on Urban Neighborhoods," *Neighborhood Planning for Community Revitalization and the Center for Urban and Regional Affairs,* 1996, https://conservancy.umn.edu /handle/11299/204427

22   Luke Fiederer, "Pruitt-Igoe Housing Project / Minoru Yamasaki," *Arch Daily,* https://www.archdaily.com/870685/ad-classics-pruitt-igoe-housing-project -minoru-yamasaki-st-louis-usa-modernism, accessed April 30, 2024.

23   Theodore Dalrymple, "The Architect as Totalitarian", *The City Journal* (Autumn 2009), https://www.city-journal.org/article/the-architect-as-totalitarian.

24   For more on the history, see the film, Chad Freidrichs (Director), *The Myth of Pruitt-Igoe.* Available at https://vimeo.com/ondemand/thepruittigoemyth.

25   Jackie Dana, "The failed promise of Pruitt-Igoe, Unseen St. Louis," Feb. 10, 2022, https://unseenstlouis.substack.com/p/the-failed-promise-of-pruitt-igoe.

26   Amity Shlaes, *Great Society, A New History* (New York: Harper, 2019), 241.

27   Photo by Paul D'Amato.

28   Anthony Effinger, "A $28 Million Low-Income Apartment Complex Descends Into Chaos in Just Two and a Half Years," *Willamette Week,* June 7, 2023, https: //www.wweek.com/news/2023/06/07/a-28-million-low-income-apartment -complex-descends-into-chaos-in-just-two-and-a-half-years/

29   Oral argument transcript, James v. Valtierra, at 13, available at https://www .supremecourt.gov/pdfs/transcripts/1970/70–154_03–03-1971.pdf.

30   See *The Myth of Pruitt-Igoe.*

31   Village of Arlington Heights, 465 U.S. at 265.

32   465 U.S. at 266.

33   "Candidate Carter: 'I Apologize,'" *Time Magazine,* April 19, 1976, 14.

34   *Id.*

35   See "Forum," *Time Magazine,* May 10, 1976, 9 (where this book's author notes Carter's remarks would not destroy his campaign because they reflected the public's "sympathy for racism.")

36   Boraas v. Village of Belle Terre, 367 F. Supp. 136, 138 (E.D. N.Y. 1972).

37   Boraas v. Village of Belle Terre, 475 F. 2d 806, 809 (2nd Cir. 1973).

38   Boraas v. Village of Belle Terre, 367 F. Supp. at 146.

39   Boraas v. Village of Belle Terre, 475 F. 2d. at 816.

40   *Id.* at 818.

41   Village of Belle Terre v. Boraas, 416 U.S. 1 (1974).

42   Village of Belle Terre, 416 U.S. at 9. This language is reminiscent of Justice Douglas's paean to a community that is "beautiful as well as healthy, spacious

as well as clean, well-balanced as well as carefully patrolled" in Berman v. Parker, 438 U.S. 26, 35 (1954), a case that justified the destruction through redevelopment of an integrated neighborhood which is discussed in a subsequent chapter.

43 Sean Keenan, "The city of Morrow abruptly evicted 22 low-income renters. Why?," *Atlanta Civic Circle*, September 13, 2023, https://atlantaciviccircle.org /2023/09/13/morrow-abruptly-evicted-22-low-income-renters/.

44 Stephen Council, "San Francisco officials open investigation into $700-ka-month tiny bed 'pods,'" *SFGate*, September 27, 2023, https://www.sfgate.com/local /article/bed-pods-downtown-startup-unworried-18392385.php?utm_campaign =CMS%20Sharing%20Tools%20 .

45 Megan Fan Munce, "S.F. Mint Plaza $700-a-month deemed illegal, unsafe by building inspectors," *San Francisco Chronicle*, October 4, 2023, https://www .sfchronicle.com/sf/article/mint-plaza-sleeping-pods-18407067.php.

46 Moore v. City of East Cleveland, 431 U.S. 494 (1977).

47 *Id.* at 498.

48 Moore, 431 U.S. at 498 quoting Cleveland Board of Education v. LaFleur, 414 U.S. 632, 639–40 (1974).

49 431 U.S. at 508, (Brennan, J., concurring.)

50 431 U.S. at 509.

51 Later, in 1985, the Court also found an ordinance prohibiting group homes for people who were then called "mentally retarded" violated the Equal Protection Clause of the Fourteenth Amendment because it was based on irrational prejudice. City of Cleburne, Texas v. Cleburne Living Center, 473 U.S. 432 (1985).

52 Lee Micklin, "Caroline Rosenberg Kline Galland," *HistoryLink.org*, Dec. 16, 1988. https://www.historylink.org/File/544.

53 "Our History, Brick by Brick, Generation to Generation," Kline Galland, https://www.klinegalland.org/about/our-history/, accessed April 30, 2024.

54 State v. Roberge, 256 P. 781 (Wash. 1927).

55 Photo in public domain, from Klinegalland.org.

56 *Id.*at 782.

57 *Id.*at 783.

58 State of Washington ex rel. Seattle Title Tr. Co. v. Roberge, 278 U.S. 116 (1928).

59 *Id.*at 121.

60 *Id.*at 122.

61 In 2008, the measure was extended to 2058 by a vote that garnered over 62% in favor. See "Napa County 'Save Measure J Initiative', Measure P" (November 2008), *BallotPedia*, https://ballotpedia.org/Napa_County_%22Save_Measure_J _Initiative%22,_Measure_P_(November_2008) .

62 Today, most workers must commute into the valley. As discussed in a later chapter, the City of Napa soon enough recognized the housing shortage and now demands that builders of new homes subsidize affordable housing. Home Builders Association of Northern California v. City of Napa, 90 Cal. App. 4th 188 (2001). This practice just makes other housing more expensive and does little to solve the problem of demand with more supply—supply reduced by the ballot box zoning.

63   DeVita v. County of Napa, 9 Cal. 4th 763 (1995). The author and Pacific Legal Foundation filed a friend of the court brief in support of the builders.

64   DeVita, 9 Cal. 4th at 791–92.

65   DeVita, 9 Cal. 4th at 776.

Chapter 6

1   Photograph by Eric Schenk, see https://www.co.burlington.nj.us/1960/Noteworthy-Burlington-County-Women.

2   The story of the attempt by the residents to build affordable housing is retold in David L. Kirp, John P. Dwyer, and Larry R. Rosenthal, *Our Town, Race, Housing and the Soul of Suburbia* (Rutgers University Press, 1995.)

3   https://en.m.wikipedia.org/wiki/File:Jacob%27s_Chapel,_A.M.E._Church_in_Mount_Laurel,_Burlington_County,_NJ.jpg

4   Kirp, *Our Town,* 3; See also, David L. Kirp, "Here Comes the Neighborhood," *New York Times*, Oct. 19, 2013, https://www.nytimes.com/2013/10/20/opinion/sunday/here-comes-the-neighborhood.html.

5   *Id.* A variation of the story has the mayor saying, "you'll just have to move." Josh Getlin, "Home Is Where the Hurt Was," *Los Angeles Times*, Nov. 5, 2004, https://www.latimes.com/archives/la-xpm-2004-nov-05-na-mountlaurel5-story.html.

6   Ethel Lawrence Halley: Habitat for Humanity (2021) https://vimeo.com/543714451. See also Ethel Lawrence: The Rosa Parks of Affordable Housing Trailer, https://www.youtube.com/watch?v=O5ISax2G87g.

7   Josh Getlin, "Home is Where the Hurt Was."

8   Southern Burlington County N.A.A.C.P. v. Mt. Laurel Tp., 336 A. 2d 713, 716–17 (1975).

9   Mt. Laurel, 336 A. 2d at 717.

10   *Id.*

11   *Id.*at 725.

12   *Id.*

13   *Id.* at 723.

14   *Id.*at 724.

15   Southern Burlington County N.A.A.C.P. v. Township of Mt. Laurel (Mt. Laurel II), 456 A. 3d 390.

16   456 A. 2d at 458.

17   *Id.*at 456.

18   Robert Hanley, "After 7 Years, Town Remains Under Fire for Its Zoning Code," *New York Times*, Jan. 22, 1983, 31, https://www.nytimes.com/1983/01/22/nyregion/after-7-years-town-remains-under-fire-for-its-zoning-code.html.

19   See In re N.J.A.C. 5:96 & 5:97, 110 A.3d 31 (NJ 2015) and In Re Declaratory Judgment Actions Filed by Various Municipalities, 152 A. 3d 915 (NJ 2017).

20   In re Declaratory Judgment Actions Filed by Various Municipalities, 227 N.J. 508, 514, 152 A.3d 915, 918 (2017) quoting Mt. Laurel II.

21   Jugal K. Patel, Tim Arango, Anjali Singhvi, and Jon Huang, "Black, Homeless and Burdened by L.A.'s Legacy of Racism," *New York Times*, December 22,

2019, https://www.nytimes.com/interactive/2019/12/22/us/los-angeles-homeless
-black-residents.html

22   Andy Bosselman, "Denver built its neighborhoods around racist housing policies. But 'neighborhood defenders' refuse change,". *Denver Post*, June 13, 2020, https://www.denverpost.com/2020/06/13/bosselman-denver-built-its -neighborhoods-around-racist-housing-policies-but-neighborhood-defenders -refuse-change/.

23   Photograph from Office of Policy Development and Research, Evidence Matters, Spring/Summer 2014, available at https://www.huduser.gov/portal /periodicals/em/spring14/highlight1.html.

24   Taylor Allen, "Before the viral video, Black Mount Laurel residents rewrote the law on fair housing," *WHYY*, July 12, 2021, available at https://whyy.org /articles/before-the-viral-video-black-mount-laurel-residents-rewrote-the-law -on-fair-housing/.

Chapter 7

1   See Daniel Harsha, "Minneapolis Is Using Zoning to Tackle Housing Affordability and Inequality," Harvard Kennedy School Ash Center for Democratic Governance and Innovation, June 10, 2019, https://ash.harvard.edu/articles /minneapolis-is-using-zoning-to-tackle-housing-affordability-and-inequality/).

2   Nigel Jaquiss, "Oregon House Bill 2001 Ended Single-Family Zoning Across the State. That's Causing Some Pushback," *Willamette Week*, Nov. 6, 2019; Jack Rogers, "Arlington, VA Eliminates Single-Family-Only Zoning," Gobest.com, March 27, 2023. https://www.globest.com/2023/03/27/arlington-va-eliminates -single-family-only-zoning/?slreturn=20240325204324#:~:text=In%20a%20 fundament%20shift%20away,single%2Dfamily%2Donly%20zoning.

3   Rebecca Eliss, "Portland overhauls zoning code to allow for duplexes, triplexes, fourplexes," OPB, Aug. 12, 2020. *See also* Residential Infill Project | Portland .gov.

4   Daniel Woislaw, "California law gives people the right to build ADUs. Cities need to let them," *Daily Journal*, Sept. 17, 2021.

5   Pacific Legal Foundation has a litigation project dedicated to supporting the right to build ADUs. *See, e.g.,* "Holding local California governments accountable for banning granny flats." *Pacific Legal Foundation,* https://pacificlegal.org /case/riddick-adu/., accessed April 30, 2024.

6   Jeff Collins, "78% of Southern California neighborhoods don't allow apartments, study finds," *Orange County Register*, March 2, 2022, https://www .ocregister.com/2022/03/02/78-of-southern-california-neighborhoods-dont -allow-apartments-study-finds/?utm_email=14EA2553A%E2%80%A6.

7   *Id.*

8   David Albouy, Gabriel Ehrlich, Yingi Liu, "Housing Demand, Cost-of-Living Inequality, and the Affordability Crisis, Working Paper 22816," *National Bureau of Economic Research*, November 20, https://www.nber.org/system/files /working_papers/w22816/w22816.pdf.

9 "*SB 9 and SB 10*: In Sacramento Bee Ad, 'Housing Is A Human Right' Urges Newsom to Oppose Both Bills," Business Wire, Aug. 26, 2021, https://www.bing.com/search?q=SB+9+and+SB+10%3A+In+SacBee+Ad%2C+'Housing+Is+A+Human+Right'+Urges+Newsom+to+Oppose+Both+Bills+%7C+Business+Wire.+City+News+Service%2C&cvid=21da47393a744fa1b5d62e9a62fa3d35&gs_lcrp=EgZjaHJvbWUyBggAEEUYODlBCDMoMzBqMG0oqAIIsAIB&FORM=ANAB01&PC=U531.

10 Contributing Editor, "AIDS Healthcare Foundation Files Lawsuit Against Controversial Housing Bill," mynewsLA.com, September 23, 2021, https://www.bing.com/search?q=%2C+AIDS+Healthcare+Foundation+Files+Lawsuit+Against+Controversial+Housing+Bill+%7C+KFI+AM+640+(iheart.com).&cvid=76969f66407347fdad5985ea695b2fe9&gs_lcrp=EgZjaHJvbWUyBggAEEUYODlBCDE5ODJqMG0oqAIIsAIB&FORM=ANAB01&PC=U531. The suit alleges that the initiatives are inconsistent with California's Supreme Court decision upholding ballot box zoning in DeVita v. County of Napa, 9 Cal. 4th 763 (1995).

11 Gennady Sheyner, "Court ruling deals blow to housing law on split lots," *Palo Alto Online*, April 25, 2024, https://www.paloaltoonline.com/housing/2024/04/25/court-ruling-deals-blow-to-housing-law-on-split-lots/#:~:text=In%20a%20decision%20that%20could,is%20invalid%20in%20charter%20cities.

12 Rick Cole, "California cities find ways to live with SB 9," *Press Enterprise*, Dec. 11, 2021, https://www.pressenterprise.com/2021/12/11/california-cities-find-ways-to-live-with-sb-9/.

13 See note 9, supra (AIDS Healthcare Foundation advertisement).

14 See Cole, "California cities find ways."

15 348 U.S. 26 (1954).

16 See James Burling, "Property Rights for the Politically Powerful," *Brigham-Kanner Property Rights Journal*, 6 (2017): 179, 196.

17 Conor Dougherty, *Golden Gates: Fighting for Housing in America*, (Penguin Press, 2020), 47–48 and 179.

18 Angela Swartz, "Woodside decides it's not a mountain lion habitat, allows developers to propose housing under SB 9," *Palo Alto online*, February 7, 2022, https://www.paloaltoonline.com/news/2022/02/07/woodside-reverses-course-on-controversial-mountain-lion-moratorium-on-housing-projects; Maanvi Singh, "Wealthy California town cites mountain lion habitat to deny affordable housing," *The Guardian*, Feb. 5, 2022, https://www.theguardian.com/us-news/2022/feb/05/california-woodside-mountain-lions-development.

19 *Id.*

20 *Id.*

21 Angela Swartz, "Worried about wildfires and denser housing, Portola Valley residents petition for fire district to take more control over development," *The Almanac*, December 21, 2021. https://www.almanacnews.com/news/2021/12/21/worried-about-wildfires-and-denser-housing-portola-valley-residents-petition-for-fire-district-to-take-more-control-over-development.

22 Andre Coleman, "Attorney General's SB9 Letter Draws Mixed Reaction from Pasadena Residents," *Pasadena Now*, March 18, 2022, https://www.pasadenanow.com/main/attorney-generals-sb-9-letter-draws-mixed-reaction-from-pasadena-residents.

23 *Id.*

24 Aldo Toledo, "Palo Alto moves forward with plan to preserve dozens of homes to keep lot-splitting away," *The Mercury News*, March 22nd, 2022, https://www.mercurynews.com/2022/03/22/palo-alto-moves-forward-with-plan-to-preserve-dozens-of-homes-to-keep-lot-splitting-away/?utm_email=448A35936402F5F5358214AC81&g2i_eui=&g2i_source=newsletter&lctg=448A35936402F5F5358214AC81&active=no&utm_source=listrak&utm_medium=email&utm_term=%3a%2f%2fwww.mercurynews.com%2f2022%2f03%2f22%2fpalo-alto-moves-forward-with-plan-to-preserve-dozens-of-homes-to-keep-lot-splitting-away%2f&utm_campaign=bang-mult-nl-sunday-weekend-morning-report-nl&utm_content=manual

25 Randal O'Toole, *American Nightmare: How Government Undermines the Dream of Home Ownership*, (Washington, D.C. :Cato Institute, 2012.)

26 Randal O'Toole, "The Folly of 'Smart Growth,'" *Regulation*, Fall, 2001, 20, at 21.

27 *Id.*

28 *Id.* at 23.

29 Randal O'Toole, "Oregon Must End "Economic Apartheid," *Cascade Policy Institute*, Jan. 2, 2017, https://oregoncatalyst.com/34577-oregon-economic-apartheid.html.

Chapter 8

1 Thomas H. Kean, et al., Not in My Back Yard, 1, https://www.huduser.gov/portal//Publications/pdf/NotInMyBackyard.pdf.

2 *Id.* at 3.

3 Lawrence Katz and Kenneth T. Rosen, "The Effects of Land-Use Controls on Housing Prices," *Center for Real Estate and Urban Economics*, (1980), https://www.huduser.gov/portal//Publications/pdf/NotInMyBackyard.pdf.

4 Cynthia Kroll, J. Landis, D. Belzer, "Assessing the Impacts of Residential Growth Caps—The San Diego Experience," *Center for Real Estate and Urban Economics*, 1988.

5 Stephen Malpezzi, "Housing Prices, Externalities, and Regulation in the U.S. Metropolitan Areas," *Center for Urban Land Economics*, 1996.

6 Edward L. Glaeser and Joseph Gyourko, "The Impact of Building Restrictions on Housing Affordability," *National Bureau of Economic Research*, (2003), https://www.nber.org/system/files/working_papers/w8835/w8835.pdf.

7 Edward L. Glaeser and Bryce A. Ward, "The Causes and Consequences of Land Use Regulation: Evidence from Greater Boston," NBER Working Paper 12601, October 2006, cited in Benjamin Harney, "The Economics of Exclusionary Zoning and Affordable Housing," *Stetson Law Review* 38 (2009):459.

8   Joseph Gyourko and Raven Molloy, "Regulation and Housing Supply, NBER Working Paper no. 20536," *National Bureau of Economic Research,* October 2014, www.nber.org/papers/w20536.

9   Edward Glaeser and Joseph Gyourko, "The Economic Implications of Housing Supply," *Journal of Economic Perspectives,* 32, No. 1 (2018), https://www.aeaweb.org/articles?id=10.1257/jep.32.1.3

10   Chang-Tai Hsieh and Enrico Moretti, "Housing Constraints and Spatial Misallocation," *American Economic Journal: Macroeconomics* 11, no. 2 (2019): 1–39, https://pubs.aeaweb.org/doi/pdfplus/10.1257/mac.20170388.

11   See Ilya Somin, "Exclusionary Zoning is Even Worse than Previously Thought," *The Volokh Conspiracy,* Reason, April 10, 202, https://reason.com/volokh/2021/04/10/exclusionary-zoning-is-even-worse-than-previously-thought/. *But see* Ilya Somin, "Controversy Over an Important Article Finding Large Negative Effects of Zoning," *The Volokh Conspiracy,* November 29, 2023 (discussing possible errors in article,) https://reason.com/volokh/2023/11/29/controversy-over-an-important-article-finding-large-negative-effects-of-zoning/.

12   Paul Emrath, Caitlin Sugrue Walter, "Regulation: 40.6 Percent of the Cost of Multifamily Development," *National Association of Home Builders,* June 27, 2022, https://www.nahb.org//-/media/NAHB/news-and-economics/docs/housing-economics-plus/special-studies/2022/special-study-regulation-40-percent-of-the-cost-of-multifamily-development-june-2022.pdf .

13   Bernard H. Siegan, *Land Use Without Zoning,* (D.C. Heath & Co, 1972,) *Reprinted* by Rowan and Littlefield (2020).

14   Siegan, *Land Use Without Zoning,* 76, n. 8.

15   Siegan, *Land Use Without Zoning,* 122.

16   James Saltzman, "Houston Says No to Zoning," *Foundation for Economic Education,* August 1, 1994, https://fee.org/articles/houston-says-no-to-zoning/.

17   Jason Furman, "Barriers to Shared Growth: The Case of Land Use Regulation and Economic Rents," remarks delivered to the Urban Institute, The White House, November 20, 2015, as quoted in Richard V. Reeves, *Dream Hoarders, How the Middle American Middle Class is Leaving Everyone Else in the Dust, Why That is a Problem and What to Do About It,* (Washington, D.C.: Brookings Institution Press, 2017,) 105.

18   Jonathan Rothwell and Douglas Massey, "Density Zoning and Class Segregation in U.S. Metropolitan Areas," *Social Science Quarterly* 91, no. 5 (Dec. 2010,) at 1123–43 as quoted in Reeves, *Dream Hoarders,* at 106.

19   Reeves, *Dream Hoarders,* 106.

20   Gray, M. Nolan, *Arbitrary Lines: How Zoning Broke the American City and How to Fix It* (Washington, D.C.: Island Press, 2022), Kindle, 52–53.

21   Todd Litman, "Parking Requirement Impacts on Housing Affordability," *Victoria Transport Policy Institute,* June 30, 2023, 1, https://www.vtpi.org/park-hou.pdf.

22   Jeffrey Spivak, "People Over Parking, in Planning," *American Planning Association,* October 2018, https://www.planning.org/planning/2018/oct/peopleoverparking/.

23 See Lewis Lehe, "Minimum parking requirements and housing affordability," *The Journal of Transport and Land Use,* 11, no. 1 (2018): 1309–21, https://www.jtlu.org/index.php/jtlu/article/view/1340.

24 White House, Housing Development Toolkit, September 2016, https://obamawhitehouse.archives.gov/sites/whitehouse.gov/files/images/Housing_Development_Toolkit%20f.2.pdf .

25 President Obama, remarks to the U.S. Conference of Mayors, January 21, 2016, https://obamawhitehouse.archives.gov/the-press-office/2016/01/21/remarks-president-us-conference-mayors

26 Executive Order, June 25, 2019, https://trumpwhitehouse.archives.gov/presidential-actions/executive-order-establishing-white-house-council-eliminating-regulatory-barriers-affordable-housing/.

27 Affirmatively Furthering Fair Housing, 80 Fed. Register 42272 (July 16, 2015).

28 *Id.*

29 Department of Housing and Urban Development, AFFH Fact Sheet: The Duty to Affirmatively Further Fair Housing," http://web.archive.org/web/20171119063642/https://www.huduser.gov/portal/sites/default/files/pdf/AFFH-Fact-Sheet.pdf.

30 80 Fed. Reg. 42272, § 5.152

31 Tracy Jam, "Federal judge dismisses lawsuit accusing HUD Secretary Ben Carson of dismantling Obama-era fair housing law," *The Washington Post,* August 18, 2018, https://www.washingtonpost.com/business/2018/08/18/federal-judge-dismisses-lawsuit-accusing-hud-secretary-ben-carson-dismantling-obama-era-fair-housing-law/.

32 Donald J. Trump and Ben Carson, "We'll Protect America's Suburbs," *Wall Street Journal,* August 16, 2020, https://www.wsj.com/articles/well-protect-americas-suburbs-11597608133?mod=searchresults&page=1&pos=5.

33 Jonathan D. Salant, "Trump keeps claiming Biden will bring crime to the suburbs and Cory Booker will lead the way," *NJ.Com* , Sept. 2, 2020, https://www.nj.com/politics/2020/09/trump-keeps-claiming-biden-will-bring-crime-to-the-suburbs-and-cory-booker-will-lead-the-way.html. See also https://www.youtube.com/watch?v=ytonHk4C1_I.

34 Note 32, *supra.*

35 For a bit more on Silas Lynch, see Davarian L. Baldwin, "'I Will Build a Black Empire'" *The Birth of a Nation* and "The Specter of the New Negro," *The Journal of the Gilded Age and Progressive Era,* 14 (2015): 569–603, https://www.jstor.org/stable/43903543.

36 The White House, Fact Sheet: The American Jobs Plan, March 31, 2021, https://www.whitehouse.gov/briefing-room/statements-releases/2021/03/31/fact-sheet-the-american-jobs-plan/.

37 William A. Fischel, *The Homevoter Hypothesis: How Home Values Influence Local Government Taxation, School Finance, and Land-Use Policies,* (Cambridge, Massachusetts: Harvard University Press, 2005), Kindle.

38 *Id.*, Ch. 10, Kindle loc. 3292.

39   Clayton Nall, Christopher S. Elmendorf, and Stan Oklobdzija, "Folk
      Economics and the Persistence of Political Opposition to New Housing"
      (April 29, 2024), SSRN: https://ssrn.com/abstract=4266459 or http://dx.doi.org
      /10.2139/ssrn.4266459.

40   *Id.* at 6

41   *Id.* at 41.

42   *Id.* at 5–6.

43   *Id.* at 40–41.

Chapter 9

1   Van Horne's Lessee v. Dorrance, 2 U.S. 4304, 307 (1795).

2   Sources vary from 300 to 1000 families. The latter figure comes from Janice
      Llamoca, "Remembering The Lost Communities Buried Under Center Field,"
      Code Switch, National Public Radio, October 31, 2017, https://npr.org/sections
      /codeswitch/2017/10/31/561246946/remembering-the-communities-buried
      -under-center-field. The 300 number from Zinn Education Project, "This Day
      in History May 8, 1859: Mexican American Communities Evicted." https:
      //www.zinnedproject.org/news/tdih/chavez-ravine-evictions/ Accessed May 1,
      2024. For a pictorial history see https://laist.com/news/la-history/dodger-stadium-
      chavez-ravine-battle.

3   Zinn Education Project, "This Day in History."

4   Id.

5   Eric Nusbaum, *Stealing Home, Los Angeles, the Dodgers, and the Lives Caught in
      Between* (New York: Public Affairs, 2020), 161, Kindle.

6   Hector Becerra, "Decades Later, Bitter Memories of Chavez Ravine," *Los
      Angeles Times*, April 5, 2012, http://www.articles.latimes.com/2012 /apr/05/local
      /la-me-adv-chavez-ravine-20120405. See also the video by Jordan Mechner,
      Chavez Ravine: A Los Angeles Story, https://www.youtube.com/watch?v=eBOt
      KhAAUHs.

7   Joseph P. Bishop, PhD, Lorena Camargo Gonzalez, Edwin Rivera, "State of
      Crisis, Dismantling Student Homelessness in California," *UCLA Center for
      Transformation of Schools*, 2020, 2, https://secureservercdn.net/198.71.233.214/38e
      .a8b.myftpupload.com/wp-content/uploads/2020/10/CTS_state-of-crisis
      _report_FINAL_10.19updates.pdf; Daniel Cassady, "Number of Homeless
      Students in California Could Fill Dodgers Stadium 5 Times, Study Finds,"
      Forbes, Oct. 21, 2020, https://www.forbes.com/sites/danielcassady/2020/10/21
      /number-of-homeless-students-in-california-could-fill-dodgers-stadium-5
      -times-study-finds/?sh=5f19c8dae5b7.

8   Also attributed to Herald-Examiner Collection/Los Angeles Public Library
      Collection.)

9   "Suzette Kelo," *Institute for Justice*, March 12, 2015, https://ij.org/client/susette
      -kelo/. For more on the case, see Ilya Somin, *The Grasping Hand,* Kelo v. City
      of New London *and the Limits of Eminent Domain* (Chicago: University of
      Chicago Press, 2015.)

10 "Transcript, Kelo v. New London Connecticut," 39, https://www.supreme
    court.gov/pdfs/transcripts/2004/04–108.pdf.

11 Kelo v. City of New London, Conn., 545 U.S. 469, 503 (2005) (O'Connor, J.
    dissenting.)

12 "Suzette Kelo's Experience Seeing Her Own Story on the Big Screen,"
    YouTube, Build Series, April 16, 2018, https://www.google.com/search?q
    =susette+kelo&source=lmns&bih=923&biw=1920&hl=en&sa=X&ved
    =2ahUKEwi-p-7AjdiCAxU8MkQIHTuKB5wQopQJKAB6BAg
    BEAI#fpstate=ive&ip=1&vld=cid:366ac864,vid:-bRWDJKJKtY,st:0.

13 Patrick McGeehan, "Pfizer to Leave City That Won Land-Use Case," *New York
    Times*, Nov. 12, 2009, https://www.nytimes.com/2009/11/13/nyregion/13pfizer
    .html.

14 Kelo v. City of New London, 545 U.S. 469 (2005) (undefined support facilities
    for pharmaceutical company).

15 Photograph from Institute for Justice https://ij.org/client/susette-kelo/.

16 Photo from Institute for Justice.

17 *See* Somin, *The Grasping Hand*, 47B54.

18 Timothy Sandefur, "A Natural Rights Perspective on Eminent Domain in
    California: A Rationale for Meaningful Judicial Scrutiny of 'Public Use',"
    Southwestern University Law Review 32, (2003):635.

19 Gideon Kanner, "Do We Need to Impair or Strengthen Property Rights in
    Order to Fulfill Their Unique Role? A Response to Professor Dyal-Chand,"
    University of Hawaii Law Review 31, (2009):447.

20 Kanner, "Do We Need to Impair," 447.

21 Poletown Neighborhood Council v. City of Detroit, 304 N.W.2d 455 (Mich.
    1981).

22 Kelo v. City of New London, 545 U.S. 469 (2005) (The ostensible purpose of the
    redevelopment (or destruction) of a middle-class neighborhood was to facilitate
    jobs. In reality, the project was for the benefit of the Pfizer corporation.); *see also*
    Somin, *The Grasping Hand*, 16. (Documents obtained by *The Day* . . . show that
    the . . . condemnations were undertaken in large part as a result of extensive
    Pfizer lobbying of state and local officials.)

23 For a longer list of cases where private property has been taken for the benefit
    of industrial and corporate interests, see Kanner, "Do We Need to Impair," 467
    nn.185B203.

24 Eric Avila, *The Folklore of the Freeway: Race and Revolt in the Modernist City*,
    (Minneapolis: University of Minnesota Press, 2014), 14, Kindle. Avila argues
    that the growing resistance to urban highways that began in the 1960s still
    pitted the white elites against poor minority communities.

25 Avila, *Folklore of the Freeway*, Location 754, Kindle.

26 *Id.*at Location 845, Kindle.

27 *Id.*at Location 866, Kindle.

28 *Id.*at Location 913, Kindle.

29 Rosen et al, "Housing is Critical Infrastructure," 13.

30   For the origins of this metaphor, see Stephen L. Carter, "Destroying a Quote's History in Order to Save It," *Bloomberg Opinion*, Feb. 9, 2018, https://www.bloomberg.com/opinion/articles/2018–02-09/destroying-a-quote-s-history-in-order-to-save-it.

31   See Kelo v. City of New London, 545 U.S. 469 (2005).

32   See generally James S. Burling, "Blight Lite," *American Law Institute-American Bar Association Continuing Legal Education, ALI-ABA Course of Study, Eminent Domain and Land Valuation Litigation*, January 9B11, 2003, at 3, 43, 2003 WL SH053 ALI-ABA 3, 43 (noting that one of the standard factors for determining blight is Adversity of ownership and general dilapidation); Somin, *The Grasping Hand*, 84 (discussing expansion of meaning of Ablight).

33   See Randal O'Toole, *The Best-laid Plans: How Government Planning Harms Your Quality of Life"* (Washington, D.C.: CatoInstitute, 2007,) 80. See also Denis C. Theriault, "San Jose's well-heeled Naglee Park poised to escape redevelopment list," *San Jose Mercury News*, Feb. 7, 2009, https://www.mercurynews.com/2009/02/07/san-joses-well-heeled-naglee-park-poised-to-escape-redevelopment-list/.

34   See, e.g., Somin, *The Grasping Hand*, 135–180 (summarizes political responses to *Kelo*); see, e.g., Jennifer Zeigler, et al., "50 State Report Card: Tracking Eminent Domain Reform Litigation Since Kelo," *Institute For Justice* (Aug. 1, 2007), http://www.ij.org/wp-content/uploads /2015/03/50_State_Report.pdf. But see Timothy Sandefur, "The ABacklash@ So Far: Will Americans Get Meaningful Eminent Domain Reform?," 2006 Michigan State Law Review 2006, (2006): 709 (arguing that the legislative response has often been ineffectual and coopted).

35   See, e.g., Brad Kuhn, "It's Baaacckkkk. . . . Redevelopment Returns to California," *California. Eminent Domain Report*, (Sept. 28, 2015), http://www.californiaeminentdomain report.com /2015/09/articles/redevelopment /its-baaacckkkk-redevelopment-returns-to-california/ (chronicling the return of redevelopment in California).

36   U.S. Const. amend. V.

37   For numerous examples of undercompensation for taken property, search for blog posts with the title, *Lowball Watch*, in Gideon Kanner's blog, *Gideon's Trumpet* [hereinafter Kanner, *Lowball Watch*], https://gideonstrumpet.info /?s=low+ball+watch, accessed May 1, 2024.

38   County of Los Angeles v. Anthony, 224 Cal. App. 2d 103, 105, *cert. denied*, 376 U.S. 963 (1964). See Wendy Horowitz, "Here Lies Liberty: Steve Anthony and His Fight Against Eminent Domain," *Central Library Blog* (Apr. 2, 2014), https://www.lapl.org/collections-resources/blogs/lapl/here-lies-liberty-steven-anthonys-fight-against-eminent.

39   Poletown Neighborhood Council v. City of Detroit, 304 N.W.2d at 459 (Mich. 1981.)

40   See Manuel Roig-Franzia, "The Time Donald Trump's Empire Took on a Stubborn Widow and Lost", *Washington Post* (Sept. 9, 2015), https://www.washington post.com/lifestyle/style/the-time-donald-trumps-empire-took-on-a-stubborn-widow-and-lost/2015/09/09/f9cb287e-5660–11e5-b8c9–944725fcd3b9 _story .html?utm_term=.0a08259f3930; *see also* Kanner, *Lowball Watch*.

41 For a dramatic video, see "Trump Plaza Implosion: The Atlantic City casino came down this morning," NJ.com, *Youtube*, https://www.youtube.com/watch ?v=8IwHZD8Qnv8 , accessed May 1, 2024.

42 See Gideon Kanner, "Eminent Domain Projects that Didn=t Quite Work Out," American Law Institute-American Bar Association Continuing Legal Education, *ALI-ABA Course of Study, Eminent Domain and Land Valuation Litigation*, Jan. 8 B10, 2009, at 17, 2009 WL SP006 ALI-ABA 17.

Chapter 10

1 See Ilya Somin, "Putting Kelo in Perspective," 48, *Connecticut Law Review* 48, No. 5, (2016): (symposium on Kelo), https://papers.ssrn.com/sol3/papers.cfm ?abstract_id=2850695#.

2 Somin, *The Grasping Hand*, 3.

3 Jeff Jacoby, "The Supreme Court can't be absolute," *The Boston Globe*, January 1, 2012, https://www.bostonglobe.com/opinion/editorials/2012/01/01 /the-supreme-court-can-absolute/gp7sg853zm9jTatBjLcJfL/story .html?outputType=amp.

4 For a sense of the public outrage, see, for example, Avi Salzman & Laura Mansnerus, "For Homeowners, Frustration and Anger at Court Ruling," *New York Times*, June 24, 2005, http://www.nytimes.com/2005/06/24/us/for-home-owners-frustration-and-anger-at-court-rul ing.html?_r=0; Jonathan V. Last, "The Kelo Backlash: What the Supreme Court Touched Off with Its Eminent Domain Decision," *The Weekly Standard*, Aug. 21, 2006, http://www.weekly standard.com/the-kelo-backlash/article/13716.

5 Paul Samuel Reinsch, *English Common Law in the Early American Colonies*, (PhD diss. University of Wisconsin, 1898): 16, https://archive.org/details /englishcommonlaooreingoog accessed May 1, 2024.

6 VanHorne's Lessee v. Dorrance, 2 U.S. (2 Dall.) 304 (1795).

7 Calder v. Bull, 3 U.S. (3 Dall.) 386 (1798).

8 *Id.* at 388B89.

9 Wilkinson v. Leland, 27 U.S. (2 Pet.) 627, 657 (1829).

10 *Id.* at 658. This proscription against private takings is consistent with Blackstone's admonition against a set of individuals taking private property even for a public purpose like a road. See 1 William Blackstone, *Commentaries on the Laws of England*, 135. While Blackstone continued that the government, and only the government, may take private property for such purposes, he did not say that government may take from one individual just for the benefit of another individual or set of individuals; to do so would have made his invective nugatory.

11 Or in *Calder*, 3 U.S. (3 Dall.) 386, which involved a legislative incursion in an inheritance dispute.

12 West River Bridge v. Dix,47 U.S. (6 How.) 507, 537 (1848).

13 *Id.* at 537 (McLean, J., concurring) (emphasis added.)

14 Hairston v. Danville & W. R. Co., 208 U.S. 598 (1908).

15 *Id.* at 608.

16 See Timothy Sandefur, "Natural Rights Perspective," 599B609) (extended historical treatment of eminent domain by mills and railroads).

17 Berman v. Parker, 348 U.S. 26 (1954).

18 See Amy Lavine, "Urban Renewal and the Story of Berman v. Parker," *Urban Lawyer* 42, (2010):451–52. Lavine recounts that while there were serious concerns about bad conditions in and around alleys that characterized many neighborhoods in Washington, D.C., the twenty-three thousand people living in these areas were not all anxious for their redevelopment.

19 Photo by Joseph Owen Curtis. DC Public Library, The People's Archive, Joseph Owen Curtis Photograph Collection, Streets and Buildings.

20 *Berman*, 348 U.S. at 32 (segueing a discussion of the power of eminent domain executed for a public purpose to the application of the police power to municipal affairs).

21 See, e.g., United States v. Carolene Products, 304 U.S. 144, 152 n. 4 (1938).

22 *Berman*, 348 U.S. at 33 (emphasis added).

23 *Id.* at 32.

24 Hawaii Housing Auth. v. Midkiff, 467 U.S. 229 (1984).

25 The previous dalliance with land reform in the United States occurred on Puerto Rico where sugar plantations, already made less viable by a World War II era condemnation for naval purposes, were condemned for redistribution to farmers. See Puerto Rico v. E. Sugar Assocs., 156 F.2d 316 (1st Cir. 1946).

26 Gideon Kanner, "Is the Public Use Pendulum Reaching the End of Its Swing?," American Law Institute-American Bar Association Continuing Legal Education, *ALI-ABA Course of Study, Land Use Institute: Planning, Regulation, Litigation, Eminent Domain, and Compensation* 709, 711 (Aug. 22B24, 2002) 2002 WL SH018 ALI-ABA 709.

27 Letter, May 9, 1984, from Harry Blackmun to Sandra Day O'Connor. Available from Library of Congress and author.

28 For more on this saga, see James Burling, "Private Property for the Politically Powerful," 6 Brigham-Kanner Property Rights Journal 6, (2017): 196–98.

29 Kelo v. City of New London, 545 U.S. 469 (2005).

30 *Id.* at 475 (homes were unblighted). See also Somin, *The Grasping Hand*, 12 (description of neighborhood).

31 See Kelo, 545 U.S. at 473B75; Somin, *The Grasping Hand* ,16B19 (outlining Pfizer=s role in the redevelopment).

32 Of course, the public should know better than to think words mean what they mean. See:

    "When I use a word," Humpty Dumpty said, in rather a scornful tone, "it means just what I choose it to mean, neither more nor less."

    "The question is," said Alice, "whether you can make words mean so many different things."

    Lewis Carrol, *Through the Looking-Glass, and What Alice Found There* (London, Ward Jock & Co. Ltd., (1896):106, https://archive.org/details /ThroughTheLookingGlass/page/n103/mode/2up.

Chapter 11

1   See, e.g., Michael Malamut, "The Power To Take: The Use of Eminent Domain in Massachusetts, White Paper No. 15." Pioneer Institute (2000); Steven M. Crafton, "Taking The Oakland Raiders: A Theoretical Reconsideration of The Concept of Public Use And Just Compensation," Emory Law Journal 32, (1983):857; David Kochan, "Public Use And The Independent Judiciary: Condemnation in An Interest-Group Perspective," *Texas Review of Law & Politics* 3, (1998):49; Peter J. Kulick, "Rolling the Dice: Determining Public Use in Order to Effectuate A Public-Private Taking: A Proposal to Redefine Public Use, 200 *Law Review of Michigan State University-Detroit College of Law 2000* (Fall 2000): 639; Wendell E. Pritchett, "The 'Public Menace' of Blight: Urban Renewal and the Private Uses of Eminent Domain," Yale *Law & Policy Review 21* (2003):4; Laura Mansnerus, "Note, Public Use, Private Use, And Judicial Review in Eminent Domain," *New York University Law Review 58*, (1983):409.; Derek Werner, "Note, The Public Use Clause, Common Sense, and Takings," *Boston University Public Interest Law Journal 10* (2001): 335. For more articles, see, Timothy Sandefur, Freespace, Bibligraphy on public use, https://sandefur.typepad.com/freespace/2004/08/bibliography_on.html, accessed May 1, 2024.

2   Kelo v. City of New London, 545 U.S. 469, 505 (2005) (O'Connor, J., dissenting).

3   *Id.* at 521 (Thomas, J., dissenting).

4   National Academies of Science, Engineering, and Medicine, et al, "Consensus Study Report, Permanent Supportive Housing: Evaluating the Evidence for Improving Health Outcomes Among People Experiencing Chronic Homelessness," https://nap.nationalacademies.org/catalog/25133/permanent -supportive-housing-evaluating-the-evidence-for-improving-health-outcomes; "Appendix B, The History of Homelessness in the United States, Homelessness Through the Early 20th Century," Washington, DC: The National Academies Press, https://www.ncbi.nlm.nih.gov/books/NBK519584/.

5   Kelo, 522.

6   Joel Schwartz, *The New York Approach,* 297.

7   *Id.*

8   Pritchett, "The 'Public Menace' of Blight," 6.

9   See Leland T. Saito, *The Politics of Exclusion: The Failure of Race-neutral Policies in Urban America* (Stanford, CA.: Stanford University Press (2009):4–5.

10 Pritchett, "The 'Public Menace' of Blight," 47.

11 See James Baldwin, *Negro and the American Promise, PBS* (1963), http://www .pbs.org/wgbh/americanexperience /features/bonus-video/mlk-james-baldwin/.

12 *Id.*

13 See Lavine, "Urban Renewal," 449. Lavine also notes that the planners apparently forgot to consider the four thousand families *already* on the waiting list for decent low-cost housing.

14 *Id.* at 448.

15 See Kanner, "Do We Need to Impair," 455B56.

16 *Id.*at 456.

17   *Id.*at 455 n. 127.
18   See *Id.*, at 435 n.48. (citing sources for estimates that 2.38 million urban hous-
     ing units were destroyed by redevelopment, and by the 1960s, "some 111,000
     families and 17,800 businesses were being displaced by urban redevelopment
     annually.")

Chapter 12

1   See, e.g., Paul H. Brietzke, "Urban Development and Human Development,"
    Indiana Law Review 25 (1991): 773 (1991) ("Edifice Complex projects have come
    to be emphasized over those promoting social welfare because elites who pay
    the planning piper get to call the tune.").
2   Pritchett, "The 'Public Menace' of Blight," 4.(footnotes omitted)).
3   For more on property rights and blight eradication see *Miller v. Schoene*, 276
    U.S. 272 (1928), holding that the removal of cedar trees to save the apple trees
    was not a taking.
4   That's not to say that private developers can't profitably invest in troubled
    neighborhoods without subsidies. See, Jim Schutze, "One Dallas Developer's
    Secret: Bigger Isn't Always Better," *D Magazine*, November 2020, https://www
    .dmagazine.com/publications/d-magazine/2020/november/one-dallas-developers
    -secret-bigger-isnt-always-better/?fbclid=IwAR2RjyqDyRKuVCUpNJN_
    RTNZ6Qe-fVuvmQHphoAwerJuh6rL4n5uZndHb7c#.X6nC3E2wf4s
    .facebook.
5   This is generally the case unless they employ the Trump model of business by
    bankruptcy.
6   See, e.g., Kanner, "Do We Need to Impair."
7   See Somin, *The Grasping Hand*, 235; see also, Kanner, "Do We Need to Impair."
8   See, e.g., Naikang Tsao, "Ameliorating Environmental Racism: A Citizens=
    Guide to Combatting the Discriminatory Siting of Toxic Waste Dumps," *New
    York University Law Review* 67 (1992):366 (noting prevalence of toxic waste sites
    in minority neighborhoods).
9   Richard Rothstein, *The Color of Law*, 57. Kindle.

Chapter 13

1   See, e.g., C. Jarrett Dieterle, "The Sandbagging Phenomenon: How
    Governments Lower Eminent Domain Appraisals to Punish Landowners,"
    Federalist Society Review 17 (2016):38B39 (In other words, governments attempt
    to dissuade landowners from holding out for more compensation by punishing
    those that do so, which results in governments getting away with systematic
    undercompensation in eminent domain proceedings. In essence, a sandbagging
    government says to landowners, "if you think our initial appraisal is too low,
    just see how low we'll go if you take it to court!"); Kanner, Lowball Watch, See
    also United States v. Norwood, 602 F.3d 830, 834 (7th Cir. 2010) (The fact that
    "just compensation" tends systematically to undercompensate the owners of
    property taken by eminent domain underscores the fact that such a taking is
    not a wrongful act).

2   See, e.g., Olson v. United States, 292 U.S. 246, 257 (1934) (It is the "amount that in all probability would have been arrived at by fair negotiations between an owner willing to sell and a purchaser desiring to buy." Likewise, the Court held that a condemnee is "entitled to be put in as good a position pecuniarily as if his property had not been taken. He must be made whole but is not entitled to more. It is the property and not the cost of it that is safeguarded by state and federal constitutions.").

3   *Id.* at 257 (eminent domain fair market value and value of speculation).

4   Saint Thomas Aquinas, Summa Theologica, Question 58 (Of Justice), Art. 1 https://www.newadvent.org/summa/3058.htm

5   Transcript of Oral Argument at 34B35, Kelo v. City of New London, 545 U.S. 469 (2005) (No. 04–108), 2005 WL 529436.

6   See, e.g., Gideon Kanner, 'Fairness and Equity,' or Judicial Bait and Switch? It's Time to Reform the Law of 'Just' Compensation," *Albany Government Law Review* 4 (2011), 42. (While fair market value of the taken property is certainly a proper element of compensation, standing alone it ignores a variety of incidental economic losses that are inevitably inflicted by forcible displacement of people from their homes and businesses, and thus falls short of being genuinely just compensation).

7   Kanner, "Fairness and Equity," 46–47.

8   Thomas W. Merrill, "Incomplete Compensation for Takings," *New York University Environmental Law Review* 11, (2002):111. cited in Kanner, "Fairness and Equity," 56.

9   Michael R. Klein, "Eminent Domain: Judicial Response to the Human Disruption," University of Detroit Urban Law Review 46 (1968): 21.

10   *Id.*, 3.

11   Kanner, "Fairness and Equity," 46, n. 31.

12   Kanner, "Fairness and Equity," 41 n. 9.

13   See John Gavin, "Estimating Assemblage Value to Help Buyers and Sellers," *NEREJ* (New England Real Estate Journal) Aug. 15, 2013, https://nerej.com /65220.

14   See, e.g., Santa Clara Cty. v. Ogata, 240 Cal. App. 2d 262, 268 (Cal. Dist. Ct. App. 1966) (The possibility of integrating parcels is a factor which may be considered in determining market value, provided such integration would have been reasonably practicable without the exercise of the power of eminent domain.")

15   United States v. Powelson, 319 U.S. 266, 281 (1943).

16   See Kanner, "Lowball Watch," http://www.gideonstrumpet.info/ (last visited Dec. 19, 2016).

17   See generally Jarrett Dieterl, "The Sandbagging Phenomenon," 38, http://www. fed-soc.org/library/doclib/20161110_DieterleSandbagging.pdf.

18   These allegations were made in United States v. 480.00 Acres of Land, 557 F.3d 1297 (11th Cir. 2009), *cert. denied*, 558 U.S. 1113 (2010).

19   This procedure was unsuccesfuly challenged at the Sixth Circuit. See Brief of Plaintiffs-Appellants, Brott v. United States, 858 F.3d 425 (6th Cir. 2017). New challenges are anticipated.

20 Darius W. Dynkowski, "Preparing a Business Damage Claim," American Law Institute-American Bar Association Continuing Legal Education, *ALI-ABA Course of Study, Condemnation 101: How To Prepare and Present an Eminent Domain Case* 251, 253 (Jan. 8 B10, 2009), Westlaw SH018 (Many jurisdictions do not permit compensation for business damages and the determination of whether business damages are compensable in a particular jurisdiction depends mainly on legislative grace or a broad interpretation of the jurisdiction's common law definition of just compensation. Moreover, in jurisdictions that allow business damages only certain elements of business losses are compensable.); see Note, "The Nature of Business Goodwill," *Harvard Law Review* 16 (1902):135) (discussing business goodwill as definable property interest).

21 See Lynda J. Oswald, Goodwill and Going Concern Value: Emerging Factors in the Just Compensation Equation, *Boston College Law Review* 32 (1991):284. (A number of state courts and legislatures have begun to recognize that losses of goodwill, going-concern value, or profits are real losses for which the property owners should be compensated.); see also Gideon Kanner, "(Un)equal Justice Under Law: The Invidiously Disparate Treatment of American Property Owners in Taking Cases," *Loyola Los Angeles Law Review* 40 (2007):1090 n.110, ("Before the legislature made loss of goodwill compensable in eminent domain under some circumstances, the court got around that inconvenient statutory scheme by simply asserting that business goodwill, though incontestably property, is not "the form of property" that is protected by the Constitution in eminent domain, implicitly suggesting that property, sort of like ice cream, comes in different flavors, some more and others less appealing to the courts.").

22 S. Lafourche Levee Dist. v. Jarreau, 192 So. 3d 214, 226 (La. Ct. App.), *writ granted*, No. 2016–00904 (La. Sept. 6, 2016), 2016 WL 4991620, and *writ granted*, No. 2016–0788 (La. Sept. 6, 2016), 2016 WL 5001347 (reversing "trial court determin[ation] that just compensation for the Jarreau tract included the fair market value of the property plus economic/business losses for lost profits associated with the value of the excavated dirt").

23 Kanner, "Fairness and Justice," 74.

Chapter 14

1 See Somin, *The Grasping Hand*, 141 (on legislative reform).

2 Fla. Const. art. X, ' 6(c) (Private property taken by eminent domain pursuant to a petition to initiate condemnation proceedings filed on or after January 2, 2007, may not be conveyed to a natural person or private entity except as provided by general law passed by a three-fifths vote of the membership of each house of the Legislature.).

3 See Sandefur, "The Backlash So Far," 751.

4 See Somin, *The Grasping Hand,* 159, 175.

5 See California Redevelopment Ass=n v. Matosantos, 53 Cal. 4th 231 (Cal. 2011) (statutes requiring windup and dissolution of redevelopment agencies do not violate constitutional provision limiting State's ability to require payments from redevelopment agencies); Maura Dolan, et al., "California High Court

Puts Redevelopment Agencies out of Business," *Los Angeles Times* (Dec. 29, 2011), http://www.articles.latimes.com/2011/dec/29/local/la-me-redevelopment -20111230 (noting political and tax reasons for abolition).

6   See Kuhn, "It's Baaaccckkkk. . . ."

7   Hathcock v. Wayne City, 684 N.W.2d 765, 786 (Mich. 2004).

8   See, e.g., City of Norwood v. Horney, 853 N.E.2d 1115, 1141 (Ohio 2006) (citing Hathcock's criticism of economic development positively). Kentucky and Illinois supreme courts have also pointed out that the economic development rationale provides no logical limits. The Kentucky Supreme Court noted that every new legal business provides some sort of benefit that could be described as economic development. City of Owensboro v. McCormick, 581 S.W.2d 3, 8 (Ky. 1979) (quoting 26 Am. Jur. 2d *Eminent Domain* 34, at 684B85 (1966)). Thus, if mere economic development is a public purpose, there is no limit that can be drawn.; *Id.* The Illinois Supreme Court dismissed the economic development rationale by explaining: "If property ownership is to remain what our forefathers intended it to be, if it is to remain a part of the liberty we cherish, the economic by-products of [an interest group's] ability to develop land cannot justify a surrender of ownership to eminent domain." Sw. Ill. Dev. Auth. v. Nat'l City Envtl., 768 N.E.2d 1, 10 (Ill. 2002) (quoting lower court decision).

9   Man "seeks out, and is willing to joyn [sic] in Society with others who are already united, or have a mind to unite for the mutual Preservation of their Lives, Liberties and Estates, which I call by the general Name, *Property.*" John Locke, (P. Laslett rev. ed., 1988), 123.

10 Thomas Hobbes, *The Leviathan or the Matter, Forme, & Power of a Common-Wealth Ecclesiastical and Civill [sic]* ch. 14 (1651). Project Guttenberg from Pelican Classics Edition, https://www.gutenberg.org/files/3207/3207-h/3207-h .htm.

11 See, e.g., Gordon Tullock, *The Rent-Seeking Society*, ed. Charles K. Rowley in Volume 5, *The Selected Works of Gordon Tullock* (Carmel, Indiana, Liberty Fund Books, 2005).

Part III

1   See, e.g., Paul R. Ehrlich, *The Population Bomb* (New York: Ballantine Books 1968).

2   See, e.g., Rachel Carson, *Silent Spring* (Houghton Mifflin Company, 1962).

3   His death was reported in a *Time* cover story. "Is God Dead?," *Time*, Apr. 8, 1966, available at http://www.time.com/time/covers/0,16641,19660408,00.html.

4   42 U.S.C. ' 4321, *et seq.* (1970).

5   42 U.S.C. ' 7401, *et. seq.* (1970).

6   33 U.S.C. ' 1251, *et seq.* (1972).

7   16 U.S.C. ' 1531, *et seq.* (1973).

8   15 U.S.C. ' 2601, *et seq.* (1976).

9   42 U.S.C. ' 6901, *et seq.* (1976).

10 Love Canal was the site of a toxic waste site that later became a residential neighborhood. It became the subject of national and international attention

in the mid-1970s. See Eckardt C. Beck, "The Love Canal Tragedy," *EPA Journal*, (January 1979,) https://www.epa.gov/archive/epa/aboutepa/love-canal-tragedy.html.

11   42 U.S.C. ' 9601, *et seq.* (1980)."

12   For a complete list, see United States Environmental Protection Agency, *"Laws and Regulations*, https://www.epa.gov/laws-regulations accessed May 2, 2024.

13   See Bill Deval & George Sessions, *Deep Ecology, Living as if Nature Mattered* (Gibbs Smith 1985). For an account of the deep ecology, the forests, and the spotted owl, see Alston Chase, *In a Dark Wood: The Fight Over Forests and the Myths of Nature* (New York: Houghton Mifflin, 2001).

Chapter 15

1   16 U.S.C. ' 1531, *et seq.* (1973).

2   For a description of the impacts of the ESA and suggestions to reform the act, see Johnathan Adler, Editor, *Rebuilding the Ark: New Perspectives on Endangered Species Act Reform* (Washington, D.C.:American Enterprise Institute for Public Policy Research, distributed by Lanham, MD: Rowman & Littlefield, 2011).

3   16 U.S.C. Sec. 1532 (19).

4   See e.g. Weyerhaeuser v. U.S. Fish & Wildlife Service, 139 S. Ct. 361 (2018) (unoccupied (and allegedly unoccupiable) habitat protected for the Dusky Gopher Frog.)

5   In Tennessee Valley Auth. v. Hill, 437 U.S. 153 (1978).

6   TVA v. Hill, 437 U.S. at 162 (emphasis in original).

7   An exception is made for dangerous pathogens. There is no requirement under the Act to save the polio virus, bacterial meningitis, mad cow prions, or any loose COVIDians.

8   Tennessee Valley Auth. v. Hill, 437 U.S. 153, 184 (emphasis added).

9   While the Fish and Wildlife Service has delisted some species –usually because they are extinct or were mistakenly listed in the first place—the God Squad has never delisted a species. See Jonathan Adler, *Failure to Recover, The Endangered Species Act at 50*, PERC, October 17, 2023 https://www.perc.org/2023/10/17/failure-to-recover/.

10   Stuart L. Somach, "What Outrages Me About the Endangered Species Act," *Environmental Lawyer* 24 (1994):804.

11   U.S. Fish & Wildlife Service, "Northern Spotted Owl," https://www.fws.gov/arcata/es/birds/nso/ns_owl.html.

12   As a practical matter, for most of the existence of the Endangered Species Act there has been no practical difference between the regulatory treatment of species listed as endangered versus those merely threatened with endangerment.

13   Jim Petersen, "Owl Be Damned," *Wall Street Journal*, Feb. 18, 2006. https://www.wsj.com/articles/SB114022159215877610

14   Victor M. Sher, "Travels with Strix: The Spotted Owl's Journey through the Federal Courts," *Public Land Law Review* 14 (1993):41.

15   See California Department of Fish and Wildlife, "Cannabis and the Environment," https://wildlife.ca.gov/Conservation/Cannabis/Environment#:~:text=Removing%20forest%2C%20grasslands%2C%20or%20other,increased%20sediment%20delivery%2C%20and%20erosion. Accessed May 2, 2024.

16 Environmental Protection Agency, "Learn more about Threatened and Endangered Species" https://www.epa.gov/endangered-species/learn-more-about-threatened-and-endangered-species#:~:text=There%20are%20over%201%2C300%20endangered,in%20the%20United%20States%20today., accessed May 2, 2024.

17 See, e.g., California Department of Fish and Wildlife, "Delta Smelt," https://wildlife.ca.gov/Conservation/Fishes/Delta-Smelt, accessed May 2, 2024.

18 Holly Doremus & A. Dan Tarlock, "Fish, Farms, and the Clash of Cultures in the Klamath Basin," *Ecology Law Quarterly* 30 (2003):279 (2003).

19 See, e.g., Christy v. Hodel, 857 F.2d 1324 (9th Cir. 1988), *cert. denied sub nom.* Christy v. Lujan, 490 U.S. 1114 (1989) (holding that depredation by protected bears is not a taking); Brian N. Beisher, "Are Ranchers Legitimately Trying to Save Their Hides or Are They Just Crying Wolf? What Issues Must Be Resolved Before Wolf Reintroduction to Yellowstone National Park Proceeds," 29 *Land & Water Law Review* 29 (1994): 417.

20 16 U.S.C. ' 1538 (1973), aka Section 9 prohibits taking protected species without federal permission.

21 16 U.S.C. ' 1536 (1973), aka Section 7, requires federal agency consultation for federal actions affecting protected species.

22 See, e.g., Strahan v. Coxe, 127 F.3d 155 (1st Cir. 1997) (permitting by state regulators of lobster fishing, which may interfere with endangered whales, could be a take in violation of the Endangered Species Act).

23 Jonathan Adler, "The Leaky Ark: The Failure of Endangered Species Regulation on Private Land," in *Rebuilding the Ark,* 16.

24 *Id.* at 17.

25 Jonathan Remy Nash, *Mark to Ecosystem Market: Protecting Ecosystems through Revaluing Conservation Easements,* in *Rebuilding the Ark,* 120.

Chapter 16

1 United States v. Mills, 817 F. Supp. 1546, 1548–49 (N. D. Florida 1993).

2 *Id.* at 1548.

3 Mills v. United States, 36 F. 3d 1052 (11th Cir. 1994).

4 Sackett v. Environmental Protection Agency, 506 U.S. 120 (2012).

5 See, e.g., *Rapanos,* 547 U.S. 715.

6 Statement of Malcolm Stewart, Transcript, Sackett v. Environmental Protection Agency, 26, https://www.supremecourt.gov/oral_arguments/argument_transcripts/2011/10–1062.pdf.

7 Sackett, 506 U.S. at 133 (Alito, J., concurring).

8 See map at https://www.flickr.com/photos/pacificlegalfoundation/52327630835/in/album-72177720301408375/

9 547 U.S. 715, 719 (2006).

10 Rapanos v. United States, 547 U.S. 715, 721 (2006).

11 See e.g. Megan Haines, Jennifer A. Smokelin, Sara M. Eddy & Randa M. Lewis, "In Light of Sackett, EPA Announces 'Revised Definition of "Waters

of the United States'" Rule" August 31, 2023, https://www.ehslawinsights.com
/2023/08/in-light-of-sackett-epa-announces-revised-definition-of-waters-of-the
-united-states-rule/#:~:text=On%20August%2029%2C%202023%2C%20the,
the%20Supreme%20Court's%20Sackett%20v.

Chapter 17

1   Richard F. Babcock and Charles L. Sieman, "The Zoning Game Revisited,"
    (Cambridge, Massachusetts: Lincoln Instute Of Land Policy (1990):203.

2   See, Louis Sahagun, "Environmental group and Tejon Ranch agree on
    plan to build 19,300 zero-emission homes," *Los Angeles Times*, Dec. 1, 2021,
    https://www.latimes.com/california/story/2021–12-01/tejon-ranch-will
    -build-19–300-zero-emission-homes; Maanvi Singh, "California developers
    want to build a city in the wildlands. It could all go up in flames," *The
    Guardian*, June 29, 2021, https://www.theguardian.com/us-news/2021/jun/29
    /tejon-ranch-housing-centennial-california-wildfires.

3   Jane Braxton Little, "Development plans test a decade-old conservation
    deal," *High Country News*, Feb. 7, 2019, https://www.hcn.org/issues/51–5
    /deserts-was-californias-great-environmental-compromise-worth-it/.

4   Patrick Hedlund, "Tejon Mountain Village Impact Report Review Clock Ticking
    Down," *The Mountain Enterprise*, June 5, 2009, https://mountainenterprise.com
    /story/tejon-mountain-village-impact-report-review-clock-ticking-down-15D6/.

5   Nicolas Lemann, "No People Allowed," *The New Yorker*, Nov. 22, 1999, https:
    //www.newyorker.com/magazine/1999/11/22/no-people-allowed .

6   Center for Biological Diversity v. Kern County; Tejon Mountain Village, 2012
    WL 1417682, (5th DCA, April 25, 2012).

7   *Id.*

8   Sam Morgan, "Tejon Ranch Grapevine project prevails in court against a law-
    suit from Center for Biological Diversity," *Bakersfield.com*, Jan. 25, 2021, https:
    //www.bakersfield.com/news/tejon-ranch-grapevine-project-prevails-in-court
    -against-lawsuit-from-center-for-biological-diversity/article_a0a0ea84–5f5d
    -11eb-a6b5–2750d6b7c175.html .

9   Press Release, Center for Biological Diversity, "Appeal Targets U.S. Wildlife
    Agency's Refusal to Consider California Condor's Significance to Tribal
    Groups in Approving Luxury Resort" (Feb. 2, 2021), https://biologicaldiversity
    .org/w/news/press-releases/appeal-targets-us-wildlife-agencys-refusal-to
    -consider-california-condors-significance-to-tribal-groups-in-approving-luxury
    -resort-2021–02-02/

10 Press Release, "Tejon Ranch, Federal Court Ruling Upholding Habitat
    Conservation Plan on Tejon Ranch Stands," (Oct. 5, 2021), http://ir.tejonranch
    .com/news-releases/news-release-details/federal-court-ruling-upholding
    -habitat-conservation-plan-tejon.

11 Jeff Collins, "A tale of two housing projects: Tejon Ranch and Newhall Ranch
    developers take different paths on global warming," *Los Angeles Daily News*, Apr.
    10, 2021, https://www.dailynews.com/2021/04/20/a-tale-of-2-housing-projects
    -tejon-and-newhall-ranch-developers-take-different-paths-on-global-warming/.

12 *Id.*

13 Center for Biological Diversity, Press Release "California Judge Revives Lawsuit Against Controversial Tejon Ranchcorp Development," January 14, 2022. https://biologicaldiversity.org/w/news/press-releases/california-judge-re-vives-lawsuit-against-controversial-tejon-ranchcorp-development-2022–01-14/.

14 Center for Biological Diversity, Press Release "Judge Deals Another Blow to Tejon Ranchcorp Project," March 27, 2023 https://biologicaldiversity.org /w/news/press-releases/judge-deals-another-blow-to-tejon-ranchcorp-project -2023–03-27/

15 Ben Bradford, "Is California's Legacy Environmental Law Protecting the State's Beauty or Blocking Affordable Housing," *KQED Capital Public Radio,* July 10, 2018, https://www.kqed.org/news/11679835/is-californias-legacy-environmen-tal-law-protecting-the-states-beauty-or-blocking-affordable-housing.

16 *Id.* and Holland and Knight Press Release, "Holland and Knight Achieves Favorable Settlement for Habitat for Humanity in Legal Battle over Proposed Affordable Housing Development," July 26, 2018, https://www.hklaw.com/en /news/pressreleases/2018/07/holland—knight-achieves-favorable-settlement-for.

17 *Id.*

18 *Id.*

19 Comments on Facebook page, Redwood City Residents Say: "What?" https: //www.facebook.com/groups/709200909129615/permalink/1231874330195601/.

20 Christian Britschgi, "While Homeless Population Balloons, San Francisco Residents Use Environmental Lawsuit to Stop Homeless Shelter*," Reason,* July 15, 2019; Liam Dillon and Benjamin Oreskes, "Homeless shelter opponents are using this environmental law in bid to block new housing." *Los Angeles Times,* May 15, 2019, https://reason.com/2019/07/15/while-homeless-population-balloons-san -francisco-residents-use-environmental-lawsuit-to-stop-homeless-shelter/.

21 Homeless Shelter Opponents, *Los Angeles Times.*

22 *Center for Biological Diversity v. California Department of Fish and Wildlife,* 361 P. 3d 342, 62 Cal. 4th 204 (2015).

23 See Collins, *A Tale of Two Projects.*

24 See The Sierra Club v. California Coastal Commission, 2019 WL 1292887, unpublished opinion, case No. B283652, Second Appellate District, Div. Three, March 21, 2019. The neighborhood streets reportedly had no names.

25 Joshua Emerson Smith and Kristina Davis, "Judge Strikes down envisioned Otay Ranch housing project, citing wildfire, climate change," *San Diego Union-Tribune,* October 7, 2021 https://www.sandiegouniontribune.com/news /environment/story/2021-10-07/adara-otay-ranch-development.

26 Blake Nelson, "Judge halts 3,0000-home project in San Diego suburb over wildfire concerns," *Los Angeles Times,* March 12, 2022. https://www.latimes. com/california/story/2022–03-12/court-rejects-santee-housing-develop-ment-over-environmental-concerns?utm_id=50239&sfmc_id=311771; See also, Preserve Wild Santee v. City of Santee, Minute Order, March 3, 2022, https: //www.biologicaldiversity.org/programs/urban/pdfs/Fanita-Ranch-court-ruling.pdf.

27   For an extensive and critical look at CEQA over a three-year period from 2010 - 2012, see Jennifer L. Hernandez and David Friedman, "In the Name of the Environment: Litigation Abuse Under CEQA," Holland & Knight, 2015 https://www.hklaw.com/en/insights/publications/2015/08/in-the-name-of-the-environment-litigation-abuse-un#:~:text=Analyzing%20all%20CEQA%20lawsuits%20filed,social%20equity%20and%20economic%20priorities. For a follow-up of the subsequent three years, see Jennifer Hernandez, "California Environmental Quality Act Lawsuits and California's Housing Crisis," *Hastings Law Journal* 24 (2018):21.

28   See *Id.*

29   See *Id.*

30   *Euclid*, 272 U.S. at 388.

31   Hernandez, *Housing Crisis*, 32.

32   *Id.* at 39.

33   *Id.* at 41.

34   *Id.* at 44.

35   Cicero Institute, "Align incentives for neighborhoods to build," https://www.housingforcalifornia.org/proposals/incentives.

36   *Id.*

37   See e.g. Janet Smith-Heimer & Jessica Hitchock, "CEQA and housing production: 2018 survey of California cities and counties," *Environmental Practice* 21 (2019, Issue 2). https://www.tandfonline.com/doi/abs/10.1080/14660466.2019.1609848?af=R&journalCode=uevp20. The conclusions in this study by environmental professionals was based on a survey of cities with a 9% response rate.

38   David J. Breemer, "What Property Rights: The California Coastal Commision's History of Abusing Land Rights and Some Thoughs on the Underlying Causes," *UCLA Journal of Environmental Law and Policy* 22 (2004): 247.

39   Erin Rode, "'Getting out of hand': Legislator blasts California Coastal Commission on housing," *SFGATE,* April 25, 2024.

40   Lloyd Billingsley, "Legacy of Zealotry," *City Journal,* June 28, 2012, https://www.city-journal.org/article/legacy-of-zealotry.

41   Erika Ritchie, "Coastal Commission says San Clemente homeless site may violate Coastal Act," *Orange County Register,* September 30, 2019.

Chapter 18

1   For more on the factual background of Munn v. Illinois, see Edmund W. Kitch and Clara Ann Bowler, "The Facts of Munn v. Illinois," 1978 Supreme Court Review, (Chicago: University of Chicago Press, 1978):313, https://www.jstor.org/stable/3109535?read-now=1&seq=3#page_scan_tab_contents.

2   *Id.*

3   It is debatable how much power the farmers actually wielded in the legislature compared to the elevators and railroads, and whether their power translated into significant benefits. *Id.*

4   94 U.S. 113 (1877).

5   *Id.* at 138 (Field, J., *dissenting*).

6   *Id.* at 142 (Field, J., *dissenting*) (emphasis added).
7   41 Stat. 298 (Oct. 22, 1919), available at https://www.loc.gov/law/help/statutes
    -at-large/66th-congress/session-1/c66s1ch80.pdf.
8   256 U.S. 135 (1921).
9   258 U.S. 242 (1922).
10 Hirsh v. Block, 267 F. 614, 621 (D.C. Cir. 1920).
11 Block v. Hirsh, 256 U.S. at 156.
12 In Pennsylvania Coal v. Mahon, 260 U.S. 393, 415 (1922), Justice Holmes opined
    that "while property may be regulated to a certain extent, if regulation goes too
    far it will be recognized as a taking."
13 256 U.S. at 158.
14 256 U.S. at 158.
15 *Id.* at 165–66 (quoting Ex parte Milligan, 71 U.S. 2, 120–21). In *Milligan*, the
    Court found that the non-combatant civilian living in a non-rebel state was
    entitled to a trial by jury in a civilian court.
16 Edgar A. Levy Leasing Co. v. Siegel, 230 N.Y. 634, 638, 130 N.E. 923, 925 (N.Y.
    1921), *aff'd*, 258 U.S. 242, 42 S. Ct. 289 (1922).
17 *Id.*
18 Edgar A. Levy Leasing Co., 258 U.S. at 246.
19 See Plunz, *A History of Housing,* (describing the early tenements).
20 James Madison, "Federalist No. 10," in Alexander Hamilton, James Madison,
    and John Jay, *The Federalist Papers* (New York, Bantam Books (1982):42. A "rage
    for paper money" refers to popular pressure for governments to print enough
    paper money for farmers to pay off their debts. This would cause inflation
    which, in turn, would reduce the value of their debts.
21 Chastleton Corp. v. Sinclair, 264 U.S. 543, 547–48 (1924).
22 Army Service Forces, "Chart 37, Returns to Civilian Life," contained in *Logistics
    in World War II: Final Report of the Army Service Forces, Center for Military
    History,* (1993)218, https://history.army.mil/html/books/070/70–29/CMH_Pub
    _70–29.pdf.
23 74 Pinehurst LLC v. New York, 601 U.S. ___ , 2024 WL 674658 (Mem.) (2024)
    (Statement of Justice Thomas).
24 G-Max Management v. New York, Supreme Court Docket No. 21–2148.
25 The infamous "Chicago Seven" trial refers to case where seven political activ-
    ists who led protests against the Vietnam War at the Democratic National
    Convention in Chicago in 1968 were tried in federal court for criminal conspir-
    acy and incitement to riot. Their convictions were overturned on appeal.
26 See National Apartment Association, "Rent Control: Policy Issue," https:
    //www.naahq.org/rent-control-policy accessed May 2, 2024.
27 Under California law this is okay, even if the rents decline year after year, so
    long as the landlord receives a fair return – as calculated by the local rent board.
    See Birkenfeld v. City of Berkeley, 17 Cal. 3d 129 (1976).
28 Ballotpedia, Proposition 21, https://ballotpedia.org/California_Proposition_21,
    _Local_Rent_Control_Initiative_(2020), accessed May 2, 2024.

29   Carla Marinucci and Victoriea Colliver, "Powerhouse AIDS organization faces scrutiny for use of federal money," *Politico*, August 19, 2019 https://www.politico.com/states/california/story/2019/08/19/powerhouse-aids-organization-faces-scrutiny-for-use-of-federal-money-1147976.

30   BallotPedia, Proposition 10 https://ballotpedia.org/California_Proposition_10, _Local_Rent_Control_Initiative_(2018) , accessed May 2, 2024.

31   Victoria Antram, "The third California rent control initiative in four election cycles sponsored by the AIDS Healthcare Foundation qualifies for the 2024 ballot," Ballotpedia News, July 28, 2023 https://news.ballotpedia.org/2023/07/28/the-third-california-rent-control-initiative-in-four-election-cycles-sponsored-by-the-aids-healthcare-foundation-qualifies-for-the-2024-ballot/, accessed May 2, 2024.

32   Christopher Cadelago, "California proposal would sideline a prolific ballot measure player," *Politico*, August 30, 2023, https://www.politico.com/news/2023/08/30/california-proposal-ballot-measure-00113475.

33   *Id.* (citing David Autor, Christopher J. Palmer, Parag A. Pathak, "Housing Market Spillovers: Evidence from the End of Rent Control in Cambridge Massachusetts, NBER Working Paper No. 18125," June 2012, https://www.nber.org/papers/w18125.pdf).

34   *Id.* at 43.

35   A copy can be found here: https://www.congress.gov/bill/116th-congress/house-bill/5072/text, accessed May 2, 2024.

36   The "Housing for All" campaign platform can be : https://berniesanders.com/issues/housing-all/, accessed May 2, 2024.

37   Alabama Association of Realtors v. Department of Health and Human Services, 594 U.S. 758 (2021).

38   30 F. 4th 720 (8th Cir. 2022).

39   *Id.* at 730.

40   *Id.* at 731, 733.

Chapter 19

1   Assar Linbeck, *The Political Economy of the New Left* (Harper & Row, 1972), cited in *Rent Control: Myths and Realities*, edited by Walter Block and Edgar Olsen, (Vancouver: The Fraser Institute, 1981): 213, 230.

2   Foreign Minister Nguyen Co Thach, *Journal of Commerce*, quoted in Dan Seligman, "Keeping Up," *Fortune*, February 27, 1989. See also Walter Block, "Rent Control," found in *The Concise Encyclopedia of Economics*, Library of Economics and Liberty website, https://www.econlib.org/library/Enc1/RentControl.html, accessed May 2, 2024.

3   Block, et. al, eds, *Rent Control, Myths and Realities*, 3, 35, 53, 85, 105, 123, 149, 161, 169, 187, 199, 231, 247, 265, 283.

4   Riis, *How the Other Half Lives*, 9.

5   Walter Block and Edgar Olsen, *Bomb Damage or Rent Control? The Answers*, in Block et al., eds., *Rent Control: Myths and Realities*, 320..

6 Richard M. Alston, J.R. Kearl, Michael B. Vaughan, "Is there a Global Consensus Among Economists in the 1990s?," *Papers and Proceedings of the Hundred and Fourth Annual Meeting of the American Economic Association* (May, 1992):201, 204, https://www.jstor.org/stable/2117401 accessed May 2, 2024.

7 Chicago Booth, Kent A. Clark Center for Global Markets, "Rent Control," February 7, 2012. https://www.kentclarkcenter.org/surveys/rent-control/.

8 Bengt Turner and Stephen Malpezzi, "A Review of Empirical Evidence of the Costs and Benefits of Rent Control," *Swedish Economic Policy Review* 10 (2003):11–56, https://www.government.se/contentassets/6e57e1d818bb4b289ac5 12bb7d307fa5/bengt-turner—stephen-malpezzi-a-review-of-empirical -evidence-on-the-costs-and-benefits-of-rent-control.

9 Paul Krugman, "Reckoning, A Rent Affair," *New York Times*, June 7, 2000.

10 Rebecca Diamon, Tim McQuade, Franklin Qian, "The Effects of Rent Control Expansion on Tenants, Landlords, and Inequality: Evidence from San Francisco," *American Economic Review* 109, No. 9, September 2019, https://conference.nber.org/confer//2017/PEf17/Diamond_McQuade_Qian.pdf.

11 *Id.*

12 David Autor, Christopher J. Palmer, Parag A. Pathak, "Housing Market Spillovers: Evidence from the End of Rent Control in Cambridge, Massachusetts," *Journal of Political Economy* 122, no. 3, (2014):661–717, 2012227 661..727 (mit.edu).

13 The Editorial Board, "The Housing Shortage in Profile," *Wall Street Journal*, Jan. 5, 2020, https://www.wsj.com/articles/the-housing-shortage-in-profile -11578263733?mod=searchresults&page=2&pos=3

14 Will Parker and Konrad Putzier, "After New York Rent Reform, Some Landlords are Falling Behind," *Wall Street Journal*, October 26, 2019. See also, Josh Barbanel, "New York Landlords Slow Apartment Upgrades, Blame New Rent Law," *Wall Street Journal*, Dec. 19, 2019 (noting that landlords can no longer fully pass on upgrade costs to tenants) https://www.wsj.com/articles/new-york -landlords-slow-apartment-upgrades-blame-new-rent-law-11576756800?mod =searchresults&page=2&pos=9; Daniel Geiger, "Blackstone halts Stuy Town upgrades in wake of rent-regs overhaul,"*Crain's New York Business*, July 12, 2019 https://www.crainsnewyork.com/real-estate/blackstone-halts-stuy-town -upgrades-wake-rent-regs-overhaul?mod=article_inline.

15 Josh Barbanel, "Wealthy, Older Tenants in Manhattan Get Biggest Boost from Rent Regulations," *Wall Street Journal*, June 12, 2019.

16 D.W. Gibson, "The Benefits of Living in the Same Place for a Long Time," *The New York Times*, April 1, 2024 (also noting that before moving in she was paying four-times that amount in rent.) https://www.nytimes.com/2024/04/01 /realestate/not-moving-benefits.html?unlocked_article_code=1.hko.cZw6 .oUECO65pYOuD&smid=url-share.

17 Will Parker & Konrad Putzier, "New York Landlords in a Financial Bind From New York Rent Law," *Wall Street Journal*, June 24, 2019, https://www .wsj.com/articles/new-york-landlords-in-a-financial-bind-from-new-rent -law-11561201200.

18   Will Parker & Konrad Putzier, "After New York Rent Reform, Some Landlords are Falling Behind," *Wall Street Journal*, Oct. 26, 2019. Sales of multifamily apartment buildings in Brooklyn fell 74% in September 2019, when compared with September of 2018. See Cate Corcoran, "Multifamily Sales Volume Plunges in Brooklyn Following Rent Regulation Reform," *The Brownstoner*, Nov. 5, 2019.

19   See e.g. Suzanne Cavanaugh, "Another rent-stabilized landlord faces foreclosure," *The Real Deal*, September 6, 2023 https://therealdeal.com/new-york/2023/09/06 /city-skyline-faces-foreclosure-on-four-rent-stabilized-buildings/

20   Peter Grant and Will Parker, "Investors Aim to Avoid Rent Control in New Apartment Deals," *Wall Street Journal*, January 21, 2020, https://www .wsj.com/articles/investors-aim-to-avoid-rent-control-in-new-apartment -deals-11579630224.

21   *Id.*

22   *Id.*

23   Josh Barbanel, "Sales of New York City Rent-Regulated Buildings Plummet After New Law," *Wall Street Journal*, February 27, 2020, https://www.wsj.com /amp/articles/sales-of-new-york-city-rent-regulated-buildings-plummet-after -new-law-11582754189.

24   Sam Rabiyah, "NYC Had 88,830 Vacant Rent-Stabilized Apartments Last Year, City Housing Agency Estimates," *The City*, October 20, 2022.

25   Sam Rabiyah, "Rent-Stabilized Apartment Tally Drops Further, as Some Landlords Try to Rent at Market Rates," *The City*, December 11. 2023, https://www.thecity .nyc/2023/12/11/rent-stabilized-apartment-tally-drops-landlords-rent-market/.

26   Plunz, Richard. *A History of Housing*, 122. Kindle.

27   Rebecca Diamond, Tim McQuade, and Franklin Quian, "The Effects of Rent Control Expansion Tenants, Landlords, and Inequality: Evidence from San Francisco," *American Economic Review* 2019, 3368.

28   Diamond, McQuade and Quian, "Effects," at 3393.

29   The study is available from the author.

30   *Cert denied* 526 U.S. 1131 (1999). The case was filed in state court because, at the time, takings cases against local governments could not be filed in federal court under a Supreme Court rule that Pacific Legal Foundation attorneys were able to get overturned by the Supreme Court only in 2019 in Knick v. Scott Township, 473 U.S. 172 (2019).

31   Rebecca Diamond, "What does economic evidence tell us about the effects of rent control," *Brooking Policy 2020,* available at https://www.brookings.edu/research /what-does-economic-evidence-tell-us-about-the-effects-of-rent-control/.

32   The Editorial Board, "Rent Control Backfires Again in St. Paul," *Wall Street Journal*, Nov. 10, 2021, https://www.wsj.com/articles/rent-control-backfires -again-in-st-paul-ballot-initiative-11636584789.

33   Ahern, Kenneth Robinson and Giacolleti, Marco, "Robbing Peter to Pay Paul? The Redistribution of Wealth Caused by Rent Control," *Abstract, NBER Working Paper No. w30083,* (May 2022), SSRN: https://ssrn.com/abstract=4122812.

34   *Id.*at 34.

Chapter 20

1 San Remo Hotel L.P. v. City and Cty. of San Francisco, 27 Cal. 4th 643, 692 (2002) (Brown, J., dissenting).

2 Sheetz is also being represented by Paul Beard of the law firm FisherBroyles in Los Angeles. From 2003 to 2014 Beard worked for Pacific Legal Foundation. While there, he argued *Koontz v. St. Johns Water Management District* at the Supreme Court.

3 Ben Christopher, "Supreme Court case about impact fees could have huge consequences for housing in California," *CalMatters*, January 9, 2024, https://calmatters.org/housing/2024/01/impact-fees-supreme-court/.1

4 Sarah Mawhorter, David Garcia and Hayley Raetz, "It All Adds Up, The Cost of Housing Development Fees in Seven California Cities," *The Terner Center for Housing Innovation, UC Berkeley*, March 2018, https://ternercenter.berkeley.edu/research-and-policy/it-all-adds-up-development-fees/. The lower figures come from Sacramento, the higher ones from Fremont.

5 *Id.*at 17.

6 Hayley Raetz et al, "Residential Impact Fees in California, Current Practices and Policy Considerations to Improve Implementation of Fees Governed by the Mitigation Fee Act," *The Terner Center for Housing Innovation*, UC Berkeley, August 5, 2019, 22, https://ternercenter.berkeley.edu/wp-content/uploads/2020/08/Residential_Impact_Fees_in_California_August_2019.pdf.

7 The proportion of impact fee costs borne by the landowner, builder, and home buyer will demand on the particulars of supply and demand in a community. In other words, the tighter the supply the more the costs can be imposed on the home buyers. See illustration of demand curve, *Id.* at 22.

8 *Id.* at 21.

9 *Euclid*, 272 U.S. 365, involved only areal use and size restrictions on buildings and was based on an expansive notion of apartment buildings as parasitic nuisances.

10 Pennsylvania Coal Co. v. Mahon, 260 U.S. 393, 415 (1922) ("[W]hile property may be regulated to a certain extent, if regulation goes too far it will be recognized as a taking.").

11 *Lucas*, 505 U.S. at 1019 ("[W]hen the owner of real property has been called upon to sacrifice *all* economically beneficial uses in the name of the common good, that is, to leave his property economically idle, he has suffered a taking.").

12 Penn Central Transportation Co. v. City of New York, 438 U.S. 104, 124 (1978) ("The economic impact of the regulation on the claimant and, particularly, the extent to which the regulation has interfered with distinct investment-backed expectations are, of course, relevant considerations. So, too, is the character of the governmental action.")

13 See chapter 23.

14 *Lucas*, 505 U.S. at 1025 n.12.

15 There is a certain irony considering that the regulatory constraints imposed on homebuilding are the chief cause of the escalation in home prices. For more on inclusionary zoning, see James S. Burling & Graham Owen, "The Implications

of Lingle on Inclusionary Zoning and Other Legislative and Monetary Exactions," *Standford Environmental Law Journal* 28 (2009):397.

16   See Mining Law of 1872, 30 U.S.C. § 28 (2019) (specifying a one-hundred-dollar annual work requirement); United States v. Locke, 471 U.S. 84 (1985) (noting an annual registration requirement).

17   Frost v. R.R. Comm'n of Cal., 271 U.S. 583, 593–94 (1926) (The state legislation conditioned the right to use public highways on the dedication of personal property to the State for public uses.).

18   Perry v. Sindermann, 408 U.S. 593, 597 (1972) (citation omitted).

19   16. F.C.C. v. League of Women Voters of Cal., 468 U.S. 364, 370, 398 (1984).

20   Nollan, 483 U.S. at 828–29.

21   Nollan, 483 U.S. at 835.

22   Nollan, 483 U.S. at 838.

23   Nollan, 483 U.S. at 837 (emphasis added).

24   Dolan v. City of Tigard, 512 U.S. 374 (1994).

25   Transcript of Oral Argument at *27, Dolan, 512 U.S. 374 (No. 93–518), 1994 WL 664939.

26   Dolan, 512 U.S. at 385.

27   "Dolan v. Tigard: Owner Gets $1.4 Million From City –at Last!," *Realtor® Magazine*, July 1, 1998, https://www.nar.realtor/rmomag.NSF/pages/lawyoujul 1998b?OpenDocument

28   Dolan v. City of Tigard, 512 U.S. at 385.

29   570 U.S. 595 (2013).

30   Dave Jolly, "Property Rights Case Before Supreme Court Tomorrow," *Washington Examiner*, January 14, 2013. Available at https://thewashington sentinel.com/property-rights-case-before-supreme-court-tomorrow/

31   St. Johns River Water Mgt. Dist. v. Koontz, 77 So. 3d 1220, 1230 (Fla. 2011).

32   *Koontz*, 570 U.S. at 606.

33   *Id.* at 604–05.

34   Parking Ass'n of Ga., Inc. v. City of Atlanta, 515 U.S. 1116, 1116 (1995) (Thomas, J., dissenting from denial of certiorari, joined by O'Connor, J.)

35   David L. Callies, "Regulatory Takings and the Supreme Court: How Perspectives on Property Rights Have Changed from Penn Central to Dolan, and What State and Federal Courts Are Doing About It," *Stetson Law Review* 28, (1999): 567–68 (1999). See also Steven A. Haskins, "Closing the Dolan Deal—Bridging the Legislative/Adjudicative Divide," *Urban Lawyer*, 38, (2006):514, (describing the difficulty in drawing a line between legislative and administrative decision-making in the land use context). "Quasijudicial" is a legal weasel word meaning the hearing is not quite judicial, like a court, but not quite legislative, like a city council, and not quite executive, like an administrative body such as a zoning board.

36   Sheetz v. County of El Dorado, California, 144 S. Ct. 893 (2024).

37   *Id* . at 900.

38   For an extended discussion of legislative exactions and affordable housing mandates, see Burling & Owen, "The Implications of Lingle."

39 See, e.g., Home Builders Ass'n of Northern California v. City of Napa, 90 Cal. App. 4th 188 (2001) (describing the ten-unit threshold).

40 See, e.g., Cherk v. Cty. of Marin, No. A153579, 2018 WL 6583442, at *1 (Cal. Ct. App. Dec. 14, 2018) (review denied Mar. 13, 2019) (describing the $39,960 that was demanded in exchange for dividing a single parcel into two lots). A petition for writ of certiorari was denied by the Supreme Court. 140 S.Ct. 652 (2019).

41 Emily Hamilton, "Inclusionary Zoning and Housing Market Outcomes," *Mercatus Center*, 2019. See also Benjamin Powell, "'The Economics of Inclusionary Zoning Reclaimed': How Effective are Price Controls?," *Florida State University Law Review* 33, (2005) 474. For a contrary view see Barbara Ehrlich Kautz, "In Defense of Inclusionary Zoning: Successfully Creating Affordable Housing," *University of San Francisco Law* Review 36 (2002):1020, (discussing the nexus study in Santa Monica).

42 See, e.g., 616 Croft Ave., LLC v. City of West Hollywood, 3 Cal. App. 5th 621 (2016), *cert. denied*, 138 S. Ct. 377 (2017); California Bldg. Indus. Ass'n v. City of San Jose, 61 Cal. 4th 435 (2015), *cert. denied*, 136 S. Ct. 928 (2016); See also Home Builders Association of Northern California v. City of Napa, 90 Cal. App. 4th 188 (2001) (case not ready for review because it wasn't yet applied to a home builder.)

43 61 Cal. 4th 435, 351 P.3d 974 (2015), *cert. denied*, 136 S. Ct. 928 (2016).

44 California Bldg. Indus. Ass'n v. San Jose, 61 Cal. 4th at 461, 351 P.3d at 991.

45 *Id.*

46 *Id.*

47 Dolan v. City of Tigard, 512 U.S. 374, 385 (1994).

48 This is essentially what Justices Thomas and O'Connor said in dissenting from the denial of certiorari in Parking Ass'n of Georgia v. City of Atlanta, 515 U.S. 1116 (1995). "The distinction between sweeping legislative takings and particularized administrative takings appears to be a distinction without a constitutional difference." *Id.* at 1118 (Thomas, J., dissenting).

49 California Bldg. Indus. Ass'n v. City of San Jose, 136 S. Ct. 928, 928 (2016) (Thomas, J., concurring in denial of writ of certiorari) (citations omitted).

Chapter 21

1 Words spoken, repeatedly, to the author on a Sacramento light rail car by a homeless man, after kicking the author's laptop out of his lap and into his face, January 2016.

2 367 F. Supp. 808 (D.D.C. 1973).

3 Paul R. Friedman, "The Mentally Handicapped Citizen and Institutional Labor," *Harvard Law Review* 87 (1974): 570 quoting Bickford, "Economic Value of the Psychiatric Inpatient," *LANCET* (March 30, 1963):714.

4 Souder, 367 F. Supp. at 813.

5 Scoles & Fine, "Aftercare and Rehabilitation in a Community Mental Health Center," *Social Work* (July, 1971): 75, 78, quoted in Michael Perlin, "Therapeutic Work Programs," Seton-Hall Law Review 7, (1976): 321(1976).

Chapter 22

1 "Souder v. Brennan," Mental Illness Policy Org, https://mentalillnesspolicy.org/legal/min-wage-souder-brennan.html#:~:text=Usery%2C%20thatthose%20sections%20of%20the,labor%20in%20state%20mental%20hospitals. Accessed May 2, 2024.

2 E. Fuller Torrey, M.D., *Out of the Shadows: Confronting America's Mental Illness Crisis*, (1997), Chaps. 1, and 3 and Appendix, as quoted in "Deinstitutionalization: A Psychiatric 'Titanic.'" *Frontline*, PBS.org, https://www.pbs.org/wgbh/pages/frontline/shows/asylums/special/excerpt.html accessed May 2, 2024.

3 Geraldo Rivera, *Willowbrook: The Last Great Disgrace*, https://www.youtube.com/watch?v=IRKoLO-9ZYk, accessed May 2, 2024.

4 *Id.*

5 O'Connor v. Donaldson, 422 U.S. 563 (1975).

6 *Id.*

7 *Id.*at 575

8 *Id.*

9 Addington v. Texas, 441 U.S. 418 (1975).

10 See Dough Smith and Benjamin Oreskes, "Are many homeless people in L.A. mentally ill? New findings back the public's perception," *Los Angeles Times,* Oct. 7, 2019.

11 See e.g. Debra A. Pinals, "For Too Many With Mental Illness, Incarceration is the Default," *Pew Trend Magazine*, December 8, 2023, https://www.pewtrusts.org/en/trend/archive/fall-2023/for-too-many-with-mental-illness-incarceration-is-the-default.

Chapter 23

1 See Miller v. United States, 357 U.S. 301, 307 & n.7 (1958) (citing The Oxford Dictionary of Quotations 379 (2d ed. 1953)) (attributed to William Pitt, Earl of Chatham).

2 Ludwig von Mises, *Liberalism in the Classical Tradition*, trans. Ralph Raico (San Francisco: Cobden Press (1985):63.

3 Hugo Grotius, *The Rights of War and Peace Including the Law of Nature and of Nations,* trans. Archibald Colin Campbell, (Washington, London, M.W. Dunne (1901): ch. 1, ' X (1625).

4 John Locke, *Second Treatise on Government*, § 123–24.

5 Thomas Hobbes, *The Leviathan*, Chs. 13, 14, 18.

6 While Locke's *Second Treatise* refuted the notion of an absolute monarchy on political and philosophical grounds, his *First Treatise on Government* argued on religious grounds against such a divine right of kings. Tracing man from Adam through the biblical kings, Locke finds no biblical support of the notion of an absolute monarchy.

7 Locke, *Second Treatise*, 222.

8 James Madison, "The Federalist No. 10",49. see also James W. Ely, Jr., *The Guardian of Every Other Right: A Constitutional History of Property Rights 3d ed.*, (New York: Oxford University Press, 2007) (recounting the founding

generations respect for private property). Of course, there are contrary views. See, e.g., David Abraham, "Liberty Without Equality: The Property-Rights Connection in a 'Negative Citizenship' Regime," 21 Law & Society Inquiry 21 (1996):1 ("property less and less the 'guardian' of other rights, and more transparently a form of individual and class domination.")

9   His reaction to paper money was in response to the practice of some states to print near worthless money that mostly farmer debtors could use to pay off their debts.

10   See, e.g., 2 William Blackstone, *Commentaries,* 2.

11   Semayne v. Gresham, 5 Co. Rep. 91a, 92b, 77 Eng. Rep. 194, 195 (K.B. 1604).

12   Miller v. United States, 357 U.S. 301, 307(1958) citing *The Oxford Dictionary of Quotations* (2d ed. 1953), 379.

13   Margaret Jane Radin, "Property and Personhood," *Stanford Law Review* 34 (1982) :957.

14   1 William Blackstone, *Commentaries,* 135.

15   *Id.*

16   See generally Hamburger, *Is Administrative Law Unlawful?* (2014).

17   *Id.* at 279.

18   *Id.* at 493B94.

19   See Scott J. Hammond, Howard Leslie Lubert, and Kevin R. Hardwick et al. eds, James Otis, "Oral Argument Against Writs of Assistance" (Feb. 24, 1761), *in* 1 *Classics of American Political and Constitutional Thought,* (Hackett (., 2007):151–52.

20   See generally John Adams & William Tudor, Novanglus and Massachusettensis: or Political Essays, (Boston: Hews & Goss, 1819).

21   See James Otis, "Oral Argument," 152.

22   See Ilya Somin, *The Grasping Hand.*

23   See, e.g., James Madison, "The Federalist No. 47," 246 (James Madison) (quoting Charles-Louis de Secondat, Baron De Montesquieu, *The Spirit of the Laws.*)

24   But a more positivist view is that the 1st Amendment is about government fostering speech, "the more, the better with public funds if necessary." Michael McGough, "Supreme Court Justices Can Pick from Two 1st Amendments," *Los Angeles Times,* June 29, 2011.

25   See, e.g., U.S. Const. amend. I, IV, V.

26   Ashcroft v. Free Speech Coalition, 535 U.S. 234, 253 (2002) (A First Amendment case, Justice Kennedy wrote, "The right to think is the beginning of freedom.").

27   See David Spangler, "The Meaning of Gaia: Is Gaia a Goddess or Just a Good Idea?," *Earth & Spirit,* (Winter 1990):44, reprinted in *In Context,* (1997), https://www.context.org/iclib/ic24/spangler/.

28   For more, see *Tree Worship,* Wikipedia, http://en.wikipedia.org/wiki/Tree_worship.

29   Worship of The Great Pumpkin was first recorded in 1959. See "Religion of the Great Pumpkin," *Comic Book Religion,* http://www.comicbookreligion.com/?c=24710&The_Great_Pumpkin, accessed May 2, 2024.

30   "I want to be alone." Greta Garbo in *The Grand Hotel* (1932) See https://www.bing.com/videos/riverview/relatedvideo?q=greta+garbo+i+want

+to+be+left+alone&mid=4CF0ADE8EB0285F8456C4CF0ADE8EB0285F
8456C&FORM=VIRE accessed May 2, 2024.

31 Philip A. Hamburger, "Trivial Rights," 70 *Notre Dame Law Review* 1 (1994)
    quoting Helen E. Veit et al. eds., *Creating the Bill of Rights,* (1991) (statement of
    Theodore Sedgwick, Aug. 15, 1789).

32 U.S. Const. amend. IX.

33 James Madison, "Property," https://constitutingamerica.org/on-property-by
    -james-madison-reprinted-from-the-u-s-constitution-a-reader-published-by
    -hillsdale-college/. Accessed May 2, 2024. The initial quote is from William
    Blackstone, *Commentaries on the Laws of England*, Ch. 2.

34 *Id.*

35 Franklin D. Roosevelt, State of the Union Address (Jan. 6, 1941) https://www
    .americanrhetoric.com/speeches/fdrthefourfreedoms.htm.

36 Andy Blunden ed , Karl Marx and Fredrick Engels, *The Communist Manifesto
    (1848),* trans. Samuel Moore, 1888, https://www.marxists.org/archive/marx
    /works/1848/communist-manifesto/ See also David Abraham, Liberty Without
    Equality .

37 Jean Jacques Rousseau, *On the Inequality Among Mankind, Part II,* at 1, http:
    //www.bartleby.com/34/3/2.html.

38 Marx and Engels, *The Communist Manifesto.*

39 Richard Pipes, *Property and Freedom* (New York: Alfred A. Knopf, 1999):116

40 Jean Jacques Rousseau, *On the Inequality among Mankind,* Part I, at 9, http:
    //www.bartleby.com/34/3/1.html. Accessed May 2, 2024.

41 Woodrow Wilson, "Socialism and Democracy," (1887) (unpublished essay),
    http://www.origin.heritage.org/initiatives/first-principles/primary-sources
    /woodrow-wilson-on-socialism -and-democracy. Accessed May 2, 2024.

42 August Heckscher, *Woodrow Wilson: A Biography,* Scribner, 1991):260.

43 Kathleen L. Wogelmuth, "Woodrow Wilson and Federal Segregation," 44
    Journal of African American History 44 (1959):158–59.

44 See, e.g., Eric R. Claeys, "Euclid Lives? The Uneasy Legacy of Progressivism
    in Zoning," 73 *Fordham Law Review* 73 (2004):731; United States v. Carolene
    Products, 304 U.S. 144, 152 n.4 (1938).

45 This is still thought, apparently, by some today. See, e.g., Abraham,"Liberty
    Without Equality."

46 See, e.g., Vill. of Eucl*id* v. Ambler Realty Co., 272 U.S. 365, 394 (1926).

47 Bernard H. Siegan, *Property Rights: From Magna Carta to the Fourteenth
    Amendment* (New Brunswick:Transaction Publishers 2001); Richard Pipes,
    Property and Freedom; Bernard H. Siegan, *Property and Freedom: The
    Constitution, The Courts, and Land-Use Regulation* (New Brunswick:Transaction
    Publishers 1997).

48 See, e.g., John W. Whitehead & Steven H. Aden, "Forfeiting Enduring Freedom
    for Homeland Security: A Constitutional Analysis of the USA Patriot Act and
    the Justice Department's Anti-Terrorism Initiatives," 51 *American University
    Law Review* 51 (2002):1081.

49 See, e.g., Thomas J. West, "The Constitutionalism of the Founders versus Modern Liberalism," *Nexus Journal of Opinion* 6, 2001):75, 89 (noting that progressive era theories of constitutionalism rejected traditional understandings of rights); Richard A. Epstein, *How Progressives Rewrote the Constitution*, (Cato Institute 2006).

50 Lynch v. Household Finance, 405 U.S. 538, 552 (1972) (emphasis added) (citing J. Locke, *Of Civil Government* 82B85 (1924); J. Adams, *A Defense of the Constitutions of Government of the United States of America*, in F. Coker, *Democracy, Liberty, and Property* 121B32 (1942); 1 William Blackstone, *Commentaries* ,138B40).

Chapter 24

1 Pennsylvania Coal v. Mahon, 260 U.S. 393 (1922).

2 While some credit the case with being the very first regulatory takings case, others find an older history. To be sure, the doctrine did not originate with Pennsylvania coal but was revived in that case. See generally Kris W. Kobach, "The Origins of Regulatory Takings: Setting the Record Straight," *Utah Law Review (1996):*1211; Andrew S. Gold, "Regulatory Takings and Original Intent: The Direct, Physical Takings Thesis 'Goes Too Far,'" *American University Law Review*, (1999): 228–38; Eric R. Claeys, "Takings, Regulations, and Natural Property Rights," *Cornell Law Review* 88, (2003):1549; David A. Thomas, "Finding More Pieces for the Takings Puzzle: How Correcting History Can Clarify Doctrine," *University of Colorado Law Review* 75 (2004): 519–33 (2004).

3 260 U.S. at 415

4 260 U.S. at 419–20 (Brandeis, J., dissenting).

5 Mugler v. Kansas, 123 U.S. 623 (1887).

6 260 U.S. at 422 (Brandeis, J., dissenting).

7 Miller v. Schoene, 276 U.S. 272 (1928).

8 For more on the background of the dispute between the competing owners of these two types of trees and why the claim may have failed, see William A. Fischel, "The Law and Economics of Cedar-Apple Rust: State Action and Just Compensation in Miller v. Schoene," *Review of Law & Economics* 3 (2007).

9 Armstrong v. United States, 364 U.S. 40, 49 (1960).

10 See e.g. Agins v. City of Tiburon, 24 Cal.3d 266, (1979), 447 U.S. 255, (1980)

11 See, e.g., Frank I. Michelman, "Property, Utility, and Fairness: Comments on the Ethical Foundations of 'Just Compensation' Law," *Harvard Law Review* 80 (1967):1165; Joseph L. Sax, "Takings, Private Property and Public Rights," *Yale Law Journal* 81, (1971):149, William B. Stoebuck, "A General Theory of Eminent Domain," *Washington Law Review* (1972): 553; Fred Bosselman, David Callies, and J Banta, *The Takings Issue: An Analysis of the Constitutional Limits of Land Use Control*, (Council on Environmental Quality, 1973).

12 Keystone Bituminous Coal Ass'n v. DeBenedictis, 480 U.S. 470 (1987). The opinion was written by Justice Stevens, joined by Justices Brennan, White, Marshal, and Blackmun. Justice Rehnquist wrote the dissent, joined by Justices Powell, O'Connor, and Scalia.

13 480 U.S. at 499.

14   First English Evangelical Lutheran Church of Glendale v. County of Los
     Angeles, 482 U.S. 304 (1987).
15   San Diego Gas & Elec. Co. v. San Diego, 450 U.S. 621, 655–57, n. 22 (1980)
     (Brennan, J. dissenting) quoting Longtin, "Avoiding and Defending
     Constitutional Attacks on Land Use Regulations," 38B *NIMLO Municipal Law
     Review* 192–193 (1975).
16   Ultimately, on remand to the lower courts, no taking was found. But the prin-
     ciple of compensation for a temporary taking remains intact.
17   Of course, California being California next devised a rule wherein invali-
     dation of a regulation might only be part of the normal permitting process,
     during which no compensation is due. See, e.g., Landgate v. California Coastal
     Commission, 17 Cal. 4th 1006 (1998), 575 U.S. 876 (1998).
18   483 U.S. 825 (1987).
19   Lucas v. South Carolina Coastal Council, 505 U.S. 1003, 1009 (1992).
20   Lucas, 505 U.S. at 1025.
21   Transcript of oral argument in Lucas v. South Carolina Coastal Council, at 33.
     1992 WL 687838 (U.S.), 33 (U.S. Oral. Arg., 1992). To listen to the argument,
     see https://www.oyez.org/cases/1991/91–453.
22   Id, transcript at 31.
23   Joshua Braver and Ilya Somin, "The Constitutional Case Against Exclusionary
     Zoning," (February 15, 2024). *Texas Law Review*, Forthcoming, George Mason
     Legal Studies Research Paper No. LS 24–05, Univ. of Wisconsin Legal Studies
     Research Paper No. 1796, SSRN: https://ssrn.com/abstract=4728312.
24   *Id*. 54.

Chapter 25

1   Attributed to Yogi Berra.
1   Michael Burrows and Charlynn Burd, "Growth in Home-Based Work Decreased
     Manhattan's Commuter-Adjusted Population by 800,000" *United States Census
     Bureau*, July 5, 2023. https://www.census.gov/library/stories/2023/07/commut-
     er-adjusted-population.html.
2   "Higher income respondents were also more likely to work remotely." Marlon
     G. Boarnet, et al, "Commuting During and after COVID-19: The Impact of
     COVID-19 on Shared Mobility and Extreme Commuting in the Bay Area
     – Central Valley, A Research Report" *Pacific Southwest Region University
     Transportation Center*, Dec. 2022, 31, https://rosap.ntl.bts.gov/view/dot/67908/
     dot_67908_DS1.pdf.
3   Marissa Morrison, "Remote or RTO?: Employers and Workers Meet in the
     Middle." October 11, 2023, https://www.ziprecruiter.com/blog/work-arrangements
     -report/
4   Richard Glaeser, *Triumph of the City: How Our Greatest Invention Makes Us
     Richer, Smarter, Greener, Healthier, and Happier*. (Penguin Press, 2011.) Kindle.
5   Megan McArdle, "AI is coming for the professional class. Expect outrage—and
     fear," *The Washington Post*, April 29, 2024, https://www.washingtonpost.com
     /opinions/2024/04/29/ai-professional-class-low-skill-jobs/.

6   Zusha Elinson, "Oregon Decriminalized Hard Drugs. It Isn't Working." *Wall Street Journal*, Nov. 11, 2023.

7   See Alex Epstein, *The Moral Case for Fossil Fuels* (New York: Portfolio Penguin Books, 2014.)

Chapter 26

1   Leviticus 19:18 and Matthew 22:39 KJV.

2   On the other hand, when the feds demanded that lenders give loans to people who plainly lacked the financial wherewithal to pay them back, it precipitated the foreclosure crisis of 2008. This was an unwise way of making amends.

3   See e.g. Derek Fidler and Hicham Sabir, "The cost of housing is tearing our society apart," January 9, 2019, *World Economic Forum*, https://www.weforum .org/agenda/2019/01/why-housing-appreciation-is-killing-housing/

4   *Id.*

5   *Id.*

6   See e.g. Senay Boztas, "'How will I buy?': housing crisis grips the Netherlands as Dutch go to polls," *The Guardian*, March 15, 2023, https://www.theguard-ian.com/world/2023/mar/15/netherlands-housing-crisis-dutch-elections. ("The average home costs . . . more than 10 times the modal income.")

7   Mark Baldassare, Dean Bonner, Rachel Lawler, and Deja Thomas, "PPIC Statewide Survey: Californians and Their Government," *Public Policy Institute of California*, February, 2023, https://www.ppic.org/?show-pdf=true&docrap-tor=true&url=https%3A%2F%2Fwww.ppic.org%2Fpublication%2Fppic-state-wide-survey-californians-and-their-government-february-2023%2F

8   See California YIMBY, "Housing Underproduction in California," February 2023 https://cayimby.org/wp-content/uploads/2023/09/2023-Housing_Under production-compressed.pdf/

9   See e.g. M. Nollan Gray, *Arbitrary Lines: How Zoning Borke the American City* (Island Press, 2022). Kindle.

10 For the Portland story, see Randal O'Toole, *American Nightmare: How Government Undermines the Dream of Home Ownership* (Cato Institue, 2012).

Index

1943 Emergency Price Control Act, 194

A

accessory dwelling units (ADUs), 94–96, 297

Adams, John, 262

Addington, Frank O'Neal, 247–248

Administrative Procedures Act, 168

ADUs. *See* accessory dwelling units (ADUs)

AFFH. *See* Affirmatively Furthering Fair Housing (AFFH)

Affirmatively Furthering Fair Housing (AFFH), 105–106

affordable housing mandates, 231–233

African Americans, xix, 28–31, 67–69, 71, 74–75, 92–93, 119, 136–137. *See also* racial zoning

African Methodist Episcopal Church, 86–87

AHF. *See* AIDS Healthcare Foundation (AHF)

AI. *See* artificial intelligence (AI)

AIDS Healthcare Foundation (AHF), 95–97, 196–197

Alito, Justice, 169, 172

Ambler, William, 44–45, 48

Ambler Realty, 44, 48–51, 53, 57

American Dream, xii, xvii, 291

American Federation of State, County, and Municipal Employees, 243

American Notes (Dickens), 31–32

American Revolution, 256, 259–260

anti-Semitism, 31, 47

apartment houses, 45–50, 59–60, 65–66, 70–73, 82–83, 85–87, 92, 95–97, 102, 106, 140–141, 180–181, 189, 191–196, 199, 202–208, 215–216, 224, 275, 290–291, 298

Aquinas, Thomas, 143–144

architecture, 70–71

Arlington, Virginia, 94

artificial intelligence (AI), 287

Atlantic City, New Jersey, 123–124

Audubon California, 175

August, Mayor Andrew, 91–92, 291

Avila, Eric, 119–120

B

Baker, Newton, 46–51, 54–57

Baldwin, James, 136–137

Baltimore, Maryland, 3–9, 20, 45, 60, 180

Baltimore Afro-American, 5
Bassett, Edward M., 38–39
Bay Area, xxiii, 96–98
Belle Terre, New York, 76–79
Benga, Ota, 29
Berea College, 11–12, 14, 19–20
Berkeley, California, 93, 95
Berman v. Parker, 96, 129–133,
    136–137
Bernstein, David, 14–16
Bettman, Alfred, 39, 44, 56–59
Biden, President Joe, xxvii, 107
Bill of Rights (England), 256, 265
Bill of Rights (US), 264–266
Bishop Estate-Kamehameha
    Schools, 132
Black, Justice Hugo, 67–68
Black Americans, xix, 28–31, 67–
    69, 71, 74–75, 119, 136–137. *See
    also* racial zoning
Blackstone, William, 258, 260
blight, 120–121, 140
Block, Julius, 189–190
Block v. Hirsh, 189–192
boarding houses, 77–78
Bomb Damage or Rent Control, 200
Bonta, California Attorney General
    Robert, 98
Boston, Massachusetts, 33–34, 39,
    197
Boston Guardian, 10
Brandeis, Justice Louis, 274–275
Brennan, Justice, 79, 278
Brinsmadek J. Chapin, 12
Bronx Zoo, 29
Brown, Jerry Governor, 149
Brown v. Board of Education, 11, 71
    74
Buchanan, Charles, 13–14
Buchanan v. Warley, 13–14, 23, 51,
    57, 75, 290

Burger, Chief Justice Warren, 159
Bush, President George H. W.,
    100–101, 164
"business goodwill," 148

C
Cabrini-Green, 72–73
Calder v. Bull, 127
California Air Resources Board, 298
*California Building Industry
    Association v. San Jose*, 233–237
California Coastal Commission,
    181–182, 218–222
California Constitution Article 34,
    67–68, 74
California Environmental Quality
    Act, 174–175, 177–181, 295–296
California Native Plant Society, 176
California SB 9, 94–99
California SB 10, 94–99
Callies, David, 229
Cambridge, Massachusetts, 64–65,
    197
Canada, 104
Carabell, June and Keith, 171
Carabell v. United States, 171
car-camping, xx–xxi
Carr, Geoff, 177–178
Carson, Ben, 107
Carson, Rachel, 153–154
Carter, President Jimmy, 75, 159
Centennial Project, 176
Center for Biological Diversity,
    175–177, 179
Center on Real Estate and Urban
    Economics, 101
Centers for Disease Control and
    Prevention, 199
Central Park, 30–31
Chapman, Travis, 77
Charles I, King, 255

Charles II, King, 255–256
Chase, Justice Samuel, 127
Chavez Ravine, 113–114
Cherk, Darmond and Esther,
    236–237
Chicago, Illinois, 72–73, 102,
    185–186
Chicago Board of Trade, 186
Chinese immigrants, 28, 41
cholera, 24, 26–27
cigar making, 41
Civil Rights Act, 198, 247
Civil Rights Movement, 74
Civil War, xx, 11, 183, 186–187,
    272
Clean Air Act, 154
Clean Water Act, 154, 162, 164–
    173, 293
Cleveland, Ohio, 44–45, 56, 78
Climate Resolve, 176
code enforcement, 298–299
Coke, Lord Edward, 258
Coking, Vera, 123–124
Color of Law, The (Rothstein), 180
Columbus Park, 30, 111
Commerce Clause, 53, 171
Communist Manifesto (Marx and
    Engels), 268
Comprehensive Environmental
    Response, Compensation, and
    Liability Act, 154
*Constitutional Limitations on City
    Planning Power* (Bassett), 38
Copley Square, 33–34
Costa, Jim, 196
cost-burdened households, xxi–xxii
COVID-19 pandemic, xi, xx, 32,
    198–199, 285–287
COVID eviction bans, 198–199
Cromwell, Oliver, 255–256

D
Dallas, Texas, 102
Dashiell, Milton, 5
deaths, of homeless people, xxi
Declaration of Independence,
    256–257
deep ecology, 155
Democratic Party, 75
Denver, Colorado, 93
Department of Housing and Urban
    Development (HUD), 105–106
Detroit, Michigan, 118–119, 122–
    123, 150
DeVita v. County of Napa, 83–84
Dickens, Charles, 31–32
Dickman, Edith and Judith, 76
Discourse on Inequality (Rousseau),
    269
disease, xx, 24, 26–27, 31–32,
    36–37
District of Columbia Rents Act, 189
Divine Right of Kings, 256
Dodger Stadium, 114–115
Dolan, John and Florence, 223–226
Dolan v. City of Tigard, Oregon,
    223–231, 233, 236–237
Donaldson, Kenneth, 247
Dougherty, Conor, 96–97
Douglas, Justice William O., 138,
    296
Due Process Clause, 78–79, 121,
    247, 274

E
Earth Day, 153
*Edgar A. Levy Leasing Company v.
    Siegal, 189–192*
education, 11–12
Ehrlich, Paul, 153
El Dorado County, Colorado, 213,
    230, 236

Elk Grove, California, 214–215
Ellickson, Robert, 233
Emergency Price Control Act, 194
eminent domain, 111, 113–125,
    149–151, 299–300
Endangered Species Act (ESA),
    154–155, 157–163, 294–295
Engels, Friedrich, 267–268
English Bill of Rights, 256
Epstein, Richard, 277
Equal Protection Clause, 11, 14, 67
    74
ESA. *See* Endangered Species Act
    (ESA)
Essay on Property (Madison), 266
Ethel R. Lawrence Homes, 93
Euclid, Ohio, 43–61, 63–66, 75
Euclid v. Ambler, 43–61, *43–61*,
    63–66, 75, 82, 85–86, 89, 216,
    251, 270, 289
Eutaw Place, 3–9
Evans, David, 179
Everglades National Park, 146
eviction bans, 198–199
exclusionary zoning, xii, 22, 58, 60,
    66, 80, 85–93, 102, 107, 215,
    231, 282, 285–286, 289, 296

F
Fair Housing Act, 105
Fair Labor Standards Act, 242
fair market value, 128, 143–147
F.C.C. v. League of Woman Voters,
    218
Federal Housing Administration
    (FHA), 136
Federal Housing and Rent Act, 194
Federalist Papers, 257, 263
FHA. *See* Federal Housing
    Administration (FHA)
Field, Justice Stephen, 188

Fifteenth Amendment, 11–12, 276
Fifth Amendment, 121, 260, 265,
    276, 278
First Amendment, 218, 265
*First English Evangelical Lutheran
    Church of Glendale v. County of
    Los Angeles*, 277–279
Fischel, William, 108
Fish and Wildlife Service, 176
Floyd, George, 92
Food Control Act, 189
Forman, Allen, 30
Fourteenth Amendment, 11–12, 20,
    49, 74, 79
Fourth Amendment, 265
Fraser Institute, 200
Frederickson, George M., 29–30
Furman, Jason, 103

G
Galland, Caroline Rosenberg Kline,
    81–82
General Motors, 118–119, 122–
    123, 150
gentrification, 95–97
germaphobia, 31
Giddings v. Brown, 127
Glaeser, Edward L., 101–102, 286
Glorious Revolution, 256
Granger movement, 186
Grant, Madison, 29
Grapevine Project, 176
Great Depression, xx, xxvii–xxviii,
    xxviii
greenfield development, 98
Green New Deal, 271
Grotius, Hugo, 254
Gyourko, Joseph, 101–102

H
Haines, Mayor William, 86–87

Hairston v. Danville & W. R. Co., 128
Hamburger, Philip, 261
Hamilton, Alexander, 257, 263
Hamilton, Emily, 233
Hamilton College, 241
Harris, Arthur, 12–13
hate speech, 264
Hawaii Housing Authority v. Midkiff, 132–133
Hawaii Land Reform Act of 1976, 132
Hawkins, Phil, 196
Hayden, Tom, 196
height ordinances, 33–36
Heights Apartments v. Walz, 199
Hernandez, Jennifer, 180–181
Hirsh, Louis, 189–190
Hobbes, Thomas, 150, 255–256
Hollywood Museum, 122
Holmes, Justice Oliver Wendell, 17, 190–191, 273–274, 280
homelessness, xvii–xxi, xxviii, 241–249
Homevoter Hypothesis, The (Fischel), 108
Hoover, Herbert, 54
Hoovervilles, xxvii–xxviii
Housing for All, 198
Houston, Texas, 102–103
Hsieh, Chang-Tae, 102
HUD. *See* Department of Housing and Urban Development (HUD)

I
Icahn, Carl, 123
Illinois Constitution, 187
immigration, xvi–xvii, xix, 28, 30, 41, 287
inclusionary zoning, 89–90, 230–233

Industrial Revolution, 288
Institute for Justice, 115, 123
Italian immigrants, 30

J
James II, King, 256
James v. Valtierra, 74–75
Jay, John, 257
Jews, 66–68, 82, 261–262. *See also* anti-Semitism
Jim Crow, 10–11, 14
Just Compensation Clause, 143–148
Just Society: A Place to Prosper Act, 197–198

K
Kanner, Gideon, 118, 137–138, 144–146, 148
Katz, Lawrence, 101
Kawaisu Tribe, 176
Kelo, Suzette, 115–116
Kelo v. New London, Connecticut, 115–120, 122–123, 133–135, 140–141, 144–145, 150
Kennedy, Justice Anthony, 171
Keystone Bituminous Coal Company v. DeBenedictis, 277
Klamath Basin, 162
Klein, Michael R., 145
Kohler Act, 273
Koontz, Coy Jr. and Coy Sr., 226–231
Koontz v. St. Johns Water Management District, 226–231, 236–237
Kroll, Cynthia, 101
Krugman, Paul, 204

L
LA Dodgers, 114

land use regulation, xii, xxii–xxiii, 33–35, 43–61, 63–66, 75, 100–110, 174–182, 289, 292–293
Land Use Without Zoning (Siegan), 102
Lavine, Amy, 137
Lawrence, Ethel Robinson, 86–87, 93
Lazarus, Emma, xv–xvi
Le Corbusier, 70
Lee, Arthur, 260
Lee, Mike, xi–xiv
Leviathan, The (Hobbes), 255
limit lines, 99
Linbeck, Assar, 200
Little Pink House, A, 115–118
Livable California, 95
Lochner, Joseph, 16
Lochner v. New York, 14–19, 53
Locke, John, 150, 254–257, 260
Los Angeles, California, xx, xxiv, xxiv–xxv, 92–93, 113–114, 178, 180, 196
Louisville, Kentucky, 9–10, 12–13, 18–20, 23–24, 45, 50–51, 60, 180, 290
Louisville Times, 10
Lucas, David, 279–280
Lucas v. South Carolina Coastal Council, 216, 279–282
Lynch, Silas, 107

M
Madison, President James, 193, 257–258, 263, 266–267
Mahool, Mayor J. Barry, 6–7
Malibu, California, 179
Malpezzi, Stephen, 101
Marcy State Hospital, 241, 243, 249
Marx, Karl, 267–269
McKenna, Justice Joseph, 42, 191

McMechen, George, 4–9
mentally ill persons, 241–249
Merrill, Thomas W., 145
Metzenbaum, James, 54–55, 58
Mexico City, xix–xx
Miami, Florida, 146
Miller v. Schoene, 275
Mills, Ocie, 164–166, 168–169, 294
Minneapolis, Minnesota, 69, 94, 297
Moore, Inez, 79–80
Moore v. City of East Cleveland, 78–79
Moretti, Enrico, 102
Morgan, Robert, 54, 57
Mount Laurel Township, New Jersey, 85–93, 291
Mtubi tribe, 29
Mugler v. Kansas, 274
Mulberry Bend, 30, 111
Munn, Ira Y., 186–187, 189
Munn v. Illinois, 187–188

N
NAACP. *See* National Association for the Advancement of Colored People (NAACP)
Naglee Park, 121
Napa County, California, 81–84
National Alliance to End Homelessness, xxviii
National Association for the Advancement of Colored People (NAACP), 10, 12, 14, 18–20, 85–86, 88
National Association of Homebuilders, 102
National Association of Realtors, 120
National Bureau of Economic

Research, 197
National Environmental Policy Act, 161
National Forest Management Act, 161
National Historic Preservation Act, 176
National Park Service, 146–147
Natural Resources Defense Council, 175
Nectow v. Cambridge, 64–65, 77
"New Colossus, The" (Lazarus), xv–xvi
New Deal, 270–271
Newhall Ranch, 178
New London, Connecticut, 115–120, 122–123, 133–135, 140–141, 144–145, 150–151
New York Central Park, 30–31
New York City, xix, 24–42, 54, 70, 189, 191–196, 200–207, 291–292
NIMBY. *See* Not-in-My-Backyard (NIMBY)
Nixon, President Richard, 154
Noah, 154
Nollan, Patrick, 219, 222
Nollan v. California Coastal Commission, 218–222, 225–231, 233, 236–237, 279
Northern Spotted Owl, 160–161
North-Western Elevator, 186–188
Not-in-My-Backyard (NIMBY), xvii, xxiv, 47, 63, 80–81, 83, 92, 95–96, 109, 155, 174–175, 178, 249, 291, 295–296, 299
nuisance, 33, 35, 37, 39–40, 42, 55–60, 215–216, 281, 298

O
Oahu, Hawaii, 133

Oakland, California, xix–xx, 96–97
Obama, President Barrack, xxvii, 103–104, 107
Ocasio-Cortez, Representative Alexandria, 197–198
O'Connor, Justice, 116, 132, 135, 281
Oregon, 39, 73, 94, 98, 162, 205, 219, 222, 287, 223297
Orlando, Florida, 226
Otay Ranch, 179
Otis, James, 261–262, 266
O'Toole, Randal, 98

P
Pacific Legal Foundation, xvii, 161–162, 168, 170, 172, 207, 214–215, 219–220, 236, 280
Palo Alto, California, 98
pandemic, xi, xx, 32, 198–199, 285–287
Passing of the Great Race; or, The Racial Basis of European History, The (Grant), 29
Patriot Act, 270–271
Pelosi, Representative Nancy, 126
Pennsylvania Coal v. Mahon, 50, 190–191, 273–277, 280
permits, 54, 97–98, 103–104, 162–163, 167–168, 170–182, 214–235, 298–300
Perry v. Sinderman, 218
Pfizer Pharmaceutical Corporation, 115–117, 133, 140–141
Pipes, Richard, 268–269
Pitt, William, Earl of Chatham, 259
Plessy, Homer, 10–11
Plessy v. Ferguson, 10–11, 13–14, 19–22
Plunz, Richard, 26
Poe, Solicitor Edgar Allan, 6–7

Poletown, 118–119, 122
police power, 35–36, 53–54, 56
population growth, xxiii, 291–292
Portland, Oregon, 39, 287
Portola Valley, California, 97–98
Powell, Justice, 74
Power, Garett, 4, 57
Pritchett, Wendell, 136, 139
property rights, 20–22, 51–54, 56,
    63–64, 251, 253–271, 289–300.
    See also eminent domain
Proposition 10, 196
Proposition 13, 80
Pruitt-Igoe, 69–74, 291–292
publicly-funded housing, xxiv–xxv,
    67–69
Public Use Clause, 129, 131, 142,
    151

R
racial zoning, 3–23, 28–31, 67–69,
    71, 74–75, 92–93, 251, 290, 296
Radiant City, The (Le Corbusier), 70
Rapanos, John A., 170
Rapanos v. United States, 170–172
rats, xx
Reagan, President Ronald W., 174
redevelopment, 30, 75, 96–97,
    116–118, 120–121, 130, 135–
    138, 140–142, 148–149, 151,
    291, 299
Redwood City, California, 177–178
Reeves, Richard, 103
reform, urban, 23–32
regulatory takings, 272–282. *See also*
    land use regulation; takings
Rehnquist, Chief Justice, 225
rent control, xxvi, 183, 185–210,
    298
rent prices, xxi–xxii
rent-seeking, 15–16

rent stabilization, 195, 205–206,
    210
Republican Party, 5
Resource Conservation and
    Recovery Act, 154
return to office, 286–287
Revell, Keith, 35, 38, 40–41
Rights of War and Peace, The
    (Grotius), 254
Riis, Jacob, 26–32, 36, 39, 59, 110
Ris, Joseph, 202
Rivera, Geraldo, 247–248
Robinson, Judge Aubrey E. Jr.,
    242–243
Rochester, New York, 105–106
Roman, Nan, xxviii
Roosevelt, President Franklin D.,
    267
Rosen, Kenneth T., 101
Rothstein, Richard, 142, 180
Rothwell, Jonathan, 103
Rousseau, Jean Jacques, 268–269

S
Sackett, Mike, 167–169, 173,
    293–294
Sacramento, California, xviii, xx,
    214–215
Saito, Leland, 136
San Clemente, California, 182
Sanders, Senator Bernie, 198
San Diego, California, 179
San Francisco, California, xxv,
    77–78, 96–97, 137, 181, 196,
    203–204, 207
San Jose, California, 67, 121, 196,
    233–237
San Mateo County, 67
Santa Monica, California, 196,
    208–209
Saxe, John Godfrey, 187

Scalia, Justice Antonin, 144, 171–173, 216, 221, 279–280
Schmitter, Aman, 16
Schwartz, Joel, 30, 39
Scott, George L., 186–187
Seattle, Washington, 39–40, 81–82, 93
Second Treatise of Government (Locke), 254–257
Section 8, 198
Sedgwick, Theodore, 265
segregation, 10–12, 18, 71, 74–75
Seneca Village, 30
Separate but Equal, 10, 13, 19
Sheetz, George, 213–214, 229–230 236–237
shelters, xx–xxi
Shlaes, Amity, 71–72
Siegal, Jerome, 191–192
Siegan, Bernard, 102–103
Sierra Club, 160–161, 175
Silicon Valley, xxiii, 62, 285–286
Simpson, George, 55
slums, 23–32, 138
"smart growth," 63
snail darter, 158–159, 161
Snow, John, 36
Souder v. Brennan, 242–244, 246
South Bronx, 200–201
Spencer, Herbert, 17
Stahl, Andy, 160–161
Star Chamber, 261
State of Washington ex rel. Seattle Title Tr. Co. v. Roberge, 82–83
Statue of Liberty, xv–xvi
St. Johns, Michael, 207
St. Louis, 69–74, 291–292
St. Louis World's Fair, 29
Stone, Justice, 58
Story, Justice Joseph, 127
St. Paul, Minnesota, 209–210

subsidized housing, 213–237
supply and demand, xi–xii, xxv, xxvi, 108–109
Sutherland, Justice George, 55, 58–60, 63–65, 180, 216, 270

T
Taft, Chief Justice William, 55
takings, 155, 157–163, 260–261, 272–282
Takings Clause, 224, 273–274, 276, 278, 280
Takings Doctrine, 251
Takings: Private Property Rights and the Power of Eminent Domain (Epstein), 277
tax increment financing, 139–142
Tejon Ranch, 175–177
Tellico Dam, 158–159, 161
tenements, 23–32
Tennessee Valley Authority v. Hill, 158–159
Thach, Nguyen Co, 200
Thirteenth Amendment, 11–12
Thomas, Justice Clarence, 136
Tigard, Oregon, 222–225
tobacco, 41
toilets, xx
Toxic Substances Control Act, 154
traffic mitigation fee, 229–230
Trinity Church, 36
Triumph of the City, The (Glaeser), 286
Trump, President Donald, xxvii, 104–107, 123–124, 294
Trump Plaza, 123

U
U2, 179
Unconstitutional Conditions Doctrine, 217–222, 226–231

United States Army Corps of
  Engineers, 164–165, 171, 173,
  293–294
urban limit lines, 99
urban planning, 139–140
urban reform, 23–32
urban renewal, 135–138

V

Van Horne's Lessee v. Dorrance, 133
Vargas, Aurora, 113–114, 119
Venice Beach, California, 178
Victoria Transport Policy Institute,
  104
Vietnam War, 120
*Village of Arlington Heights v.
  Metropolitan Housing Commission*,
  69, 74–75, 78
Village of Belle Terre v. Boraas, 76–79

W

Ward, Bryce, 101
Warley, William, 10, 13–14
Washington, District of Columbia,
  137–138, 188–189, 193
Washington Growth Management
  Act, 108
Westenhaver, Judge D.C., 48–50,
  52
West River Bridge v. Dix, 128
wetlands, 164–173, 293–294
Whitten, Robert H., 38–39
Wilderness Act, 155
Wilkinson v. Leland, 127
Willowbrook State School, 247–248
Wilson, President Woodrow, 28,
  269–270
Wolf, Michael Allan, 41–42, 47, 52
Woodside, California, 97–98
World Trade Center, 70
World War I, 183, 188–189, 207

World War II, 183, 194
Writs of Assistance, 261–262

Y

Yamasaki, Minoru, 70
Yes-in-My-Backyard (YIMBY),
  96–97

Z

zoning, xii, xxii–xxiii
comprehensive, 38–42
economic impact of, 100–110
eminent domain and, 113–125
end of single-family, 94–99
environmental consciousness and,
  154–155
in Euclid, Ohio, 43–61
"Euclidean," 62
exclusionary, 85–93, 265
inclusionary, 89–90, 230–233
judicial influences, 62–84
in Los Angeles, 92–93
in New York City, 24–42
racial, 3–23, 28–31, 67–69, 71,
  74–75, 92–93, 251, 290, 296

Suggested Reading

There are many books on land-use law and housing. These are some of the best:

Bryan Caplan and Ady Branzei, *Build, Baby, Build: The Science and Ethics of Housing* Regulation, (Cato Institute, 2024).

> *The best graphic novel ever written on the housing crisis. Well, it's the only one, but it is highly entertaining and informative.*

James W. Ely, Jr., *The Guardian of Every Other Right: A Constitutional History of Property Rights*, 3d ed. (New York: Oxford University Press, 2007).

> *A highly readable account of property at the beginning of the Republic.*

Richard A. Epstein, *Takings, Private Property and the Power of Eminent Domain* (Cambridge, Massachusetts: Cambridge University Press, 1985).

> *The property rights manifesto that began the modern era of property rights.*

Edward Glaeser, *The Triumph of the City: How Our Greatest Invention Makes Us Richer, Smarter, Greener, Healthier, and Happier* (New York, New York: Penguin Books, 2011.)

   A paean to urban living.

John Locke, *Two Treatises on Government,* P. Laslett rev. ed. (Cambridge, England: Cambridge University Press, 1988).

   The philosophy that launched the American Revolution.

Nolan M. Gray, *Arbitrary Lines: How Zoning Broke the American City and How to Fix It* (Washington, DC: Island Press, 2022).

   A wonderfully readable book on the ills of modern zoning.

Ilya Somin, *The Grasping Hand: Kelo v. City of New London and the Limits of Eminent Domain* (Chicago, Illinois: University of Chicago Press, 2015).

   A compelling account of the case revealed the national disgrace of eminent domain abuse.

Richard Rothstein, *The Color of Law* (New York, New York: Liveright, 2017).

   This book must be read. Period.

Bernard H. Siegan, *Property and Freedom: The Constitution, The Courts, and Land-Use Regulation* (New Brunswick, NJ: Transaction Publishers, 1997).

   Property and freedom cannot be separated.

Bernard H. Seigan, *Land Use Without Zoning* (Lanham, Maryland: Rowman and Littlefield, 1961 and 2022).

Why zoning does little besides raise the cost of housing.

Michael Allan Wolf, *The Zoning of America: Euclid v. Ambler* (Lawrence, Kansas: University Press of Kansas, 2008).

A compelling account of the story behind the case that made zoning legal in America.